Y0-ARR-278

WRITING AND SELLING SPECIAL FEATURE ARTICLES

PRENTICE-HALL JOURNALISM SERIES

Kenneth E. Olson, Editor

WRITING AND SELLING SPECIAL FEATURE ARTICLES

BY

HELEN M. PATTERSON

ASSOCIATE PROFESSOR OF JOURNALISM
UNIVERSITY OF WISCONSIN

WITH AN INTRODUCTION BY

GRANT MILNOR HYDE

DIRECTOR OF THE SCHOOL OF JOURNALISM
UNIVERSITY OF WISCONSIN

New York
PRENTICE-HALL, INC.
1945

First Printing.....................July 1939
Second Printing....................May 1941
Third Printing...............February 1942
Fourth Printing...................April 1944
Fifth Printing.................August 1944
Sixth Printing................January, 1945

PRINTED IN THE UNITED STATES OF AMERICA

INTRODUCTION

The writing of special feature articles was one of the first subjects developed in the pioneer university departments of journalism. In 1909, when the course was first introduced at the University of Wisconsin, the entire curriculum offered by the journalism staff included only three other courses—reporting, copyreading, and editorial writing. The subject appeared in other universities at about the same time and is now a part of the curriculum in all well-equipped schools of journalism. It is also one of the most popular and profitable courses in the rapidly expanding list of specialized projects in journalistic training.

The popularity of the course in writing special feature articles from the viewpoint of either the student or the teacher, results from several advantages that may or may not be obvious at first sight: (1) for the student who is seeking training in specialized writing, it is a step beyond news writing in interest and in literary qualities; (2) for the student who is taking his first steps toward professional writing, the special feature article is much easier to master than the short story—and may prove to be a preliminary to later success in fiction writing; (3) to the young student who is tired of trying "to write out of his head," the course offers a chance to do something worth while with actual facts; (4) for the teacher who seeks a tangible measure of success in his teaching, the feature article is sufficiently within the range of undergraduate accomplishment to bring the goal of publication to the student while he is still a member of the class; and (5) to any person who has an urge to write, the size and ramifications of the special feature market offer the most immediate possibilities of financial return—even to the free-lance.

Perhaps because of its special appeal to the type of student who was early attracted to the embryo classes in journalism, the course in special features got its start in such departments. It has, however, since grown far beyond the province of journalism departments and has been adopted by many departments of rhetoric and English composition as a specialized writing course of value to any college student.

The pioneer teacher of special feature writing was probably the late Dr. Willard G. Bleyer, founder of the journalism curriculum of the University of Wisconsin, although several other professors began offering the course at so nearly the same time that the identity of its inventor is difficult to establish. At any rate, Dr. Bleyer began developing the course in 1909, and in 1919 brought out the first textbook for such a course. Subsequently, the course was handled by various other teachers on the Wisconsin staff, including myself. But no one on the staff has had greater success—measured in actual sales of articles by the students—than the author of this new book, Miss Patterson, who has conducted the course since 1929. Under her direction the class has included as many as 90 students a year, handled in two sections and in many small discussion groups. Annual sales of the class have attained $3,800, even during the "Great Depression."

The secret of Miss Patterson's success with the class would appear to be her emphasis on the study of markets and on the adaptation of articles to particular markets. That secret, together with many other special techniques of teaching which she has developed, I believe she has written into this book so clearly and so effectively that they will not escape the notice, of either the student in a university class or the ambitious writer approaching the subject alone without the aid of a teacher. If she has done that, she has made a contribution to the literature on "how to learn to write."

As a colleague of the author, who has watched with interest

her achievements in teaching special feature writing, I am delighted to assist at the launching of this book and to add my best wishes for its successful voyage.

GRANT MILNOR HYDE

PREFACE

This book has been prepared for those who have the urge to write and who desire remuneration for their efforts. A salesmanship approach to the technique of writing feature articles for newspapers and magazines has been made in order to aid beginners in attaining success.

Many amateurs attempt to write fiction because they feel they will have more freedom and will be happier doing that type of writing. They do not realize that they are competing with hundreds of authors whose names are well known. When they learn of the opportunities for unknown journalists in feature writing, of the freedom in style, of the wealth of subject matter about which they may write, and that they can earn while they learn, they take up the subject—whether in the classroom, writing clubs, or alone in their dens—with an enthusiasm that borders on fervor. They do not find the study of writing to sell a drudgery but a merry adventure. Students like to write features because they do not have to wait until graduation to be compensated for their efforts. Adults turning to it as an avocation find they can get results almost immediately, since they learn to slant and market as they write. Why should amateurs be encouraged to write if they are not taught how to sell what they write?

It is not the purpose of this book to teach writing for writing's sake, but to aid the beginner in methods of seeing ideas, gathering material, interviewing tactfully, slanting accurately, planning and outlining painstakingly, writing enthusiastically, and selling satisfactorily: If a beginner is taught to work as a professional, he will sell to publications with a sectional or national circulation. If he is taught to work as an amateur, he will be lucky to have his work printed—without even thanks—in the semi-annual or quarterly school periodical with its limited campus circulation.

The ideas and plans outlined in this book are the result of the author's experience in writing and buying features and in teaching hundreds of students in her classes in the School of Journalism at the University of Wisconsin not only to write but to sell articles. That the methods outlined are practical is proved by the students' sales, which for a recent year totaled more than $3,800.

The book is planned to be helpful to four types of persons: first, the undergraduate majoring in journalism or advertising, who takes the course to meet the requirements of the curriculum and to be prepared to do this type of writing upon graduation; second, the undergraduate who elects the course because he wants to write to sell even though his major is in some other field; third, the graduate student who is preparing himself for a profession or business which offers material that would make acceptable articles or who may be called on, in his chosen work, to write articles; and fourth, the adult writing without guidance but who has ambition and leisure and aspires to learn the fundamentals of writing and marketing either for immediate profit or for an avocation after he retires.

Since writing should be fun, the content of the book was planned with but little emphasis on the actual writing techniques before Chapter 11. An assignment to write will thrill a student rather than bore him, if he feels free from the restrictions of rules that are necessary in the beginning composition class. After his new-found writing freedom allows him to write as he wishes, he very soon will be aware of his lack of ability and will then seek information from his instructor or from rhetoric and composition books that will aid him in presenting his ideas effectively. A desire for knowledge of technique will follow successful salesmanship. Throughout the chapters the fact is stressed that feature writing is just as much a problem of thinking as of writing. Particular emphasis is placed on methods of slanting material in order to aid the free-lance writer in selling his manuscripts. The Publication Analysis at the end of each chapter will aid him in acquiring market knowledge of what editors wish to buy.

To serve as inspiration to the novice, by showing him what other beginners have accomplished, Part II consists of amateurs' first articles, reprinted with permission from the authors as well as from the publications that bought them. A short sketch of the source of the ideas and the methods of gathering, slanting, writing, and marketing precedes each feature. The student-written articles were selected from the hundreds that have appeared in periodicals, with the idea that they also could be used by the student in the classroom or by the self-teaching adult in analyzing organization of material and style of writing.

In using this book, the beginner, whether studying under an instructor or teaching himself, should scan Part I to get a survey of what it contains that will aid him in the production of his first feature. As he writes, he will then know where to turn in the book to find the solutions to his problems as they arise. Teachers long have realized that there is only one way to learn to write, and that is to write and learn the technique afterward. The book is based on that theory. The first draft of the first article should be written as soon after the hurried scanning as is possible. The interested beginner will be anxious to re-read the chapters to find all help available and to check his manuscript for ways in which he can present the material more effectively to interest the reader.

If the amateur has the opportunity of having his manuscript criticized in small discussion groups, or in the classroom, or by groups of other beginners, or even by a friend, he will be benefited immeasurably by the reader point of view.

A chapter a week should be read thoroughly if the course is a semester one, or a chapter every two weeks if the course runs a year, as it does in many of the nonprofessional classes. Weekly or daily assignments of the exercises at the end of the chapter will serve as a teacher-check to inspire a second and thorough reading. For year courses, the publication studies at the end of each chapter may be assigned in alternate weeks, or additional magazines may be analyzed.

Several books on magazine writing have been published during the last two decades, and since the author had read and had used in her classes most of these volumes as supplementary texts, she is glad to acknowledge indebtedness to those authors. Much credit is due particularly to the late Professor Willard G. Bleyer, whom she assisted and whose book she has used as a text during the time she has had charge of the feature courses. It is not possible to thank, in this brief space, the hundreds of students who—by proving the author's tenet that beginners not only can write effectively but can sell successfully—have made Part II of this book possible.

In presenting this book, the author desires to express her special debt of gratitude for the many helpful suggestions and the assistance given by Professor Grant M. Hyde, Director of the School of Journalism at the University of Wisconsin, who gave generously of his advice during the preparation of the manuscript.

The author feels especially indebted to newspaper and magazine publishers and the number of distinguished writers for their gracious permission to reprint complete copyrighted articles, or extracts from them. They are: *American Farm Youth; American Home; American Magazine,* Dr. Walter A. Wells, and Mrs. Marie Beynon Ray; *American Miller; American Paint and Oil Dealer; Beach & Pool; Better Homes and Gardens; Boot and Shoe Recorder* and Miss Caroline E. Iverson; *Boot and Shoe Recorder* and Mr. Alvo Albini; *Brooklyn Daily Eagle; Capper's Farmer; The Christian Home; Christian Science Monitor Weekly Magazine Section; Chicago Daily News; Cleveland Plain Dealer Sunday Magazine; Collier's* and Mr. W. B. Courtney; *Co-operative Merchandiser; Country Gentleman* and Mr. Wade Mosby; *Dance; Detroit News; Forum and Century* and Mr. Ellis O. Jones; *Good Housekeeping* and Miss Lonore Kent; *Good Housekeeping* and Mr. Julian R.

Meade; *Hobbies; Hygeia; Indianapolis News; Insurance Salesman; Ken* Magazine and Mr. Arthur Bartlett; *Ken* and Mr. James F. Sheer; *Kansas City Star; Leisure; Milwaukee Journal; Nature Magazine; New York Herald Tribune; New York Times Magazine* and Mr. Harlan Miller; *New York World-Telegram; Northwestern Druggist; Outdoor Life; Parent's Magazine; Physical Culture* and Miss Ellen Sorge; *Popular Mechanics; Popular Science; Portland Oregonian,* King Features, and Miss Ida Jean Kain; *Saturday Evening Post* and Mark R. Byers; *Scribner's* (now *Scribner's Commentator*) and Mr. Stanley Jones; *St. Louis Post-Dispatch; This Week; Woman's Home Companion* and Mr. Wallace Biggs; and *Woman's Home Companion* and Mrs. Anna Steese Richardson.

H. M. P.

CONTENTS

PART II

ILLUSTRATIONS

WRITING AND SELLING SPECIAL FEATURE ARTICLES

which they might look forward on that day when they retire from the monotonous routine of their jobs. They may then spend their days writing feature articles, and thereby have something interesting with which to occupy their time as well as to add to their incomes.

Even Beginners Sell. Young people, just average juniors and seniors in a university school of journalism, who never before had written a feature article, have applied these principles of feature writing. As a result, they have written features that perennially brought the class in magazine article writing a total of $2,500 to $3,800 a semester. If college students can, as some of them have, become entirely self-supporting, while in school, by means of writing features, it seems likely that others, no matter how inexperienced, may be successful, provided they have the necessary qualifications. Of course, one should not plan to be dependent upon an income from free-lancing until he has become established and has acquired some reputation in particular fields, or has made successful contacts with enough magazines to be assured at least of a certain degree of success.

Definition of a Feature Article. The special feature article is similar to a news story in that it gives the reader facts in an interesting form and is adapted to rapid reading. But it goes beyond those facts by amplifying them with study, research, and interviews, to instruct, guide, or entertain readers who know about the subject as well as those who do not.

The news story is written to inform the reader. The feature article not only informs but instructs, guides, or entertains. Where the news story presents the bare facts, the feature article dramatizes and supplements them by giving in detail information that will appeal to the reader's imagination. The reporter writes of what he sees; the feature writer relates not only what he sees but the causes or background of the story. The news story may, of necessity, be hurriedly written. The special feature article seldom has to meet a "deadline," and can be written at greater leisure. Thus, it affords the writer greater opportunity to make use of moving narration and vivid description, as well as clear exposition, in order to dramatize his writing. The news story and the magazine article are similar in that they interest the person who knows all about the subject and the one who knows nothing about it. In many respects, feature writing is reporting—at least it amplifies the work of the reporter.

Ability to Write May Be Acquired. Many persons feel the creative urge to write but hesitate to market their manuscripts because they believe that successful writers possess occult powers that they themselves do not have. But writing for publication is not mysterious; it must be reduced almost to a formula if one would write successfully. It is true that there are born writers; but as in almost every other kind of work, one may acquire the knack or mastery through practice and experience. Some have an inherited or natural aptitude for writing, but anyone who can write English correctly can write features if he will cultivate the following qualifications: (1) the ability to be curious and interested in the things about him and the desire to share that interest; (2) the capacity to recognize subjects that will interest readers and that may be developed into features; (3) the confidence and the enthusiasm and the ability to inspire those qualities in his readers; (4) the sympathy and understanding to enable him to see human interest elements in the facts about which he is writing and to make the article appeal to the readers; (5) the qualities of observation, thoroughness, and accurateness, to give the reader as well as the editor confidence in the writer; (6) skill in interviewing, in order to obtain interesting facts; (7) the ability to write clearly, accurately, and with imaginative appeal, to hold the reader's interest to the end of the article; and (8) the realization that feature writing is a business requiring a practical knowledge of the markets and the skill to "slant" articles to appeal to the publications.

Writer Must Be Sincere and Enthusiastic. Just as the advertising copy writer must be convinced that the product he is describing is the best the customer can buy, so must the feature writer convince or, as the advertising writers say, "sell" himself on his own idea for the feature that he is about to write.

Unless it is written with sincerity and enthusiasm, the article will never sell. Even as he plans the article before beginning to write it, he will want to visualize his reader—he will want to have a sincere desire to help, guide, or entertain him. If, as he plans and writes his article, he can picture the reader in his home sitting under the light of the reading lamp, in his hand the magazine containing the article, the writer will be able to write enthusiastically and sincerely.

Curiosity Is Source of Ideas. The person who is interested in people from all walks of life, who is curious, and who is always asking "why" of everything he sees and hears and does, or sees others do—and thus cannot be content with telling it to one or two friends but must tell it to hundreds, thousands, or millions—will find newspaper feature sections and magazines the most satisfying means of communicating his interests to others.

A young journalist passed a florist shop window that displayed, in miniature, a whirling windmill, a fast flowing brook, and a cool placid pool on whose moss-covered bank little, bright-colored flowers were growing. He stopped along with many morning shoppers, for he, too, was attracted by the movement in the small but realistic scene. He wondered what made the little windmill go, what power kept the water forever flowing in and out of the tiny lake. He was curious. He wanted to know "why." He entered the shop and asked the proprietor the explanation of the mechanism. As he left the store, he met a fraternity brother, a law student, and as they walked back to the campus the young writer told what he had just learned about the window display. At the first opportunity, the lawyer asked if the journalist were going to Chicago for the football game. The novice realized that his audience of one was not interested; but he felt that someone must be interested in that clever device that attracted so much attention to the window.

In answering his own question as to who would be interested, he thought of other florists, and he wondered what they read. Retracing his steps, he asked the florist what he read, and was invited into the manager's office to see copies of several florist's trade journal and business magazine. Some time later the young writer's story of the window display, including snapshots of it (which had been made on "glossy" paper) and the blueprint of the motor and the machinery employed to keep the little windmill and the water moving, appeared in one of the leading floral trade papers. The young man cashed a check for $35, which he felt was a fair reward for his first feature article and for his first assignment in his magazine-writing class. Because it was written with intense enthusiasm and sincerity, and almost absolute correctness, his professor had recorded a grade of "A" for him. Although he occasionally had received a few "A" grades, it was the first time he had ever received a check for a class assignment.

A young woman in the same class passed the window several times and was impressed by the crowd watching the display every time she went by. Each time she passed she noticed that a number of window shoppers went into the florist shop and made purchases. She wondered how much new business the window display was bringing the owner. A fifteen-minute interview with him gave her the material for her first feature article. A few minutes spent that night taking a flashlight picture of the window display, and her interest in wanting to tell other florists how they could attract more customers through interesting window displays, resulted in an article that was accepted by another florist's trade paper and for which she received a check for $25. Her article was shorter and was not quite so practical, because she did not send a drawing to show how the mechanism worked, as the young man did. Her ability to sense news, store news though it was, and to recognize a subject that would interest readers of a business journal, brought the writer the satisfaction of seeing her article in print and enabled her to earn her first money by means of her journalistic training.

A third student observed another display in the opposite show window of the same shop. It contained an aquarium with tropical fish, which were coming into vogue. She was interested in the kinds and types of fish bowls and, in talking with the manager, she became interested in them from the point of view of interior decoration and types best suited to the various periods of furnishings. They also talked about the care of the little fish. The young interviewer became so enthusiastic about her idea, or "tip," for her first feature that she wrote it up immediately. Her article was informative and entertaining, but she was not satisfied with it. She went to the library to read all she could find on the subject of small-fish life and rewrote the article entirely. She changed words, sentences, and paragraphs until she had an article that compared favorably with those that appear in many magazines. Before rewriting, she had studied the magazines that appealed to home-owners and housewives, and finally selected one whose readers she thought would be interested in her article. She sent it out, and in due time received a letter of acceptance. Upon publication of the article, she received a check for $50.

Here were three young students, ages 20, 21, and 22, juniors and seniors in a university school of journalism, who never before had written a feature article, but who sold their first. After the magazines were on the subscribers' desks, two of the writers received "fan mail," or letters inquiring further about the subject matter and expressing interest in the articles.

To Succeed One Must Be Careful Thinker. Let us see why these three students, and hundreds of others too, were successful in selling their first articles. The answer is easy: in each case the young writers had the eight qualifications for feature writing. Although all three became interested in the same floral shop, each saw a different thing when he looked in the window. Each saw a different angle appealing to a different reader. But they were all interested; they all recognized the news or interest value to other people; they were confident they could write the article to interest others. Through their understanding and sympathy of the problems of florists and home-owners they made their articles practical enough to appeal to the readers, who were practical people. They were skillful in getting the florist to give them the information, and they were observing and accurate in writing the facts into articles that editors would buy for their readers. They were businesslike in: (1) deciding who would want to know these facts; (2) learning what the shopkeepers and home-owners read; and (3) studying the markets before they began to write their articles.

Perhaps one might conclude that these students had worked on school publications and had had courses in survey of journalism and news reporting, and, because of even that small experience, were better prepared to write features that would sell. That was true of one of the three, but the other two had not had journalism experience or previous journalism courses. In the same class, sitting in nearby seats, were other students who had never had a previous course in journalism and had never worked on a student publication. They, too, wrote articles that sold. (Some of the articles are reprinted in Part II of this book.) There was the mother who had come along to college with her son and daughter, whose interest in an unusual corner drug store netted a check for $65 from a drug-trade publication. There was the college professor's wife whose children were in school. She had leisure time in which to learn to write of her home-making experiences. There was the seventy-year-old grandmother who wrote three times as many articles as were required in the course; and she sold them all. There was the minister who later became so successful as a free-lance writer that he abandoned his pulpit for the typewriter. There was the young physician, the lawyer, the high-school teacher, as well as eighty others who were just college juniors and seniors who had enrolled in the course because they wanted to write—and to write to sell.

They wrote about all kinds of subjects for all kinds of publications; they wrote of their own experiences, and the experiences of others; they wrote all types of articles because they were interested in everything—and they were so enthusiastic that they just had to share their interest with others. They were successful in selling their manuscripts, not because they were upperclassmen or held degrees of higher learning (for some of them who had not completed a high-school course were enrolled as adult specials), but because they were willing to apply what they learned concerning the technique of writing features. Their success was not due to their education or their lack of it, but to their interest, enthusiasm, and observation; to their ability to gather and verify facts, use a library, and write simply, clearly, and entertainingly; and to their businesslike procedure in studying newspapers and magazines to find markets and in keeping systematic records concerning their manuscripts (the cost of paper, stamps, envelopes, pictures, drawings, and other expenses, the time spent in gathering and writing the material, the dates on which the articles were mailed out and returned, and the list of publications to which they were sent).

Aptitude for Writing Is Essential. The gift for writing features, whether native or acquired, is absolutely essential. But by no means is it a talent with which one must be born. If, however, a person thinks he would like to learn to write for print, he should, first of all, take stock of his native abilities and his likes and dislikes. He should determine, in so far as possible, his capacity for overcoming his dislikes and the traits of character that would hinder his success in writing feature articles.

As important as the desire to express himself in writing, and to share or communicate his knowledge of facts with others, is his high regard for truth and accuracy. A writer must never be willing to disseminate false statements or facts, or even to imply untruths. His inaccuracies will find him out. Then he will lose the confidence of both the editor to whom he submits his manuscripts and the reader who detects the false statements. The latter will in turn lose his faith in the publication to which he has subscribed. Equally significant is the writer's willingness to search out and dig for facts and to go to no end of trouble to ascertain the truth in order to inform the reader correctly. If one finds that he is bored by searching for facts, and if he is not curious or interested in the people and things about him, and if he does not wish to know what others like to read for their information, guidance, and entertainment, he should hesitate to take up writing either as an avocation or as a career.

Skill in Interviewing Is Important. If a writer is to gather facts from authorities, he must develop skill in interviewing, in order to draw from the expert the information that he desires for the readers. He must learn to be not only a good listener but an enthusiastic one. If he does not show interest in the subject upon which he is interviewing, the person interviewed (or the "interviewee," as the journalists say) will not be enthusiastic or interested either, and the result will be a lifeless article.

If the interviewer does all the talking, or most of it, the interviewee will not have an opportunity to give his expert opinions, and then the interviewer will have nothing of importance to write or quote. The good interviewer has been termed a "human sponge," or a "blotting paper." He must be able to absorb and assimilate what he is told, and to think through his material clearly, in order to be able to appeal to the reader's interest. The person who is content with foggy thinking will not have readers to whom to appeal, because editors will not buy his manuscripts.

Slanting Manuscripts to Markets. To succeed, a writer must be willing to study the markets. If he cannot sell his manuscripts, he will never attain success. He must be able to adapt his material to conform to the policy and style of the publication that he thinks might be interested in the article. When writing for print, the writer should never think of the editor but of the 100,000 or 500,000 subscribers. He should visualize one of those readers—a typical reader of the newspaper feature section or of the magazine to which he is submitting his manuscript—and then he will be better able to write his material for that reader and for the thousands of other similar readers. If he has selected, in his imagination, a typical reader, he will be less likely to go beyond the mental grasp of that reader. Thus, he will avoid writing down to or over the reader's head. Before beginning to write the first draft of the article, the writer must determine the markets to which he will send his article, in order to fit it to the style of the publication and to know what pictures or drawings he will need for it.

In appealing to the reader's interest, one must write about the things in which the reader will be interested. Yet many young beginners yearn to write their own opinions. A writer will never develop a reader following unless he writes from the point of view of the reader rather than from his own opinions. Very young writers often try to impress their readers with their individual style of writing, which in many cases is merely a poor imitation of some freakish style popular for the moment in some of the magazines that are more interested in fads than they are in facts. Or the embryo writers may refuse to conform their style of writing to that of the publications that they are hoping will buy their articles, because they feel it will ruin their so-called "individual" style. Some beginners have such confidence in their own writing ability that they feel it is a waste of time to organize their material or to write from an outline. There are others who write the first draft enthusiastically but who refuse to edit their copy to correct careless or slovenly writing, bad spelling, and faulty punctuation. Their personal vanity is hurt when they are required to prepare their manuscripts in the professional manner of experienced writers. Many beginners are wordy or they fail to use the right words to express their ideas. They express themselves awkwardly because they do not think through the sentences before they start to write them. They have little regard for the rules of punctuation and grammar or for accuracy in spelling. Editors will not have confidence in careless manuscripts and will reject them even though the facts may sound new and interesting. They feel that the authors of such manuscripts may be equally careless in their fact-gathering. Editors have to be careful to avoid making their publications ridiculous in the eyes of their readers and of editors of other publications.

Writers Must Use Businesslike Methods. The successful writer does not wait until he "feels like writing," or "until the spirit moves him," but he has a definite time for his writing and he lets nothing interfere with his work. Though he thoroughly enjoys writing, he writes for money rather than for "the love of writing." Some sensitive people who are afraid to get a rejection slip say they do not care to write for money because they prefer to write for "the love of writing." There are dreamers who refuse to write practical ideas or to be businesslike in their writing or work. They refuse to keep their files of material and clippings in an orderly manner, and they just cannot be bothered with keeping records concerning the expense and whereabouts of the manuscripts they have written. They think it is artistic to be careless, unsystematic, slovenly in their thinking and writing, and unbusinesslike in looking after the financial side of their avocation or career.

The enthusiastic beginner who is ambitious to overcome his faults; desirous of adapting the content and style of his article to that of a possible market; willing to work hard, study publications, and analyze possible markets for his manuscripts; always thoughtful of the readers; always thinking of that typical reader as he writes; never satisfied with his manuscript but always anxious to revise it in any way he can to improve it; careful to prepare his copy in a professional style; and sensible enough to write about things in which people are interested—he will be a success. His own fervor will help him to overcome his faults. If he will be businesslike in keeping his files in order, always to have material on hand, and systematic in keeping his records of profits from his writings, he will soon pass from the stage of the beginner to that of the professional.

Some who start writing features have one or all of the faults enumerated, but because they have a burning desire to express their thoughts and to write for print, they are willing to learn to write in the professional manner. Of course, it is hard work and requires great patience; but in the end they win and their names are seen in the by-lines over leading articles in magazines today, simply because they were determined to write and to write well.

Some Beginners Never Attain Success. Many who would

write remain amateurs because they are not willing to adjust their ideas to conform to editorial policies. They fail because they wish to write their own opinions, and, as a rule, beginners do not have opinions of enough value to interest readers. They are not authorities in some specialized field. There are self-satisfied souls who write because they wish to express themselves; they do not want to include opinions of people whose ideas would be new and interesting to readers or whose names would lend weight to the article. These self-centered folk may sell one or two of their opinion articles, but they never progress far in writing for publication. They are not observant, nor are they desirous of learning what readers want to read. Others never climb above the round of the amateur on the writer's ladder because they will not work regularly or systematically; they wish to wait to write until they "feel like writing," until they are "inspired." They are the type who spurn the writing of anything practical that will inform, instruct, or entertain readers.

Others fail to succeed because they will not interview people who have new ideas or who are authorities. They do not desire to share credit for anything in the article with anyone. Many will not adjust their ways of writing to conform with the policy of the magazine or will not prepare a manuscript to meet the requirements for publication. They feel their way is superior. They do not want to be informed on the topics of the day because they feel that to do so is not "being literary." As a result of their attitude, their articles are always behind the times, and editors will not buy them. No matter how well written others are, manuscripts on current subjects are preferred by editors. Or there is the type of would-be writer who cannot bear to send anything out for publication until he has developed a "style." The result is that he writes but little, and therefore never attains the style he is seeking. Some lose their courage at the sight of a rejection slip and become so depressed that they never attempt to send out the manuscript again, or to revise it, or to write another one. They are the cowards of the writing world. Others are too lazy to think:

(1) who will read their articles; (2) why will they read them; and (3) how much will they want to read. The consequence is that no one ever reads the articles. They are written so carelessly and contain so little that is informative, instructive, or entertaining that editors will not buy them.

Many remain beginners because they are content to send out manuscripts that are written hastily and superficially; the vocabulary is poor; sentences and paragraphs are not thought through; and the writers are satisfied to write merely what they saw, without telling the reader what was back of what they saw, or what caused what they saw. They are neither enthusiastic nor confident about the subject matter; they write to be writing, but they do not give any thought to the reader and to his likes and dislikes.

Writer's Attitude Helps or Hinders. The unknown writer has as good an opportunity as the well-known one to have his articles accepted, provided that his manuscript is as well done as the experienced writer's. Editors depend upon free-lance writers for most of their fact material. They are more interested in the content of the article and how it meets their publication needs than they are in the author's name, or by-line, over the article. The amateur's by-line will be welcome to any editor if the writer will adopt the professional way of writing and the attitude of the professional toward his work.

The professional feature writer admits that he writes for money, whether it is to provide his entire income, or, as an avocation, to add to his salary from his regular profession or work. The writer whose by-line is familiar has the spirit of the eager pioneer or adventurer, because he, too, seeks the new, works regularly, and writes systematically. He not only is willing, but desires to do his work in the professional way. He knows what he is doing, how to do it, and, upon its completion, where to send it for publication.

He succeeds because he gives thought: (1) to the subject about which he is going to write; (2) to the reader and to how much the reader will be interested in the subject; (3) to the publications that people interested in the subject will read;

(4) to the sources he will go to for help or ideas; (5) to the person, or persons, he will interview; (6) to the pictures, drawings, and illustrative material that he can use to add to the interest in the article; (7) to the plan of development of the facts, in order that they will have the greatest appeal to the reader; and (8) to writing it in a way that will make the article effective in its appeal to the reader.

Through experience he has learned that writers must be curious, observant, accurate, and well informed. He has found that when he is confident and enthusiastic and has faith in the article, he writes more easily and better. He has acquired the scientific spirit, for he is willing to search for facts until he gets what he wants; then he desires to share them with others through the printed page. By studying the markets assiduously and knowing how to slant his articles to fit the policy of the publication to which he sends them, he avoids rejection slips. He is businesslike in filing the material that he gathers from observation, interviews, experiences of his own and of others, clippings, and notes from his readings. He tries to know a little about everything and to know all he can about several fields of special interest. He does not wait for inspiration to write, but inspires himself by writing regularly, whether or not he feels like doing it.

Often one hears it said that success in writing is just a matter of luck; but success in writing is a matter of hard thinking and careful workmanship. Those who enjoy it are rewarded with the satisfaction that their work has been well done and with the knowledge that the financial remuneration can be as little or as big as they desire, the amount depending upon their determination.

The Amateur Acquires a Journalistic Face. The novice who becomes a success undergoes a metamorphosis before he becomes a professional writer, because a free-lance must develop "a journalistic face." In looking for the new about which to write interestingly, the feature writer develops "a nose for news," as the journalist says; in looking for appeals to the emotions to brighten up the facts, he acquires "an ear for human interest"; in finding fact material that will entertain or inform the reader, he enlarges "his eye for feature stories"; and in learning to slant his material to a market that may buy his article, he strengthens "his jaw of determination" to succeed. In reality, the professional achieves more than a journalistic face, because back of and above his face he must have a mind that is sympathetic, understanding, and desirous of knowledge; and he must have a conscience that will let him write only the truth.

In the eyes of the craft, the amateur becomes a professional writer when he has made his new journalistic features a part of his physiognomy, or his professional face. He gathers his material, writes his facts, and markets his manuscripts in the professional manner. Any beginner who will read and apply the proper techniques can be transformed from an amateur into a professional as soon as he acquires the qualifications that will enable him to write articles that subscribers will want to read, to study markets as diligently as the investor studies the financial pages of his newspaper, and to write his manuscript as carefully as does the professional writer.

Learn to Write by Writing. There is only one way to learn to write for publication, and that is *to write*. Creative writing, which is largely self-taught, actually is only a small part of writing. If one could break feature writing up into ten parts, he would find: one part gathering facts; one part interviewing; four parts thinking and planning; three parts knowing how to analyze the editorial policy in order to slant the article and to know where to submit the manuscript; and one part writing—but excellent writing.

The tyro must force himself to write whether he feels like it or not, because creative work of any kind is seldom the result of some spontaneous inner power. The writer can compel or inspire himself by various methods to become so interested in what he is writing that he will forget to go to lunch or will write far into the night without realizing the hour. If a novice will set a time to start his "research," or preparation, for his article, he can call forth the impulse to write by: (1) reading all he can find on the subject; (2) investigating facts; (3) observing things that might apply to the material; and (4) interviewing authorities. By the time he has collected all his notes, material, pictures, or drawings, he will have given his article so much thought and become so enthusiastic about it that one could not keep him from writing. Even before he sits down to his typewriter, he will have formulated a plan or outline of the material he will wish to include. As he was walking down the street, or perhaps he just was dozing off to sleep, or just had turned off his alarm clock, a striking idea may come to him for a clever "lead," or beginning, for his article. Attention-getting captions, or headlines, and leads usually come to one like a flash after he has given the subject matter of the entire article the necessary thought that spurs the imagination to produce clever ideas with reader appeal.

Some beginners find that to form the habit of writing every day at a regular time develops not only the urge to write, but improves their ability and skill. For others, unusual events often serve as the stimulus to invoke the urge to expressing themselves on paper, or perhaps a unique experience which the beginner wishes to share with others serves as the incentive to begin his article. A sense of obligation will conjure so-called inspiration for undisciplined writers who must meet a "deadline," even a self-made one, in order to get started; or making a vow to start often aids one in doing so. The hope of compensation, either a financial reward or renown and fame, frequently is sufficient incentive to begin the manuscript. The fervent desire to communicate ideas or experiences with others who may be interested may fire the novice's enthusiasm to the point where he sits down and types off an outline from which he develops his article. Writing will not come by waiting for the impulse or inspiration; it does come by regular and continued practice.

One learns to write by writing, provided he has some ability and skill in using the fundamental rules of composition or the willingness to learn them. He will be successful if he will write about things that will interest the many people represented by thousands or millions of subscribers to which the publications go, and if he acquaints himself with the editorial policies of as many publications as possible.

Difference Between Amateurs and Professionals. Feature writers are classified into two distinct groups: amateurs and professionals. Amateurs are those who find pleasure in writing out their thoughts but who are too interested in their own self-expression to give thought as to possible readers. They write only for the praise they hope to receive from their friends or fellow members of writing clubs, whose main purpose may be to entertain visiting authors at tea. The amateur works spasmodically and usually takes pride in writing only when he "feels the urge." He glories in the fact that he is not businesslike, he refuses to slant his copy to any particular publication, and he says he spurns the idea of writing for money.

The professional's attitude toward writing is quite the opposite. He writes regularly either to keep in practice, if his writing is an avocation, or, if it is a career, to earn his livelihood. He plans a schedule of articles to be written; he studies and analyzes publications of all kinds to know their editorial and advertising content. Even though he is not writing editorials, fiction, or advertising copy, a careful study of those phases of a magazine may show a writer the kind of readers for whom the editor plans his magazine. A survey of the advertising in a publication will give one an idea about everything he needs to know concerning the readers for whom he hopes to write, because the advertising is written to appeal to them. A fair estimate of the reader's income, buying power, living standards, likes, and interests may be determined from the advertising, as explained in Chapter 9, "Slanting Articles to Publications." The veteran writer takes pride in his sales, which are the result of his careful work.

The amateur will remain an amateur until he is able to adjust his attitude toward writing and his writing habits to conform with the standards set up by experienced writers in the craft and demanded by editors. He must: (1) follow the accepted technique in order to do the articles as editors would want them done; (2) be observant in order to develop the nose for news and the eye for features; (3) gather interesting facts that will instruct, inform, or entertain his readers; (4) have ability to use the writer's tools—words, sentences, and paragraphs—correctly and effectively; and (5) never be satisfied with his writing until he feels that it has real merit.

The feature writer is a reporter, who, like the aviator, has a sixth sense. He knows what the general public likes to read and he knows where, when, and how to market his manuscripts. Like the reporter, he must keep on studying, experimenting, and setting himself newer and harder tasks in the writing field. Feature writing is the reporter's normal side line.

Equipment for Writing. Of all the arts, writing requires the least financial outlay. A good typewriter is the first requisite. A supply of a good grade of typewriting paper, carbon paper, and copy paper are necessary; one should always save a carbon of anything he writes for print, in case the manuscript may be lost in the mails. Two sizes of manila envelopes, the outside one, 13 x 10 inches, and a smaller one 12½ by 9½ inches (to fit easily inside the larger one, to be used if it is necessary to return the manuscript), and government postal cards for the editor's acknowledgment of the receipt of the manuscript, are necessary. Bristol board, a smooth lightweight pasteboard, or any other that takes India ink, should be used for drawings and sketches if articles lend themselves to that type of illustration. Every feature writer should, as soon as possible, have a good camera, since informal snapshots are preferred by editors. A professional writer has his office or study equipped with file cases in which he files notes taken from his readings, clippings, bulletins, and other reference material. He will find a small postal scale of great convenience in weighing his manuscripts. His professional library should include a recent, recognized dictionary, a thesaurus, a synonym book, a handbook for writers, a World Almanac, and an atlas—all instruments of his craft. Market books listed under "The Free-Lance Writer's Library," in the Appendix will be suggestive of ideas for articles as well as markets, as are the writer's magazines listed there. Access to libraries where newspapers, trade or business papers, magazines, periodicals, and bulletins may be studied is essential if the writer is to achieve craftsmanship.

Pretentious equipment is not necessary for the beginner. He may rent a typewriter and a camera. He will find that a pasteboard box large enough to hold manila folders will serve well as a file case. He may buy the necessary supplies (typewriting paper, carbon paper, envelopes of two sizes, post cards, and stamps) as he needs them, in order not to purchase too heavily at a time. Because many people think that they want to write but, when they get at it, find they do not have the aptitude for it, one should be cautious about investing in too much equipment until he is confident that he wants to make writing either his avocation or his career.

Rewards for Writing Features. If a beginner enters the field of feature writing with the determination that he will not be discouraged by rejection slips, disgruntled by the long waiting for either the rejection or the acceptance of his articles, or disappointed by the uncertainty of the financial remuneration, he will find great satisfaction in writing articles—whether he makes it an avocation or a profession.

In considering the benefits and rewards as an avocation, the beginner will find mental satisfaction in self-expression and in the communication of his ideas to others. It affords an incentive to improve his writing and to develop a style as well as providing opportunities for meeting and interviewing successful people. It also serves as a training school for short-story and fiction writers, in that it stimulates initiative and imagination. Intellectual curiosity and scientific desire for investigation are stimulated in the search for facts, which makes a feature writer a student throughout his life. He is always adding to his knowledge in many fields, because he cannot write features without becoming better informed himself. Since a great variety of material is available to the free-lance, he writes only that which he chooses. The opportunities for his manuscripts to be published are almost unlimited.

The novice should not depend upon feature writing as a means of livelihood, because the markets and the financial remuneration are too uncertain until one has become established in the profession. There have been a few clever and gifted students in almost every journalism school, however, who have abandoned dishwashing as a means of attaining a college degree. They have found free-lancing easier, more pleasant, and more profitable. They have received from $500 to $2,200 for their articles. But they had acquired the eight desirable requisites for successful writing of features.

The beginner is paid from one-fourth of a cent to two cents a word or more, the rate depending upon his ability to write effectively and to slant his material to meet the editor's approval. As skill is developed and experience is gained throughout the years in writing and marketing, many adults have added from $1,000 to $6,000 to their incomes in addition to their business or career. Many people find free-lancing a means to attain little luxuries and pleasures that they could not otherwise have. There was the housewife, for example, who wanted more than anything else to go to Europe. Financially it was impossible; but upon hearing of the success of writers in a beginning class in magazine writing, she enrolled, determined to learn to write and sell articles. She received $3,000 for her articles over a period of about two years. Then, with her husband, she went to Europe on the money earned. She has been writing ever since. The money has enabled her to enjoy other things that she had always wanted.

Widens Professional Opportunities. Professional satisfactions include personal influence, public recognition, respect of others, and fame—to at least some degree. Ability to write acceptable articles and to be paid for one's ideas often serves as a cause for promotion or a salary increase in almost any business or profession, as well as increasing the opinions of others as to the value of one's ideas. Doctors, lawyers, ministers, professors, teachers, business people, engineers, housewives, farmers, and others may add to their incomes by sharing their expert knowledge or experiences with readers who are interested.

Fortunately for the journalist, many experts do not have the time nor the inclination to write about their specialities; or they may write too technically for the average reader. Their shortcomings enable the feature writer to interview them and to write the information in a way that will appeal to readers. By submitting features to newspapers and magazines, free-lance writers may make contacts that will bring them offers of positions as correspondents, staff reporters, feature writers, or associate editors. A young woman in a feature class wrote an article concerning the coal and fuel business and sent it to a coal dealers' trade paper. The editors were so well pleased with it they asked her to send in an article a month and made her an associate editor. Numerous other students and free-lance writers have developed similar opportunities through their articles. Feature writing offers many opportunities to enter any of the several fields of creative writing and serves as the door that may lead to the writing of fiction.

Feature Writing as a Career. For the person who has the ability and has established a reputation for himself in the journalistic field, writing as a profession has just as much to offer from the financial point of view as has any of the other professions, provided one likes to write and has the determination to succeed. The income of the professional varies with his ability to slant his material for the more remunerative markets and with his capacity to turn out a large number of articles in a year. The income of the proficient writer varies from $5,000 up to $20,000, and in a few cases even higher. He is paid from two to ten cents a word, although a number of the big names are paid as high as a dollar a word.

The road to success as a writer is long and arduous, but no more so than in such professions as law and medicine. To the creative writer, however, it is never laborious nor boresome. His work brings him in contact with successful, happy people, whom he enjoys meeting. Even though one is never certain of his income, if he is businesslike and keeps a score or more of articles in the mail at the same time, and if he is able to turn out from two to three articles a week, like the physician and the lawyer, he will soon establish definite sources of income from markets upon which he can depend. As some free-lance writers become specialists in a particular field, they give up writing for the other fields. They feel it is better to concentrate on one. They depend entirely upon querying the editors of the field in which they have specialized and in which they are known and writing only upon order. Many class magazines pay from $500 to $1,000, or even more, for an article written upon order by a writer whose by-line will add to the reputation of the publication.

Professional writers who prefer to have a definite and assured income may become associated with publications as assistants, associate editors, or as editors-in-chief when the opportunity arises. Their salaries range from $3,000 up to $25,000 a year. Even though one may not have become a renowned writer, there are many openings for experienced writers as editors of trade, industrial, fraternal, professional, class, and general publications in addition to opportunities in writing fiction, nonfiction, syndicated features, publicity, and radio continuity. Such experience gives one background if he wishes to start his own magazine, as many free-lance writers do when they are interested in the business as well as in the editorial side.

The World Is the Writer's Workshop. Whether one makes writing an avocation or a career, he will succeed only because he likes to write, he enjoys meeting people, and he has a professional attitude toward his work. To the novice and the professional alike, there is a keen pleasure in writing features, for the whole world may become the writer's workshop. His search for facts to interest readers takes him into all sorts of paths and byways at home or abroad, because wherever one goes or wherever one looks, there are more ideas for feature articles than one can write in a lifetime. In this golden age of the magazine there are more markets than free-lance writers can ever hope to oversupply.

Exercises

1. What are the names of the magazines that are on sale at your nearest news stand or corner drug store?
2. List those with which you are familiar.
3. Check the names of those in Exercise 1 that contain special feature articles.
4. List five metropolitan newspapers that have feature sections to which you think you might be able to sell feature articles that you could write.
5. In your two favorite general magazines list the fiction (short and continued stories) and the feature articles that you find in the table of contents. What does this comparison tell you about the reader's interest in each magazine?
6. What is the circulation of your favorite metropolitan newspaper as listed in the N. W. Ayer & Son's *Directory of Newspapers and Periodicals* or in the directory in the International Year Book Number of *Editor and Publisher—The Fourth Estate*.
7. What is the circulation of your favorite general magazine as listed in the last issue of the magazine and farm paper section of the *Standard Rate and Data Service* or in Ayer's *Directory?*
8. Question yourself concerning the eight qualifications of a feature writer listed in this chapter. Grade each question good, fair, or poor. Which qualifications do you need to develop more fully?
9. Go through the advertising in your favorite magazine and make an estimate of the subscriber's income, living standards, and his interests.
10. On the basis of your survey of the advertising in Exercise 9, what kind of subjects for feature articles do you think the subscribers would like to read?

Publication Analysis

Milwaukee *Journal* and Kansas City *Star*

Do not spend more than three hours in analyzing and typing this report.

An analysis of the feature articles in the Milwaukee *Journal* and the Kansas City *Star*. (Glance through the state, local, and national features in one or more issues of the Sunday *Journal* and Sunday *Star*.)

1. Notice length of features. What did you like about them? What did you find less interesting?
2. What did you learn that was suggestive to you in writing your own feature articles?
3. What did you like or dislike about the captions or headings of the feature articles?
4. With what subject matter were the feature articles concerned?
5. What was the average number of pictures used to an article?
6. What kind of readers do you think read these special feature articles?
7. Which article in each paper would you have liked to have written and why?
8. List two tips for feature articles that you could write that were suggested to you by this study. List three markets for each tip or suggested article.

(Reports are to be typed, double spaced, written on one side only. *Not to be more than 500 words* if you do not use outline form. Fold papers crosswise and out. In upper left-hand corner write your name, course number, name of course, and your instructor's name. In middle of top margin write name of newspapers you are analyzing.)

2

FINDING IDEAS AND MATERIAL FOR FEATURES

Recognizing Material for Articles. The inexperienced writer marvels at the variety of subjects for feature articles that the professional finds. But everywhere there is material that even the beginner may write into marketable articles as soon as he develops the ability to recognize possibilities in material about him. In searching for ideas, he develops (1) "his nose for news"; and in finding the facts with which to entertain or inform the reader, he develops (2) "his eye for special features." The amateur must train himself to look at every person, every experience, every event, and at everything he sees, hears, tastes, and even smells with a view of seeing what possibilities there are for features in which readers would be interested.

Qualifications for Finding Ideas. A writer, to be successful, must have: (1) an inquiring mind; (2) a keen eye that is all observing; (3) a nose that senses the new and unique; and (4) an indispensable notebook in which to record the inspirations, or "tips," immediately, or they will be lost to memory. With this equipment he will never need be concerned as to what to write about. If he has the curiosity to dig beneath the surface, he will find "gems" for acceptable articles for which the editors and the reading public are eagerly awaiting.

Sources Are Everywhere. There is never a lack of subjects. The alert writer will find within his own world a perpetual supply of ideas for profitable articles. It is not necessary to have a specialized training, or extensive travel, or a particular location in order to find ideas, or "tips," for articles. These advantages, of course, will increase the supply and variety of suggestions. Yet if similar ideas cannot be seen and developed into successful features from one's immediate surroundings, the chances are that one will not have the "special feature eye" when he reaches the location of his desire. Everywhere one turns, everything one reads, everything one sees contains possibilities for subjects about which to write. Good material for articles goes to waste every day because no one writes it into features. But in order to train oneself to see features, one must constantly ask "why" of everything he sees, hears, feels, and does. When a writer says that he cannot find anything to write about, he is confessing that he is not alert, or observing, or curious. If he were, he would see material everywhere, along every street, on the train, in the street-car or bus, in the newspaper, or in daily conversation. Wherever one goes there are more ideas than one possibly can find time to write, even if his working day were twenty-four hours.

Even in the most commonplace environment there is unlimited material. One can always find something unusual, unfamiliar, and unexpected. Even the usual and familiar things in one community may be unusual enough in other communities that readers there would enjoy reading about them. Wherever there are people, things are happening. Back of these events there may be interesting ideas, personalities, discoveries, or experiences upon which the alert writer can easily capitalize.

The feature writer in search of ideas is like a first-class reporter who associates with all classes of people in order to learn their points of view, their interests, and their ideas. Through these contacts he picks up ideas for stories of hobbies, avocations, and all sorts of unique and unusual things. He finds ideas in conventions, addresses, sermons, newspapers, periodicals, bulletins, advertising, publicity, catalogues, fairs, conversations, exhibits, museums, industries, trades, businesses, professions, educational institutions, holidays, anniversaries, or weather conditions. As the beginner becomes more experienced, he will find that "tips" will "pop" into his mind. With practice it will become second nature to discover subjects that deal with concrete ideas.

Three Classifications of Sources. Because editors consider content more valuable than form, even a writer who is clumsy in his style may draw generous checks if he has the faculty for seeing everything through his "special feature eye." Even though one is not born with this ability, he can soon train himself to see features all about him. The more one writes, the more he will find about which to write. As one readily can see, it is difficult to classify sources as to types, because in many instances an article may seem to have its origin as much in experience as in observation, or even in printed material. But for the sake of examining the sources from which ideas come, we shall classify the sources into three divisions. In so doing, we must keep in mind that the sources overlap, and in some cases it is impossible to classify an idea as definitely coming from one source. Three main sources of ideas and material for special features to be written for newspapers and magazines are: (1) observation; (2) experience; and (3) printed material.

Sources of Ideas Are Unlimited. Observations of one's own, or of others, are rich with ideas and suggestions for acceptable articles. (1) A locality, (2) a prominent person, (3) the new and unusual, (4) conventions, (5) professions, businesses, and trades, (6) farm life and activities, (7) homes and gardens, (8) family problems, (9) recreations, (10) organizations, and (11) the arts—all, by means of observation, will provide unlimited sources of ideas to the beginner as well as to the professional.

The Locality. Wherever one lives, if he walks down Main Street, or through the neighborhood or community, or takes a ride in the country, he will have ample opportunities for observation and for excellent ideas. To see things happen on the streets, in public places, or at meetings and gatherings will suggest ideas that anyone who enjoys writing will find interesting and lucrative. The ease with which a writer may find subjects and material is best shown by specific examples.

Seeing people enjoying their picnic lunches in the park gave a woman writer a good subject for a historical treatment of this custom and its many variations throughout the world. The article was published in the New York *Times* magazine section in July, a picnic month.

A beginner in feature writing stepped into a drug store to buy some paper for her first article. She was informed that only drugs were carried in this store. She became interested in the owner's business policy and asked so many questions that she found she had a better idea for her first article than the one she had planned originally. She wrote up the druggist and his store and sold it to the *American Druggist.*

Prominent and Interesting Persons. The great or near great are valuable as a source for articles, because everyone likes to read about them. In almost any community are persons who would become more famous if the outside world only knew more about them. The alert writer may be the means of bringing deserved recognition to an interesting personality, and thus give him and his friends pleasure. The fun of writing and the financial remuneration will be the writer's reward. One can capitalize upon the ambitions of those who may not have attained greatness by encouraging them to talk about the hidden secrets and desires of their lives that may be so written as to inspire readers.

An interview with a Madison Street bridge tender not only told of the crew's work in saving lives in Chicago, but made the readers of the Chicago *Daily News* feel that they knew Paddy Culhane. An account of two young women hiking their way to Mexico to study social and economic conditions and taking turns in carrying the portable typewriter and camera made a feature in the Brooklyn *Daily Eagle.* Because of his unique ideas concerning the education of young women in the college of which he is president, and because of his prominence in the educational world, Dr. James M. Wood made an interesting subject for an article in *The American Magazine.*

The New and Unusual. Since human nature is always interested in the unique and the modern or newest, editors are always on the lookout for articles of that type. As the range of subject matter is unlimited, an ever-watchful writer will find this source a lucrative one. It may be a new way of doing something, a new invention, a new idea that has improved old conditions, a new point of view, the unusual things made by man or nature. In fact, anything that is new and unusual in or on the universe will develop into saleable features. Such articles contain many elements of the news story, because they concern the new and, like the news story, must supply the answers to who, what, why, when, where, and how. Although the object about which one is writing may be old to that particular community, it may be new and unique to readers in other places, and this increases the range of "tips" for this type of article.

Noticing, while on a short motor trip, that numerous small towns in Missouri, Kansas, and Nebraska had adopted city planning and that unsightly buildings were vanishing from the main streets to be replaced by modernized business sections, an observer made some inquiries at the local chambers of commerce and wrote an article on "Main Street in the Middle West is Going Modern." It was both new and unusual, and was published in the Kansas City *Times*. The great eroding power of rivers and streams and the colossal carving power of glaciers was described graphically as the unusual in *Nature Magazine*.

Conventions. Speakers at meetings of all kinds are usually experts in their fields and are good sources of material. Their talks often are based upon the results of years of research, or upon valuable experience, or upon the presentation of new ideas, any one of which would make interesting articles for magazine readers. From such a source came the following:

Attending a meeting of the American Road Builders Association, a writer gathered information that provided material for an article on building highways with cotton because it was more enduring and the upkeep cost less than present road construction materials. The story was printed in the New York *Herald Tribune*.

Professions, Businesses, and Trades. All kinds of professions, businesses, occupations, and trades offer innumerable opportunities for articles for professional, business, and trade magazines, which number 1,585, with 31,736 issues annually. Anyone who is successful in his profession or adept at his business or trade will be glad to tell the feature writer what distinguishes his work from that of others. The story must be based upon the worker's originality, ingenuity, skill, or technique. The writer must get all the information he can and must ascertain how much time, trouble, or expense the professional or occupational worker saves and the pleasure he derives from his tasks, which thus enables the reader to improve his methods, save his time or his money, or add to his pleasures. Pictures, sketches, or drawings, no matter how rough or sketchy, are necessary to show the construction or use if the article concerns the construction of some device that the reader may wish to make. The beginning writer should observe different kinds of professions, businesses, and trades by visiting offices, stores, and shops. The wealth of suggestions he will see will bring in checks. It is easier to sell to this field of publications than almost any other.

An article on a young woman physician whose profound knowledge astounded research men, published in the Milwaukee *Journal,* and one on court judges who show an understanding sympathy, printed in the Chicago *Daily News,* show the ease with which one may find articles concerning professions. Stories on the Christmas-tree business, in the New York *Herald Tribune,* on the turkey-raising industry, in the Kansas City *Star,* on how delivery trucks build sales, in *The Cooperative Merchandiser,* and one on a harness maker whose business continued to flourish in spite of changed customs, which was used as the lead article in *The Spokesman and Harness World* —all indicate what a writer may find in occupations and trades when he is observing and alert.

Farm Life and Farm Activities. Since it has been estimated that 32,500,000 people live on the 6,500,000 farms in this country, farm interests provide a wide range of features that will find a ready market in the 3,974 farm publications with their 202,662 issues annually. The editors of these journals are in the market for all kinds of manuscripts concerning the farm. The marketing of farm products, the cutting of production costs, improving farm sanitation, modernization of farms, crop rotation, erosion control, increased production of dairy products, poultry, livestock, grains, gardens, short cuts in the farm kitchen, canning made easy, decorating the farm home, and planning the farm family's wardrobe—all have reader appeal. Articles on novel sidelines—such as raising bees for profit, growing evergreens to finance the children's education, or conducting a wayside market—are found in magazines because the editors know that they will be read by millions of readers and that they will be a means of helping them physically or financially.

A young woman observed birds eating bugs on grains growing in her father's fields. She interviewed a zoology professor and obtained material for an article, "Birds Aid in Pest Control," which was published in *Capper's Farmer*. "New Grades for Baby Chicks" gave the readers of *Country Gentleman* information and guidance in purchasing baby chicks, which, if followed, doubtless saved the readers thousands of dollars and resulted in stronger and healthier flocks.

Homes and Gardens. Even if one does not have a home, he hopes to have one some day, and that explains the almost universal reader interest in this subject. It is upon this human desire that 18 well-known home and garden magazines, with 208 issues annually, are founded. Women's magazines and newspapers devote pages and whole sections to these two subjects, which, in many publications, are expanded to include articles concerning not only exteriors and interiors, but interior decoration, home management, household equipment, selection and preparation of foods, textiles, needle-craft, and fashions. Material of this type is to be found everywhere, for every home, however humble, may have article suggestions. The writer's own home and garden, or those of others that he observes, may be the source of checks. One writer, who says everything in and around the home is "grist for her mill," has earned more than $10,000 writing for home magazines since she took a course in magazine writing.

A young writer was attracted by an artistic and colorful window display of linens and bedding. She interviewed an expert in interior decoration and buyers in stores and acquired information that would enable anyone to shop more efficiently for a good night's sleep if they read the issue of *American Home* in which the article was printed.

"Highlights in the Colonial Kitchen" was suggested by observing a display of kitchen utensils. It gave the readers of *Better Homes and Gardens* information in keeping their pots and pans as attractively as did the colonial housewives. Giving guidance and information to the reader, the author of "Going Native with Rock Gardens," in *House Beautiful,* gave definite directions in selecting the location and the soil and in choosing the plants for the sunny and shady places among the rocks.

The Family and Its Problems. Not only the social but the physical welfare of the family is a perpetual source of ideas in which a writer will find unlimited opportunities. Many publications are devoted entirely to the subject, and almost all of the 58 home and women's magazines, with their 714 issues annually, use one or more articles concerning the family and its life. Many observing housewives and mothers who have an aptitude for writing and who are alert to their opportunities find that articles on the problems of the family sell as easily as do those written for the home and garden publications. The subject matter may range anywhere from dressing the child for indoors or outdoors, helping the man of the house to overcome his grouchy spells, or meeting the problem of the unpopular daughter.

A young mother told a writer of her experiences, with the aid of a psychologist, in helping her small son overcome his fear of dogs. The article, which was sold to *Hygeia,* aided many other mothers to teach their children to like rather than to fear their pets. Hints of what a summer vacation at home or away might mean to the various members of the family were given to the readers of *Woman's Home Companion* in the article "Vacation Time."

Recreation, Outdoor Life, and Health. Because modern inventions and labor laws have provided more time for play, and apostles of good health have championed the desire for relaxation through play, articles concerning recreation, outdoor life, and health are much in demand by 106 publications, with their 1,417 issues a year, in this field. Since people are much interested in outdoor and indoor sports and games, particularly those beneficial to one's health, a writer will do well to familiarize himself with as many different kinds of sports and recreation as possible and to utilize this information in articles that will sell to outdoor, recreation, sports, and health magazines.

In "Games for Players," in *Woman's Home Companion,* the author emphasized that sports must be fun and not work. "Curling, the Quaintest of Sports," in *Leisure,* gave an interesting history of this ancient Scotch game, which resembles bowling. "Hit That Ball" tells the young readers of *The Open Road for Boys* how they can improve their skill. "Rolling Your Own Home Over Wide America" in the New York *Times* magazine section is equally instructive.

"Let's Make Winter Sports Safer," in *Hygeia,* "Here's a Way to Better Casting," in *Outdoor Life,* and "The New Road to Mexico City," in *Sports Afield,* show the interest in life outdoors, whereas such articles as "The Corrective Value of Swimming," in *Health and Physical Education,* "Sports by Which Hollywood Keeps Its Waist Line Down," in the New York *Herald Tribune,* "That Waistline Slump," in *Ladies Home Journal,* and "It's the Way You Walk," in *Hygeia* indicate that readers are interested in sports as a means to keep or gain health.

Organizations. Commercial clubs, merchants' associations, civic and industrial organizations, church groups, and study and cultural clubs may be the sources of articles if the writer is observing and alert to what the groups are doing more efficiently or effectively to hold and increase their members' interests and to be of greater service in their communities. There are hundreds of special publications for such organizations that pay well for fact articles. One free-lance writer has earned $20,000 from publications that paid less than a cent a word by writing up church and club affairs and methods of church and club management. The hundreds of editors of church publications clamor for such articles, as do editors of the hundreds of club and association magazines.

The Arts, Statuary, and Carvings. Pictures, to the observant writer, are possible incentives for the production of articles. They may be snapshots in a camera book; illustrations in papers, magazines, books, or advertising copy; or paintings in homes, public buildings, or art museums. A writer may find profitable germ-thoughts in statuary—carvings in soap, wood, and stone—and works of art of all kinds. The picture of a bridge spanning the Royal Gorge in the Colorado Rocky Mountains suggested to a writer an article on great bridges and their engineers in the United States.

A young woman going into the library in search of ideas for her first feature admired a statue so much that she asked a librarian about it, she learned that the sculptor at one time had lived in the city and that her work was outstanding. It happened the librarian had known the sculptor as a child. The novice recognized her first feature "tip," did more interviewing, took pictures of the statue, and was able to get one of the sculptor as a young woman. She wrote up articles that sold to Sunday sections of the Washington *Star,* New York *Herald Tribune,* and Boston *Transcript,* because the sculptor's statues were in those cities. She became so interested in the woman's personality that she was able to write a sketch that sold to an art publication. By using her powers of observation, this young woman received four checks for one idea. An interview with a sociology professor and the director of the art department of the University of Oregon related the success of an experiment of a class in sculpture at the Oregon state penitentiary. It was sold to the *Christian Science Monitor.*

Realistic Experiences Are in Demand. Experiences of one's own or of others are a second source for factual material. One can always write better of that which he knows from personal experience or the personal experience of those whom he interviews. Not only is the technique and method of the experiences known to the writer, but also the desires and purposes back of them. A novice will find his own experiences easier than those of others to handle because he is familiar with the facts and can make them appear real and vital to the reader. Beginners, since they are desirous of gathering material far afield, overlook the possibilities of what they, or others, have done or are doing that would appeal to readers.

In the early development of the feature articles in the '90s, owing to the rise of popular magazines and of magazine sections of daily newspapers, feature writers assumed the roles of persons whose experiences they wished to relate. The article might tell of the adventures of deep-sea diving; or a professional writer might feign insanity or confess to a crime, in order to be assigned to an institution to tell of the life there; or he might ride in the basket of a balloon to get material to interest his readers. Such articles and methods are out of date. Present-day editors prefer experiences of people who regularly do the things about which they write, or about which they are interviewed, rather than to have a stunt writer relate his impressions, which frequently are inaccurate. Also, readers soon tired of the early type, because the articles were impractical. It is no longer necessary to go far afield or to do stunting to obtain experiences. This is the age of reality, and editors want realistic experiences. One's own (1) university campus, (2) pioneers and old settlers, (3) crafts, mechanics, and hobbies, (4) confessions, (5) travel, and (6) conversations are suggestive of sources for ideas based on experience. That opportunities are unlimited is shown by a few examples of good sources.

University Campus. A gold mine for student writers is the campus. Every day in classrooms and laboratories new knowledge is being imparted, new inventions are being made, and many experiments are conducted, all of which make excellent feature articles. One student writer, whose sales ran into high figures, said he found "editor's checks breezing across the hall, fluttering up the steps of the library, and draping the windows of every college building." Professors, he found, were passing out greenbacks with every daily assignment, and their lectures were as so many gold pieces.

From material in his applied psychology class he wrote an article on the lie detector machine, which he sold to a scientific publication; a botany professor's experiments with fruit trees, which resulted in increased production, suggested a story that was sold to a fruit raiser's journal; an interview with a chemistry professor yielded two articles, one on the health value of nuts and the other on the advantages of cane sugar as a sweetening in bakery commodities, which were purchased by bakers' trade papers. New ways to serve tomatoes, appropriate clothes for the school child, planned household finances to cut increased living costs, and temper tantrums overcome at nursery school were articles based on interviews from the department of home economics and sold to women's magazines. Interviews with professors in the College of Agriculture who had done research in corn production, rural zoning, growing soy beans, and erosion control developed into articles that were sold to farm publications. The laboratories in the Medical School were the source of ideas for an article on dogs in medical laboratories that save hundreds of lives, which was printed in the magazine section of the Milwaukee *Journal;* for one on a new cure for athlete's foot that was accepted by *Hygeia;* and for an article on a Chinese interne who discovered a relief for colds that was purchased by a scientific magazine. These were only a few of the articles that this student free-lance wrote during his junior and senior years, from which he cleared more than $2,000 in the two years. Two other students, who had part-time jobs and were carrying a full study program, earned $950 and $785 respectively from the feature articles they wrote during their senior years after they had studied magazine writing in their junior years. All of their articles were based either on their own experiences, or on those of others, and the majority of the ideas were found on the "runs" or "beats" that these young writers developed just as do news reporters.

Pioneers and Old Settlers. Good experience articles may be developed from historical subjects by interviewing old settlers. These old-timers are happy to have the opportunity to recall other days and other events that will add incidents and human interest to the dry facts obtained by the writer in libraries and historical files. New light may be thrown upon present-day problems by the point of view gained from interviewing those who have lived long in a community.

The bare facts of the history of a drug store that played an important part in the pioneer history of making Kansas a free state, and in the development of the town of Lawrence and the state university, were made interesting to the present generation. The feature writer was not content with the facts gained from her reading in the library, but interviewed one of the old-timers, who related many incidents of those early days when the North and the South were each struggling to control the vote that would determine whether the state was to be slave or free. She gathered so much material that she was able to develop it into three articles: one compared the early days with the present, for the magazine section of the Sunday Kansas City *Star;* another emphasized the part New England played in the history of Kansas, for the Boston *Transcript;* and the third showed the influence of a druggist, not only in making state history, but in setting a high standard for the drug business, and suggested how drug stores may still be an important factor in community life. This latter story was accepted by the *American Druggist.* "Wheels Go Round, But—," a feature comparing the pleasures of bicycle riding in the '90s with those of the '30s, was based on interviews with old-timers and was printed in the New York *Times* magazine section.

Crafts, Mechanics, and Hobbies. How-to-do or how-to-make articles, better known as utility features, have their sources in experience. It is easy to find markets for them, because many publications are devoted to useful information of this type. Mechanical, handicraft, homecraft, hobby, farm, home, garden, and women's magazines as well as trade publications are only a few that use utility articles of this type. They are much in demand, because readers always are wanting to know how to do things more efficiently or how to make things more effective, more practical, more economical, or more artistic. The sources for these types of articles are found everywhere. The mechanic's or carpenter's workshop, the home, the garden, the farm, the business place, the office, and the laboratory abound with ideas. There is a market for the articles in the many craft, mechanic, and hobby magazines if the article is so clearly written that the reader can follow directions accurately. Novices find it easy to gather material for these types as well as easy to write and to sell the features. Articles on upholstering old furniture, making puppets, or turning the basement into a recreation room are the kinds of articles that beginners find easy to sell, because all kinds of publications buy them.

"Scenic Modeling," in *The Model Craftsman,* is the story of one of the most realistic model railroads in the country. "The Story of Bridges," an article on bridge construction engineers in the same issue, shows the diversity of material in the same publication. "Making Modern Dressing Sets," "Jackknife Sculpture," and "Care and Use of Tools" found markets in *Popular Home Craft.* "Tricky Cards for Christmas Made on the Typewriter" was bought by the Pittsburgh *Telegraph.* "Help Your Microscope with Stains and Reagents," in *Popular Science,* and "Color Piano Plays Melody on Rods of Glass," in *Popular Mechanics,* had their sources in university laboratories. "Build This Stinson Glider from Scrapwood," in *Model Airplane News,* came from a young mechanic's experience in his own workshop. "A Collection of Old Wooden Ware," in *Hobbies,* "Book Plating as a Hobby," in *Leisure,* and "Bees in Uncle Sam's Bonnet! National Crazes That Strike Us," in the Detroit *News,* appealed to readers with or without hobbies.

Confessions. A popular form in which personal experiences of the writer or of others may be written effectively is the confession. If the confession is the writer's own experience, it is told in the first person, often anonymously. If it is well written, it is one of the most interesting forms in which to present facts and experiences. When the writer is telling of the personal experiences of another, and if he is able to obtain sufficiently detailed information to make the article plausible, he may use the form of the confession.

Confessions are usually written as though the "confessor" had told his confessions to the writer. The writer in turn tells them to the reader. This form of writing is called "ghosting." It was a device developed by writers a decade or more ago to enable them to write articles of personal experience or confessions of others, as will be discussed in a later chapter. Because the cheaper class of magazines were the first to use confession articles, and since many cheaper magazines are devoted entirely to confession articles, young writers frequently think that they are above writing confessions. The quality magazines, *Atlantic, Harpers, Scribner's,* and hundreds of other well-written and well-edited magazines, use numerous articles of this type, although the appeal is different from that in the cheaper, or "pulp," periodicals. Sometimes the articles are short; sometimes they are so long that the editors publish them in serial form, as did *Ladies' Home Journal* with "This Is My Story," by Eleanor Roosevelt. Another type of confession article, which is in part historical, is known as recollections. An example is "Washington Wife," by Nathalie Colby, which ran serially in *Harpers.* Not all confession articles are written by people whose names are well known. Beginners find that if their confessions have reader interest, they, too, can sell their articles.

A novice wrote of her experience of being left a cripple by infantile paralysis. In a confidential tone she "confessed" to the reader how self-centered and selfish she became before she realized that her friends and her family no longer found her agreeable. She not only overcame her character faults, but by her entrance into sports she overcame her physical handicaps, entered the university, and made all the honor societies. She received a check for $65 for the article, "I Refused to Be a 'Polio' Cripple," which was printed in *Physical Culture*. She was paid an additional $10 for her picture, which the editor requested. Others have sold articles about overcoming bashfulness, transforming the jolly fat girl into a sylph-like prom queen, and the mother and daughter who became pals instead of enemies. These were confession articles because the writers not only wrote of their experiences but confided their thoughts or revealed their secrets to the reader. Every writer has had experiences that he can write in confidential tones and sell as confession articles. Or if he has not had them, his friends have.

Travel. A never-ending source of ideas for experience articles is found in travel. But everyone travels nowadays, and therefore a trip does not have appeal unless it is that of a well-known person, or unless it is into unfrequented parts of the earth, or unless there is something unusual about it. The temptation of the beginning writer, when traveling, is to become too interested personally in the trip itself and to fail to see and investigate the things that would make a manuscript interesting. The writer who can see things "scriptorially"—that is, see things that will make an interesting manuscript for a travel page or travel magazine—will find excellent ideas in short trips as well as in distant travels.

Traveling will open up ideas for other types of articles. A salesman, who has an aptitude for writing, and whose work takes him through the Middle West, says that in addition to travel articles he finds material for semi-historical articles, personality stories, and all kinds of informative articles. His work takes him into industrial plants, and he contacts the publicity directors for the necessary photographs and a guide to take him through the plants. He sells articles to industrial trade publications and adds more than $2,000 a year to his income. In addition, he hears intimate stories from the strangers he meets, and from these he develops excellent confession articles that add several more hundred dollars, to bring his total income from his side line to more than $3,000 annually.

A writer does not need to take long and expensive trips to get material; but the trip itself should have something unusual about it. The expense, the manner, the plan, or the purpose may be the interesting feature that will make the article marketable. An account of an automobile trip from Chicago to Seattle, taken by three college juniors at a cost of $14.79 each, brought the young writer a check for $50 because he showed that one can travel economically. He also pointed out the educational value of such a trip to three young men reared in a city. A canoe trip from the source of the Wisconsin River down into the Mississippi was sold to a boy's publication. The article had appeal not only to youths of that age but to their parents as well, because it showed how an experience of that kind aids in a young boy's character development.

All types of newspapers and magazines use travel articles. "I Travel to See People," in *Good Housekeeping,* "Two Months in Mexico," in *Woman's Home Companion,* and "Gypsy in a Trailer," in *Harpers,* are excellent travel articles. Each tells of experiences that are different and have an appeal both to the reader who travels and to the one who cannot. Travel articles, like all others, should always have interesting pictures to illustrate them.

Conversations. Discourse with others furnishes ideas for articles. When a friend or visitor takes some of the writer's valuable time, he should make this person pay well for the call by entering heartily into the visit and conversation. The alert writer may obtain scores of ideas for future features by talking less and listening more. One should get into the habit of "listening in" not only on the radio but on conversations he hears in the bank, the grocery, the butcher shop, the bakery, the beauty shop, and the dentist's and the doctor's offices. Wherever there is conversation, one will find suggestions for features that will sell at good rates to business and professional journals.

A student journalist stopped in at an auto parts store in Dallas, Texas, and heard a conversation between a salesman and a customer. He wrote up their arguments from three different points of view into stories for three different publications. The three checks more than paid his out-of-state tuition for the second semester at the University. By listening carefully, one not only gains ideas for tips but learns the kinds of things people are interested in. The things that people talk about are the things about which they like to read. From conversations one will garner ideas for personality sketches about prominent people. He will learn about community leaders who will be excellent subjects for general and trade magazines.

Popularizing Facts Makes Interesting Features. To the writer who is willing to look about for some new angle upon which to base, or "slant," his article, printed material of all kinds supplies unlimited suggestions. By finding some person who is an authority and whose name as the person interviewed will add value to the article, one may make dry, uninteresting subjects into excellent features. Or by taking facts and explaining them in such a way as to interest the reader, or popularizing them, one may find a ready market for the new form. Printed material includes: (1) newspapers; (2) periodicals; (3) books; (4) pamphlets; (5) trade and scientific publications; (6) advertising of all types—display, classified, direct-by-mail, circulars, catalogues, store announcements, and outdoor advertising; (7) questionnaires and surveys; and (8) contents of libraries.

Current Newspapers. A necessary part of a writer's equipment is the current newspaper. It abounds in suggestions for acceptable articles. Every free-lance writer should read several good newspapers every day, because in addition to getting ideas for his own writing, he learns the trends of reader interest and is able to foresee what subjects are likely to be future features. To be a thorough newspaper reader will enable the free-lance writer to watch the trend of current news and to detect undercurrents of interest before it is too late. The writer must be able to anticipate the public's interest before the public is aware of that interest. Many free-lance writers read regularly such stanch newspapers as the New York *Times,* New York *Herald Tribune,* Boston *Transcript, Christian Science Monitor,* Kansas City *Star,* Milwaukee *Journal,* Portland *Oregonian,* and many others. From those papers they regularly get many ideas for articles. Valuable information can be garnered, which can be clipped and put into one's files. Any part of the paper from the front-page news to the death notices and the "want ads" will yield material that will offer a diversity of topics. The writer must let the material he reads, or collects, filter through his own mind, in order to absorb it and make it his own.

Newspapers in one's own city, town, or village offer "tips" that the writer easily develops into marketable material by visiting the place mentioned, interviewing the persons concerned, and gathering additional material. With practice, one soon learns to recognize in the local newspapers ideas that will develop into lively and interesting articles. Every paper, metropolitan or rural, prints events of the day that are rich in possibilities. If an article has a news angle that is timely, it stands twice as much chance of being accepted as one that does not have—and this explains why many journalists are prolific and successful magazine writers. If one is a thorough student of current and public affairs, has an inquiring mind, and even an average amount of imagination, he will do well to specialize in writing features based on the day's news. There is an added pleasure in writing features from this source, in that one feels he is not only up with the news, but a step ahead of it. A successful free-lance writer found that it paid to subscribe by mail for a newspaper from each of the twelve largest cities in his state. The many articles suggested brought checks to him of varying sizes, paid for the subscriptions and the expense of preparing the pictures and manuscripts, gave him a liberal income, and afforded him pleasure and satisfaction in his writing.

Old Newspaper Files. A valuable supply of ideas that are not limited to historical or reminiscent stories may be found in old newspaper files. Past incidents often suggest a new point of view to some current problem of civic or public interest. Comparison articles may concern prices, fashions, customs, etiquette, entertainment, recreation, anniversaries, and anything else in which there would be an appeal to the reader. Such articles find a ready market in the Sunday magazine sections of newspapers. A novice who had access to an excellent library of newspaper files specialized in writing articles of this type, which he sold to newspapers throughout the country. His problem of finding illustrations was solved by photographing articles in the museum that fitted in with those of the periods about which he was writing. The income from his Sunday features enabled him to give up his job as assistant janitor that had formerly paid for his meals and room while he was in college.

Periodicals. Factual articles, fiction, poems, and advertising in periodicals will start the mind of the free-lance thinking in terms of definite "tips." Even an incident in a short story may suggest an idea to start him making investigations that will uncover worth-while material. One magazine article may suggest another. The fact that something has been written up in one magazine is no reason to think that the subject cannot be handled again for an entirely different publication with a different appeal. Investigation in the library and interviews with authorities in the field will suggest new material and enable the author to write from a new angle. A dozen people might write upon the same subject, but their articles would not be alike. No two people approach the subject from the same angle, and one cannot write even a short article wthout putting some of his personality into the manuscript.

Trade publications devoted to specialized fields, which appeal to only one class of readers, are a source of article ideas for periodicals that have a general circulation. A beginner, while waiting in a science professor's office for an interview with him, looked at some magazines. Among them was a copy of one of the learned scientific journals. In glancing through it, he saw an article telling of the results of research on potato chips, which showed that the health value of potato chips was greatly overrated by the advertisers. The young writer read the article carefully, did considerable reading on the subject in the library, interviewed a home economics professor and obtained some recipes using potato chips, and sold the article to a woman's magazine. A few days later he interviewed a professor in the business school on advertising and then rewrote his material into an article to appeal to grocers. He suggested ideas for advertising potato chips in the store and pointed out that, although the potato chip wasn't a complete food any more than other foods, it was still a potato and contained nutritious food elements. The second article sold to a grocer's magazine. He received for the two articles two checks, which totaled $55.

Almost every trade and profession has several magazines that carry news and feature articles concerned with one kind of business activity. In addition, there are many magazines devoted to specialized fields, such as music, art, the dance, nature, and archaeology. Therefore, a writer need never be without ideas or markets to which to sell them. The advertising in these publications is also suggestive of articles to the writer.

Books. The title, as well as the content, of a book may stimulate the writer to new ideas. A novel may give some sidelight on human nature that would make a saleable article. Non-fiction often is suggestive of ideas that will grow into checks for features. Even poetry has been known to be the source of articles. Frequently the title of a book will suggest an article.

Pamphlets. Scientific and government bulletins, reports, documents, printed proceedings, and monographs giving results of research and investigations done by experts, bureaus, commissions, or committees may be had free, or for a very small charge. They are worth their weight in gold to the freelance because of their wealth and variety of ideas. Generally they are written in so technical a style that few people ever read them. The journalist may profitably popularize the material for the general public. The expert who made the scientific discovery then becomes known outside of the technical field and may even become famous through the information that the writer sells to general publications. Some time ago, a scientist working in his laboratory at the University of Wisconsin "bottled" sunshine in a way that practically meant the revolutionizing of the manufacture and production of many of the foods of the world. Up to that time his name was scarcely known outside of the world of science. Today Dr. Harry Steenbock's name is a household word because feature writers popularized his material and readers of general magazines were informed of his scientific discoveries. A writer was inspired by a government bulletin to do an article on removal of stains. It was sold to a woman's magazine, and through it she helped thousands of readers to reduce their cleaning bills and to keep their clothes attractive. She received a generous check for doing a good deed for her fellow women.

Bulletins issued by federal, state, or local governments, or by universities, are concerned with new and better methods of doing all kinds of things. They are written by experts in federal and state laboratories, universities, agricultural colleges, and home economics departments. When popularized, the material develops into articles that are easy to sell, because they are concerned with the new in the field of science and research. State commissions issue reports that are fruitful sources for timely articles on industries, insurance, health, sanitation, welfare, relief, railroads, commerce, conservation, and other subjects with which government is concerned. Official documents are seldom read by the general public, yet from them may be gleaned suggestions for the writer who will present the information in a bright, interesting manner to attract the reader. Teachers' bulletins are good sources, for the material there can be expanded and presented to appeal to parents' and women's publications.

Advertising Copy. Display, classified, direct-by-mail, and outdoor advertising, circulars, catalogues, and store announcements are rich in subject-finding material. An attractive display advertisement of linoleum suggested an article on the selection and care of linoleum. This article in turn suggested another one on various uses of linoleum in the home. The first was sold to a woman's magazine and the second to a farm publication. A classified advertisement, in a metropolitan newspaper, concerning guinea fowls for sale was investigated and resulted in another pair of articles. One was on raising guinea fowls for the market and was purchased by a farm magazine; the other was about the preparation and serving of guinea fowls, which sold to a restaurant trade paper.

A circular advertising jelly made from wild fruits and berries growing on Wisconsin hillsides turned into a success story. It told of a woman who gathered the fruit and berries, canned the juice, and, when the orders came in, made the jelly, which she put in attractive containers and shipped in neat cartons to any part of the United States. The first story, emphasizing the local state angle, sold to the Milwaukee *Journal*. The second one sold to *Capper's Farmer* and played up the angle of how this farm woman operated a thriving business in her home. Even catalogues suggest all kinds of articles if one only takes time to turn through them. An article sold to *American Home* magazine on the care of blankets had its origin in a mail-order catalogue. Many articles on flowers for garden magazines were suggested to the authors by seed catalogues.

The Survey and Questionnaire. Another source of articles, although not used so frequently because it is a rather involved and expensive method of getting information, is to get factual material by means of the survey and questionnaire. Public and private businesses and professional people usually will consent to fill in a questionnaire if it is so planned that it does not take much of their time. A student journalist was interested in a newspaper item concerning the amount of milk consumed by the students on her campus. By getting out a questionnaire and interviewing managers of dairies and the director of the student clinic, she gathered information for an article, "College Students' Drinking," that sold to *Hoard's Dairyman*. Another student, who was attending college on the income from a life-insurance policy taken out for that purpose, wondered how many other students were similarly supported. She carefully thought out the questions, and ran off several hundred mimeographed copies. With the permission of her professors, she circulated the questionnaires in her classes, tabulated the results, and wrote the article, which she sold to *The Insurance Salesman* for $25.

Libraries. Next to the daily newspaper, the library is the feature writer's biggest help. Not only must he know how to use books, but he must have an intimate acquaintance with reference books, biographical dictionaries, gazetteers, encyclopedias, and periodical readers' guides, as well as books, magazines, learned journals, house organs, and trade papers.

Anniversaries, historical events, holidays, seasonal events—all give rise to many timely articles, material for which can be found in the library. By looking over tables or lists giving significant events, a writer may always anticipate the special days sufficiently far in advance to have his material collected. Prolific writers usually start collecting material for articles for special days a year in advance.

Filed away in university libraries are hundreds of master's theses and lengthy reports of graduate research. These, boiled down and rewritten with a popular, practical slant, would make articles of the type editors clamor for, because they contain information and guidance to interest the readers.

In addition to developing the library habit, one should make friends with the librarians. A few minutes of conversation with them may open up numerous ideas for marketable articles. Then, too, a cordial friendly librarian can save hours of time for a busy writer who cultivates her acquaintance.

Keeping an Advance Book. The feature writer should keep an advance book, as does a city editor of a newspaper. When he learns of events, coming conventions, people returning from unique trips, and other news happenings that could be developed into features, he can jot down the notation. For as little as ten cents one can buy a diary with a space for each day of the year, which serves the purpose very well. A larger book, of course, has the advantage of more space under each date. By looking forward three to six weeks or more for the newspaper magazine sections, and six months or more for the magazines—because editors plan their publications long in advance—a feature writer can select subjects and gather material that will be timely and seasonable. Free-lance writers who support themselves entirely by their writing keep their advance books systematically, in order never to be without ideas about which to write. If one has his advance book full of "tips," he may start collecting material from various sources long in advance of the time he wants to start his article. Then, when he is ready to begin writing he has his material at hand.

One Feature Often Leads to Another. As one can readily see, finding subjects is the easiest part of writing magazine articles after one develops a nose for news and an eye for features. Even the amateur learns to see articles all about him, and he wonders why he ever thought it would be difficult to find things about which to write. In addition to seeking material for all sorts of features, the beginner learns how interesting it is to meet the successful people with whom his search for material brings him in contact. Their enthusiasm and happiness is contagious. He also finds that when he searches for material for one article, he is likely to uncover ideas for another. And that, in turn, uncovers other ideas for other features.

Exercises

1. Walk down Main Street and come back with six ideas for feature articles for metropolitan Sunday newspapers or for magazines. Type out and hand in at class.
2. Walk across the campus and find six suggestions that will make features suitable for Sunday newspaper magazine sections or for general magazines. Type out and hand in at class.
3. After attending one class in each of the courses in which you are enrolled, type out one "tip" for a feature article that you got out of each of the lectures, which you could develop into a newspaper or magazine feature.

4. In reading your afternoon or morning newspaper, find three ideas from local news stories for which you could gather the material and write into features that would be acceptable in metropolitan newspapers or magazines.
5. Recall recent conversations that you have had to find one idea for a suggestion that could be written up for a marketable article.
6. From a convention, a speech, or a sermon, find one idea that you could expand into a feature to sell.
7. From bulletins, advertisements, publicity, or catalogues, find two ideas for features.
8. Find a "tip" for an article from some industry, trade, business, or profession that you could sell to a trade or business magazine.
9. Suggest a "tip" from out of your own experience, or the experiences of others, that you could write.
10. From the eleven sources for ideas for features listed in this chapter, jot down one "tip" from each that you think would sell.
11. Every day during the coming week write down the ideas that have come to you from observation, experience, or printed material that you think would make good future "tips" for articles. At the end of the week transfer the good ones to your permanent "tip" notebook, or card file, and plan to write them when you can gather the material.

Publication Analysis

New York *World-Telegram,* New York *Times,* and
New York *Herald Tribune*

Do not spend more than three hours on this report.

Look at Sunday feature and magazine sections in the three newspapers.

A. 1. What can you say of the general policy of these papers toward features?
   2. How do local, state, regional, national, and international features compare in space in the three newspapers?
   3. What do you think would be your chances of selling to these papers?

B. (Put emphasis of report on this section.) In chart form classify the features as to: (1) types; (2) variety of subject matter; (3) use of cuts; (4) average length of feature; (5) type of readers to whom features appeal; (6) ones that you might have written.

C. Analyze three feature articles—one in the *World-Telegram,* one in the *Times,* and one in the *Herald Tribune*—preferably something you might have written and of the type that you are now writing for your first feature article.

D. At the end of the report—and in every report hereafter—list two tips for feature articles that you might write that were suggested to you from this study. List three possible markets for each tip.

3 THE INTERVIEW ARTICLE

No Definite Distinctions of Types. The number of classifications of feature articles is as great as the number of feature writers, for almost every writer has his own plan of grouping the various types. In any classification one arranges, considerable overlapping is likely to occur, because almost any article has elements of one or more types. In the majority of newspaper and magazine offices the editors classify them into the following types: (1) the interview; (2) the utility article; (3) personal experience story; (4) the confession article; (5) the personality sketch; and (6) the narrative. Thus, a writer will do well to adopt the journalistic names for the different types. Nevertheless, he must bear in mind that any article may contain elements of one or more of the types enumerated in addition to the predominating one.

Popularity of the Interview. The success of an interview article depends upon the interest in the interview, which is in proportion to the "interviewee's" prominence, or to the interest in the topic, or both. Any person, however, is interesting. He must have done something, and he is therefore worth interviewing. It is true that editors are more willing to buy interviews with well-known persons, because readers recognize them; but they are equally interested in unknown persons whose opinions and ideas are new and unique. The interview article offers the writer a good device for giving information. Because the material for many features is obtained by interviewing, a writer may present it more effectively by developing it as an interview article. People are questioned for the information they can impart, for their opinions, and their ideas concerning particular subjects, which may make up the major part, if not the whole of the article.

As a means of obtaining material, the interview also is used for the other kinds of articles listed, as discussed in later chapters. However, when editors speak of the interview article, they refer to one that is more concerned with one phase of a person's opinions or ideas. Usually that person must be a recognized authority on the subject about which he is interviewed or he must be so well known that his prominence gives weight to his opinions or ideas, even though he may not be an expert in the field in which he is being interviewed.

The interview article may be defined as one concerned with one phase of the opinions or ideas of a recognized authority on the subject or the opinions of a person so well known that his prominence gives value to his ideas.

Personality and confession stories are similar to the interview in that they contain opinions and ideas, but they are presented from a different point of view. In the confession article the writer confesses or confides his ideas, or "sins," whereas in the personality sketch not only the person's opinions but his or her personality and character are revealed by relating the interesting experiences in his life.

Technique of Interviewing. In looking about for ideas for interview articles, the writer is attracted to persons because they are experts or because they are distinguished in some particular field. After selecting the person to be interviewed, the writer should make an appointment, either by telephone or letter, for an interview at the time and place designated by the interviewee. One problem is to know whether it is better to meet the interviewee in his office or at his home. Some persons think better away from their desks, whereas others think better in the atmosphere of their work. When the interviewer makes the appointment, either by telephone or letter, he may solve this problem by asking whether he should go to the person's office or home.

As a rule, it is a poor policy to interview a person without giving him several days to think about the subject. One will get much more interesting material if the interviewee has had time to do some thinking. The interviewer should give his name and explain briefly that he is a free-lance writer who wants an interview for an article to be published because the person to whom he is speaking, or writing, is considered an outstanding authority in whose ideas magazine readers will be interested. He should indicate the amount of time that he thinks he will need for the interview; then he must be careful at the conference not to outstay his time, unless the person to be interviewed assures him that he may have more or shows by his attitude that he is willing to talk longer.

The interviewer should learn all he can about the subject upon which he wishes to base his interview, by: (1) looking at the periodical readers' guide and reading all the material he can find listed pertaining to the subject, in order to be as well informed as possible and to ask intelligent questions; (2) looking in all available sources, such as *Who's Who,* or the *Who's Who* of the special fields in which the interviewee might be listed, for the facts about the person's life; and (3) talking with friends and acquaintances of the interviewee to learn about his hobbies, his pet theories, his likes and dislikes, in order to plan the interview carefully. If the writer acquires this knowledge before he meets the interviewee, he not only will save time, but will be able to start the discussion from the angle he desires and to control the interview. By being well prepared, he will gain the person's confidence and respect, because he knows what he wants and because he is accurately informed.

Interviewing the Interviewee. A series of questions, perhaps as many as twenty-five, should be planned and memorized by the writer in advance of meeting the person to be interviewed, in order to acquire the exact information he desires. The questions should be cleverly phrased, to arouse the interviewee's interest. In planning the questions, the writer constantly must keep his readers in mind and think of the questions that they would ask the interviewee if they had the opportunity to talk with him. For this reason the writer should pretty well determine, even before he has had his interview, to which markets he will submit his manuscript. Thus he will have some idea as to who his readers will be and in what phases of the subject they will be interested. Nothing is more irritating to a person whose time is valuable and who has granted a twenty-minute interview, than to have a feature writer take an hour of his time because he knows nothing of the subject and did not have his questions planned in advance. Nothing labels a person as a beginner more quickly than the lack of adequate preparation and the failure to carry on the interview in a businesslike manner and thus save time for the interviewee as well as for himself.

One should be on time, or a few minutes ahead of time, for his appointment. He should be attractively and appropriately dressed, as is any successful professional writer. It is only in the movies and fiction that journalists go about their business hatless and slovenly dressed, dashing past secretaries without presenting their cards or names, instead of waiting to be asked into the interviewee's office. It is only the young writer portrayed on the silver screen who achieves success by entering his interviewee's office chewing gum or smoking and who sits slumped in his chair, hat on the back of his head, while he takes a few notes on any scraps of paper he has at hand. The successful writer is extremely careful to see that his personal appearance is attractive and that his manner is gracious and considerate toward office boys and secretaries as well as toward the interviewee. As much care and thought should be given to these matters as by a person who is going to apply for a position. Like the employer, the interviewee forms his impressions of the writer as he enters the room. If that impression is favorable, the writer will be more likely to get better material for his article, and perhaps the way will be opened to more features.

Writers find that business cards with their name, the words "Free-Lance Writer," and their address and telephone number, to present to the interviewee upon entering his presence, serves to bridge over any awkward pauses following the self-introduction. The card may later aid the interviewee in getting in touch with the writer in case he wishes to correct some statement or wishes to add to the material he has already given. Even young journalism students find the cards useful. If they do not have engraved or printed cards, they can type the necessary information on blank cards, and these serve the purpose until more professional looking ones can be obtained.

CARLETON D. SMITH

FREE-LANCE WRITER
429 PROSPECT AVENUE
TELEPHONE FAIRFAX 9753

FIG. 1. FREE-LANCE WRITER'S BUSINESS CARD

A well-trained memory is preferable to a notebook or folded pages of copy paper, unless the feature writer knows that the interviewee wishes to be quoted verbatim or that he is accustomed to being interviewed. Some people feel there is less danger of misquotation if the interviewer takes notes in their presence. A person less experienced in being interviewed will feel ill at ease and self-conscious of his speech and expression if he sees a writer taking notes. Such note-taking may result in an atmosphere of formality that will prevent his giving all of his interesting information. The writer must remember that the interviewee may be frightened, because many people hold writers, even beginners, in great reverence, if not in awe. Or he may be nervous for fear the writer, whom he recognizes as an amateur, will misquote him and make him appear ridiculous in print. The free-lance should conduct the interview in as cordial and informal a manner as possible, and thereby put the interviewee at his ease. The interviewee can be tested to see whether he will be more comfortable when notes are taken, or when they are not. A good device is to get him talking and then ask, "May I write that down?" The writer can see the interviewee's reaction to such writing down of the quotations, and then he will know whether or not to take notes during the remainder of the interview.

Like a psychologist, the interviewer, to be successful, has to know how to judge people and how to draw them out to say the things that will make a good article. If one feels that he is not clever in drawing people out to say the things that he wants them to say, he should practice on his friends, classmates, and anyone with whom he comes in contact. To interview successfully, knowledge of human nature will help one more than anything else. One must be alert, enthusiastic, and interested in the person he is interviewing as well as the subject. By his own interest he will elicit greater interest and better material from the interviewee.

A young writer may find that he is inclined to let the interviewee lead him astray from the topic, not because he wants to, but because it is human nature to ramble in conversation. The interviewer may be kept off the subject for several hours by a too talkative interviewee, whereas he could have obtained his material in twenty minutes. The interviewer must put a value on his own time just as do people in such professions as medicine, dentistry, and law. Even though one is only a beginner and evaluates his time at only one dollar an hour, he cannot afford to spend two hours in an interviewee's office to obtain material that could be his in a tenth or a sixth of that time.

Although it is the interviewer's place to keep the conversation moving by means of questions, to draw out the interviewee, and to keep the discussion in the direction that he wishes it, he must remember that his chief business is that of a listener. When he sees that he has taken as much of the interviewee's time as he had asked for, he should suggest that perhaps he should leave. If the person is willing, of course, the interviewer should stay until he has all the desired information; but if the interviewee is busy, then the writer should ask if he may have another appointment to complete the interview.

If the material is of a technical nature, the free-lance should ask the interviewee to be kind enough to read the copy of the interview for approval before it is submitted for publication, in order to avoid any inaccuracies. Experienced writers find it to their advantage to have an interviewee's approval on a completed article, even if it is not at all technical. It is easier to deal with objections before rather than after publication. When the final draft has been approved by the interviewee, indicate this in the note to the editor on the cover sheet (as explained in a later chapter) by saying: "This article has been approved by Mr. Blank." When the editor knows that the interviewee has seen and approved the manuscript, he will feel more secure in printing the article, especially if the writer is a stranger to the magazine.

A considerate writer will remember, when he leaves, to thank the expert, or authority, for his valuable information and for the time that was so graciously given. The information the interviewee has given the writer may be the result of a lifetime of study and research. The time that was given by the interviewee for the conference may be worth ten dollars an hour to the expert. If the interviewer has taken fifteen minutes of his time, he should consider that the expert has given him $2.50. For such generous gifts, the writer should express his appreciation.

Preparation for Writing the Interview. Immediately, or as soon after the interview as possible, the writer should fill in the exact words and phrases and complete his notes whether or not he took notes during the interview. If he has done a good job of interviewing, the interviewee's words will be ringing in his ears. Now, with the quotations in hand, he may wait to write the article until he has: (1) thought through his material carefully; (2) investigated possible markets thoroughly; (3) decided how to "slant" the article to give it the greatest possible reader interest; (4) selected the style and form in which he can write it most effectively; (5) planned the type and number of photographs or snapshots; (6) and arranged for other illustrative material, such as drawings, maps, and charts.

A well-written feature is the result of careful thinking and planning before one begins to write. For this reason, it is essential that the interviewer should transcribe his notes completely, in order that he can take time to think and plan his interview into the type of article that will market easily and profitably. He should manage to relate his interview to someone. In the telling of it he will remember points that he forgot to include in his notes, and new ideas of development may occur to him as he talks about it.

The interview article may consist (1) almost entirely of direct quotation, with a limited amount of explanatory material concerning the person to be interviewed; or it may (2) be made up partly of direct and partly of indirect quotation, combined with necessary explanations; for greater variety it is advisable (3) to alternate direct with indirect quotation; and (4) a description of the person and his surroundings, generally by way of introduction, gives the reader a distinct impression of the individual under characteristic conditions.

Although a good beginning is important in any article, it is even more so in the interview article. Unless one puts a great deal of thought into organizing his material, the beginning, or "lead," is the hardest part to write. But if he has thought through the plan carefully, he will be able to introduce the person interviewed to the reader in the lead paragraph or paragraphs by giving a vivid description of him, his appearance, and mannerisms, his surroundings, or his background. Thus he will give a distinct impression of the individual and make the reader feel he really knows the person as well as what he says and thinks. Or the writer may feature in the lead something unusual or a striking statement, followed by a paragraph of description of the interviewee, just as a news reporter includes the "W's" in his speech story.

No matter which type of lead is used, early in the article, probably in the second or third paragraph, an explanation should be given the reader as to why the interviewee was interviewed, and a brief sketch of him should be included. In the paragraphs following the feature and the identification of the interviewee, the writer may continue with the direct and indirect quotations, description, narration, and exposition in any order that will add to the effectiveness of the article, just as though he had not interrupted himself to give the interviewee's background or the reason for the article. The following interview with John Masefield, in the New York *World-Telegram,* illustrates this technique.*

Dig beneath the surface of a man who writes copy for mouthwash in an advertising agency and you are likely to find a frustrated poet, John Masefield, poet-laureate of England, said today.

Tall, a trifle stooped, and gray, Mr. Masefield arrived with his wife on the Aquitania, for a visit of eight days. He will spend three days in Boston, where he will read a poem dedicated to Harvard tercentenary.

The poet laureate, once a handyman in Luke O'Connor's saloon at Christopher and Greenwich Sts. in Greenwich village, did not hold out much hope for poets in these days of economic uncertainty. As he sees it, their lyric voices are stilled by the necessity of becoming barkers for nationally advertised brands.

"Poets," he said sadly, "are no longer able to reach large audiences by word of mouth. They have been squeezed out of the theater.

"A book is a haphazard way of reaching an audience. It very often takes fifty years before they appreciate what has been written.

"Poets found they were not wanted. They took to drinking and riotous living and finally wound up writing advertisements and little booklets."

The artistic writer keeps himself in the background entirely, remembering that his readers are interested in the interviewee rather than the interviewer. He avoids writing so that his questions stand out. He knows his readers are interested in the answers rather than the questions. He refrains from mentioning that there was an interview, for that is obvious to the reader.

In many ways the interview article has an advantage over

* Reprinted by permission of the New York *World-Telegram*.

the other types, in that readers are attracted to it because they like to feel they know prominent or successful people. If they cannot know them personally, they like to read about them, and that is why editors buy interview articles to supply the subscriber demand. Verbatim quotations give life to the article and make the reader feel that he is conversing with the person interviewed. Descriptions of him or of his surroundings make the reader feel that he has seen the speaker, and the statements of an authority have greater weight than those who are not well known or experienced in a particular field.

The symposium interview is developed in the same way as the interview, except it is based upon interviews with several authorities whose opinions on the same subject may or may not agree. The writer may compare or contrast the opinions, according to the "slant" he decides to give the article. This type generally is more dependent upon the prominence of the persons interviewed than upon their opinions.

Rewards Are Many. Beginners often are surprised at the willingness of prominent people to be interviewed and at their generosity with their time. They do not realize that even the well known are not averse to becoming better known; and in most professions, businesses, and trades, people interviewed are benefited by favorable publicity. For that reason they are not only agreeable to being interviewed but are extremely grateful to the writer for making them, their views, or their work better known to the public. Although the interviewer is asking valuable information and time from the interviewee, the latter will be more than compensated by the favorable publicity when the article appears in print.

Sometimes, however, the reverse is true. One may have to exercise his ingenuity in approaching the interviewee. Not all experts and celebrities are easily seen, and many of them become interview-weary. A writer tried to see Fritz Kreisler but was not admitted. However, she did not give up. During the last encore number at the concert she slipped back stage, and as Mr. Kreisler was entering his dressing room, she said, "I'm interested in one thing about your violin."

The great musician beamed down upon her and, although he would not talk about himself, he would talk about his violin, for he loves it. Before he realized it, he was being interviewed; but he did not object, because the writer had given him an opportunity to talk about what he wanted to talk about.

An ingenious interviewer will have little difficulty in approaching those whom he wishes to interview if he hits upon the celebrity's main interest, which, of course, requires a knowledge of the interviewee's likes and dislikes.

Rewards to the writer who interviews are numerous. He learns how to meet people tactfully and how to adjust his personality to theirs in order to get the information he desires. He meets successful, happy people, and this in itself is an interesting experience. In getting one article, frequently he gets material for others. While he is interviewing to earn, he also learns, and thereby adds to his own knowledge. From these contacts he acquires new acquaintances and friends, many of whom may prove valuable in years to come. From a financial point of view, the free-lance finds that well-written interview articles are always in great demand. Every Sunday newspaper and almost every magazine, as well as scientific and trade publications, is in the market for this type of article.

As a writer, one does a great deal of interviewing, not only for interview articles alone, but for most of the other types for which the material generally is gathered by interviewing people. For that reason, much of the discussion of the technique of gathering and writing the interview article applies to developing other types of features.

Examples of the Interview Article. An analysis of the articles that follow will show how the writers gathered their materials and arranged them for the effective presentation. The first interview conveys to the readers why air hostesses like their work. It was published in the St. Louis *Post-Dispatch* and was illustrated with photographs of the interviewee, two other hostesses, and of a fourteen-passenger transport making 200 miles an hour from Los Angeles to New York. The second example, a signed article taken from the New York *Herald Tribune,* shows how an expert in some field may write out his own opinions. How a writer may interview anyone who has ideas and experience, even though that person is not well known, is illustrated in the third article, taken from *Collier's.* However, a free-lance does not have to go to far places to find material that he can treat in a similar style. Even a beginner may find in his own community articles that he can write in an interesting way if he will study the manner in which the author developed this article. Five excellent photographs of the "pilgrim," his family, his home, and his livestock added to the reader interest in the article. The fourth example, a symposium interview, appeared in *Good Housekeeping.* It shows how the writer presented the opinions of nine women on gardening. Ten pictures were used to show authors and their gardens. A writer does not have to get opinions of well-known people, but may develop a symposium interview by talking with people in all walks of life, as did the writer in *Woman's Home Companion,* in the fifth example.

(1)

AIR HOSTESS *

The Young Women Who Look to the Comfort of Plane Passengers Must Pass Pretty Exacting Requirements, but Find Plenty of Compensations

By Marguerite Martyn

When Transcontinental Western Airlines let it be known last fall they were about to employ "hostesses" on their passenger planes, there were 16,000 applicants for the first training class. Six weeks later another class was opened with twice as many applicants. From this host of aspirants 49 young women have qualified for jobs, four from St. Louis, Miss Florence Oden, Miss Martha Early, Miss Edith Galyen and Miss Dorothy Hutchings.

* Reprinted by permission of the St. Louis *Post-Dispatch.*

What does it take, what are the duties, how does one qualify for this much coveted new vocation for women? Obviously a lot of girls would like to know.

Florence Oden, who made the grade in the first class, was assigned to the Western flight Dec. 1, and now, by seniority rates her preference for the Eastern flight. She was home on leave visiting her sister, Mrs. T. N. Everett, 1018 Art Hill place, and such questions as she did not answer verbally and generously were answered even more eloquently in her own personality.

The first impression is that it takes a very pretty girl to be an air hostess. Pictures of all the girls show them strikingly good looking. Miss Oden, so attractive that McClelland Barclay, on his way to Hollywood to judge a beauty contest, was inspired to make a sketch of her during a landing at Indianapolis and asked if she'd pose professionally for him in his New York studio.

She is slim, making her seem taller than the required minimum. Blonde, with fair skin, blue eyes and pale gold hair. Trim and smart she looks in the beautifully tailored gray flannel suit, topcoat lined with red, scarlet blouse, "overseas" cap with winged insignia, gray oxfords and gray hose, the regulation uniform provided by the company. She is one of nine sisters all similarly endowed with what's known as looks if numerous photographs in the apartment are not too flattering evidence. Three of them are trained nurses.

* * *

But it was an enthusiastic air mindedness, her attitude of devotion to the service and of understanding and responsibility toward her passengers which probably in large measure led to Florence Oden's selection midst much competition.

"I was completely sold on flying long before I went into the service," she said. "Whenever I had a vacation while taking nurses' training and afterward on private duty, I would fly home to Cainsville in North Missouri. I love to fly and I like to see other people enjoy it.

"Most of the passengers are business men to whom the speed element is important, or movie people rushing back and forth between New York and Hollywood, people hurrying on urgent missions or people who have been everywhere and seen everything. The contacts with celebrities are interesting. It is nice to observe Lionel Barrymore as studious, fatherly, dignified, off the screen as on. He learned my name and always addressed me punctiliously,

'Miss Oden.' Lupe Velez and Johnny Weismuller cut up all the way, scrapping, throwing pillows. Kay Francis was as fastidious, Sylvia Sidney as demure, as they seem in pictures. Wallace Beery, though, leaves his villainous role behind. The boys who wrote 'The Music Goes 'Round and Around' sang it from sheer exuberance. It's amusing to identify newly-weds by the way they hold hands across the aisle. But all these people are more or less preoccupied. Many of them sleep nearly all the way or spend time checking off distances on the time table. Or they eat. You develop the most amazing appetite in the air.

"The passengers I like best are those to whom flying is a new experience, like the farmer and his wife who got on at Indianapolis. You could see they had planned and looked forward to this vacation trip a long time. All their neighbors and relatives were there to see them off at 4:30 in the morning. I advised the elderly couple to get some sleep so they could enjoy the sights when they flew over the Painted Desert, Grand Canyon and the mountains. 'I'll see that you are awakened when you get to Albuquerque,' I told them. But, no, they weren't going to waste a minute sleeping. They had to see it all.

"The T. W. A. prefers to call us hostesses rather than stewardesses, and stresses the graces as well as routine duties," she chatted on. "I provide card tables, get up bridge games, serve the luncheons we pick up fresh and appetizing in boxes at airport restaurants, distribute cigarettes and chewing gum, devise pastimes for whiling away monotonous stretches. But it is when we get out where the scenery begins to get grand and passengers just have to sit up and take notice that I thrill with them. There is one sight that never fails to strike even the most blase speechless and breathless. That's our first glimpse of Los Angeles. After crossing long desert stretches, then the San Bernardino range, suddenly, all at once, a great city comes into view, shimmering in the sunset or with millions of lights twinkling, the ocean beyond, Catalina Island and Long Beach also visible.

"The Western flight," she continued, "on the big Sky Chief has its thrills, but it has its monotonous stretches. We fly so high and at 12,000 feet little is distinguishable, especially at night, except the beacons and emergency landing fields flashing by every 30 miles. It was exciting during the holidays when we flew in two sections and so many people were going to the Rose Bowl game. But I really prefer the Eastern flight with more frequent stops. We had a thrill Sunday before last when, with a 70-mile tail wind, we flew into Newark an hour and four minutes ahead of time, averaging 280 miles an hour and breaking a record. The passengers were all agog about it and even Pilot Parker, who had been with a Byrd expedition, was thrilled.

"I enjoy telling passengers of all our safety precautions, how planes passing keep always to the right of the beacons; eastbound flying at even numbered altitudes, say, 6,000 feet, westbound at odd numbers, 5,000 or 7,000. I used to like to take them up to the cockpit and have the co-pilot explain the instruments. It took the mystery out of flying and left them with such a safe feeling. It was a great selling point, but since the mysterious crash recently on American Air Lines in Arkansas, a new rule has been made that passengers are not allowed in the cockpit. I am sorry about that. They enjoyed it so much."

Getting back to less personal, more arbitrary standards by which a girl qualifies for the job: "You are judged by personal appearance and behavior," admitted Miss Oden, "but that is by no means the only test. You must weigh not more than 118 pounds, stand no more than 5 feet 4 inches in height, be not more than 26 years old when you apply. You are judged by the way you wear your clothes. You must be neatly groomed and careful about your makeup. It mustn't be excessive. You must stand a rigid physical examination. This includes eyes, ears, heart and nervous conditions, also mental and psychiatric tests. Many applicants are eliminated because of some emotional or temperamental quirk. But first of all, and the most limiting factor naturally, you must be a registered nurse. I don't know why this training should be considered essential. I never have had occasion to use my knowledge of nursing. We don't have air sickness any more. With the automatic pilot and stabilizers the planes ride more smoothly than they used to. The company does not anticipate illness, but they believe, I suppose, this special training stands an air hostess in good stead because a nurse already has learned to take a lot on the chin.

"You must have recommendations from your training school and former employers," she went on. "I had had two and a half years of private duty in which I traveled extensively with patients and some public health and institutional experience, after graduating from the Missouri Baptist Hospital training school.

"Then you must attend the training school at T. W. A. headquarters in Kansas City for six weeks. There you learn enough accounting so you can take entire charge of tickets as a train conductor does. Quite large sums are involved and your reports must tally with the ticket agents'. A certain amount of meteorology, so you can answer passengers' questions about air conditions. You must be able to tell about air pressures, what causes fogs, air pockets, bumps; what is meant when a radio report comes that we are likely to be locked in by fog or low ceilings ahead or grounded by ice-forming conditions. You are given some study of plane construction. And then there is the manual.

"The manual is the big thing. It lays down rules and laws intended to govern conduct under every imaginable situation aloft or in port. The watchword is uniformity, military uniformity for every hostess on the line. There is a rule for everything. You learn these by heart and it would seem you can't go wrong.

"There is a certain place you must stand as you greet passengers. You must identify each one, seat him and thereafter be able to address him by name. You must sit in the rear of the plane with an eye ahead, alert for each passenger's wants and as you respond you must stand facing toward the rear, not leaning over so that you turn your back to the passenger in the seat opposite. All the formula you must learn and then there is something else. I guess it's discretion, intuition, tact or something you are born with. We saw one girl after another, who was letter perfect in the rules, eliminated for some indefinable fault in manner or behavior. It was odd how four of us girls who manouevered ourselves together to share an apartment, all landed regular duty.

* * *

"The severest test one which eliminated all save the 20 who finally qualified from our class, was when we were invited one at a time to meet the 'benzine board,' that is, the president, vice-president, secretary, and treasurer of the company. This, I presume, was to see how we would meet personages we felt were important. It wasn't quite a fair test, some of the girls complained, because you are always more awestricken by a prospective employer than by any other person, however high and mighty. Some were so jittery they said afterward they knew there were eight men in that room instead of four. Comparing notes, I seemed to have been the only one who went boldly in and shook hands all around.

"After you are assigned to a regular flight you are given two days' rest between each trip and five days' holiday every six weeks. When there is a vacant seat I usually spend mine traveling on passes over the line. It's just fun to fly with no responsibilities. The pay is $125 a month with $4 a day for expenses while on duty."

She loves to tell about her job, emphasizing the advantages, minimizing the disadvantages. "It worried my mother at first, but now she is reconciled and I have promised that the first family pass I am entitled to, she is to make a flight. With a family of 10 children she hasn't had much chance for adventure, but the instinct for it is still latent, we find. My grandmother, who was 91 when she died lately, gave me more encouragement than anyone else.

"We were warned," concluded the air hostess, "that we must not get unduly friendly with passengers nor with pilots. I pooh-poohed this. I never had become too friendly with doctors, internes or patients with whom I was associated on business terms. At first there was no danger. The pilots resented us as a new element they could very easily do without. Now they are pleased to find we don't add to, but relieve them of all responsibilities back in the plane. And we find the pilots—well—different from other men. They regale us with thrilling stories of adventure and danger when they flew the mails without the safety precautions we have now. They are so in love with their work, so keen and r'aring to go. The company keeps them impatient to be in the air by demanding they spend twice as much time resting as flying. Well," she confessed reluctantly when goaded to it, "we do hear of romances between pilots and hostesses blossoming all along the line."

(2)

MODERN TRENDS IN EDUCATION *

Scholar Called School Asset, But Classroom Practice Held Most Important to Student

Prof. Withington, of Smith, Says Good Teachers Often Pass Unnoticed; Describes Ideal as One Who Combines Love of His Subject With Broad View of It and Interest in Classes

By Robert Withington
Professor of English, Smith College

The perennial question concerning the relative value of competence in research and teaching ability, as a prime requisite for

* Reprinted by permission of the New York *Herald Tribune*.

academic advancement or as a measure of computing the worth of professorial service, continues to occupy the attention of educators, both of the faculty and the administration. Should scholarship be a means or an end? Does investigation help or hinder pedagogy? Can it reasonably be expected that a man can be both an inspiring teacher and a distinguished investigator? These are some of the questions which continually arise and which are variously answered.

To begin with the last: it is perhaps generally agreed that if a teacher is interested in his subject he will keep up with the latest developments in it, and that if he does this he will want to join in such investigations as are in progress. Some will go so far as to say that unless he does this he cannot be a good teacher. It is, of course, obvious that every teacher must have a certain mastery of his subject, and it should be equally obvious that no great teacher can repeat a course unchanged over a long series of years. There is, it need not be remarked, a difference in the kind of teaching required, say, in school and college and university; a difference between that of the first two years in college and the last two; between that suitable to a freshman and to a graduate student. The same man can often change his method to suit demands, and does so; he would hardly give the underclassman the tough meat which the advanced student needs, nor would he hold that the gruelling training for the doctorate should include much mental pabulum of the consistency of pap. Surely the graduate student, coming to his course with a certain preparation and interest, does not need to be spoonfed, and the investigator can regard him in the light of a potential colleague whose chief lack is experience.

Care of Undergraduate

But for the undergraduate the case is altered. Scholarship, in a narrow sense, is not likely to be his chief interest. He has, he will say, come to college to learn; he wants his degree, and takes an interest in grades as a means to that end. He will do enough to "get by with," as he expresses it and may find in the course of his academic career that an unexpected interest has been aroused by some of his teachers. (In a few unusual cases, the interest is already there; in these circumstances the teacher has the delight of nurturing it to greater development.) H. G. Wells's question, "What brand can ever be lit at altars that have borne no fire?" but echoes Carlyle's "How shall he give kindling, in whose inward man there is no live coal, but all is burnt out to a dead grammatical cinder?" Many of us have known teachers who were so wrapped up in their subjects that they forgot their students: "I call it his subject," says Stevenson, "but I think it was he who was subjected."

Unfortunately, the course leading to advanced degrees and to a career of scholarship is just as likely to extinguish a native fire as to kindle one. The administrators who seek scholars at the expense of teachers forget this sometimes. The distinguished faculty member is widely known and brings glory to the institution—but how about his classrooms? The outside world knows little of them, and perhaps cares less; one wonders if the administrator cares much. So long as he has the kudos of the famous name on his staff the other things do not count. He pays for that, and the teaching can be done by smaller fry.

All Scholars Not Dull

I must here not be misunderstood. I do not mean to imply that all great scholars are dull—many of them are far from it—or that if a man is interested in a subject he cannot be interested in his students. Ruskin went so far as to say, "Where investigation is necessary, teaching is impossible," and a certain kind of scholar is described by Goethe:

> "That brain alone not loses hope whose choice is
> To stick in shallow trash for evermore,
> Which digs with eager hands for buried ore,
> And when it finds an angleworm, rejoices!"

There is, undoubtedly, a happy medium in all things; and a teacher, without sticking forevermore in shallow trash, can do enough research to keep him out of a rut.

The deeper question now presents itself; Is scholarship an end in itself, or is it important as a means to improve teaching? Must the scholar interrupt his investigations in the classroom in order to gain his livelihood; or should teaching be his aim, improved by his research? Are more students attracted to a college by the fact that it has very distinguished members of the faculty than because it has good teachers (some of whom are not widely known outside the college walls)? Do the teachers or the scholars (unless a man is both) claim a greater share of alumni affection? And then, of course, comes the question: How is good teaching measured? Is any teaching so bad that it does not have an inspiration for somebody?

A list of distinguished scholars can easily be made, and the university which has the most is often considered the greatest. Administrators make every effort to get and keep such luminaries; colleges capitalize the famous names of present and past celebrities; memories of past greatness lend a glory to the campus of our day, making its shades more soothing, its sunlight more dear than descends on less privileged earth. Sometimes present greatness is recognized and cherished; more often—such is human nature—the scholar is not truly honored until his presence is a memory. When the teacher goes he lives in the minds he has formed, scattered over the earth; his name gradually fades unless he lives in undergraduate tradition—and even this is a tenuous immortality. He is rarely known outside the classroom, and is consequently of less value to the administration than one who draws attention because of wider fame.

Research Costs Money

Universities are beginning to recognize that research costs not only time but money. Some have funds from which grants are made to faculty members carrying on an investigation; others give no such help, except in the form of an occasional leave, and yet expect their teachers to carry on like their more fortunate colleagues. It is, perhaps, surprising that so many teachers are willing to invest not only their time but their substance in research; the answer lies not only in their personal interest in the subject, but in their hope that they may gain that recognition expressed in increased salaries or calls to a larger field of service, which also will be more lucrative. The research thus becomes a form of investment. Those teachers whose interest lies primarily in pushing back the bounds of human ignorance are often on the lookout for a post which will give them more graduate students than undergraduate, in which they can direct advanced work, while carrying on their own investigations, which will remove the routine of the classroom and the drudgery of elementary instruction. There are not many of these "plums," and competition is keen.

We may now ask just what is the primary purpose of our institutions of learning. Is it to add to the sum of human knowledge, or to develop human beings? Upon our answer to this question depends our attitude toward the relative importance of teaching and of research. It must be clear that, if our graduate schools are concerned with the development of scholars, the faculty must be made up of scholars—men who have done research, and are still carrying on the investigation of problems. As the distinction is being made between the junior and the senior college, perhaps we need scholars in the latter, too; for frequently we expect more from our upper classmen than mere parrot repetition. The development of judgment can best be carried on under the influence of a scholar; but he does not want to work on material which has not been prepared for the advanced work of a seminar.

It must be assumed that both teacher and scholar are men of intellectual integrity. It also may be taken for granted that both will encourage intellectual honesty in their pupils. The "scholarly attitude" of mind implies a frankness in facing facts, as well as an ability to add to the sum of human knowledge. This is possible both for the investigator and the teacher—who are, often, united in one man. The question still remains, however, as to which aspect of his activities is more productive of good for his own development, of value to the institution he serves. Perhaps no categorical answer can be given to this question; perhaps both kinds of men are necessary for every faculty—assuming again that every teacher is somewhat of a scholar, and most scholars teachers of a kind.

The good teacher, like the good poet, is born, not made. There are not many of them lying around, and lucky is the college that gets one. Long centuries ago, Chaucer discovered that "The gretteste clerkes been noght the wysest men." The Prince, in "Rasselas," found in a scholar one of the sages whom he should understand less as he heard him longer. The ideal teacher is one who combines a love of his subject, not so pronounced, however, as to make him lose his breadth. He sees the importance of his subject to the individual student, and is as much interested in the pupil as in the subject-matter of the course. He is an authentic man, who can take a line of his own, and can feel intellectual passion. He should make his mark outside of the school, if only to show that he carries a living soul into it. Often, as H. G. Wells has pointed out, nothing is so fatal to a schoolmaster's career as to do that. This is perhaps true in politically-run institutions of so-called learning; but not, we like to think, in the best American colleges and universities.

(3)

PILGRIMS' PROGRESS *

Four Years Ago A Handful Of Pioneer Farmers, Tired of Droughts and Dust Storms, Were Given A Fresh Start in Virgin Territory in Alaska. And Now Look At Them

BY W. B. COURTNEY

We stood in a clearing where yesterday there had been old trees and primeval shadows and the matting and tangle of the years. Peter, broad and Nordic, stooped and filled both hands with virgin soil and worked it under his stubby thumbs. There was a light on his face like the flash of a plowshare when it turns at the field's edge.

"This is fine dirt, Mister!" said Peter.

It was moist and dark and glowing with rich and secret hints of fertility; in it lay distilled the gifts of time and weather, of sky and bracken and wilderness creatures—the bounty of the centuries waiting in a fortunate land.

"I seen two farms blow away from me back in the States!" said Peter.

Mayta, his wife, came near and stared with us at the fisted earth. She was tall and slim and young, and their baby was in a sling upon her back. Peter reached across her shoulder and rubbed a bit of earth between the baby's gaping eyes until Mayta slapped down his arm.

"This one ain't goin' to blow away from us, Mister!" said Peter.

Mayta was girlishly trim in a blue overall; a brightly dotted handkerchief restrained her corn-tassel hair. There was certitude and grace and the discipline of pride in her swaying body as she drove the horses; a mobile, pliant fullness that was in mysterious affinity with the new field. Peter walked behind the plow. He looked backward from his uneven, plunging stride.

"The woman is the most important thing up here. A feller's lost if his wife ain't got no git-up and git-out. If she's okay they'll eat, you bet, and be warm, too, and have good things to wear!" said Peter.

This was the picture you carried away from Matanuska: a young American family, innocent of national or party destinies, of catch-

* Reprinted by permission of *Collier's*.

words or theories, of economic laws or political controversies—knowing only that here was a country that did not go without rain for months, here was soil that would not turn to dust and blow away for all your hard work, here was a place where strong and willing folks could make a go of things.

Now the long days have come again to that far-off valley: steel blades have unlaced winter's bindings from the earth, and the furrows turned like eager wounds to the gentle sun and the nurturing rain. Down the Susitna from the great Alaska Range, down the Matanuska and the Knik, down a hundred creeks and a thousand brooks, down the aisles of the spruce woods and the rough grooves of the foreland moraines, the water hurries, its skimmed-milk color telling of glacial birth. Springtime in this land of emphatic seasons is a lusty upheaval in men and beasts and ground alike. And the colonists of Matanuska, the latter-day pioneers, turn grateful eyes to the summits where the eternal snow is a pledge against crops withered in the row and cattle dead of thirst.

Their eyes come back quickly to immediate things; to horse and plow and seed bag, to fork and disk. For in the shape of events, this will be for them a momentous year; when the colonists must walk diligently in a middle road, armed against meddling friend and captious foe alike. The purse strings in Washington are closing; Matanuska is on its own, to justify its existence or to be marked down as another crackpot experiment in patent-medicine sociology; to flourish as a milestone in sound and practical depression relief, or to be shrugged off as another five-million-dollar rooking of taxpayers that will piddle away and be forgotten.

No other single welfare project of modern times in the United States was so spectacular as this uprooting of two hundred-odd families, a thousand men, women and children with a variety of pets and household goods, and transporting them more than three thousand miles over prairie, mountain, ocean and valley to a new world; a romantic public adventure with a throwback to the early history of the Republic; an exodus that sometimes took on spiritual fervor, when the women cried and sang hymns, the men shouted psalms, and there were exhortations and emotional joinings in prayer. Public attention dogged the strange, pathetic flight; advocates minimized each delay and stupidity, critics howled up each mistake; the pilgrims themselves were infected and there were fights and sickness and hysteria and some who stood around with their hands out, while delegates were actually dispatched to Washington to charge parsimony to a bewildered and beneficent uncle. In those days you could not see the waves for the spray; shirkers and homesick, the unfit and the misfit, had not yet departed to give you a clear view of the Peters and the Maytas.

"This is our fourth year," Peter says, "and now you can begin to get a pretty good idea of how things stand and how they ought to go. Last season about 150 tourists a week came to see us and we think it's good because they go back and tell folks at home what's going on up here. Funny thing, a lot of them come with chips on their shoulders."

Peter and Mayta and the baby typify the 170 families left in Matanuska Colony of the 245 that were chosen, all told, in the first and succeeding years. Not a bookish fellow, Peter; but a simple, earthy one, who lets down his suspenders when he relaxes beside the radio after supper. Historical parallels you will have to round up for yourself; for example, how favorably Matanuska's desertion of less than one-third compares with the stories of early colonizations in America. From the group of 120 settlers, dispatched in 1607 by the Plymouth Company to the mouth of the Kennebec River, who went home in a mass the next year; through Plymouth, the Bay, Maryland and Virginia settlements and plantations, there was a constant wholesale flow of faint hearts back to the homeland. It has been estimated that only one in ten of the early colonists in America survived; incredible hardships and Indian raids accounted for many of the nine; desertion the rest. But the nearest Peter comes to a reference is when he tells you:

Why Not Cream-Puff Pioneers?

"We saw in the papers a lot of names for us. Sometimes we hear tourists whispering, too. We are 'cream-puff pioneers,' and 'plush-lined pioneers' and a lot of other things. They say we are spoiled because things are made too easy for us; and I guess they are sore because we don't have the same hardships like the Pilgrim Fathers, who had fevers and starvation to fight as well as Indians. Well, there ain't no Indians to fight up here, that's so, and we have been helped a lot; but I still think we got hardships of a kind. I don't understand why some people who have got jobs expect that a great, rich country should send its poor out to live like the poor lived three hundred years ago. After all, I figure a hardship in any time is when you ain't got all the nice things that's available to other ordinary people in the same times. We got a good life here and I ain't kickin', but it's a new, strange world and we're away from our friends and relations and probably won't never see most of them again, because it costs plenty of money to travel all the way back, and we're stuck here in the valley, with only local roads; and the cost of living for everything except what we make or grow is awful high on account of the Alaska Railroad's freight rates; and if you think breakin' new land is for sissies, a cream-puff job, just lend me a hand with this here stump, Mister!"

The mystery of Matanuska, so far as laymen at home are concerned, is why Alaska was selected for a resettlement project; a distant and unbroken land, with initial costs for transportation and ground preparation so great that only a relatively small number of needy families would be aided.

Many conjectures have been made; some in whispers. It is likely, however, that Matanuska is the result of no single idea or motive, either superficially benevolent or slyly ulterior.

The military advantage of a widely tilled and settled Alaska is, perhaps, the incentive principally credited: indeed, the colonists themselves have a vague idea of being part of some mysterious provisions for national defense strategy. Alaska has been much talked up in recent years as an outpost of United States arms. And when you discuss in Washington the question of the disproportionate cost of the Matanuska Resettlement Project, officials lay fingers alongside their noses and shut one eye and give coy visual interpretations of air raids and machine guns.

A vast land, Alaska offers nearly ten square miles of room for each of its inhabitants, compared with the sixteen or so acres each one of you here at home must be content to swing your elbows in. It has about 30,000 white residents, who live chiefly out of tin cans imported from the States. But it lies far out at the crown of the Pacific Ocean, extends west of Hawaii and comes within eyeshot of Russia, like a sentry box guarding the main routes over which invaders from Asia—when and if any—would have to approach us. However, even a Saturday-afternoon militarist can see that it would take scores of Matanuskas—thousands of families—before Alaska will be competent to provision and comfort an embattled American defensive army up there; a condition hardly attainable, except by ruinous expenditures, within half a century or more.

"I figure," said Peter, "it's just one of them things for which you can't blame nobody and it comes out good anyhow."

In mankind's annals there have been many such instances; movements, actions, tides in human affairs for which neither legal justification nor clear purpose can be discerned, but after a while you see that it had to happen. Alaska is a "natural," in these days of international hunger for good land.

The flow there on a large and organized scale was inevitable—with our agricultural population crowded over the edges of nonarable land, running far ahead of irrigation projects and possibilities, robbed by lack of attention in the past to conservation fundamentals.

Alaska was bought from Russia for about two cents per acre, or $7,200,000—thus, only a couple of million dollars more was paid for the whole territory than has been expended so far on Matanuska colony alone. That was in 1867, and the wags called it "Seward's Folly" and "Seward's Icebox"—after the Secretary of State who made the deal—also "Icebergia," "Walrussia," "Zero Island," and a lot of similar rib-splitters. Alaska contains nearly 600,000 square miles—it is about one fifth as large as the entire United States, twice as large as Texas and 14 times the size of Ohio.

Alaska's Three Belts

Alaska is divided into three climatic belts—Arctic, Interior and Coastal. Forget the first, the zone within the "Circle," for colonization purposes; although some vegetables actually are raised in the inch or two that in the brief summer thaws into a sort of grease on top of the perpetually frozen ground. The Interior has drastic weather; 60 to 70 below zero in the long winters, occasionally 90 or more above in summer—and, incredibly, a semiarid precipitation record. Fairbanks averages about 11 inches of rainfall, and 50 of snow. Conditions here and elsewhere in the interior sometimes approximate drought. The Coastal region has lots of precipitation, luxuriant vegetation, and escapes prolonged severe cold. Lowest winter temperatures here do not approach those of the Midcentral States from which the Matanuska settlers came. The Japan Current does for Alaska's coast what the Gulf Stream does for the British Isles and Scandinavia.

Government experts hold that Alaska contains 65,000 square miles of land suitable for tilling; 35,000, in addition, ideal for grazing. The potential agricultural land, therefore, nearly matches the whole area of the combined New England States and Pennsylvania and should be able to support an equivalent population—about 18,000,000.

Alaska, thus, has a farmable area of about 65,000,000 acres with a population now of only 60,000, including Indians and Eskimos. Finland has a cultivated area of less than 6,000,000 acres; and a population of more than three and a half millions. Yet Finland's people are decent and sturdy, enjoy an unusual per capita use of the most progressive features of science and economics, and Finland manages to be one of the few solvent nations; the only European country to pay fully its foreign debt obligations. Alaska, being infinitely richer in natural resources, intelligent and persistent colonization should endow its future and increase the sum total of our national prosperity and security.

"My folks came from Finland," says Peter, "and I bet they would say this is swell, better than the old country. A lot of the folks here is Finns, and most of the others is Swedes or Norwegians. All from North Europe, anyhow. You see, I guess the fellers in Washington did figure this thing all out pretty well."

Mightier Than the Plow

The most important ability of these Scandinavian-Americans from the north Middle West, however, to safeguard the general plan of colonization of Alaska, lies in their economic traditions; they have farming in their blood. For Alaska has been, essentially, a mining and fishing civilization, with fur and lumber tagging along. These are fields of quick huge profits today; and there is no thought for tomorrow.

Since the purchase, Alaska has been exploited, looted and wrung by rich speculators and by adventurers. These are industries that pay good wages, bring high costs of living on their margins, and do not have the will nor the incentive nor the inherent structures to support large populations at their sources or to confer local benefits. Both fisheries and mines attract, even transport, hordes of transient workers for their brief season—men who have no civic interests in Alaska. Both are represented only seasonally by managers and superintendents; and for the greater part of the year, merely by watchmen. Here are all the curses of absentee landlordism; and it has bred an inferiority complex into resident Alaskans. Young people grow up to feel they are nobody unless they have been "outside"

—the great shibboleth word of Alaska, which indicates hectic social competition and a state of mind that recently drew a scathing editorial in "The Farthest North Collegian," the official newspaper of the University of Alaska. Except for certain professional men and government employees, only the drones stay on in Alaska the year through.

There have been farmers in the territory heretofore. Many of them, however, are men who failed as miners and went off to scratch the ground just enough to make a living for themselves. In the old days grubstakers used to raise potatoes in the sod roofs of their hovels. Few independent Alaskan farmers can find local markets, for the mines and the fisheries not only import men, they fetch up all their needed food and make Alaska a tin-can civilization. Nor can the farmers ship produce to the United States; partly because of the terrific freight rates, and partly because you can't raise things in a $6-a-day labor market, such as Alaska, and send it to a $2-a-day labor market, such as the Pacific Northwest. So it is difficult to get energetic men to remain on the soil; moreover, there is a gamble involved in mining that gets into the blood.

Nearly every professional man I talked with in Alaska—dentists, aviators, railroaders—either has a stake in a large property, or a "field partner" (a prospector whom he finances), or entire ownership of a small quartz mine. I met one farmer from Oregon, a skilled and experienced countryman, who had a good home on a farm that, together with incidental work under the auspices of the university, guaranteed him a living for himself and his family and $1,600 cash profit each year. But he chucked this to go to work at $6 a day for five months on a gold dredge. In the winter, the miners who don't or can't return outside hole up in the back rooms of saloons and play an endless card game until the spring thaw. It's the old lure of the chance that you might strike a big pot overnight; something cabbages and beans will never do for you.

I asked Peter whether he thought any of the Matanuska colonists might succumb to the fever that has made the tin pan a mightier weapon than the plow in Alaska.

"Mebbe," said Peter, "although once a feller signs the various agreements with the government and the co-operative—and nearly everybody has signed now—it won't be a light matter for him to pull stakes again. Me, well, look at this soil. The government agents tell me that in some places around here it is 18 feet deep. This looks like a sure thing to me. This is my kind of pay dirt, and I ain't goin' off after rainbows."

If present and future colonists hold true with Peter, Alaska may have in its nearly 100,000 square miles of still undeveloped arable land a resource that one day will overshadow her traditional activities, supplement them, and give them a sounder relationship both to Alaskan and to national values.

The Kuskokwim is one of the great rivers of Alaska; it drains the territory southwest. The Yukon is one of the greatest rivers of the earth: roughly, it bisects Alaska, piercing the Arctic Circle at one point. Both rivers flow into Bering Sea; and both have in their valleys millions of untrod acres, now a mat of spruce and birch, that could be made available for grazing and some crops.

Colonel Ohlson's Pet

The grassy inlands off the southwest coast line—including Kodiak, home of the giant bears—offer ideal livestock ranges. Lack of transportation facilities, the greatest handicap to Alaska's progress, make organized settlement of all these districts unlikely for generations to come. The airplane and the dog sledge are the only carriers that have ever been seen in those valleys; the mail boats visit major points along the island chain once each month, and ranchers must provide themselves with small boats for journeying from their homes to the nearest scheduled dock. These seas can be rough and wild; and in stormy weather you'd better stay home and take a chance on getting provisions and mail next month.

Tanana Valley, north of the Alaskan Range, has nearly five million tillable acres, of which few have been turned; however, it is one of Alaska's business farm belts. There is an experiment station at the university; grain, potatoes, berries and some truck are grown—with lilacs, certain roses, and a few hardy old favorites like Cotoneasters possible if you want to make your place homey. In Tanana your crops grow above permanent frost; eight to eighteen inches of surface thawing, depending upon the length and temperature of the summer. Dry spells are frequent, but of little moment; for the plants get moisture by capillary attraction from the ice beneath.

In the opinion of experts, the Kenai Peninsula—which runs along Cook Inlet from a point near Anchorage, southwest into the Gulf of Alaska—has the best land and the best climate in Alaska; the latter more temperate than that of New England. Large numbers of settlers and homesteaders are going to Kenai now, but there can be no boom until highways and transportation are provided.

The Matanuska Valley, north of Anchorage—brightest and cleanest and most get-along-minded town in Alaska—and dabsmack on the Alaskan Railroad, is, therefore, the favored zone at present. Its town is Palmer, about 150 miles from the chief Alaskan port, Seward. Matanuska, like Kenai, is south of the Alaskan Range—the Rocky Mountains of Alaska—and outside the area of permanent frost. If you want to find Matanuska in your atlas look between parallels of latitude 61 and 62 north; and meridians of longitude 149 and 150 west.

Colonel Otto Frederick Ohlson has known where Matanuska is, and many other things about it, for a long time.

Colonel Ohlson is general manager of the Alaska Railroad, which is owned by the government. It has cost about $75,000,000 to date, and was finished in the Harding Administration. Colonel Ohlson is a demon card player, and a demoniacal driver of the automobile, equipped with special wheels, that he uses for traveling on the railway. It is his job to hold down the annual operation deficits of the road; part of his method for accomplishing this is to charge freight rates that cause howls that can be heard as far away as Washington.

The Matanuska Project is Colonel Ohlson's pet; he is president of the Alaska Rural Rehabilitation Corporation, and parent body. But he is a tough pappy; and the colonists kick bitterly over the cost of having things shipped up from the States.

Colonel Ohlson is generally acknowledged to be the originator of the movement that eventually brought a federally blessed colonization project into the valley. Years ago, when he took over his job, he realized that his railroad and the towns beside it would find security only upon a base of sound and permanent agriculture. He surveyed the potentialities, then sent candy-tongued scouts into Oregon and Washington and other states to entice settlers. Many came; and some prospered modestly. A number of these "old settlers" have received financial aid from the Matanuska Project; membership in its co-operative is available to them, and widely taken advantage of.

When drought and dust storms and wind erosion brought distress to the West, and put thousands of country families on relief, the current administration got up its program of resettlement. Colonel

Ohlson's heart leaped; his valley was made to order for this. He set a pregnant word in Secretary Roper's ear, and first thing you know the Matanuska idea was born in Washington.

There were mistakes from the beginning; but there was shrewdness, too. The emergency dictated haste, and many blunders can be traced to that. Orders went out to field workers of the WPA to nominate families from the relief lists of Wisconsin, Minnesota and Michigan; a section that, it was calculated, would offer least climatic variation. The welfare people were, moreover, strictly charged to pick only experienced farmers, preferably of Scandinavian origin and not more than 40 years old, and warned not to overpaint the promised land.

"But some of them agents, in some counties, told whopping lies," said Peter. "They said moose came to the back doors begging to be shot, you had to shoo the rabbits and quail out of your bed, and just drop a line out the kitchen window once to catch enough salmon for a year. Us farm men took it all with a grain of salt, but the way we felt, after what we had been through, we figured any land where it rained would be good land. But they picked a lot of guys who didn't know an 8-8-4 mixture from a pie recipe—plasterers, steamfitters, streetcar motormen, and some plain loafers."

You will find in Matanuska that officials will discuss the mistakes as candidly and readily as the colonists. Men, for example, like Dr. H. M. Colvin, general counsel in Washington for the WPA, or Leo B. Jacobs and Stewart Campbell, general manager and administrative assistant respectively of the project. Wisdom dictated this policy for some of the pioneers departed from the popular general conception of Scandinavian inarticulateness, and no sooner did the jams begin than they took pens in hand.

A Capital in the Making

Plus the loose selections, there were two other primary errors: one in not having tools and implements available for the colonists when they reached the valley, another in permitting unrestrained, almost reckless, building up of debt loads by some. The latter has been the project's sorest problem; any solution apparently would set a premium on brashness, and penalize thrift.

"Some trouble, I guess, has been on account of what they call this here government red tape," said Peter. "Like the wheat thing. Last year we planted spring wheat to use for chicken feed, only when it came up it turned out to be red Russian winter wheat, and that ain't for poultry feed. The seed was sent up from a central buyin' place in the States. That system has given us lots of headaches. We see things like clothes or tools, say, in a mail-order catalogue for a dollar, but we may have to pay three dollars for the very same thing in the colony store. I kin tell you some more mistakes, too. But I figure that's water over the dam, and as we get on our feet the government won't have so many chances to make mistakes for us. If there are going to be any more, we kin have the fun of making them ourselves."

You will have a visual surprise when you come to Matanuska Colony, in the storied territory of sourdough and musher; of the hairy men of Rex Beach and Jack London and the bitter trail of '98 over Chilkoot Pass and up to Dawson. You alight, from train or bus, at Palmer and immediately you perceive the American institution of a community divided by railroad tracks into sheep and goats; quality folks and the unanointed.

On the one side is the noncolony Palmer, the original little frontier post that mushroomed with the coming of government largess to the valley. Here is a single rank of nondescript buildings, gaudy to shabby, facing the tracks and looking over them to the mannered community.

Palmer is the Washington, the Albany, the Sacramento, the Austin and Baton Rouge of Matanuska Valley. The main administrative buildings have a sour-cream tint and are grouped in a loose quadrangle around a park; you can see that one day this is going to be an impressive and beautiful capital. There is a large school, which has been turned over to the territorial government and is open to all children of the valley. It runs through grade and high school, and is unusually well staffed and equipped—as good, in these respects, as the best in the States—for a high class of teacher was attracted by the novelty of the project. This is likewise true of the hospital, also in the group.

Facing Their New World

There is a dormitory where you can live and eat Matanuska products during your visit. Eventually this will be an inn when more homes for nurses and teachers and other workers are ready. There is an office building and a general store called "Trading Post" by the more romantic pioneers. Scattered beyond the quadrangle are co-operative buildings, blacksmith and machine shops, garage, a big hatchery and whatever buildings you would expect in an up-to-date budget farm colony.

The school is, of course, the center of social activities, with clubrooms of various natures, and with a huge auditorium in which movies, dances, the emotings of the drama societies, receptions to visiting firemen, mass political meetings, boxing matches and such goings on are housed.

"I think we got it better than the nicest small towns back in Minnesota," said Peter. "Only if it makes you want to come up here, remember they got more than fifteen thousand applications now in Washington."

The colony is scattered over more than 10,000 acres in the Matanuska Valley, and by no means exhausts its potential farm land. Within the colony boundaries there are only 150 miles of newly built roads, so that each tract is accessible, by highway, from Palmer. A road of any kind is like a fine, cool well in the Sahara. The colonists gad about on horseback a great deal, and a row of Dobbins hitched to the fence alongside the taxi stand gives a frontier touch to the handsome modern community. Many colonists have small cars, though, and farm electric-light plants. You remember these families were all on relief and you wonder; the soldiers' bonus, paid since Matanuska was founded, is the answer to such luxuries.

The latest census of the colony shows 170 families. The pioneers, arriving in two contingents in the summer of 1935, consisted of 201 families; and that many tracts were originally surveyed. They lived in tents while the houses were being constructed that summer and fall, and 75 families quit. Only 173 houses were finished, therefore; of these, two burned down and one is on a plot where a well has not been found. The project heads therefore decided to hold the colony to 170 families. Twenty families, of the number of replacements needed to attain this strength, were handpicked from a waiting list of about 3,000 in the States, by Stewart Campbell, a government expert from Matanuska. The others were selected from a number who, at their own cost, actually went to Alaska to "crash" the colony.

Brothers Under the Skin

The houses in which these modern pioneers face their new world vary in size according to family requirements: they were built from specially designed plans, which differ enough both in exterior and interior treatment and materials to lend variety and to give play to individuality. They are paneled, insulated, warm; advantage has been taken of the latest architectural knowledge to get comfortable, inexpensive homes. Framed by wood lots of spruce and birch, set against a backdrop of snowy Alpine ridges, this is indeed a picture-book farming community.

The people who live in these houses—well, Nelson and Septka, Johnson and Laako, Anderson, Stebbins, Wagner, Erickson; the same as the Nelsons, Johnsons, Wagners, and Ericksons of Pennsylvania, or Florida, or Nevada, or Rhode Island. With that little extra something in the heart that comes from hands that know the joy of primitive grips; of feet alive to the rhythm of new furrows, the first cuts in a virgin earth.

"It's working out here like every place where you git a thousand people together," said Peter. "Some man is better than other man. Some never done working. There's that Mrs. Novak: she has a family, but she finds time to drive a taxicab, work in the store —anything to make a little for getting on the feet. Then when we come up here first there was that girl who opened a beauty shop to curl the ladies' hair while her mother and father worked on their tract. Some of us is self-supporting already. That means, don't have to git no more help from the government, but raise enough, or earn enough by working outside your own tract, to pay for your own livin'. Joe Puhl and Virgil Eckert were the first two to declare their independence, back in July, 1936, only a year after they got here. There's been more than a dozen other families since. Pretty good, hey, for people who started from the poorhouse, like you could say, only three years ago!"

If Matanuska is a part, however, remote, of the national defense plan, if it is only the beginning of a farsighted scheme to husband resources, it is cheap; for it has cost, altogether, scarcely more than the price of a modern destroyer. Purely on relief grounds, it is not easy to justify.

Total federal grants, with respect to the Matanuska Project, fall just short of $5,000,000. Of this, three fifths has been expended on roads, public improvements, facilities and buildings, and similar phases. Old settlers in the valley borrowed some $26,000 from the project. About $1,300,000 has been loaned, or is available for lending, to the colonists and secured by mortgages on their farms and chattels. This is the money that will be repaid by the colonists to the government over a 30-year period. In their home districts it was costing the government about $500 a year to maintain each of those families in relief, and there was scant hope of their getting off the rolls.

To Keep Out Speculators

Under the original terms, the government paid transportation for each colonist, his family, and 2,000 pounds of household goods from the home town to Matanuska Valley. This was not charged against him, but every subsequent advantage, save community facilities at Palmer, was counted into the sum he would have to repay. He received 40 acres of land, of which the government undertook to clear 15 acres. He received materials and help to build his dwelling; and could draw livestock, equipment, and farm machinery in line with his personal desires and requirements. In addition, the government promised subsistence, food and clothing to each family until it should be able to provide for itself.

There were two sad features here. The government's system of bulk purchasing and shipping made commodities higher—even at cost price—and caused much grumbling as the indebtedness piled up. Moreover, there was little check on each colonist's drawing of livestock and other equipment, and some reached for the moon. It was a pat laboratory adventure in character—thrifty people lived thriftily; wasteful people lived prodigally. Some pioneers ran their debts as high as $16,000; an insane burden for a 40-acre farm in a remote land of dubious markets, and one that never could be repaid. It was soon plain that a readjustment would have to be made, an equalization of indebtedness, if the government were to get anything. Now the first really grave crisis in the history of the colony arose: families who had managed well, and kept their debt low, found they were in prospect of having it hiked up to bring down the average of the spendthrifts. Eventually a debt commission was established. This called in each colonist and his wife for a review of their situation and a joint decision as to the lumped amount they should repay.

When peace has been restored to each such conference, three papers are signed: a satisfaction agreement, a realty sales contract, and a chattel mortgage. The average settlement comes to about $5,000, which the colonist promises to repay fully through amortization over a period of 30 years, with interest at three per cent per annum. You never can sell your farm without permission from the government; even when you own it free and clear! A stipulation designed to keep out speculators.

The colonists have formed the Matanuska Valley Farmers Co-operating Association to prepare and market their products. Membership is available to old settlers, as well as pioneers. The project had an income of $200,000 last year; and for the first six months paid its members a 3½ per cent dividend. "Matanuska Maid" dairy products are being proudly displayed in Anchorage windows.

Colonel Ohlson writes up dreams of a million-dollar market along his railroad for Matanuska products, and has figures to give them substance. He sees the colonists eventually making incomes of more than $4,000 each, which is more than four times the average farmer's income in the States. Certainly the canneries and the mines, which now fetch up all their provender to a land where fresh vegetables have been almost unknown, will afford a market when the Matanuska output is consistent and dependable; the steamship officials told me they hope to be able to take aboard fresh Matanuska things at Seward, instead of filling their larders in Seattle for the round trip.

"You kin figure it this way," says Peter. "Me and the other fellers ain't goin' to git rich off 40 acres, although I guess we'll be able to buy more land some day because this is a big valley. Good farmers will make a livin' here okay. And I guess you won't see a more beautiful place no matter where you go. Of course scenery doesn't help your crop none, but it doesn't hurt your life none, either, when other things is good, too. And this is a swell climate, and you got all the things a feller wants when he ain't workin'. You got moose, if you look hard enough; and black bear; and plenty of smaller game. And you got trout and salmon; last year Mayta put up 12 dozen cans of salmon, along with all the other things."

Light in the Distance

You have seen Matanuska, then, and it is your impression these farmers live, not luxuriously, but a little better than average farmers in the States. Government aid in financing and building a fine model community is partly responsible for this; climate has more to do with it. But this seems true—the government will get back much of the money it has put into Matanuska. Meanwhile, it has taken a group of good Americans who were pauperized through no fault of their own and given them self-respect. It has made an important, if unwitting, step in national defense. It has turned the searchlight of American public interest, and of scientific investigation, upon a virgin agricultural land that, in expert opinion, can support in health, comfort and modest prosperity a population of 18,000,000.

When you come away from Matanuska, you will be filled with statistics and theories; with views of mistakes and gains; with claims and charges. You may have no better idea of the wisdom or soundness of the experiment than you had when first you came: I didn't. But gradually those matters fade into a larger, clearer picture of a band of lost, frightened people who came out of a swamp of hopelessness and were set on a firm road. It may lead through uncertain years, but in the distance there is light. And then you have the largest and clearest picture of all. . . .

We stood in a clearing where yesterday there had been old trees and primeval shadows and the matting and tangle of the years. "This is fine dirt, Mister!" said Peter. It was moist and dark and glowing with rich and secret hints of fertility; in it lay distilled the gifts of time and weather, of sky and bracken and wilderness creatures—the bounty of the centuries waiting in a fortunate land. Mayta, his wife, came near and stared with us at the fisted earth. She was tall and slim and young, and their baby was in a sling upon her back. "I seen two farms blow away from me in the States," said Peter. "This one ain't goin' to blow away!"

(4)

SPRINGTIME PILGRIMAGE *

To The Gardens
Of Nine Women Who Wield A Spade
As Well As A Pen

By Julian R. Meade

Who would not like to make a spring journey from Vermont to Colorado and visit nine lovely gardens of nine old friends? Don't say, because you live in Georgia or Oregon, that you have no gardening friend so far away as Vermont. If you have read a writer's stories or poems, laughed or wept with the characters she has created for

* Reprinted by permission of *Good Housekeeping* and Mr. Julian R. Meade.

you, you would not be meeting a stranger if you walked with her in her garden and heard her talk of her favorite flowers. Certainly you would find a friendly welcome in the garden near Arlington, Vermont, where this pilgrimage begins.

Dorothy Canfield Fisher's house lies on the side of Red Mountain and overlooks the valley of the Battenkill stretching away to the Green Mountains. The location of her garden was almost decreed by geology, for there was only one level place on that mountainside big enough for a garden—a slope facing south. This tract of flat land, sixty by seventy feet, is surrounded by a low stone wall. In the exact middle of the garden is a still fountain made from marble bought in Manchester, where marble for the New York Public Library was quarried. Mrs. Fisher paid $2.25 for some of the short ends of the great building's columns, had them set in a base of cement, and had water piped from a near-by spring.

Gardening is but one of Mrs. Fisher's many interests, yet you wonder if the tranquil expression on the gardener's face and the calm tone of her voice are not inspired in part by hours she spends in cultivating the iris, delphiniums, and lilies, which are her favorite flowers. There is no need to wonder, for she answers the question cheerfully:

"The reason I garden as I do is because I want to enjoy it. The best I have in the way of vitality and intelligence belongs to my family and my work. I put my faith in gardening, not on my own vitality, but on that of the plants. Mine is strictly a Darwinian garden, based on the survival of the fittest. I have a simple rule about the choice of what flowers to have: those that stand a severe climate without being fussed over. I give them plenty to eat and drink and a slope facing the southern sun, and try to keep the worst of the weeds out—if I don't happen to be too busy when weeds are flourishing! The rest they have to do for themselves, and if they don't, I don't even have to bother to throw them out. They vanish!"

Mrs. Fisher is modest, and when you see the healthy plants which fill her border with waves of color from April through October, you know her flowers do not do all the work for themselves What she means is that she's not going to worry if you discover a few dead blossoms on her iris or stray chickweed in her sweet alyssum.

"I love beautifully kept gardens filled with rare and lovely flowers," she smiles, "but I mourn over the harassed face of the gardening lady if the effort is too hard for her. The reason why I think people ought to know about my kind of garden is that I'm sure there are many people with absorbing, exacting work, who would really like to garden and are scared off by the professionals—"

"The professionals?"

"Yes," Mrs. Fisher laughs, her eyes glowing. "Especially the professionals who call themselves amateurs. I'm sure there are people who would enjoy, as I do, the occasional hour or so of work in the earth, surrounded by the poignantly beautiful miracles of growth. People who would return to their work, as I do to my desk, refreshed, and at the same time not be obliged (although there is no greater fun) to brood and hover and continually think about their gardens."

As Mrs. Fisher shows you about her place, you know that every visitor to this home goes away with treasured memories. On the mountain above her house she owns acres of woodland which for twenty-four years she has been reforesting with white pines. She bought these young trees from the State Forestry Department at $5 a thousand, and, as she says, "what they need chiefly is some waste land, time, and a little prayer, rather than much money." Every day of her life Mrs. Fisher walks among these clean-smelling pines. And then she strolls to the bubbling spring which was the reason for her family's settling on this Vermont mountainside in 1764. The spring has deliciously soft water, and Dorothy Canfield's grandmother insisted on settling near by so she would have soft water for her washing.

"I'm so grateful to my grandmother!" Mrs. Fisher exclaims.

No wonder she's grateful. There is peace beside the spring, just as there is peace within the stone wall of the garden where pansies hail the return of spring and twenty-year-old delphiniums bloom in summer against a background of old-fashioned hollyhocks.

Now for another hilltop garden, south of Vermont. Several miles from the village of Austerlitz, New York, a maple-edged hillside lawn surrounds an inviting white clapboard house which was once a small farmhouse. Wandering from this lawn, you have your choice of a hardy garden, a rock garden, or a sunken garden. The head gardener at Steepletop is a small woman with a delicate, visionary face, red-gold hair, and lovely blue-green eyes. By her assistant gardener she is referred to as "she," but to the world she is Edna St. Vincent Millay.

Because she is a great lyric poet you might not think of Miss Millay as a very practical gardener. But as she herself is quick to tell you—

her firm little chin raised up and her voice melodious but insistent—

"I use the spade *myself,* and I'm not unskillful at it, either. On occasion I've been known to swing a mean pickax! As a weeder I think that I'm unsurpassed, but I'm a bad transplanter. When I find that the hole I've dug for a rosebush is too small and I have to drag it out and dig some more, or when roots which I've carefully spread out curl back and slap at me, I become irritated. My husband will spend hours transplanting one rose. He has infinite patience. I haven't."

Besides her husband, Miss Millay has one helper for her heavier labor, a man who is clever at transplanting but knows very little about flowers.

"When I'm at work in my study," she says, "and know that he's at work in my garden, I don't know whether to feel elated or depressed."

If any horticultural sins have been committed in this garden, the enchanted visitor will not detect them. The hardy garden, as Miss Millay calls it, is blessed with thriving beds of oriental poppies and lupines. The delphiniums, according to the head gardener, are sadly in need of spraying, but flower growers from warmer climates will say they are handsome enough and will not see the black edges which worry the poet. Peonies, especially the big double white *Festiva Maxima,* are very fine. In the rose beds hybrid teas have been carried through the bitter winters with unusual success. At the back of this perennial garden a summerhouse is covered with Easlea's Golden Rambler, which takes the place of an Emily Gray that had saffron-colored buds and shiny foliage for several years and then died—much to the gardener's distress, for she considers Emily Gray the most beautiful climbing rose she has ever seen. An unusual feature of this summerhouse is a painting, done in automobile paint by Charles Ellis, which stays out in all weathers. It is of two little cherubs resting on clouds. One of the lovely small figures is blowing the trumpet, and the other looks at a cedar waxwing which has alighted on his finger.

The rock garden at Steepletop (that name, incidentally, honors a native shrub which Austerlitz farmers call hardhack or steepletop) is natural.

"These rocks are really perennial," Miss Millay says. "They have been in exactly the position in which they are now for, I imagine, some millions of years. The only flowers which seem to intend to compete with them in hardiness are the harebell, which seeds itself everywhere, and the red wild columbine which I dug up and brought down in my lap from the top of a mountain near here. Hollyhocks also do well in this rock garden, here, and in the driveway—they refuse to grow anywhere else!"

Miss Millay loves especially her sunken garden, which was constructed within the stone foundation of an old barn which burned down a long time ago. Two small lawns have been made here. Each is bordered by tall arborvitae, and each contains a fountain. At the end of one secluded alley of evergreens is a statue, exquisitely done in marble by Randolph Rogers, of an absurd little boy dressed up as an Indian. A terrace leads from the sunken garden to a swimming pool bordered with Japanese iris.

"They are the finest Japanese iris I've ever seen anywhere," the head gardener confesses, "and I'm not excluding Japan. We grow them on the place from seed, and we're very proud of them."

Miss Millay's lovely voice would never be raised to tell you of what goes on within her study, of sonnets that are acclaimed by critics and are best sellers, too. But when a gardener can raise Japanese iris *from seed*—well, that's no time for modesty.

When you reach Virginia, there are all about you famous gardens full of ancient boxwood and gnarled crepe myrtles. But there's one small garden which some of us would rather see than the grounds of any mansion. It lies behind Miss Ellen Glasgow's gray stone house of Georgian design at the corner of Main and Foushee Streets in Richmond. This dwelling has been there for a hundred years and now is unperturbed by changes which have brought rooming houses and garages as neighbors. An iron fence, hung with twisted wistaria vines, encloses the small yard where box trees and a towering magnolia frame the house. Window boxes, both upstairs and downstairs, bear the rich green of dwarf box and trailing ivy.

The garden at the rear of the house is completely shut in by gray walls. When you first glimpse this retreat, you remember that living garden of "The Sheltered Life":

"In the garden, which was reached by stone steps from the back porch, splendour flickered over the tall purple iris that fringed the birdbath, and rippled like a bright veil over the grass walks and flower beds. A small place, but it held beauty. Beauty, and that deep stillness through which time seems to flow with a perpetual rhythm and pause . . ."

Change the iris fringing the birdbath to boxwood, and you have a likeness of the novelist's own garden. Miss Glasgow's own "small place" is still and secluded. No wonder visitors want to say the novelist writes here rather than behind the closed door of her upstairs study!

On the railings of the back porch overlooking the garden are more window boxes. Sunlight of warm months falls upon pink geraniums and soft blue ageratum. Stone jars mark the top steps, and down below are antique urns with petunias tumbling from their sides. At one edge of the garden there is a maple, and there are crepe myrtles and mimosas. A flagstone path crosses the grass center; forsythia, snowball, almond, and weigela make a background for bulbs and perennials.

Miss Glasgow likes such a variety of plants, and you will find so many different kinds of flowers in bowls on the Sheraton and Chippendale tables of her house, that it is difficult to say which are her favorite blossoms.

"I love all flowers, I think," she declares with the mingled humor and tenderness so characteristic of her books, "except the beds of cannas which politicians plant in our parks. For a garden I prefer what I call poetic flowers, meaning flowers that create an atmosphere of poetry. How much of this may be from association with English poets I do not know. But I love the poppy, the single—never the double—hollyhocks against a paling fence, a row of tulips, and always clusters of lilies (especially the old tiger lilies), and Canterbury bells, blue or purple. I love best the simple, familiar flowers."

In Ellen Glasgow's novels you meet women who delight in borders of cowslips and wallflower or a bed of bleeding hearts and lilies-of-the-valley. In "Vein of Iron," *John Fincastle* says, "I put by enough seeds from one year to the next," and *Mrs. McBride* is busy mulching her rosebushes with straw and manure. Such gardeners are created by a writer who spends much time in her Richmond garden, and who knows the abiding satisfaction of working in the earth.

"My tiny plot, hemmed in by city streets, appears to me entirely too simple to merit attention," Miss Glasgow declares, and you have to remind her how much beauty that small place has given to the world.

The next stop of this random journey is in South Carolina, between Columbia and Charleston. You drive through flat country—wide fields of cotton and other crops with occasional colonies of moss-hung trees overarching the roadsides. If you arrive at Lang Syne Plantation on a hot afternoon, the driveway through a grove of live oaks and elms is wonderfully shady and welcoming. Julia Peterkin's home is a comfortable frame dwelling with porches on each side. Around the front porch grow magnificent bushes of gardenias—Cape jessamines or "funeral flowers," as the Negroes call them.

A side porch is enclosed as a conservatory, and from it steps lead to a fenced-in oblong plot which is Mrs. Peterkin's flower garden. Grass grows in the middle of this retreat, and flowers bloom along the borders by the fence. Blossoms come early and stay late in this garden. Sometimes in the middle of November Mrs. Peterkin walks out on her side porch and looks down at blooming roses, chrysanthemums ("October roses," according to Lang Syne's Negroes), petunias, verbenas, tea olives. On her Hallowe'en birthday she picks gardenias which surpass the florists' best.

In autumn the novelist's friends in New York were begging her to come to the city for a visit.

"Days here are too lovely to leave for the roar and hardness of any city," she pleaded. "I'd like to see my friends. But sweet peas and larkspur and pansies are all coming up. Winter grass and evergreen trees make a fabulous contrast with crimson leaves of crepe myrtles and golden nut-tree leaves. I wish I could paint them."

Sometimes Mrs. Peterkin claims she is a very lazy woman, despite the fact that she has reared a son, helped her husband manage a big plantation, kept up her piano music, hunted and fished, and won fame as a novelist. To see how far from lazy she is you should watch her working her vegetables with a wheel plow, or hoeing her flower beds. She does hard labor until her family complains bitterly. But when you see her youthful walk—and what older Southerners would call her "queenly carriage"—you feel that she knows what is good for her.

Mrs. Peterkin, a handsome, auburn-haired woman, looks at you with candid blue eyes and talks frankly in a voice that is quiet and yet full of animation. She will tell you how excited she is about the way all her cuttings root, how she grows winter vegetables to make up for her distaste for canning, how her love of gardening began.

"What fun it has been," she reflects smilingly. "What great good it has done me! Love plants, and they reward you generously. My debt to them is enormous. Once when I was ill, despairing of health, failing to respond to treatment in hospitals, my father, who was a doctor, said, 'Let's try digging in the earth.' I began with five minutes a day. Soon a whole new world appeared, and such an exciting world! I discarded all books for catalogues of seedsmen. My enthusiasm crowded out my ill health in an odd, miraculous way. And it has lasted all these years. The earth can afford to be kind, since it knows that sooner or later it will make us itself."

Mrs. Peterkin's gardening debut caused much talk. Daddy Champagne, the ancient Negro gardener at Lang Syne, had always been most arrogant. Even the cook was not allowed to go into his vegetable garden, and Mrs. Peterkin was expected not to put her foot into it. But things changed when "Missus" started her competing garden. She began with a plot twenty by thirty feet and set out six tomato plants and other vegetables in the same meager proportion. At first Daddy Champagne sniffed scornfully at the tiny plot. Then he began to marvel at the way things inside it grew. Before his death he and his rival became close friends, and he wanted to pass on to her his gardening wisdom. He told her about the moon, how to save seed, when to plant for sunshine or shade, which wild plants are for healing.

Now Mrs. Peterkin has a young gardener, black Willie Powell. Willie has the same growing hand his mistress has. And he has more, for he knows how to mix magic with his horticulture. He puts a grain of corn in every hole for a plant so the roots will not be lonesome and die. He is careful to plant blossom seed on the sign of the Holy Virgin; beans on the sign of the fish; melons on the sign of the lion. Willie attributes much of his success to his use of magic.

You listen spellbound to the picturesque philosophy which the Negroes preach as they dig in this loamy earth of the low country. You marvel at the scuppernong arbor which adjoins the vegetable garden. If you have nursed a sprig of yellow jessamine in a greenhouse or in some sheltered corner of a Northern garden, you will never forget the fragrant jessamine vines which entangle redbud and dogwood trees at Lang Syne's woods. Most of all you will remember the faith in life which Julia Peterkin attributes to her nearness to plants and earth.

Down in New Orleans lives a gardener whom all the world knows as Dorothy Dix. Her real name is Elizabeth Meriwether Gilmer.

Her town house is out on the edge of New Orleans' famous Audubon Park. There is a tale about Audubon Park's being Mrs. Gilmer's private garden, and this is how the tale was born. A few years ago, while Mrs. Gilmer and a friend were in Europe, they met a newly rich woman who boasted endlessly of her Palm Beach home and her Fifth Avenue apartment and her Adirondacks lodge and her parlor maids and footmen.

Finally Mrs. Gilmer could stand it no longer, so she said to her friend: "Helen, you can't tell this woman that your house is one of the most historic ones in the South, that it was the old Spanish customhouse when Spain owned Louisiana, and that your butler's pantry was the prison. But the next time she starts bragging you might break in casually by saying: 'Dorothy Dix has quite an interesting place. She has eight hundred acres in her front yard. A lagoon runs through it, and there are little motorboats in which you ride around to see white and black swans' nests. She has a formal garden that people come hundreds of miles to see. She has lions, tigers, elephants, and marvelous tropical birds in her aviary. And the best part of it all is that it doesn't cost her a cent. The city keeps it up for her.' "

Mrs. Gilmer heard no more boasting from the newly rich woman, and that is why Audubon Park is jokingly referred to as "Dorothy Dix's garden."

But Mrs. Gilmer has a beautiful garden of her own, and it is one of the things she loves best. It is a feature of her home at Pass Christian, on the Gulf Coast not far from New Orleans. Like Gaul, she says, it is divided into three parts. The front garden lies around the long, low white house that was built during the Mexican War, and along its entire length she has planted a hedge of camellia japonicas that from Christmas to Easter are a mass of blooms—crimson, pink, and white. There is a lovely garden at the back of the house where plants indigenous to the Gulf Coast are carefully preserved. In her big middle garden at the side of the house, Mrs. Gilmer really indulges her growing hand. Here are two rose plots, sweet pittosporum, oleanders, and many plants that grow luxuriously in this semitropical land. Here azaleas make splashes of color. Here are old-fashioned shrubs that grew in the garden of Mrs. Gilmer's grandmother. Mrs. Gilmer says that if *Scarlett O'Hara* and *Melanie* and *Rhett Butler* came strolling through her middle garden, she knows they would feel perfectly at home.

This wise and friendly woman whose youthful zest makes you forget her white hair talks enthusiastically about her garden.

"Strictly speaking," she says, "it isn't a garden at all. It's just a bouquet flung at the feet of giant live oaks that have guarded my bit of earth for more than two hundred years. There's something so austere and majestic about these trees—one of them has a spread of more than a hundred and eighty feet—well, it would be incongruous to try to prettify them by making flower beds among them."

"But the 'middle garden,' as you call it?"

"Yes," she smiles, a merry twinkle in her eyes—"there I have flung discretion to the winds and have planted all the things I love best. But the back garden I've left as God made it, a primeval forest of whispering pines—"

With so much color and stillness around you, it seems silly to ask Mrs. Gilmer if she has a favorite spot. But she ponders the question tolerantly.

"Well, the azalea garden is my pride and glory. And it absorbs most of my spare cash!"

"So the azaleas—"

"Oh, it's as hard to say which is your favorite spot in a garden as it is to say which is your best beloved child. But the place where I go to rest and commune with my soul is where a little babbling brook goes singing on its way through the lilies. It's almost covered by the calla lilies on either bank that bend their white chalices above it. They are flanked by rows and rows and rows of yellow, white, pink, and red lilies. What a gorgeous spot of color! They look as if some prodigal hand has flung a magnificent Persian carpet on the grass.

"Often in the twilight I seek this enchanted spot. Above my head a scarlet tanager flies in and out among the waxen blooms of a Cherokee rose that climbs a hundred feet up the trees. A mockingbird hymns the dying day. The air is heavy with the fragrance of honeysuckle, wild azaleas, orange blossoms, magnolia *frascati*. Then I know there is a God, and I know why he put the first man and woman in a garden. Nowhere else can we so surely find peace and forgetfulness of our worries and sorrows as in a garden."

It is a day's journey from New Orleans up to Dallas, Texas, where Grace Noll Crowell lives on a quiet little street with her husband and three sons. The house and garden of this woman whose poems are read from one end of America to the other are simple and unpretentious, and Mrs. Crowell says: "How could my little garden possibly mean anything to anyone else? You should go to some of our big estate gardens here in Dallas."

But when you remind her that the most magnificent estate in Texas could not mean so much to the rest of the country as the small garden which has inspired such poems as hers, she smiles and says: "Well, I know this much: no individual flower or tree could be loved more than I love mine. I'll gladly tell you a few of the lovely things that have come to me from the earth. I remember, for example, one little rose cutting I set out beneath glass on a bleak November morning, and how that rose gave me a poem that became loved by many, if I'm to judge by letters I received.

"Then the Rose Lovers' Association of America chose it as the Rose Poem of America at the Sesqui-Centennial. A nursery company in Arkansas propagated a gorgeous rose and named it for me—all that because of one little rose cutting. So, after all, nothing of beauty is really unimportant."

Mrs. Crowell must consider three boys before she caters to plants, so the plot of grass in her garden gives first place to a screened-in portable room where her sons sleep during the hot Texas summers. But all around the lot she has a bed four feet wide which contains a variety of plants, many of which came from admirers of her poetry. Peonies from the North that had two blooms on one bush in spite of the climate, bleeding hearts from Indiana, chives from Idaho—gifts to make a real Friendship Garden.

"How can I have a favorite flower?" Mrs. Crowell asks as she looks about the garden full of plants she nurses with her own hands. "The pussy willow which has silver catkins up its stems for the first day of spring? The old-fashioned four-o'clocks which bloom under my window?"

Like so many gardeners, Mrs. Crowell confesses at last that what comes nearest to being her favorite flower is the one she cannot grow successfully. In her case it's the lilac. Lilacs in Texas, she says, are small and wear a look of struggle compared with the great purple plumes of Northern bushes. Having spent her girlhood in the North, she cannot forget the lilacs along a road she used to travel when she was young.

Flowers fill this poet with a great sense of reverence.

"Who could fail to see God in the heart of a lily or a rose?" she asks. "Heavenly blue morning-glories can take me as near to heaven as I'll be able to get here on earth. In a bed of scarlet poppies— But you don't want me to say anything else, or I'll burst into poetry right now!"

Mrs. Crowell laughs at her own wave of enthusiasm, enthusiasm that all garden lovers appreciate.

"I feel shy about mentioning such a small garden," Mrs. Crowell adds. "But it's mine, and I love the feel of upturned earth and the smell of growing things. I have a sense of worship knowing that I'm working with God whenever I plant the tiniest seed or the hardiest root that may grow and give joy to those who may see perfected flowering."

Leaving that garden, you remember the poet's sincerely spoken words and the serene expression on her face as she stands by a large sun-loving lantana which is as much at home in that Texas garden as she is.

In the first paragraph of her novel, "A Lantern in Her Hand," Bess Streeter Aldrich says of the Cedartown where her story is laid, "It is beautiful only in the eyes of those who live here." Some people said what Mrs. Aldrich wrote of Cedartown would also be true of Elmwood, Nebraska, where she lives. It all depends upon that word "beautiful." One kind of stranger coming to Elmwood might see a commonplace road leading into the village, and another stranger might see, as Mrs. Aldrich does, the low rolling hills, the dip of the ripening wheat, the field of sinuously waving corn, and catch the elusively fragrant odor of alfalfa.

Mrs. Aldrich has won success as a writer, and she could move away to some big city if she wanted to. Her husband is dead, and her children are grown. But there is no far-off place to lure her from this friendly town to which she came as a bride twenty-seven years ago. She has traveled widely, but for her all roads lead back to Main Street, Elmwood, and to the comfortable brick house which is so full of binding memories. On the cement driveway are the initials "C. S. A.," the mark of one of her sons who used to establish monuments to himself on every piece of new cement. Such small things are eloquent in showing why a famous writer prefers to stay in her own town.

There is another anchor: the growing things which Mrs. Aldrich has planted herself and cared for throughout the years.

Mrs. Aldrich's lot is only one hundred by one hundred and seventy-five feet, and in planting her space she chooses things that can stand the hot, dry summers. She goes away each summer, so she has given up things which require midsummer care. Spring, she says, is her gardening season. She delights in her tulips and narcissi. She has a lilac hedge fifty feet long; the bushes are nine feet high and fourteen years old. They were slow in growing, and she was despairing of seeing any blossoms when the bushes finally reached a glorious maturity. On the lawn of the Aldrich home are ten Russian olives, a few poplars, spruces, and junipers, and a tamarack. The fourteen-year-old bridal wreaths, which are massed against the house, withstand the dry months wonderfully, and their white blooms are chief among the novelist's springtime pleasures.

Mrs. Aldrich says she has learned that native things survive when imports perish. Even barberry hedges succumb to weeks of blistering Nebraska sun and no rain. English ivy died out on the brick walls while hardy American woodbine went on growing unperturbed.

This cheerful, likable woman would never tell you a word about the success of her books, but there's one accomplishment she'll tell you about with glowing enthusiasm.

"Last year I had such beautiful red geraniums!" she exclaims. "Two long porch boxes of them which, with water every day, withstood the heat beautifully. In fact, they were on a portion of the porch which is roofless and got the full heat of the sun for part of each day. I kept my large geranium plants in the house all winter and in May stripped every branch from them, setting these out in my well-mulched boxes. It wasn't long before they were blossoming profusely with over one hundred blossoms."

"That's sound horticulture, Mrs. Aldrich."

"Oh, no," she hastens to say. "I'm no great authority on horticultural things. But I do love growing plants and shrubs."

What greater authority could you ask?

Now for a very different garden. Katharine Newlin Burt's home in Jackson Hole, Wyoming, is 6800 feet high—a mountain valley surrounded by huge forested ranges, the highest of which, the snow-clad Grand Teton, rises to 13,800 feet. In winter there is a blanket of snow averaging six feet.

The view from the garden adjoining the Burts' ranch house is across meadows and over a heavily wooded ridge of fir and pine to three snow-covered peaks. For its frame the garden has converging hills, laden with wild flowers.

Mrs. Burt is as frank as she is amusing, and she will tell you at once that she is one of those superintending gardening ladies whom so many husbands deplore.

"It is distinctly the man of this house who does the actual gardening," she declares. "I deal liberally in criticism and advice. But it's my idea of heaven to sit comfortably under a tree and watch a man I'm fond of work."

The man in this case is Struthers Burt, also a celebrated writer. And Mr. Burt says it's "our garden." Whoever the gardener may may be, and however the teamwork operates, to the visitor it's the successful performance that counts. Every flower bed surrounding the Burts' ranch house has by it a deep, narrow, running brook. Jackson Hole is in irrigation country, and no flowers, save wild ones, will grow without constant watering. The best thing is to have a small irrigation ditch running all the time. Then almost any flower does splendidly. Iris, larkspur, pansies, asters, sweet William, bachelor's-buttons—all grow in profusion, almost Alaska fashion, until the heavy frosts of middle September. What sounds marvelous to gardeners from other parts of the country is that these Wyoming flower beds are never ravaged by pests.

"Except the stock," Mrs. Burt remembers. "If it weren't for the fence, they'd come right in, kneel down, then stand on their hind legs and eat all our flowers!"

The country around Jackson Hole is like Switzerland or Norway, in scenery, climate, and soil. As in all high altitudes the growing season is short—perhaps twenty days—but anything that can grow at all is exceptionally large and hardy and brilliantly colored.

"Wyoming is the finest gladioli country I know," says Mrs. Burt's husband-with-the-hoe. "We have enormous blooms, radiantly colored, about twice the size of Eastern gladioli. And we have splendid iris. As for pansies, they're actually perennial. To my astonishment we've been able to transplant that most delicate thing, the wild rose, with no more ceremony than digging it up when it's in full bloom."

This is one of the most famous wild-flower sections in the world. Approximately 130 varieties have been isolated in the vicinity of Jackson Hole, and many are not yet counted.

"Almost everything the Garden Club ladies grow in the East grows wild out here," Mrs. Burt explains, "I've counted 75 different sorts of flowers from my horse, while I was riding through these mountain meadows. For blue we have monkshood, gentian, flax, harebells, lupines—it goes on like that for miles. We've done well with transplanting many of these to our flower beds at the house. Yes, flower gardening is lots of fun, particularly if the man does the hard work!"

Lest some beginner at gardening thinks we've visited too many experts, let's make our last visit to a Colorado flower grower who insists on saying her work is not always blessed with blossoms. Lenora Mattingly Weber belongs to that valiant tribe who keeps right on planting things in spite of any defeat. Behind her rambling white house in Denver there is a fenced-in garden where she practices horticulture with results which, if we are to believe her own hilarious confessions, are sometimes as pathetically comical as any story she has written.

"When I was a child growing up on our ranch," Mrs. Weber recalls, "I could always do wonders at raising motherless lambs, patching up broken wings of pigeons, or pulling a cow through colic. But just as soon as I'd step through the garden gate everybody would yell: 'Look out! You're stepping on the cauliflower plants!' "

This author talks as convincingly as she writes, and you forget at first that she's being severe with herself.

"I've raised six husky youngsters," she continues ruefully, "even magpies and little goats. But I shudder to think of the 'angel-wing' begonias and rose geraniums I've nursed to an unsuccessful end! One spring I planted dahlias which took three weeks longer to appear above the surface than my neighbors' dahlias—because they were planted too deep and upside down. Another time I bought twenty-eight grapevines to plant along our fence. I had two left over which I gave to an old Swedish couple back of us. Now every fall they bring us a big dish of grapes, and I haven't even a grape leaf to season dill pickles!"

But you can't let Mrs. Weber laugh at her gardening any more. The truth is that she has the kind of outdoor living room most suitable for homes where romping boys must be considered before delicate flowers. She loves flowers, but, as she expresses it, "Like our furniture and friends, they have to be the sturdy, able-to-take-it kind." She cannot have fragile plants which cannot resist a football landing in their midst. She has tougher perennials—iris, hollyhocks, Shasta daisies, chrysanthemums—and flowers that come back, such as cosmos and California poppies.

At one end of her garden Mrs. Weber has a small pool surrounded by wild flowers from the Colorado mountains—columbines and wild roses and ferns. Hardy roses climb over three different arbors. There is a friendly fireplace and a pergola and a table for family picnics. One section of the back garden is devoted to a good-sized strawberry and raspberry patch. And the rest is playground where the boys are supposed to, but don't always, stay.

Mrs. Weber confesses that when she develops a "mad" she hurries to her garden and works off her ill humor with vigorous spading. Her family protest that she leaves lumps in the soil, but that does not deter her.

"Goodness knows I've tried to be a good gardener," she sighs. "At heart I'm still optimistic, though some of my very horticultural friends say I can always make one blade of grass grow where two grew before. One thing is certain: I keep getting the fever every spring."

Mrs. Weber's cheerful tale of her floral ups and downs sounds the note of all our gardening writers. They all keep getting the fever every spring. And the fever is very contagious!

(5)

WHO IS A GOOD CITIZEN? *

By Anna Steese Richardson

During one month in each year (November) the Supreme Forest Woodmen's Circle, an organization of some one hundred and fifty thousand women, concentrates on civics.

For thirty days practically every other activity of the association is pushed aside while patriotic programs, pageants and plays are presented by local circles in every state of the Union.

An interesting feature of these civic celebrations in many communities is the prize contest for essays on citizenship, written by school children. Competition is so keen that in thousands of homes parents are bombarded with questions such as these:

"Hi, Pop, what makes a citizen good?"

"Mother dear, please tell me what is good citizenship? Is it voting at every election or being honest office-holders or what?"

Probably the hundreds of teachers who read the essays and sort

* Reprinted by permission of *Woman's Home Companion* and Mrs. Anna Steese-Richardson.

them for the judges would place the emphasis on "what." For while most of the entrants quote almost literally from textbooks, not a few build their essays on personal observation of government as it is administered in their own communities or citizenship as it is practiced by their own parents.

But laying aside theoretical definitions of civic duty born of textbooks and platform oratory, I decided to learn what citizenship means to those who have attained the right to exercise it at the polls. Not professors of politics or economics; not office-holders who have acquired the perfect patter; not radio commentators or club leaders who circulate propaganda, but the folk with whom you and I rub elbows every day.

Max, the dry cleaner and presser who collects clothes in need of freshening, with a German police dog on guard in his car, lounged against my picket fence.

"You heard about that Nazi rally over in Silver Creek Park last Sunday?"

I shook my head.

"You ought to know. It ain't right. Shock troop uniforms and tin hats and Heil Hitler saluting and everything. Twenty years ago now I come to this country and start me a nice little business. Me and my wife are doing fine. Now comes over from Germany this foolish regimentation. Say, I am going to find out about this—who is bringing it. I tell you all I can learn and then we Americans got to stand together, yes, stand close, so we don't lose what we have got."

We Americans! Max is intensely American and his one idea of citizenship today is to fend off any of the European isms which might endanger his freedom and independence as a businessman. Plainly any man or woman holding office in our community will have to stand the acid test of what Max considers good citizenship and that is to keep this democracy as it was when he applied for his naturalization papers.

Astrid, my masseuse, born in Sweden, naturalized twenty-five years ago, has hands and a voice that rest and soothe the weariest of brain workers.

"Who is the good citizen?" she repeated. "Well, I say first she knows and supports the Constitution. Then she is industrious. With these two she is useful to the United States. I tell you about the Constitution. Many do not read it even. But it is what safeguards our liberty and when there is talk of changing it, all Americans had better get busy and find out why and how the change will be made. I keep my copy of the Constitution beside my Bible. Both are valuable to me.

"I know you think that all is well with the country which was once mine, but it would not be well for you or for me, now that I have lived and worked here so many years. You and I might not like cooperatives, nor the small wages, nor maybe one new dress a year, and a coat that must last a long long time. It is all in the way one starts as a girl. You cannot start over at middle age or even less. From the Constitution comes the American way in finance, in business, in wages, in living. A good citizen keeps her eye on the Constitution and what is being done to it."

Whence have come these thoughts? From the lips of the patients she pummels and kneads or from her own observations? She has spent two vacations in her native land.

"But about industry?" I prompted.

"Oh, yes, that is important. A good citizen finds out what he can do and works at it regularly, steadily. Yes, I know we have had a depression, many laid off, but before that thousands did not work because their relatives or rich neighbors took care of them. You Americans are sometimes too kind. Your washwoman or day worker used to tell you her troubles and then you and others took care of her whole family. Now they are on relief."

I murmured something about the machine age. She dug deeper.

"Yes, but always there are thousands looking for the excuse. They never wanted to work. They never will. They are bad citizens. They do not deserve the protection and care which this government gives them. I know."

Astrid will stick to her story so long as she lives. Be industrious and uphold the Constitution and you will have fulfilled your obligation to your country.

Tony, who repairs my shoes, speaks straight from the shoulder. He thinks civic obligations start and end right in your own community.

"Me? Am I a good citizen? I don't know. I pay my bills and my taxes and ain't the taxes something fierce? I read two papers a day but they don't always help. When there's an election I work like hell to kick the rotten men out and get a few good ones in but they don't stay good long.

"I talk to my customers about politics, but they ain't much interested. They got business troubles of their own. But ain't it bad politics that makes business bad? Don't those businessmen pay the taxes? And ain't all of us that work paying a city tax for a lot of loafers who could find work if they wanted it? Say, there's a feller—John—comes in here regular to have his shoes shined and he's on relief. There's a good citizen for you."

Mary Ann, plain American, thinks it her civic duty to serve two afternoons a week in a Harlem Health Center. The city gave her a fundamental education in its public schools. Her parents sent her to Teachers College, Columbia University, where she majored in home economics. Now that she is comfortably married and has leisure she feels that she must serve the less privileged. Not that she has much hope for the future of the underprivileged. She thinks that social service should be less generous and more constructive. It should educate the poor to be better managers. As for politics, well, the less said the better, observes Mary Ann.

Mrs. A—— believes that we can have better government only by electing a higher grade of men and women to office; therefore she is working day and night on the League of Women Voters' personnel committee.

Alma P—— believes that the safety of the nation lies in training for, and electing more women to, office. She thrills audiences with her appeal that her hearers sacrifice themselves on the altar of politics but she has not yet brought herself to the point of starting at the bottom and working along with men in her own ward!

The last answer to my question came from a physician whose profession carries him from clinics in crowded hospitals to the homes of the rich.

"Good citizens? Oh, I find them here and there. What is good citizenship or patriotism? I often wonder. First, there must be an understanding of international affairs. The United States has passed the point where it can isolate itself. Modern traffic, communication—"

He seemed to be thinking aloud.

"A citizen must be informed on national affairs also. Laws that regulate his taxes, affect his income. Legislation in his own state, elections in his own city or town. How can a busy man keep informed on all of this? How can he escape propaganda or recognize it when he hears or reads it? But it goes deeper than all this. He is not a good citizen unless he is a good parent. Family relations, wholesome, understanding—it's on these that the national life is built. If every man—yes, that's where good citizenship starts—in the home."

Is that statement worthy of your consideration?

Does it answer the question, who is a good citizen?

Exercises

1. Select the last issue of your favorite Sunday newspaper and go through the magazine section and list the articles that are interview articles as defined in this chapter.
2. In chart form: (1) list the captions; (2) indicate the source from which the writer probably got the article; (3) list the type of person whom you think will be interested in reading the article; (4) estimate the number of words (roughly estimating there are almost 50 words to the typical newspaper column inch); and (5) list the number of pictures or drawings for each article.
3. In the sixth column of the chart indicate which persons were interviewed because they were recognized authorities and indicate those who were interviewed because they are prominent.
4. Selecting one of the articles, list six of the questions that the feature writer probably asked the interviewee.
5. Selecting a recent issue of your favorite monthly magazine, go through the feature articles, selecting the interviews, and make a chart for them as you did in Exercise 2, except that in estimating the number of words to the magazine column inch, you will have to count the average words in a magazine line and multiply by the number of lines. (To get the average word length of a line count the number of letters, or units, as they are spoken of journalistically, and divide by the number of letters in the average word, which is seven.) Complete the chart as you did in Exercise 2.
6. Compare the two charts and write a topic of not more than 200 words on "The Difference in the Treatment of Features in Newspapers and Magazines."
7. Select one of the interview articles in the magazine and see if you can detect the questions that the interviewer asked the interviewee. List as many as you can find.
8. List five persons in your community that you might interview

and indicate whether you would interview them to give readers information or to tell their opinions or ideas to the readers.

9. Give two sources from which you could get information concerning each of the five persons you listed in Exercise 8.
10. List five questions that you would ask one of the persons you selected to interview. Check them to see if they are worded to bring forth the replies that you want and that you would be able to use for direct quotations, or could the interviewee simply answer "yes" or "no"?
11. To what five markets would you send each of the five interview articles as suggested in Exercise 8 if you actually were to write them?
12. Interview a classmate as to what he thinks the prospects are for a winning football team, but do not take any notes during the interview. Then try to reproduce on paper the exact words that the interviewee used. Check with the interviewee or others present to see if you quoted all he said, and correctly.
13. Write a beginning, or "lead," for the interview you obtained in Exercise 12.
14. Where would you obtain material for the second or third paragraph of the article or that concerned with the explanation of why the interviewee was interviewed and a brief sketch about him?
15. List one idea and three persons that you could use for a symposium interview.

Publication Analysis

Detroit *News,* Boston *Transcript,* and *Christian Science Monitor*

Do not spend more than 3 hours on this report.

Note: Turn through several issues of the papers to get a general idea of the publications as a whole before writing your report. Then discuss the following:

1. (a) What are the opportunities for a free-lance writer, such as yourself, to sell features to the Detroit *News* and the Boston papers?
   (b) Prove your answer.
2. (a) List the titles of the feature articles in each paper, and from only the titles and lead paragraphs classify the articles as to

type as listed in the beginning of this chapter, and to what class they appeal.

(b) What is the general tendency or nature as to type of the feature articles in each paper?

3. (a) How many interview articles did you find?
(b) Why was each interviewee interviewed?
(c) List the subjects that the interviewees were interviewed upon.
(d) Which interview article did you consider the best and why?

4. (a) What sections did you find in the one paper that you did not find in the others?
(b) What would be the prospects of your selling articles for these special sections?

5. What are the interesting things about the three articles (one from each paper), in reference to the *way it is written,* that you might have or would like to have written?

6. List two feature tips that you might write, including source, authorities, and markets that were suggested to you by this study.

4
THE UTILITY ARTICLE

Aim Is To Help Reader. Because it is a trait of all human beings to want to be (1) wiser, (2) healthier, and (3) wealthier, magazine readers are always interested in articles that will benefit them mentally, physically, and financially. If a writer succeeds in showing people how to be more efficient, more useful, or more practical, or how to increase their wealth, editors will buy anything he writes, provided it is well written. It is upon these three factors that all magazines are founded. If free-lances write to help and guide their readers, they will find it easy to sell.

In order to help the reader, the writer must think of the subscriber constantly. With his nose for the new and his eye for special features, he must observe things that will be useful, beneficial, or remunerative to the reader. Parts of publications, and even entire magazines, are printed on the theory that every one wants to know how to advance, how to get more pleasure out of living, how to live more easily, cheaply, or comfortably. The utility article is one that aims to help the reader in some way, by giving him definite directions and advice for doing or making something in a better way to satisfy human needs, wants, or desires.

The similarity between the utility article, the personal experiences story, the confession, and the narrative is marked. They all are written to aid the reader. They may be distinguished by remembering that the utility article guides the reader by giving him definite directions. The personal experience story may benefit the reader, but it is based on experiences of the writer or experiences of others whom he interviews. The confession article helps the reader ethically, religiously, or morally, but it does so only through confiding one's sins or shortcomings. The narrative, which is written in the third person, may help the reader as well as to entertain him, although it is written with many of the techniques used in the writing of the short story.

Sources of Subjects. Ideas for utility articles may be found anywhere and include all sorts of subjects. Anything from a recipe giving simple directions for making a salad or a cake to an account of producing new building materials or saving hundreds of dollars in business operations will develop into marketable manuscripts. The people who made the salads or devised means by which they improve their businesses will only be too glad to tell a feature writer how they did it. It is a human characteristic to like to appear favorably in print. By observation or by conversation with people in homes, industries, trades, businesses, and professions, a writer, in a few minutes, may uncover material for telling the reader how to do something or for giving him practical guidance. The technique of arranging for the interview and planning the article is the same as for the interview article.

Before deciding to write, the free-lance should ask himself: (1) whether the idea for the utility article he wishes to write is new; (2) if not, how can it be written to be of value to a certain class of readers; (3) whether it will interest a large number of readers, or, in other words, is it the type of article that could sell to any one of many publications; and (4) is the idea of the utility practical from the standpoint of the expense involved and the results that may be expected?

The illustrations for utility articles should often include drawings or charts as well as photographs. If the various steps of a process described may be shown by drawings, even very simple ones, they will aid much in making the directions clearer for the reader.

Planning and Writing. Because the purpose is to give practical guidance, the plan of writing the utility article varies considerably from that of the interview article. Any type of beginning may be used, but the writer must select one that will attract and appeal to the reader and make him curious to read on. In the shorter utility articles, dialogue makes an effective beginning. Unless it is handled well, however, it is a poor device. To dramatize the opening by putting people and their problems into the article sometimes makes the effect more realistic for the reader. If it is written in the first person, the article has the advantage of making the reader feel that the writer actually made or did the thing about which is he is writing. However, with the frequent use of the personal pronoun, the reader is likely to get the impression that the author is conceited and is "preaching." The writer can modify this tone by frequently warning the reader not to make the mistakes that he did. To give confidence and encouragement to the reader, the author may point out that although he was an amateur and did make mistakes, he finally succeeded. The simplest and most direct method is to write the article in the second person imperative; it is then easier to give the directions clearly. But one must guard against making the tone dictatorial. Recipe articles, mechanical guidance articles, and other short concise pieces of similar nature, in which the reader will prop the magazine up on his work table or bench and follow directions exactly and quickly, often are written in the second person. The third person is used in writing utility articles only when the material is unusually dramatic and entertaining and is written more in a narrative style. But in whichever style one writes it, he must get people and action into the article to make it realistic.

The questions that the readers would be likely to ask, if they were present when the method, process, contrivance, or device was explained, must be kept in mind by the writer, since it is his duty to anticipate the questions and answer them before the reader thinks of them.

In giving directions for practical guidance in utility articles, one must remember that the reader is unfamiliar with the process. Great care must be taken to explain and describe every detail and step clearly and simply. The person who made the contrivance or the expert who draws from a rich store of knowledge is inclined to forget that the reader has not had the same experience and information. As a rule, he does not write so simply and understandingly as the feature writer, who has not had the experience nor the knowledge but who does have the ability to express clearly what he sees or hears. If a single direction is omitted, it may be impossible for the reader to follow the procedure successfully. A writer should not insult the intelligence of the reader by telling him things he already knows, but he may assume tactfully that as he "may know," or that as he "remembers," or that he "may have forgotten." Perhaps the greatest problem in the writing of utility articles to give practical guidance is the avoidance of being "preachy" in tone. In giving instructions to others, one easily appears to be, in print, superior and overbearing. Young writers, because they have been preached at all their lives by their parents and teachers, are quite inclined to talk down to their readers in an imperative tone.

Throughout the body of the article, the writer must avoid choking the reader with facts. Everyone agrees that encyclopedias are excellent books because they are full of facts; but they are used only for reference. One may keep his article from sounding like an encyclopedia by getting people and action into it. An article on how to play golf could be full of facts and still be most uninteresting. But if awkward John Smith is taken out on the course by the professional for his lessons, and the reader learns along with John and profits by John's mistakes, he will be interested, whether or not he plays golf. A real person always adds to the interest of any article. After the article is finished, one must go over it, unit by unit, or paragraph by paragraph, to see that all the needed information is there, that every step of the process is clear to the reader, and that it is written concisely, since wordiness detracts from the clearness of the meaning.

Results Are Easy Sales. For his interest and efforts in giving the reader practical guidance and telling him how to do something, the writer of utility articles is rewarded by the ease with which he can find material and sell his manuscripts. Of course, he must study carefully the magazines that use this type of article, in order to "slant" it correctly. If he has the missionary urge to do good and help his fellowmen, but his temperament or circumstances prevent adoption of a religious career, he can find a sense of satisfaction by writing utility articles that will help other people by the hundreds and thousands to find life more enjoyable. Hence, editors are constantly in the market for all kinds of utility articles if the ideas are expressed clearly, accurately, and concisely.

Examples of the Utility Article. The first of the following utility features was published in the Portland *Oregonian.* It shows how a writer may interview an expert in order to get information for his readers on how to do something. The second article appeared in the New York *Herald Tribune* syndicated magazine section, *This Week.* It gives suggestions to mothers for teaching children to make gifts. Two halftone reproductions of photographs showing a little boy and girl making toys to give their friends, and five drawings, showing the simple designs that even children could draw, to use as "patterns," would encourage the mother as well as the child to try out the idea. The third, with five drawings, appeared in the *American Home;* the fourth, with six photographs showing how the painters were doing the work, was written in the second person and was printed in *Good Housekeeping;* and the fifth, written in third person, and illustrated with two pictures showing how the repairing was done, appeared in *Popular Science Monthly.*

(1)

TRAPEZE WORK COMMENDED FOR BEAUTIFYING OF FIGURE *

Noted Circus Aerialist Says Any Woman Can Work On Horizontal Bar

BY IDA JEAN KAIN

With contour control that is nothing short of perfect, the daring young maid on the flying trapeze has the slim, tapered figure of a boy and the throat of a Greek goddess.

* Reprinted by permission of the Portland *Oregonian* and King Features, and Miss Ida Jean Kain.

Eileen Larey, noted circus aerialist, believes trapeze work to be unexcelled for the development of a beautiful figure. While we can't all join the circus, Miss Larey says that any woman can have a lovelier figure by practicing a milder form of the gyrations staged at the top of the big tent. In the aerialist's traveling kit is a horizontal bar which can be secured to a doorway. This is the air star's practice bar while traveling—and a similar one can help you to beautify your figure.

Keep Feet Together

Just hanging to the bar will pull the bulge from your waistline and strengthen the arm and shoulder muscles. In two or three weeks you will be able to chin yourself—and then the real workout begins.

Grasp the bar with the hands turned forward to get the most benefit from the workout. Keeping the feet together, move the legs at the hips and slowly bring them forward to form a right angle with the body. Then, just as slowly, move the legs back to the original vertical position.

Stretching Aids Figure

"Beating" is part of the circus performer's warming-up exercise and is excellent for hip and abdominal muscles. Kick the air with vigorous movements of the legs from the hips. Then, keeping the feet together, kick backward from the hips. This kicking movement automatically brings the head backward to give more stretch to the waist, abdomen and throat muscles, while slimming down hips incorporated.

Eileen Larey flies through the air with the greatest of ease because of her beautifully supple muscles. The same strong muscles give her these streamlined measurements: Bust, 31 inches; waist, 24 inches; hips, 32 inches. Incidentally, these are the measurements of a modern airminded mother, for Eileen Larey has a 6-year-old daughter.

This performer weighs 103 pounds and is five feet tall. One of her loveliest features is her throat. It is beautiful! No lines, and no double chins! The clearly defined contour is characteristic of throat muscles that are well developed, full and rounded. "You never get a double chin in this work," is Eileen Larey's comment.

If you want to acquire a perfect figure get a horizontal bar and stretch. There are a number of stretching bars on the market. You will find various types at the department stores and at gymnasium equipment houses.

BALANCED REDUCING MENU

Breakfast—	Calories.
Orange juice, ½ glass	50
Poached egg on toast	150
Coffee, clear	
	200
Luncheon—	
Bouillon, 1 cup	30
Celery	10
Mixed fresh fruit salad (Fruit dressing).	150
Brown nutbread, 2 slices	200
Butter, ½ pat	50
	440
Dinner—	
Tomato juice cocktail	25
Roast beef—trim off fat	200
Browned potato	100
Butter, 1 level tsp.	33
Fruit jello	100
Boiled onions, 4 small	100
	558
Total calories for day	1198

(2)

CREATING CHRISTMAS GIFTS *

Give Them The Right Tools And a Little Help, and Your Children Will Find Great Delight in Making Holiday Wrapping Paper And Simple Toys To Go In It.

BY LAURA HOLMES MACDONALD

"What can I do now, Mommy?"

How many times during the day does a mother of small children hear that question—and doesn't know what to answer. For lack of something new to do, the blocks are brought out, the beads are restrung, and old magazine pictures are cut out once more. The little, restless hands are busy for a time, and then the same old question is asked: "What can I do now?"

Children have energy, enthusiasm and considerable ability; and with a little help and the right tools, they can make many worthwhile playthings. They will welcome the chance to make wooden toys for their little friends, wrapping papers for all the family, and scrap books for children who may be spending Christmas in a hospital room.

First of all, they will need a suitable room where they can saw, paint, and cut out pictures without much interference. A playroom, nursery, attic or basement may be turned into a workshop if there is good light; or if space is limited, a special corner of almost any room may be screened off for their purposes.

Making wooden toys is a fascinating occupation for children of all ages. Even sawing a straight line will keep the little five-year-olds interested and busy; and when they find that they can follow a line which will eventually turn into an elephant or a camel, their enthusiasm knows no bounds.

It is important to choose toy designs of simple outline; use soft wood (pine or white wood) about ¼ inch in thickness; and a coping saw with a medium coarse blade. The teeth of the blade point in the direction of the handle and outward. The designs are transferred up and down with the grain of the wood.

Place the wood in a horizontal position, on the edge of a table

* Reprinted by permission of the New York *Herald Tribune*.

or bench, and work the saw in a vertical position with the handle pointing toward the floor. Use long, regular strokes following the outline of the design; and move the wood to feed the teeth of the saw. A little practice is necessary to turn corners, but the wood is very soft and works easily.

When the toy is sawed out, sandpaper it well to take away any sharp corners. Cut a base of wood ¼- to ½-inch in thickness, 2-½-inches wide and as long as the toy. To this, nail two ¼-inch dowel strips, far enough apart to allow the toy to stand up firmly. Sandpaper well.

The toy is now ready to be painted. Trace the design on the sandpapered toy, carefully drawing eyes, ears, blankets, etc. Use poster or show card paint, which is an opaque water color. This is easier to use than oil, as the soft wood readily absorbs it, and there is very little waiting for the toy to dry. Use separate brushes for each color, varying their sizes for large and small areas.

When the toy is thoroughly dry, give it three coats of white shellac, allowing each coat to dry before applying another. This gives a good, hard, glossy, waterproof finish. If a softer, duller finish is preferred, use steel wool on the surface and then polish with a furniture wax.

There are three kinds of decorative papers that children enjoy making—marbleized, crackled, and block printed. They are all simple to make.

The marbleized paper is the type used for the end papers of old manuscripts. Marbling paper is an old craft that has never lost its charm. The paper used may vary from the cheapest to the finest of drawing papers. For children who will make many sheets of it, the cheapest is unprinted newspaper, which may be purchased in rolls of 100 or 200 sheets. This, by the way, is the kind of paper for children to use when they paint on easels, with large brushes and jars of paint.

Buy a few tubes of oil paint. Thin a little of two or three colors with oil, in separate dishes, until the paint is fairly thin. Next, fill a large, rectangular pan with water. Float these oil colors over the surface of the water to get the swirling effects we sometimes see on oily water. It may be necessary to stir the water slightly or blow on it.

Now lay a piece of paper on the surface of the water. The swirling design will be deposited upon it. Try different combinations of colors and spot in a little gold if you have it. The results are so interesting and varied that children will want to make papers for many different uses.

Crackled paper is nothing more than a sheet of waxed paper (the ordinary kitchen variety) carefully crushed in the hands to get a fine weblike pattern through it. Dip a sponge or soft cloth into a combination of oil paint and turpentine and rub it over the surface of the paper. The color will deposit itself in the cracks of the paper and make an interesting crackled design. Place the waxed paper on a newspaper and remove most of the wax with a medium hot iron. The result is a soft, semi-transparent, crackled paper.

A more advanced step of this craft is to take a square or rectangle of light colored silk for a scarf. Thumb-tack it to a drawing board and paint the surface with a coat of hot paraffin and beeswax (in equal amounts). Now crumple this in the hands to get the weblike lines and then immerse in a strong, cold, dye bath. The cracks will color while the wax resists the dye. Iron the silk on several thicknesses of newspaper until the wax is removed.

Block printing ranges from simple, stick printing designs to elaborate all-over patterns. For young children, stick printing is advisable. Little, wooden blocks are cut in the shape of diamonds, squares, circles, triangles, stars, etc., and then pressed on a saturated pad of color. Then they are stamped on paper in various combinations.

One very simple way to make the blocks is to cut them from a raw potato with a sharp knife. These little potato blocks are pressed into poster paint and stamped on the paper. With a little practice the right consistency of paint will be found. Cellophane makes an interesting background for these prints also.

A child who enjoys cutting and saving pictures from magazines, will like to make a scrap book. The cover of the book is made of oil cloth; the inside pages of cambric or starched, thin cotton. The edges of the cover and pages are pinked on the sewing machine. The whole is bound together with yarn or heavy mercerized thread.

The pictures, in a miscellaneous assortment, or separated into special kinds (animals, children, boats, etc.) are carefully pasted to the cambric. If the children collect pictures daily, and have an objective in view, many scrap books may be made that will make Christmas a little happier for sick children in hospitals.

(3)

APARTMENT STOWAWAYS! *

Make Space in Your Furniture for All of Those Odds and Ends

BILL BRICE

Three people and all their worldly possessions often have considerable difficulty about fitting into a very small apartment. Photograph albums and scrapbooks collect with time, extra sheets and blankets are necessities whether you have a linen closet or not, and Junior's growing assortment of baseball bats and toy trains get underfoot. At least that is the picture of our family.

When my wife realized that even if she did get a new hat and dress there would be no suitable place to put them, she decided that we must do *something* about the situation. I announced that we might design and make some furniture with all the much needed shelves and compartments, and began to sketch with great energy. Though I am not much inclined toward manual labor and the designs are still just on paper, before long I'm going to get to work with hammer and saw and actually make this furniture!

First of all, we want two shelf cabinets built along simplified modern lines for our 8 x 10 dining room. We plan to build these stowaways out of three-ply crates and the best white pine packing cases to be found in the shipping room at the office. As you see in the illustration, the design provides several very useful shelves, cabinet space, and a place on the wall side for albums, scrapbooks, and our portable typewriter as well.

Our design for a modern bed is one that should end forever the sheet and blanket problem. We expect to start with a disreputable-looking old bedstead that we found in a second-hand store on sale for a dollar, and turn it into a thing of modern beauty and usefulness. We will use the old bed's head, foot, and rails. After we cut down both ends, eliminate the gingerbread trimmings and extend the rails to the floor, we will make two spacious drawers beneath and a cabinet in each end. The wood problem is solved by my recent discovery that veneer, backed by a durable cloth, can be purchased for

* Reprinted by permission of *American Home.*

about fifty cents a foot. It can be cut with a razor blade and cemented to any flat or curved surface with the probability that it will never come off. If I ever get into action, this bed will undoubtedly be my most prized possession.

The first two ideas were just enough to inspire more designs. This time my attention fell on our sad-looking radio cabinet and our equally sad-looking old end table. Why not combine the two and dress them in the modern manner? I made a few sketches and finally produced the design you see below. It calls for cutting up the end table (all but the top), installing the radio in it, and building two shelves. Then we will curve heavy cardboard around the framework and cement some walnut veneer to it. After we run a heavy glass rod through the shelves and finish the whole piece in natural, it should be quite an addition to the living room.

Now I have still another idea—but my wise wife says she'd rather have one table in the living room than a dozen good ideas on paper!

(4)

PAINT AND PAINTING *

By Lonore Kent

It is a fascinating prospect to survey your house, color cards in hand, and to know that it is within your power to give your dwelling place an entirely new personality. While you are pondering what paint colors to select—whether to endow your house with a maroon door, with black shutters and white trim, or to add a gay note with colorful window boxes—you will be interested to know that there is a trend in some localities toward painting the body, trim, and window sash all the same color, generally a light one. Color is introduced in the shutters and doors.

You should give careful thought to color schemes before you instruct your painter what colors to use. There are several angles that should have consideration: the color of your roof, the color of neighboring houses, the style of architecture, and your own personal preference.

In planning your color scheme, however, don't forget that there are other important things to be thought of. Naturally you wish to get the greatest value for your money, the maximum protection

* Reprinted by permission of *Good Housekeeping* and Miss Lonore Kent.

for your property, and the greatest beauty of finish. In other words, when the painters leave, you want a house of which you and your family can justly be proud.

And just as you are anxious to get good results, so are the manufacturers of paint products anxious to help you get them—both those manufacturers who furnish materials from which the professional painter manufactures paint to suit his job, and the makers of ready-mixed paint. To this end, paint chemists have been working to perfect the old paint products and develop new ones. As a result, coatings of every type are reaching a new high in serviceability. With microscopes, test tubes, and ultraviolet rays chemists are developing new methods of manufacture; tests are being made constantly to create coatings that are more weather-resistant, less likely to fade, and faster drying. Some of the manufacturers have rows of painted wood samples exposed to the weather at different angles and with different exposures. Here practical tests of time and weather are tabulated.

Hundreds of synthetic (built-up) resins have been developed. These make paints, varnishes, and enamels more durable. New pigments have been produced chemically. Casein and other water paints have been improved.

But perhaps this talk of new products, new ingredients, and new methods makes you feel at sea. It needn't. In selecting materials, your guide today, as always, is the integrity of the manufacturer and of the painter you employ.

It is unwise, incidentally, to cut corners on the price of products used. After all, paint materials used on the exterior of a building represent only one-quarter of the cost of the paint job. Three-quarters is for the workmanship involved in applying it. When you consider also that the best grades of materials last longer and cover a larger area, it is easy to see why it is unwise to "economize" on paint.

The three-quarters factor of the paint job—the application—calls for just as careful consideration as the selection of materials. Be sure to entrust the painting of your home to workmen who have a reputation for their dependability and skill. Experienced painters will know how to deal with the problems of old as well as new construction—whether it is cleaning out gutters, nailing down loose clapboards or shingles, or—if necessary—burning or scraping off the old paint.

They will know, for instance, that metal which is exposed to the wear and tear of weather needs special attention. They know that if any rust is left on the metal surface when it is painted, the rust will continue its devilment. They will know that where there is still a sign of gloss in protected spots the gloss should be removed with sandpaper.

Remember that the painter must always cope with weather conditions in completing an exterior paint job. If a drenching downpour interrupts his progress, be sure to allow sufficient time for drying before a paintbrush is again laid on your house. For moisture, no matter what form it appears in, is a deep-dyed villain. If moisture is sealed into a structure with a new coating of paint, you may be sure that he will barge through to the surface, and the result may be blistering and peeling and scaling of the paint film.

And, to speak once more about colors—remember that color used on large areas looks quite different from the way it does on the small region occupied by a color chip. Also that some colors dry darker than they appear as put on—others, lighter. For this reason it is a good idea to have your selected colors brushed out on a large board and allowed to dry before you give the painter your final okay. It is wise to inquire as to the permanence of the shade and select those of enduring service even at a higher price.

(5)

STOPPING LEAKS IN SHINGLE ROOFS *

In northern districts, particularly during a severe winter, many roof leaks are reported, all similar in cause and usually occurring in houses and other buildings where the roof projects considerably beyond the walls at the eaves. This type of leak is always prevalent in seasons of heavy snowfall and is likely to cause much damage to ceilings and walls.

On a comparatively mild day, the snow on the main part of the roof melts because of the sun and the warmth of the building. As the water runs down the roof, it is likely to freeze on the wide overhang because this portion of the roof is much cooler, being more exposed to the wind and having no warmth from below. Gradually a ridge of ice forms and any water that is still flowing down is forced

* Reprinted by permission of *Popular Science Monthly.*

to back up until it works under the shingles and into the building. Ceiling insulation, of course, will help to some degree, but is not sufficient in itself to effect a complete cure.

The shingles should be removed for a strip of about 3 ft. 6 in. all along the edge of the roof, or from a still wider strip if the overhang is greater than usual. Should the shingles be laid on shingle lath or on spaced sheathing, it will have to be removed also and this portion of the roof boarded up solidly to afford a good bed. A strip of roll roofing is now laid on the exposed portion of the roof. A generous coat of asphalt roof "dope" or cement (of brushing weight) is applied to the roofing material, and the shingles are then relaid.

While the finished job has the appearance of normal shingling, it offers an undersurface completely sealed to water. The asphalt cement on which the shingles are laid has the effect of sealing even the shingle nails themselves.

It is sometimes desirable and even imperative for economic reasons to use up some of the old shingles on a job of this kind. Often when reshingling a house, for example, many of the old shingles are found to be in good shape, and throwing them away seems to be extravagantly wasteful. The usual procedure is to lay them as far as they will go and then use new, but it is better to have alternate courses of new and old shingles. This insures more protection and longer life. The old ones should be laid with the previously weathered side down. They will lie flatter this way, because of the slight curve they developed in their old position. Furthermore, the exposed portion will match the new shingles much better.—R. O. Lissaman.

Exercises

1. In any newspaper of your choice, list all the utility articles. In the first column of a chart indicate whether the article was written to aid the reader in becoming more efficient, more useful, more practical, more wealthy, more healthy, or wiser.
2. In the second column indicate the source of the material for each article listed.
3. In a third column indicate those articles that do not meet the four-pointed test that the free-lance should give himself before deciding to write.
4. In a fourth column indicate what kind of illustrative matter was used with each article.

5. Suggest one tip, gained by observation, for a utility article for your near-by metropolitan newspaper.
6. Suggest one tip, gained from conversation, for a utility article for any newspaper magazine feature section. Indicate to which newspaper you would send it.
7. In any magazine of your choice, list the utility articles. In the first column of a chart indicate the type of lead that was used for each article.
8. In the second column of the chart indicate in which person the article was written.
9. In the third column of the chart indicate the type of illustrative matter used for each article.
10. From your two charts write a paragraph of not more than 200 words. Point out the kinds of utility articles that the two publications use.
11. Suggest two tips for utility articles for magazines, and also suggest three possible markets for each one.
12. Suggest illustrations for each of the articles suggested.

Publication Analysis

Woman's Home Companion, Popular Science Monthly, and *Home Craft*

Do not spend more than two and one half hours on this report.

I. Identification: Names, publishers, editors, where published, price.

II. Make-up: Including typography, size, style, etc. What do you like about the magazines? What do you not like about them?

III. Advertising: To whom does the advertising appeal? Is there anything different about them than in the other magazines studied? From the advertising, what type of material would you expect to find in the magazines? List at least one tip suggested to you by some advertisement in *each* magazine.

IV. General Policy:

1. From the table of contents, estimate roughly the amount of different material used.
2. What do you think are your chances of selling to these publications?
3. What do you like about the magazines?

4. If you were editor, what would you change in the magazines?

V. Features:
1. What feature articles could you have written for each of the publications?
2. Which types of features seem to predominate?
3. Write a comment of not more than 100 words concerning the photographs or other illustrative devices used in the publications?
4. Analyze one feature article in each magazine in any way you wish, but do it from the point of view of what you can learn about writing your own articles.
5. How many utility articles did you find in each magazine?

VI. Slogan: Make a slogan for each magazine.

VII. Four tips: Source, authority, and three possible markets suggested by this study. (Six tips in all, including tips suggested by advertisements.)

5

THE PERSONAL EXPERIENCE STORY

Interest Depends Upon Uniqueness. The interest in a personal experience story depends chiefly upon the extraordinary and unique events with which the account is concerned. People crowd movie houses and entertainment palaces and buy millions of magazines and books because they wish to escape from the commonplace things in their own lives. To satisfy this demand for "literature of escape," editors are in the market for accounts of unusual events and novel happenings. The personal experience article is one concerned with unusual experiences of either the writer or of other people, and is written to entertain, help, or inform the reader.

This type of article, perhaps more than the others may contain elements of the interview, the utility article, and the personality sketch. Occasionally the personal experience story will contain much that, in part, might be classified as a confession article, except that it must concern the unusual or extraordinary rather than the typical. It is similar to the narrative but differs in that it deals entirely with experiences that are personal and unusual.

Ideas Exist Everywhere. Amateurs as well as professionals may write this type of article. Everyone has taken trips, has had adventures in his diversions or at work, or has done something different or something out of the ordinary that will make interesting features. Of this type were articles entitled "I've

Been Around," or "Selling My Blood to Obtain a Sheepskin," or "Thrice Married." Everywhere there is material for this type of article, which makes its possibilities for the free-lance as great as those of the interview.

The article may be the writer's own experience, written under his name or a pseudonym, or anonymously. If the experience is not his own, the feature writer, whom we will call John Jones, may: (1) write it in the third person; (2) "ghost" it, by writing it in the first person as if he were the one who had had the experience, and write it under that person's name; or (3) write the "by-line" as that of the person who had had the experience, followed by the phrase "as told to John Jones." With the advent of "ghost writing," feature writers realized that, although they were paid well for the "ghosted" manuscripts, the glory of authorship went to the person for whom they were writing. Consequently, someone devised the phrase "as told to," in order to enable the writer to put his name in the by-line, or more accurately, the second by-line underneath the by-line of the person who has had the experiences.

Style Must Be Convincing. Whatever device is used, the writer must present his material realistically and convincingly. The more personal and intimate the tone of the article, the greater the interest.

Descriptions of persons, places, and objects, conversation by means of dialogue, and vivid narrative all help to make the article more realistic and personal to the reader. Illustrations, such as photographs, drawings, and charts, add immeasurably, as they do in other types of articles, to the reader's interest.

Added Compensation Is Meeting Interesting People. Whereas the Sunday newspaper readers and magazine subscribers enjoy reading lively and well-written personal experience articles, the feature writer enjoys gathering the material and writing it. He is brought into contact with interesting people who have done something out of the ordinary, such as "Making $50,000 a year in the Turkey Business," or "Taking a Dixie Detour." As when writing the utility article, the feature writer is rewarded for his efforts in writing the personal experience story by finding material everywhere and in knowing that there are innumerable markets for this type of feature. A writer will more readily find a market if he analyzes the newspapers and magazines (as is suggested in a later chapter), in order to make his manuscripts and illustrative material conform to the policies and style of the publications to which he submits his articles.

Examples of the Personal Experience Article. The first of the following personal experiences, written in the first person, appeared in the Milwaukee *Journal,* accompanied by a halftone picture of the writer, one of her snapshots of the moose at Isle Royale, and a map of the Lake Superior district showing the location of the island. The second was taken from the Brooklyn *Daily Eagle.* The third, from *The Saturday Evening Post,* was illustrated by two halftone pictures of an editor at work in a modern newspaper office. The fourth, in *The American Magazine,* written with an "as told to" by-line, had a halftone of a cold victim propped up on his pillows in bed.

(1)

'MY WINTER ON ISLE ROYALE' *

From November to April No Word From the Mainland Was Received Except by Short Wave Radio; and Hungry Moose Became Tame Enough to Come to the Cabins, Writes School Teacher.

In a few weeks the first boat to Isle Royale will be able to crash through Lake Superior's ice and give the islanders their first contact with the outside since last November. Heavy ice which choked the Duluth end of Lake Superior and formed a perilous ice bridge to the island is several weeks later than usual in breaking up.

What it means to spend a winter on Isle Royale is told in the following article by Eva Cooley, who taught school on the island. Miss Cooley now lives in Milwaukee.

Winter on an island—the island Isle Royale, Winter Wonderland—from late November until April, cut off from the world save for shortwave radio. There it was my adventure to spend the winter,

* Reprinted by permission of the Milwaukee *Journal.*

one of the 12 people at Chippewa Harbor on the south shore of the island, where I taught school for the five children of a fisherman's family. Chippewa Harbor is protected from sweeping winds by high conglomerate ridges, balsam clad. There our small colony lived in log houses with the chinks packed with swamp moss, lined with insulating cedar bark, lit by pressure lamps, heated by sheet iron stoves.

Arriving on the island Nov. 4, there were only three weeks before the closing of navigation—time enough to realize what a boat means to an island. A note in my diary reads: "Wind, rain in torrents, the bay full of white caps, incessant thunder of the waves in the shore caves and over the shore ledges. No Winyah today, so now we shall have to wait another half week" Yes, we must wait for letters and packages, for groceries and mail orders, newspapers and magazines—that is what it meant to have storms that delayed the Winyah. Then came her last trip, Nov. 27. Late in the morning we heard her whistle in the bay and the Winyah glided in to the dock. Like Christmas and New Years in one, the crew heaped on the dock, boxes and barrels, cases and packages (Do not open until Dec. 25) and a six-month supply of letters. Nor was this all, two more winter residents arrived, Paul Hickie, state mammalogist for the Michigan conservation department and his assistant, Ellsworth St. Germaine. They had come to spend the winter investigating the condition of the island moose herd and live trapping a small number of the animals. At last the Winyah was unloaded, the hawser was cast off, and we stood among the groceries and lumber and bales of hay brought for the captive moose and waved goodby, for six months. Now we might settle down for the winter, the 12 of us.

I read my winter's supply of letters wishing me a hearty Thanksgiving, a Merry Christmas, a happy birthday, and the Top o' the Mornin' to ye on Mar. 17! Now let it snow.

* * *

There is a romantic lure about any island with its isolation, limited boundaries, and completeness. Isle Royale adds to this island lure the romance of a history beginning with the Indians who long ago approached the island in their canoes seeking the precious metal, copper. With their primitive stone mauls and the expedient of heating stones and pouring on cold water, they mined. Today their crude instruments are picked up near their ancient mining sites. Years later parties of scientist explorers visited the island, reporting on its plants, animals and mineral resources, especially copper and chlorastrolite. Chlorastrolite is commonly known as green stone. It is found on Isle Royale, along a stretch of the north shore of Superior, and along the shores of Australia, ranking seventh among the precious stones. It is dark green with faces of various shades of green.

Isle Royale would seem by its relative inaccessibility to be a locality where conditions of fauna and flora would be stable. Yet this is not so. Great have been the natural changes on Isle Royale even within its recounted history. There is a small book, "Winter on Isle Royale," written concerning the winter of 1874–'75 by one Sarah Barr Christian, who spent that winter on the island with her husband, one of the mining officials. It contains this passage, "I am sure there was but little wild life on the island at that time. But as summer came on woodsmen reported seeing occasional bears." Later there were lynx on the island and caribou in numbers.

Last winter there were no bears, no lynx, no caribou on the island. They had disappeared completely. The secret? In the case of the caribou at least it was the periodic formation of an ice bridge between the island and the Ontario-Minnesota mainland, a medium of emigration and immigration. Crossing on this ice bridge, the moose came to the island, being first reported in 1912. Today the moose are the largest and most numerous mammals on the island. In fact, they are too prevalent as they have increased in number beyond the capacity of the winter food supply. As winter advanced and the moose felt the pinch of hunger, they lost their fear of man and became more and more familiar until they slept around the house at night. We would find their beds in the morning.

One afternoon in February at about 2 o'clock Togo began the moose bark (Togo being the collie). As he persisted, the schoolroom windows were manned and, sure enough, Togo had a moose over by the house. The animal stood eating vines off the building, in magnificent unconcern as to the barking dog. But Togo was too persistent, suddenly the moose kicked at him, then disappeared into the shed, to emerge hastily in a volley of tin cans and firewood, and retreated around the corner of the house. Alas, the show was over! At 4 o'clock, however, there came another furious barking and once more from the windows we saw the moose unconcernedly eating vines. School was out and we all stole over to the house. Cautiously the boys and I climbed to the roof and crept over till we were above the moose. The animal had seemed so vivacious as we viewed it from the school window. But from this vantage point we could see the moose was thin and very feeble. At last it moved slowly off, its legs nearly buckling under it, down the trail and through the snow. Sunday we found the animal in the woods behind the boys' cabin, dead.

This was one of the many moose carcasses we found. They were not diseased; they were simply starving to death. There was nothing we could do about it except watch the success of Michigan's moose trapping experiment and hope that another year more moose could be trapped and shipped to the mainland to reduce the island herd.

* * *

During intense cold, when the water of the bay was calm, it would freeze over, once so thick and clear that we walked out on it, lay down and looked at the bottom of the bay with its silt covered ledges and our shadows cast through the ice. It was a queer feeling to be suspended so safely above the depths. Then would come a night of great activity on the bay, sounds as of some giant seamstress ripping a great seam down the length of the ice. All night we would hear this tumult and in the morning see sparkling ice free water. Twice pressure ice floated around from Canada. Great chunks were heaved into the bay and along the shores by the force of the storm. Then as the temperature fell they congealed in grotesque postures, some heaved up on end rising five or six feet into the air. This ice always looked blue.

I had an expedition in mind the first time this ice came in—along that curving shore to the southwest. As the island was 50 miles long, with an area of 229 square miles I could not explore much save in the vicinity of Chippewa harbor, but I wanted to get beyond the south point of the bay and see the stretch of the southwest shore of the island and the grand horizon of Lake Superior. Of course I must snowshoe. I had begun my snowshoeing with much pleasure and little skill, but now could at least keep one foot off the other. I started out on the ice across the bay and then close to the shore line. Out over Superior as far as I could see was an illimitable stretch of pressure ice. Never had I seen such a vast, disheveled stretch, with no apparent end.

At an accessible point I scrambled up on the ledge above. Here the balsams were stripped by hungry moose, even the ground cedar had been pawed up and the buds were nipped from the alders. The younger balsams will have a hard time staging a comeback, for added to the ravages of the hungry moose, they are infested with the spruce bud worms.

Up on the ledge the moose tracks were plentiful. I startled a couple of animals that rushed away out of sight. In a minute I came upon their beds, smelling them before I could see them. The moose lie in the snow where trees or windfalls serve as a windbreak and lying there through the night, melt their impress into the snow. These imprints are the moose beds and they have a rank, animal odor. But now it was my turn to be startled. Almost unconsciously I stepped to the right as a small flock of ducks sped past, close above the ice.

As soon as the moose were hard pressed to find food the officials' live trapping was quite successful. Finally the herd in the corral numbered 11; four calves, five cows and two bulls. The moose were really likable animals especially the tamer ones and the calves.

All during the winter we had been in communication with friends and relatives by short wave radio. At one time the whole colony was filled with consternation because the belt of the washing machine engine broke and this was the engine used to charge the batteries for the radio receiver and transmitter. The men, with the spirit of martyrs, offered their belts to be used in making another, but it was not successful. Finally on the point of reconciling ourselves to a winter of isolation, an ingenious device was improvised with a spliced rope, the belt worked, the engine charged the batteries and our communication continued—the one link across Lake Superior.

Spring really came with the first trip of the Winyah Sunday morning, Apr. 13. Now the spell of the winter was broken. Once more communication was established. We could have fresh eggs and mail, some of which had been held all winter. It was grand to see Capt. Christiansen and the jolly crew again after seeing 11 people only for so many weeks. The Winyah steamed away, and Monday began the final week of school, the fastest week of the six months.

The last morning dawned—gulls over the bay, wheeling, drifting, wheeling. The bay itself reflected the balsams half glorious in the sun and half in shadow, and white birches with pink tipped branches. Into this bay glided the Winyah, for the last time in my experience.

All too soon I was stowed on board with my luggage. There was the cry to "cast off!" the hawser was thrown on board, the Winyah turned around and headed for the mouth of the bay. This time I waved goodby from the bow of the boat. We left Chippewa harbor and steamed down the southwest shore so effortlessly—I could vividly remember snowshoeing along this shore with great difficulty. The shore of the island slipped past till at sunset we could look back and see only the southwest end and the Rock of Ages lighthouse. Shades gathered about the island, obscuring it. At last it was enveloped completely in the immensity of night, descending like a curtain upon my winter on Isle Royale.

(2)

SPEED THRILLS TOLD BY AMBULANCE DRIVER *

Judges by Expression What Other Motorists Will Do and Misses Them by Hair's Breadth, Says Methodist Hospital Employe

Next time a clanging ambulance charges down the middle traffic lane missing your fenders by no more than the breadth of a hair, don't thank the stars for your good fortune. That wasn't luck. That was psychology.

"Reading the other fellow's face is the one secret of this job," says Hall Hearn, ambulance driver at the Methodist Episcopal Hospital. "You've got to think for him and you do it by judging his expressions; that is, as soon as you come near enough to see them."

Hearn should know: He is one of the four drivers at the Park Slope institution who recently received cash bonuses from officials there for making a perfect safety record. Through snow and ice and rain, at all hours of the day and night, the quartet responded to approximately 7,500 emergency calls without the slighest mishap to either a patient or their machines. The three other drivers are Joseph Schuster, who has operated ambulances for eight years with only one minor accident; Otto Marshewka and Robert Kennedy.

Other Driver a Danger

"You've got to watch the other driver's face," Hearn says, "that, and the condition of his car. You can see fear of a crash in his eyes, or you can see recklessness. And strange as it seems, sometimes as

* Reprinted by permission of the Brooklyn *Daily Eagle*.

we break through traffic and approach other cars we can see some of them wondering what they're going to get out of an accident—insurance and all that.

"When they seem perfectly calm and in control of the situation you can shoot ahead, but when they look panicky and bewildered and reach for the emergency brake, that's the time to begin worrying."

Excited citizens telephone the Telegraph Bureau at Police Headquarters that something terrible has happened and please hurry for God's sake. The ambulances cut through traffic, dart past red lights, skirt left of slow-moving trolleys and turn corners wildly. Neither driver nor interne knows how serious the emergency is until the end of their limb-risking journey through crowded streets.

Many Times It's Trivial

"Then sometimes we find that a tooth just pulled at the dentist's didn't stop bleeding as quickly as the patient expected," says Marshewka. "We get some funny emergencies."

Neither Marshewka nor Hearn would venture to estimate how many of their calls were unnecessary. Both, however, guessed the percentage to be high. Nevertheless an emergency is an emergency until it is found to be only a headache, and for that reason there can be no let-up in the speed with which they respond to a call.

"You can never tell what the next experience will be," says Hearn. "Last Summer we rushed to a house in South Brooklyn. We ran up the stairs not knowing if someone was shot or stabbed or seriously sick. Inside a young boy was crying at the kitchen table. We could hear him in the hall, but when we opened the door he yelled louder than ever. His mother standing there was pretty calm, though, and that surprised the doc and me.

Sulky Boy Was Cause

"She didn't bat an eye when she told us why she called for an ambulance. It seems her son didn't eat his supper. She threatened to call the police and have him taken to the hospital if he didn't show more appetite. He told her to go ahead. And she did call."

"How about the boy?" the reporter asked Hearn. "Did he eat up all the spinach after the ambulance came?" Hearn grinned.

"The funny part of it is that he did—and plenty fast, too."

One of the duties of the ambulance driver is performed only the first few days in July. It consists in steadying the young internes whose ambulance service starts the beginning of that month.

"They're all keyed up, but they calm down after a day or two," Hearn says. "We help to teach them how to carry a stretcher. In return we learn something about medicine and wound dressing. We can't help learning that."

Often Aids Internes

The driver aids the interne in other ways. Recently one of the doctors had a difficult time treating a young drunk who put his hand through a windowpane and was insisting on a joy ride in the ambulance before permitting the interne to examine him. He hit the interne, a small man, twice. Hearn gave first-aid to the interne in subduing the drunk. The latter did not go to the hospital that night. Instead he went to jail.

Ambulance driving is a difficult job because of the nervous strain brought on by knowing that lives are at stake. For that reason the drivers at the Methodist Episcopal Hospital need no safety campaigns such as those conducted by the Police Department to urge them to examine their brakes frequently. The hospital drivers do all but major repairs on their automobiles. Before they are selected for the job, their driving records are carefully checked at Albany.

(3)

I WANT TO SEE THE EDITOR *

By Mark Rhea Byers

The lovely snow is coming down
On you and me and all around;
It falls on both palace and hovel,
And we all have to get out and shovel.

I have never forgotten that verse, nor the occasion on which I heard it. It was read to me from a roll of manuscript, which, I swear, was tied up with ribbon, by a young girl, whose mother accompanied her to my office in the role of manager. The visit, unannounced and uninvited, was for the purpose of obtaining publication of the verse and its many following stanzas in the small-town

* Reprinted by permission of *Saturday Evening Post* and Mr. Mark R. Byers.

daily paper with which I was then connected. Not only was the paper to be privileged to print selections from the beribboned roll, it was expected to pay for them.

We did not publish the verse, but we did promptly lose a subscriber—several, if the promises made by the mother were fulfilled. And I had received another lesson in the patience and diplomacy indispensable in the conduct of a small-town newspaper.

I suppose that the phrase "obscure journalist" fits none so well as the staffs of the small-town daily newspapers and local weeklies of the United States. Now and then, a William Allen White or an Ed Howe becomes a nationally known figure. But for the most part, they live and work in a field so restricted that none but their own subscribers reads them, and their capacity or lack of it is a matter of utmost unimportance to any outside their neighborhoods —unless it be to their colleagues with whom they "exchange."

Yet I know that I speak the mind of all of them when I say that they long for the obscurity which a kinder fate bestows upon their big brothers of the metropolitan press. For the "fierce light which beats upon a throne" is comparative privacy and immunity as against the daily atmosphere in which the small-town editor must pursue his calling.

It is customary, particularly in the movies, to represent the metropolitan newspaperman as living in a hurly-burly of excitement and feverish activity—and so he does on occasion, although the tempo of his life is much exaggerated in popular fancy. But the hurly-burly is the ordered bustle of his own city room, his natural element, in which he is at home and at peace. No indignant and protesting subscriber can pass those guarded portals without good reason given, and when the inmates write "30" on the last piece of copy for the day, they are free to depart in comfortable anonymity. Even the possessors of by-lines may step from the door of the building and be instantly lost in the stream of nameless humanity that flows past, to pursue their own devices, unknowing and unknown.

So it is not with the small-town newspaperman. He is never off duty. He has no private life worthy of the name. His office—even his home—is subject to invasion by any who may so elect, and should he try to close his door for an hour's concentration upon a piece of work, he runs grave risk of incurring that most deadly-damning of all provincial epithets: "stuck-up."

Not to be thought stuck-up, the small-town newspaperman must resign himself to every conceivable sort of interference in his work and his personal life. A large fraction of his subscribers assume, from the mere fact of having paid for the paper, a self-appointed status as members of the editorial advisory board. Now, it is perfectly true that any small-town newspaper that hopes to live must occupy the position of a spokesman for the community; it must reflect and express the aspirations and indignations of its public. But that is a very simple statement to write, and an extraordinarily hard principle to put in practice, when one takes into account the aggressive democracy of an American small town. There every item of public business and every personality among its population is a subject for discussion the most free and opinion the most positive. The result is that there are never fewer than two sides to every question—including what ought and what ought not to be printed—and that all sides of every question are indignantly vocal.

Which means in practice that the newspaper office becomes a cockpit of warring factions, since everyone of every shade of opinion or prejudice feels it incumbent upon him to lay his ideas before the editor, with a demand that they be adopted. Should the newspaper, after this opportunity to learn the truth, embrace the cause of the opposition, the editor becomes either an idiot or a corrupted propagandist, and there rise dark murmurs about the need of a competing paper to insure freedom of discussion. Everybody else in town exercises the right of free discussion of local affairs, but the right of the newspaper to do so, in the minds of most of its readers, extends only so far as the editor's judgment coincides with that of the reader.

The head of a well-known syndicate of small-town newspapers some years since caused to be framed in the editorial rooms of all his papers the following terse observation:

"Whatever a patron wants to get published is advertising. Whatever he wants to keep out of the paper is news."

And that illuminates a principal difficulty in small-town publishing: What to print? The pressure for free publication of all manner of puffery, advertising and promotion material is tremendous, and equally tremendous can be the pressure to omit news of the greatest interest, and even importance, for strictly personal reasons.

The schools, the Parent-Teachers' Association, the baseball club, the Merchants' Association, the Safety League, the women's clubs, the churches, the labor unions, the Boy Scouts, the Rotary and Kiwanis clubs—one could cover the page with a list of the groups which feel themselves entitled to free publicity to further their activities. The unfortunate part is that many of them really are so entitled, from the standpoint of public welfare and news interest. Unfortunate, because those which are not entitled to it find it hard to understand the reasoning by which one group rates headlines and pictures, while theirs does not.

"Y'gotta treat ev'body alike" is the dogged credo of the provincial democracy, and fortunate is the small-town paper, making its painful choice, which does not find its decisions attacked as evidence of personal prejudice, snobbery, or worse.

The metropolitan press has to repulse the press agent and the organized assaults of various types of group promotion. But the city paper is insulated against them by the very terms of its existence; it may choose between those it will support and those it will not on the basis of news value and public desirability alone. Any given choice will alienate a negligible fraction of its readers. Indeed, there are a few great newspapers which seem to prosper, not by pleasing but by offending great groups. Of course, this is not really true—the excellence of their news services, astute circulation methods, exclusive comics and other features, keep the readers interested in spite of an irritating editorial page and a challenging and provocative news policy.

"Keep it Out of the Paper"

But the small-town paper's circulation potential is strictly limited. Every subscriber is precious; to lose a few hundred by riding over their prejudices is a matter of concern. So, when the local Townsend Club sends in a column or two of scatter-witted economic argument, the editor does not pitch it in the wastebasket, as his good sense suggests, but finds a place for it in the letters-to-the-editor column, and hopes that not too many will be caught by the glitter of the fallacy. He knows how much his circulation and advertising can be made to suffer by the next well-paid Townsendite orator who may choose to depict him as a tool of the greedy interests, denying the suffering and the aged the right of free speech.

Yet the greater bane of the small-town paper is the pressure to "Keep it out of the paper." It may be anything from an arrest for "drunk and disorderly" to a recall petition for the city government, but there will be somebody who wants to keep it out, or at least to inject the color of his own interest into the handling of it. Ingenious social, sentimental and personal pressure is used to make refusal difficult, and it is to the credit of the small-town press that in major matters it so consistently flies in the face of its own selfish interest, and discharges the duty which is its reason for being.

Let us suppose that the editor's open door is invaded by a gentleman who has come, the morning after, full of either contrition or defiance, to suggest that nothing be put into the paper about the fact that he was just fined for driving while drunk. His car sideswiped another, and one of the occupants is in the hospital. The newspaper is conducting a campaign to keep drunken drivers off the roads, and has been urging the courts to make examples of all violators. But his case, it appears, is "different." He has an invalid mother, an expectant wife, and children in school who will be shamed.

Morning-After Visitors

Those who plead for shelter against the publicity which follows their own misdeeds invariably put their pleas on the ground of their families. It is strange how angry they get when it is suggested to them that the time to think of wife and children was before they took the last three drinks.

For always, when refused, they become righteously indignant at such treatment of a "good citizen, and a subscriber to your paper for ten years." Not unusually, they suggest, not too delicately, that they are willing to pay reasonable blackmail to have the item suppressed. If the visitor happens to be an advertiser, it is a foregone conclusion that he will threaten to withhold future patronage. Almost surely, refusal means cancellation of a subscription.

There still are many readers who believe that the newspaper's news and editorial columns as well as its advertising space are for sale. These probably comprise the more gullible of the listeners-to-politicians, the ones who believe almost any sort of extravagance, provided it is baldly enough stated and often enough repeated. To such it appears reasonable that if a newspaper disagrees with their politics or economics, it is obviously sold to the enemy, and, therefore, that bribery must be part of the editor's stock in trade. To such simple-minded persons, the enormity of proposing that a stark lie be printed, for payment, does not suggest itself, and it is hard to make them understand, even dimly, the questions of ethics and honor involved. Indignation is completely wasted, of course.

What is one to say, for example, to a mother whose son has been arrested for theft, who extracts from a shabby purse a half dollar and lays it on the desk, with the request that there be no story in the paper about the affair? I spent three quarters of an hour attempting to explain, in this particular case, why I could not take the money, and I am afraid that she left with the idea that her request was refused because she couldn't pay enough. It happened that her son was given probation as a first offender, and in keeping with the paper's policy, the boy's name was not used, in the hope that any effort to reform would be encouraged. I wonder how his mother explained the situation to herself when she read that night's paper? In the light of some other experiences, I am not sure that she did not think I was a fool for not taking the money.

Of course, foolish and ignorant people do foolish and ignorant things, and it was just funny when a ham-and-egg fighter, to whom I had handed a copy of the paper which contained some reference to himself, shoved a quarter toward me and said, with a lordly wave of the hand: "Keep the change!"

But it was not funny when, after more than a week of strenuous day-and-night effort on the part of the newspaper, a bank run was stopped and the community's financial structure prevented from crashing—not to mention saving the hide of the bank's stockholders and directors—it was not funny, I repeat, to have the cashier call to offer a few grudging words of approval—and a "tip" in the form of a check for twenty-five dollars! It will be a long time before I have as much heartfelt satisfaction as when I tore up the check and expressed my opinion.

It is the accepted credo that every town needs its newspaper just as it needs churches and schools. I suppose I am not the only newspaperman who has wondered why, considering what efforts are made to abort the best services of all three. Is there an epidemic of influenza, scarlet fever, diphtheria or typhoid in town? At the first mention, there will appear an indignant delegation from the Chamber of Commerce, anxious to suppress the facts because they will be "bad for business" by keeping the farm families from coming into town to trade. Reporting a raid on a dive is strenuously objected to as "giving the town a bad name." Is there a squabble at the union meeting or the session of the vestry? When a reporter seeks the facts, the editor will shortly receive visitors insisting the affair was a private matter, which ought not to be printed.

Woman's Inhumanity to Woman

Yet in any small town every such occurrence, and many more trivial, is public property instantly, and the newspaper that publishes these minutiae accurately does a service to the actors, for the truth is never half so sensational as rumor. Nonpublication lets the gossip run, but small-towners seem to be hardened against the most vicious sort of talk—on the autogenous vaccine principle?—while at the same time considering it imperishable disgrace to have one's name in print, except in a laudatory paragraph.

With this attitude general, it is not surprising that ill-natured folk often delight to give things to the paper which will make trouble for their "friends." Many a social item is gleaned because someone who attended a little bridge party tattles to the women's-page girl, although her hostess wanted to "keep it out of the paper" because she didn't invite all her friends. And what shall one think of the person who telephoned in the birth of a baby girl to "Mabel Blank"?

"What's her married name, please?" the reporter asked.

"It's 'Miss' Blank," was the reply, with a sniff.

"Oh," hesitated the reporter. "I don't know— Who is this, please?"

"Go ahead, print it!" rejoined the voice on the telephone. "It's true. I ought to know; I'm her sister."

A Hoax That Got Out of Hand

Some of the folks love to hoax the paper. It is a joke highly esteemed to give a reporter false information leading to publication of something embarrassing to a neighbor. Usually there is no malice. The butt of the joke is expected to grin and bear it, and the newspaper to make its retraction gracefully, all in a spirit of good clean fun. Sometimes, though, the hoax gets out of hand.

A reporter came in from his beat excitedly one morning, with a story about a lion's cub killed by an Indian not far from town. Lions are not usual in the Mississippi Valley, but there was no doubt about this one. The reporter had seen the hide, which was being dressed by a local furrier. Unimpeachable experts verified that it was indeed the skin of an African lion cub, a few days old.

Naturally, we hopped to that story. How could a baby lion be loose in our settled farming countryside? As he must have had a mother, obviously a lioness was loose among us, a menace to livestock and to human life. The furore lasted a month. Someone remembered a wagon show that had trekked through the region, and so the lioness was accounted for; she must have escaped from the show. Soon after that, imaginative persons began to report seeing the lioness. Sheep and calves began to disappear. Mothers kept their children home from the country schools. People stayed indoors at night. More than one man sat up with a shotgun to watch his calves.

A delegation of serious farmers came to town one day and stopped into the newspaper to check up. By this time we ourselves believed the story, although we had broken it the first day more or less with tongue in cheek.

We took the delegation of farmers to the fur shop and let them see and handle the skin for themselves. It was convincing. They went home and organized a great lion hunt, and for a week they beat the wood lots and hay meadows, accompanied by photographers and reporters. The Chicago papers sent special correspondents. It was a wow.

The lioness was never found—since she had never existed. Just when the headlines had swelled to banner proportions, a hint from a friend gave me the clue to the mystery, and presented me with a problem in journalistic conduct. By this time we had built the story to such proportions that we dared not puncture it. We should have had a thousand angry farmers seeking reprisal and the whole Midwest press making fun of us.

For the simple explanation was that during the engagement of a lady lion tamer who was doing an act in the vaudeville theater, one of her pets had given birth to a cub, which had died, and she had given its hide to a friend in town as a keepsake. The furrier had only thought to have a little fun with his friend.

The furrier and the owner of the hide were by now appalled. Together we swore to bottle up the facts, and we tapered off the story. Without publicity to fan their imaginations, people stopped seeing the lion, and the farmers abandoned the hunt in the belief that the lioness had left that part of the country. The story died safely away.

Alas, Poor Yorick!

I shall not forget the scene in the potter's field at the county poor farm when the body of an unknown man, found dead after the spring break-up, was exhumed for identification by his son from a distant city. The evidence was a shock to a cub reporter, but not so to the brisk young man whose father had disappeared.

"Yes," he said, lifting his father's skull, "that's dad, all right. He was bald, you know, and I'd recognize that dent in the top of his head anywhere."

He placed the skull prominently on the rim of the coffin, and asked us all—coroner, policemen, undertaker, reporter—to line up in a group around it while he unlimbered a camera.

"I want to take a picture home as a souvenir for the folks," he explained. "I'll give you each a print, and one for the paper."

He did too. It was a clear, sharp print, and the young man was aggrieved when the paper refused to publish it.

Cranks of every sort besiege newspaper offices everywhere. In the small places, where the editor's door must be open to all, they are hard to handle, sometimes. Their obsessions may range from depression panaceas and new monetary systems to downright religious mania. In the most cases they are only excitable and argumentative. I remember only one who was dangerous.

He had been writing us a long series of letters, complaining that we were leagued with the pastor of his church against him, and making incoherent threats. This is not uncommon, so we paid little attention.

But one night the editor was working alone in his office when the man came in—a huge country blacksmith. He announced that he was tired of the persecution he had been undergoing, and that "the Lord" had instructed him to "settle this thing right now."

The editor stalled for time, hoping some member of the staff would drop in to help. Becoming completely sympathetic, he offered the blacksmith his protection. He told of a refuge which had been provided against those mysterious ones who, he complained, were "after him." If the blacksmith would just slip out the back door and down the alley, at the end of the alley he would find protectors waiting to guard him against his persecutors.

Secretary to Moses

It worked. At the end of the alley was the police station, and a quick call to the desk sergeant did the rest. An insanity commission passed him on to the state asylum.

My chief told me, the next day, that the worst part of the experience was leading the way through the dark composing room to the back door. He had to go ahead to show the way, and he kept thinking of all the heavy metal objects around a composing room.

There is a fitting sequel. Three days later the country circulation man reported that the blacksmith's family had canceled their subscription because the editor had their relative put in jail.

I have a vivid recollection of returning home one evening to find my wife entertaining a grim old lady who had been waiting to see me for hours—to sell me a book by Abraham Lincoln. She was a practitioner of automatic writing, and Mr. Lincoln had spoken from beyond the grave through her pen. My wife had not known whether to be frightened or amused by the lady's anecdotes for encounters with the famous dead, for Moses and Napoleon also used her as an amanuensis.

Cranks and freaks can usually be dealt with by patience. Publicity seekers are a different breed, and they come in all sizes and shapes.

One day a country correspondent telephoned that a thirteen-pound trout had been caught in a near-by stream. If you know Middle West trout fishing, you know that a German Brown that size is news. We asked for details and a picture, and that afternoon the correspondent drove in with the banker of a neighboring village, in waders and trout rig complete. The big brown was in a gunny sack, and the banker posed for a picture with a fly rod in one hand and the trout in the other.

Our information, however, was that the fish had been snagged out of the mill pond by a youngster with a cane pole, worm fishing.

The banker admitted that was correct. He had bought the fish from the boy, and was planning to enter it as his own catch in a fishing contest conducted by a magazine.

"I figured," he said complacently, "sending a clipping of the picture from the paper would make it look good. You can just say it was caught on a four-ounce rod with a gray hackle."

We printed the picture—of the fish. We cut the banker and his fishing outfit off the print, and credited the catch to the small boy and his worm. The banker was much hurt. It is just as well that a larger trout won the contest, or he would have blamed us for doing him out of the prize money.

Any newspaperman of experience could match these anecdotes. The point is that in small-town newspaper work they have an importance out of all proportion to their real significance—importance to the paper and its publisher. He cannot simply grin or shrug. They concern people he knows and who know him. It often matters little whether the decision the editor makes—to print or not to print—is intrinsically right or wrong. The result either way is likely to be the creation of an enemy—and a grim, vindictive one often enough—for the simple reason that he knows the editor well enough to call him by his first name and took it for granted that this acquaintanceship would suffice.

If an editor does let such considerations sway him, he will regret it bitterly. For the small town's memory is long, and when a routine item about somebody else is published, that aggrieved person will come in to note, with embarrassing truth, that when the same thing happened to John Smith, it wasn't in the paper.

The involved and intensely personal and factious politics of small places is another source of grief. For the sheer mudslinging and disregard of facts, a campaign for the mayoralty or the sheriff's office will make the last stages of a presidential contest seem a picture of good feeling. Every mean prejudice is appealed to—and the newspaper is in between all factions and damned heartily throughout for sins of omission and commission. That is the only thing that all sides can agree upon.

Newspapermen are interested in politics by the nature of their calling, but most of them take little pleasure in local campaigns. Election night is an occasion of great excitement while the returns are being tabulated and the election extras prepared. To most of us, I think, half the enjoyment springs from the sense of a pressure removed. We hope that the next day friendship suspended for the duration of the campaign will be resumed, and sudden enmities that have no warrant except in fleeting political excitement will have begun to subside.

The Voice of the People

The particular grief of election campaigns is the vox-pop department, standard in every newspaper. Letters to the editor double and redouble as the campaign warms up. It becomes necessary to establish stringent rules to avoid libel and abuse of the publication privilege. Some newspapers in the small towns have even gone so far as to shut off vox pop during campaigns. They will print no political letters, so difficult is it to confine the contributions to fair argument.

Ordinarily, a newspaper will print a letter from a subscriber over a pen name, though usually the writer is required to give his own name and address as an evidence of good faith. But in campaign time it is becoming the rule to print only letters signed with the real name of the author.

Since campaign letters are more often than not vigorous personal criticisms, the criticized are sure to come in, demanding to know the name of the attacker. And that means angry criticism of the editor for allowing anonymous character assassination in his columns if the name is not given, or another indignant visit—from the writer—charging betrayal of confidence if the name is given.

The smart boys in local politics, sensing the interest vox pop has for the public, need a bit of watching. If one is not on guard against them, they will write their own letters by the dozen and feed them to the paper one or two at a time. Even the requirement of a bona-fide signature is not insurmountable. They write the letters and have their followers take turns signing them.

Toward the finish, the editor does well to forget his too easily evaded rules and rely on his own judgment, letting the howls rise as they will. And woe upon him if he prints more or longer letters from one side than from another! The rivals will stop only just this side of the criminal statutes, but the editor is expected to part his hair in the middle.

The Man Who Knows the Answers

Which may illustrate one of the reasons why the old-fashioned party organ has almost disappeared from the small-town scene. The "independence" of most of the smaller newspapers through the country, outside of the Democracy obligatory in the South, is not so much independence as a safety-first neutrality. If you are independent, no party can make claim to your services against the scoundrels on the other side.

Newspaper standards have been raised, and it is no longer economically practical to produce two or more newspapers in the smaller places. There has been an epidemic of mergers, so that there are many fewer dailies and weeklies than there were thirty years ago. That makes newspapers safer investments, but the newspaper with an exclusive field is under the obligation to be, as nearly as possible, objective in its treatment of the news. Not to be so is unfair—and as compelling is the probability that it will invite the launching of competition.

Some newspapers have gone so far as to surrender any opinion whatsoever; their editorial columns have disappeared. For the honor of the profession be it said that these are a minority. On the whole, small-town editorial comment is as vigorous, if not always so well-informed and polished, as is found in the city press. It is the point of this article to demonstrate that this condition is maintained in the face of odds, personal and economic.

There are compensations, of course. The small-town reporter or editor knows, more surely than can any metropolitan specialist, how people live and how their minds work, from Jake Wozniak, on WPA, to his town's manufacturer. He can say more truly than any other man of his time, as Aeneas said of his: "All of these things I saw, and of them was a part." For mighty little goes on in his community in which he has not a finger. His position has many rewards for the man of an inquiring nature, with an itch to watch the human mechanism operate and understand its springs of action. It leads to a catholicity of friendships and a deep and forbearing knowledge of men and women.

For, of course, the small-town newspaperman conducts, as an obligatory and unpaid side line, a kind of intellectual public-service bureau for the community. There is a simple faith among his subscribers that he knows all the answers—or that if he doesn't, he can find them out. He never knows, when he answers his telephone at home of an evening, whether the call will be from a subscriber who missed his paper, a summons to a meeting of some sort, an angry criticism, or a demand that he settle a bet. I have been dragged from bed at three A.M. to declare the number of electoral votes of Alaska. Like the parson and the doctor, I am expected to be at everybody's service.

Here is a hasty list of jobs that I have done for subscribers in the last few years, with no thought of compensation on either side: Written a speech for a lady going to a class reunion; lobbied before the state legislature for bills; written letters for a group of commercial fishermen who felt unequal to official correspondence; written parodies of popular songs for home-town shows; written a one-act play for the Chamber of Commerce; prepared speeches innumerable for officers of various groups; assisted in the preparation of a pageant; turned out yards of verse, serious and otherwise, for social occasions; headed reception committees for all sorts of visiting luminaries; prepared supposedly humorous "special editions" for conventions, banquets, and so on; written letters and made trips in behalf of seekers for political appointments. In addition, of course, I am expected to be always on tap for a talk before local groups—women's clubs, service clubs, trade conventions, and so on. I am the ex-officio chairman—and only working member—of the publicity committee of every organization to which I belong—and a newspaperman is expected to be a joiner. These activities, which produce nothing but good will, consume at least as much of my time as the actual newspaper work for which I am paid. I am no exception. I know other publishers who are much more active along these lines than I. It is a responsibility that goes with the job, which one dare not evade.

The famous metropolitan journalist whose name is known to millions is able to go his way and speak his mind with comparative immunity. He is insulated from his great audience by the fact that, off the pages of his newspaper, he is an indistinguishable individual unit in a great city.

The late Arthur Brisbane could stroll through the streets and scarcely meet a soul who would recognize him. Many of those of his own staff, indeed, seldom or never saw him. To them, as to his millions of readers, he was fourteen printed letters at the head of a column of uniquely written, excessively simplified comment and interpretation. For all his fame and power, he, personally, lived in the privacy which is the blessing of the metropolitan journalist.

It is that anonymity, rather than journalistic *réclame,* which the small-town newspaperman envies. For he lives the life of a goldfish, and someone is always trying to sink a harpoon in the goldfish!

(4)

WHY CATCH COLD? *

BY WALTER A. WELLS, M.D.

As told to Marie Beynon Ray

> An eminent surgeon of Washington, D. C., Doctor Wells is a recognized authority on the prevention and treatment of colds. He is the author of a book, "The Common Head Cold and Its Complications," widely consulted by physicians, and of numerous treatises on allied subjects. He is a Fellow of the American College of Surgeons.

"Feed a cold," Grandmother used to say, "and starve a fever."

Whereupon she'd set the table: Good, rich soup. Roast beef, gravy, mashed potatoes, string beans. An extra cup of coffee. A big slab of butterscotch pie.

"That'll fix you, son."

You remember, don't you? But did it cure your cold? Bless her heart, no!

The reason is that, like so many old adages, it isn't true. Meat and potatoes and soup don't kill a cold. Other foods are much more valuable, for they build up resistance to infection. Besides, a cold *is* a fever. There's inflammation in your chest or your throat or your head, and frequently in all three—and a few other places. Instead of overloading the body with food, you should adopt what is almost a reducing diet. And you don't have to starve yourself to do it, either. Diet is not all, but it is a mighty important part, of the newest treatment for colds

The late fall is one of the two worst times for colds. So, if you haven't a cold now, you'll have plenty of chances to catch one before the next rent day comes around. Statisticians have found that most of us have three colds a year: one now, one in February, and one somewhere in between, and that the cost to industry alone is more than $450,000,000, or 90,000,000 working days!

* Reprinted by permission of *American Magazine,* Dr. Walter A. Wells, and Mrs. Marie Beynon Ray.

Imposing figures! But even more imposing when you realize that they do not represent the entire population but only the 42,000,000 engaged in gainful industry. Then there are persons who hardly ever cough and blow, who have colds so seldom that it's hard for them to sympathize with the rest of us. They are the fortunate few, of course. But we can all be just as fortunate, for scientists have lately discovered a few things about the common cold and how to prevent it.

Some years ago they began to inquire why it is that most of us are so susceptible to colds, while a favored few are almost immune. In short, they undertook to discover the actual *cause* of colds, which, strangely enough, had never been determined. Once they could put their finger on it, they would be a long way toward a cure.

The search began in Germany in 1914. More recently it has been carried on at the Rockefeller Institute Hospital in New York, at Johns Hopkins Hospital in Baltimore, and elsewhere in the United States. It was a long, discouraging task. But at last the scientists made several interesting discoveries.

They discovered, first of all, an organism smaller than any bacteria heretofore known, so minute as to be invisible under the most powerful microscope, and capable of penetrating the pores of a porcelain filter. This tiny organism is now being put through the third degree at Johns Hopkins. Scientists believe it is the long-sought cause of colds, and they hope the cure is not far off.

Meanwhile, progress has been made along other lines. For research workers made still another discovery—the proper diet to deal with a cold. The old adage about feeding a cold, they knew, needed revision. They applied to the problem the new knowledge of vitamins, those mysterious food substances which are indispensable in maintaining health. Strange things—vitamins. They are essential to life—yet until a few months ago no one had ever seen a vitamin. Even now we know nothing of their chemical structure. They are contained in many foods, their presence may be demonstrated in a dozen different ways, yet their nature is not yet determined. The recent discoveries concerning the effects of certain vitamins on colds are among the most important that have come out of the cold-research laboratories thus far.

It was shown, for example, that the lack of Vitamin A in the diet caused experimental animals to develop symptoms similar to those of a cold. From this the scientists reasoned that the feeding of

Vitamin A should counteract a cold. And this, they found, was just what happened. But, since Vitamin A can't be taken as just plain Vitamin A, it becomes necessary to supply it in the form of food.

So there you are! The next time you have a cold—in your head, chest, or throat—go on a diet rich in Vitamin A and eat it out of existence. How? By drinking glasses and glasses of milk, as much orange juice as your wife or husband will squeeze for you, and any of the other liquids or foods which contain this vitamin in quantity: lemonade, grapefruit, cider, pineapple, and big spoonfuls of cod-liver oil. Stay on this diet for a day or two, and you'll find that, while you yourself have been exceedingly well nourished, that wretched cold has been starved to death. If it hasn't—if it lasts three days, or four—you may be sure it's a regular giant of a cold, one that normally would have developed into a long and serious illness.

But don't expect this diet to work if you obtain it at lunch counters and soda fountains during working hours. It's customary to fight a man standing up, but the only way to fight a cold is on the flat of your back. And that means bed. Drafts and chills are the breath of life to a cold, and the best way to avoid them is to sink your head deep into a pillow and tuck the covers in tight all around. That's one reason for going to bed. Another is that physical activity burns up energy which you need to fight the cold.

It's astonishing how hard it is to convince people that they're acting foolishly instead of bravely when they refuse to take their colds seriously. True, a cold doesn't make you actually sick—just confoundedly uncomfortable and a bit thick in the head. You can get around. You can continue to do your work, sit up to the table, and go to the movies. But, besides prolonging your cold, you're doing something far worse. You're a public menace. You're spreading it all over the place.

The common cold is a catching disease. By going to the office you are taking one cold and multiplying it into ten or a dozen. You endanger everyone who comes within breathing distance of you. And that's one reason why colds are so common.

If we could ever get enough people to realize this, to stay at home and keep their sniffles to themselves, we would see an amazing falling-off in the number of colds a year. It wouldn't be long before the October and February epidemics were little more than an unpleasant memory.

For fighting a cold the liquid foods I have mentioned are best. Not only are they extremely rich in the anti-cold vitamin, but they help to flush the system and are easy to digest. Cod-liver oil especially builds up resistance.

Avoid everything that is the least bit hard to digest. You are better off with only a small amount of meat and other heavy foods. Eat plenty of fresh fruits and vegetables. Avoid highly seasoned or fried foods, cheese, beans, pastry, freshly baked breads.

Solid foods which contain large quantities of the anti-cold vitamin include butter, the yolks of eggs, spinach, watercress, lettuce, celery leaves; turnip, beet, and radish tops; carrots and sweet potatoes; yellow corn, but not white; liver, kidneys, and sweetbreads.

Of course, lying there in bed with nothing to do but drink milk and wonder how the office is getting along without you, you'll probably want to hurry things along by taking a little medicine. As a rule, don't. If you have unbounded faith in some particular little pill or sirup that saved your wife's brother from the grave—well, take it. It probably won't do you any more harm than it will good. But, whatever you do, don't take quinine—quinine, pure or in any of the combinations commonly prescribed for colds. I have never heard of a cold that was cured by it, and in large doses it can actually do harm.

There is one very simple remedy, however, upon which I often fall back during the acute stage of a cold. That is the good old bicarbonate of soda. It has a most salutary effect. I advise taking a half teaspoon of bicarbonate of soda in a half glass of water three or four times a day or drinking freely an alkaline table water.

Another precaution not to be neglected is the use of a saline laxative in the early stages of the attack. No doctor ever said a wiser thing than the famous Dutchman, Boerhaave, when he wrote, "Keep the head cool, the feet warm, and the bowels open."

There are other drugs which, properly administered, according to a doctor's prescription, can give you relief—certain coal tar derivatives, for example. But the dangers of self-drugging far outweigh the advantages. Moreover, many of the medicines used for colds have a depressing effect upon the heart. And how do you know that your heart, just at this time, is able to stand the strain?

Besides, the usual effect of these medicines is not to cure the cause of the distress but merely to dull the pain. Which also may be dangerous. Likely as not the pain is one you would do better to be aware of.

This happened not long ago to a man I know. He had what he thought was a cold in the chest. He doctored himself industriously with drugs, imagining he was curing it, since he felt easier. But actually he was dulling the warning pains of a severe chest complication. When finally the pain became so severe that he could no longer subdue it, he had to be taken to the hospital. The cold had developed into broncho-pneumonia.

Local treatments, of course, depend upon the kind of cold you have. There are really only three types of colds: those caused by irritants, such as smoke, dust, pollen, volatile oils; the hay-fever cold; and the true or common cold, in which a number of germs with unpleasant names are usually present, but which is believed to be caused by that ultra-microscopic item of recent discovery.

Let's say you have what you call a head or catarrhal cold. You use a dozen handkerchiefs a day and you feel as if you were breathing, talking, and thinking through several layers of piano felt. Here local treatment, whether the cause be pollen or a virus, is decidedly beneficial. It consists of clearing the nasal passages of their accumulation of mucus, with either a spray or a douche. The treatment usually advised is to dissolve a teaspoonful of salt in a pint of warm water and, with douche or spray, introduce a small amount of it into the nose. Don't snuffle it up through the nose. Pour or spray it into the nasal passages and let it flow down into the throat, "hawk" out through the mouth, and repeat. If, at the same time, you open your mouth wide, you avoid the possible danger of forcing some of the water into the ear passages, and perhaps causing trouble. If you find that one of the nasal passages is freer from mucus than the other, it is well to introduce the cleansing solution into the tighter side first. This insures against the fluid's getting into the ear passages. And again—do not swallow while the nose is being irrigated!

Now let's consider the sore throat or tonsillitis cold, where the cause, probably the same as in the head cold, has been localized in the throat, no doubt because that happens to be your weakest point.

The tonsillitis cold usually starts with a tickle in the throat, a constriction, or a soreness. Gargling, painting, and spraying the throat are advised by many physicians. There are any number of products on the market for sprays, gargles, and douches, but there is nothing better (or cheaper) than salt or a simple alkaline antiseptic solution. The prescription usually advised is to make a solution of one teaspoonful of the alkaline solution to four equal parts of water and use it as a gargle two or three times a day.

A powerful coarse spray may be used on the throat, but never in the nose. Such sprays are particularly helpful for those half-hearted garglers who merely bubble the water in their mouths. It forces the solution deep into the passages, washes out the germs located far down in the throat.

Now, if a cold has gone to your chest, local treatment is somewhat more difficult. You can spray the nose but you can't spray the lungs, and no gargle will reach the bronchial tubes. Grandmother's method of placing a newspaper cone over a kettle of steaming water in which she had put a few drops of Friar's balsam or spirits of turpentine was not without its merits. Today the local treatment usually adopted is the same steam inhalation. Just steam alone is good, but many physicians find that quicker relief is obtained by adding some preparation of menthol to the water, or compound tincture of benzoin. They recommend placing a large paper cone over the steaming solution and breathing the fumes in deeply for ten minutes three or four times a day.

Counterirritants are also prescribed: a mild mustard plaster; oil of wintergreen, rubbed gently on the chest and covered with wool; or an electric pad. And a warm bath twice a day helps a lot—always supposing you are where you should be: in bed.

Then there is what you are pleased to call the "indigestion cold," the kind that attacks the man whose digestion is faulty and whose elimination is poor. Here diet and proper elimination are the principal treatments, but this type of cold frequently goes beyond a mere cold and becomes a true grippe or influenza. Call the doctor!

The hay-fever cold and the cold caused by irritants are often treated with a nasal spray. But this at best affords only temporary relief. The irritants—dust, pollen, volatile oils—are in the air you breathe and the only permanent cure is to prevent them from entering your system. If your job is involved—in a pet shop, or a mattress or fur factory—that's not very practicable. Great advances have been made in our knowledge of the hay-fever and asthma types of so-called "colds." It has been found possible by means of skin tests of a patient to determine the particular pollen or other substance responsible for his attack. The cause determined, the patient may change his abode or way of life to avoid it. In some cases a course of treatment by the physician with extracts containing the offending substances may make the patient resistent to it. For hay-fever, such treatment must be undertaken several months before the usual season of attack.

And finally there is the cold which doesn't confine itself to any particular area but attacks the entire body—the eyes and toes, the teeth and nerves. The patient is hot and cold at the same time, has pains in every joint and muscle, aches in jaws, forehead, and fingers, feels soreness in the very flesh. If he takes his temperature, he will probably find it somewhere between 101° and 103°. That is a true systemic infection—and that is the kind of cold you want to take particularly good care of. It is imperative to see a doctor.

When you feel a cold coming on, the wise thing to do is to take a hot tub bath or a hot mustard foot bath and go to bed immediately (even if you don't intend to stay there longer than just the night). In order still further to promote perspiration, once in bed, you may, on the authority of many eminent physicians, drink a hot lemonade punch.

The best prescription any doctor can give for immunity against colds consists of fresh air, plenty of it, in your rooms and offices day and night, outdoor exercise even during the cold months, and cold baths—one a day if possible.

We can't hope to escape colds if we live in houses and offices steam-heated up to 75 and 80 degrees and with most of the moisture removed by overheating; 68 degrees is the healthy temperature. At this temperature the relative humidity of the atmosphere is from 40 to 50 degrees, but when the thermometer rushes up to 75 degrees, the relative humidity drops to 20 degrees. Very bad! A thermometer and a hygrometer (to indicate the relative humidity—it can be bought for as low as $5) are advisable for every home; also various types of humidifiers, which return to the air the moisture extracted by overheating.

And most of us overdress as well as overheat and overeat. Women in little pink shirts are far better off than men in long woolen underwear. In the temperate zone, underwear, even for children, should be the same weight the year round. Woolen underwear is needed only by those who are constantly exposed to severely cold weather, and perhaps by the old and feeble. Plenty of outdoor exercise, cold showers, a diet rich in Vitamin A, and you should build up a regular polar-bear resistance to cold.

Exercises

1. Select a magazine section of a newspaper and list the personal experience stories in chart form. In the first column indicate the elements of the other types of articles that you find.
2. In a second column indicate whether the experience is that of the writer or of others.
3. In a third column indicate the purpose the author had in writing the feature.
4. Indicate whether the article was written under the author's name, a pseudonym, anonymously, or ghosted, and indicate the reason for the writer adopting the method he did.
5. In a brief paragraph discuss the devices the writers used to make the articles personal and realistic.
6. Select two general magazines and list the personal experience stories in each in chart form. In the first column list the sources of the information from which the writers obtained the material.
7. In the second column, in less than four words, indicate what is distinctive about each article that influenced the editor to buy it.
8. In the third column list the number of pictures, drawings, or charts for each article.
9. In the fourth column indicate whether the experience is that of the writers or of others.
10. In a paragraph of not more than 300 words enumerate the points that you learned to make the personal experience stories you write more realistic and personal in order that editors will buy.
11. List a tip for each of the following types: personal experience of your own; personal experience of others; and a ghosted or "told to" story. Indicate three markets for each.

Publication Analysis

Hygeia, Outdoor Life, and *Field and Stream*

Do not spend more than two and a half hours on this report.

I. Identification: Name, publisher, editor, where published, price of each magazine.

II. Make-up:
1. What do you like about each magazine?
2. What do you dislike about each magazine?

III. Advertising:
1. What is the difference in the appeal in the advertising of the magazines?
2. From the advertising what kind of a reader do you visualize for each publication?
3. One tip from the advertising of each magazine (three tips in all).

IV. General Policy:
1. If you were editor, would you change either of these magazines in any way?
2. Give reason for above answer.
3. What types of articles could you submit to each magazine?

V. Feature Articles:
1. What types of articles do you find in each publication and to whom do they appeal?
2. Analyze a personal experience article in each magazine and list five suggestions for improving the writing of your own feature articles.

VI. Four tips: Two from each magazine; source, authority for the articles suggested, and three possible markets for each one that were suggested by the study of this magazine.

6 THE CONFESSION ARTICLE

Popular Because of Tone. The confession article is popular because readers like: (1) unvarnished tales related in a confidential style, in which the writer confesses or reveals his "sins" or shortcomings; or (2) exposés of conditions in classes of society with which the reader is unfamiliar. It may aid the reader by showing how personal faults and problems, which may be similar to his own, have been overcome either by the writer or the person about whom he is writing. An article of this type is "How I Improved My Disposition." Or it may present to the reader an intimate revelation that will give him an insight into some phases of life with which he is not familiar. His attention may be attracted in order to have him become interested in helping to remedy conditions or in aiding the solution of problems revealed. Such an article was "The Life of a Summer Hotel Waitress."

The confession article is a feature in which the writer reveals in a confidential tone: (1) personal and intimate experiences of his own, or those of someone else, which he would not care to give in a signed article; or (2) the "inside story" of conditions or problems normally unknown to the average reader. It may entertain, reform, or inform the reader.

Although the confession is similar to the personal experience article, it is different in that the things related, revealed, or confessed should be typical rather than exceptional or unusual. A writer may relate his own confessions, or he may obtain interesting revelations of others. Existing conditions may be criticized constructively and entertainingly by the device of the confession article. The reader's concern in problems about which he previously knew little or nothing may be aroused. The tone, however, must always be confidential—as though the writer were whispering in the reader's ear.

Experiences Must Be Typical. The experiences described must be typical of those of other human beings. Facts and figures may be incorporated to prove that the incidents are not unusual. The nearer the writer can make the problems correspond to those of the reader, the greater will be the appeal.

Illustrative material for this type of article is more difficult to plan. Frequently the person, or persons, concerned in the confession article does not wish his picture included. Sometimes the confession is of such a nature that charts or graphs add to the clarity and simplicity. In confessions written anonymously, photographs cannot be used because they might reveal the identity of the confessor. Pen and ink sketches often make good illustrations.

Plan and Style of Writing May Vary. The personal or psychological confession may be written to show the author's fall from a happy, prosperous existence to one of continuous calamity. It may present forceful examples to the reader, to warn him to avoid similar failures. Or, if the article is of the opposite type, which is so popular, the author will show how errors of judgment or faults of character were overcome and how in the end he triumphed over all. The reader is thus told how he, too, may do the same. Such articles were "I Cured Myself of the Blues," "The Dentist Made a New Man Out of Me," and "The Confessions of an Undergraduate."

By writing anonymously, or under an assumed name, a confessor may write more freely and intimately, since a large part of the success of the article depends upon the confidential tone in which the revelations are related to the reader. To write anonymously, however, is no excuse for poor workmanship. Simplicity and directness characterize the style of the confession article. The more straightforward the manner in which it is written, the more effective it will be. If the writer is "ghosting" the confessions of another, he must try to put himself in that person's place and reveal his thoughts and experiences as clearly as though they were his own. Even though this type of article may be written anonymously, readers are keenly interested. On the printed page it takes the place of the confidential neighborhood gossip that people like to hear, even though they are reluctant to admit their interest. The happy ending is greatly in favor. No matter how realistic the confession is, the writer should always show that there was a reformation or that experience taught its lesson. If one writes with faith in his own story, he may present many good sermons that will leave the right impression without appearing didactic. If the author wishes his confession to appear without his name, he may so indicate in the note to the editor on the cover sheet. This is explained in the chapter on "Preparation of the Manuscript."

Writer Rewarded by Self-Analysis. In addition to the financial reward and satisfaction of seeing one's confessions (or those of others) in print, there is the added advantage that the writer may benefit from the self-analysis, or analysis of others, that he makes in revealing his problems or existing conditions to the reader. In helping the reader, the writer may help himself.

When considering the markets, the writer must ask himself who buys magazines containing confession articles. He will find that housemaids and policemen, housewives and business men and women, priests and gamblers, spinsters and bachelors, youths and maidens, laborers and professional men, the young and the old, and everyone else are readers of these tales. They all want to read about something that might have happened to them. Markets are abundant and of great variety. Many pulp magazines consist largely of confession or "true story" articles, and almost every general and class publication includes at least one confession article in each issue. The successful writer of confessions studies all the magazines that print such articles. Their policies concerning the kind of confessions they print differ widely, and he must know the differences in order to "slant" his articles accordingly.

Examples of the Confession Article. For obvious reasons, newspapers buy more articles of the exposé type than of the personal or psychological confession. Of this type is the first one of those following, which was printed in the St. Louis *Post-Dispatch.* It was illustrated with three pen and ink sketches of the "chiselers" at work. The second, which was printed in *Ken* is similar in type. It too warns the reader, by revealing methods of high-pressure promoters. The third, written by a college junior, appeared in *Physical Culture.* It illustrates the type of personal and psychological confession in which the writer confides in the reader. The fourth, from *Forum and Century,* reveals a new racket to the reader.

(1)

THOSE HIGH-POWERED RACKETS *

Vanity, Generosity, and Even Misfortune,
Are Preyed Upon, Often Successfully,
By Gentry of Easy Conscience.

By Virginia Irwin

Mr. Williams is out $50. In the parlance of the profession, Mr. Williams has been taken—in plain English, swindled. And Mr. Williams is in a bad humor. Not because he is going to actually suffer financially by the loss, but because it's pretty hard to admit, even to himself, that he is a sucker. Mr. Williams holds his head and remembers the day he received that letter from the editor of an executive's magazine. It was right after he received his promotion.

The letter contained proof sheets of an article which had been prepared by the magazine—sort of a biographical sketch, lengthy, of course, of Mr. Williams. They proposed running it in an issue devoted to the country's rising young executives and Mr. Williams thought they had done a pretty good job of finding out just how smart he was. After the proof sheet was corrected and sent back, there was a long distance call, advising Mr. Williams that the issue was just going to press and suggesting that he order at least 200 copies at 50 cents each for distribution to friends and customers.

* Reprinted by permission of the St. Louis *Post-Dispatch.*

Mr. Williams modestly ordered 100 when informed that the magazine was sold only by subscription and never on the news stands. He knew a lot of folks who would turn green when they read that he was one of the "country's rising young executives."

* * *

The magazines arrived and Mr. Williams gasped. Cheap pamphlets—with sketches of himself and several men of whom he had never heard. He wanted to throttle somebody, but instead tied the little "magazines" up in a neat bundle and took them home and threw them in the furnace.

That was the vain Mr. Williams' $50 introduction to the puff sheet racket. Serves him right, you say? But how about the widows who pay dearly for puff sheets on their dear departed? A widow with a little money is also easy prey for the unscrupulous slicker who scans the death notices and then mails anything from a Bible to a billfold to the address of the dead man. The letter accompanying the goods usually thanks him for the down payment and requests the balance due. If the widow demurs, she is raked over the coals in a letter informing her that she is making a dead beat out of her dead husband. Usually, the widow pays up, rather than be annoyed in her time of distress.

Most expert of all the swindlers who know how to make emotions produce dollars, are the charity chiselers. Thousands of dollars are collected annually in St. Louis by these unfeeling gentry whose pockets bulge with dollars donated in the name of charity. They have their sucker lists and actually hold schools in salesmanship for petty larceny racketeers who want to break into a big-money game.

The high-powered expert in charity chiseling will handle anything from a small campaign for funds for a new church carpet to the drive for the yearly quota for a national fraternal order. He goes into a town, approaches the operating director of an institution and convinces him that the old-fashioned method of taking whatever people want to give is out of date. "You set the quota, pay me a commission, and I'll do all the work," he proposes. It sounds business-like and the prospect signs on the dotted line. Then the charity chiseler sets up his "boiler room" with its battery of phones and puts his solicitors to work on the sucker list. The solicitors, or "dynamiters," get verbal promises of donations over the telephone, likely as not by using the name of the head of the institution, and then the "leapers" get on the job. Girls are usually employed as "leapers" to go after the checks or cash promised, and always pose as charitable souls donating their time and energy in the interest of the organization.

Comes the reckoning. The drive has been a big success, far beyond the wildest hopes of the managing director, but when the chiseler's commission, operating expenses, etc., are deducted, there is comparatively little left for charity. The contract is brought out and the well-meaning managing director discovers that the institution's share is but 20 per cent of the amount collected. The racketeer pockets the balance and departs for the next town, where he will use the success of the St. Louis drive to jockey another sucker into letting him handle another charity campaign.

Nearly all big racketeers work from sucker lists. One catalogued index, taken in a raid on a boiler room by the Better Business Bureau contained 5000 names. Mr. Jones was listed as a sucker for anything to do with orphans; Mrs. Smith was a "lily" (polite name for a sucker), guaranteed to go for the crippled children gag. And it is from sucker lists such as this that the charity racketeer operates—oftentimes without even bothering to actually contract with an organization for a drive. In some cases he just pockets everything collected, and the church or lodge doesn't hear until days later that they have been making an appeal for funds.

One reformed charity chiseler confessed that he never dabbled in anything but milk funds. "Haunt 'em with the picture of babies without milk and they'll dig down nine times out of 10," he explained.

It costs a lot of money to operate a racket on the big-time circuit, and occasionally the sucker market is demoralized by publicity in a certain section of the country. When the per capita income gets so low a promoter can't make a decent living, he turns to such things as good luck charms and Biblical plants to eke out an existence until the depression lifts.

The peddler of Biblical plants tries out the "good luck" approach. If the housewife doesn't believe in charms he switches to their beauty as ornaments. He promises to send out an expert the next day from the company's offices to see that the plants are properly set out. Of course, the expert never appears, and the housewife discovers that she has paid $3 for a 10-cent cactus. The pie tin salesman is another of the tribe of petty larceny crooks. He represents a company in the pie-selling business. The housewife merely buys a certain set of pie tins and recipes and the company guarantees to take so many pies a day from her. It's all up to her, how much money she wants to make. She buys the pie tins and the recipes, bakes a flock of pies, and awaits the pick-up truck. In the end her family eats the pies.

Gypping the unemployed is certainly the lowest type of racket but the heartless hoodlums have worked out more variations of this type of swindle than any other.

Taking a dollar or two from an unemployed man, with the promise of sending literature pointing a way to earn a living at home, is perhaps the most common of all methods. The literature arrives, perhaps outlining in roseate hues the profit that can be made whittling watch charms out of peach stones. Of course, the sucker must either buy the peach stones from the company at an exorbitant price or buy peaches from the market and save the stones, but the real hitch comes in when you try to whittle on a peach stone. There's quite a trick to it and what the whole scheme amounts to is that the unemployed man has poured another dollar, or more, into the insatiable maw of the fakers.

Ever since women took up the dieting fad, the "obesity cure" racket has flourished. One preparation analyzed contained 2¼ cents worth of soya bean flour faintly flavored with cocoa and malt. The smart boys got hold of a sucker list of fat women somewhere and cleaned up selling their preparation at $2 a package.

* * *

How these specialized sucker lists are obtained is not always easily explained, but once you bite, the fraternity of crooks hand your name about among the brotherhood with the notation that you're an easy "tap." It's easy enough to get on a sucker list, but not quite so easy to get off.

A St. Louis doctor has a prescription. He actually received a formal notice from one high-binding sharpshooter that his name was scratched from the sucker list. When the doctor received an unordered box of ties and a bill for $1.00, he sent a box of pills in return, a bill for $2.00, and a letter saying he would keep the ties for $1.00, and all the company owed him was the dollar balance on his bill. The company returned the pills and asked the doctor to return the ties and call it square. Again the doctor wrote, said it was a half block to the nearest mail box, that he always charged

$2.50 for leaving his office, but if the company would send the $2.50 he would be glad to mail the ties back. The next letter from the company told the doctor to keep the ties and forget the whole matter, because his name had been removed from their list.

(2)

GOLD IN THE GRAVE YARD *

High pressure promoters discovered an easy-to-sell item in the bronze-markered "democracy in death" Memorial Park. Folks with money tied up in depreciated securities are first on their sucker list. They trade cemetery lots for whatever you have, promising to pay full value plus profit on your securities when and if they sell a flock of graves for you. Meanwhile cashing in your securities and pocketing the market value. You wait for graves to sell, ignorant of the fact that the promoters have provided our cities with enough cow-pasture Memorial Parks to inter two centuries of not-yet-born.

By Arthur Bartlett

For thirty-two years the two maidens had kept house for their three brothers, there in Dayton, and life had been placid and uneventful. Then, one by one, the brothers had died, and now the last one was gone, and their entire life savings of $5,700 were tied up in the Building and Loan—and only worth about half the face value—and they hadn't even been able to pay the undertaker for Brother's funeral. And then this nice man had come.

The way they understood it there was some new ruling by the Governor, or something, and this nice man was going to get them the full face value of their Building and Loan certificates within two years, and pay them $10 a month on it in the meantime. But he talked so fast that, land sakes, a body couldn't get it all straight at once. They didn't know. . . . They weren't quite sure . . . .

He was so nice and sympathetic that he decided to make a special arrangement whereby they would get an immediate check to pay the undertaker's bill of $482.98. So Miss Sarah and Miss Mary went upstairs to get their Building and Loan certificates from the back of the bureau drawer. It wasn't until several days later, when a niece came to visit them and began reading the fine print on the official

* Reprinted by permission of *Ken* and Arthur Bartlett.

papers, that the old ladies realized that they had exchanged their Building and Loan certificates for 22 lots in a cemetery called Crown Hill Burial Park.

The cemetery was real—quite a beautiful park, indeed, of 256 acres, between Cleveland and Akron, with an imposing entrance gate, a funeral chapel, and even some people buried in it. But the Misses Palfrey didn't want any cemetery lots. And because the nice salesman hadn't said anything about selling them cemetery lots, the District Attorney got their Building and Loan certificates back for them. Therein their case differed from thousands of others.

The salesman had outsmarted himself. Perhaps he hadn't paid close enough attention in the salesmanship class conducted by the Crown Hill Development Trust back in Cleveland. Anyway, while he was selling the Misses Palfrey by his somewhat evasive methods, a large crew of his fellow-alumni of the salesmanship class were selling many of the Misses Palfrey's fellow-holders of the depreciated Building and Loan certificates by franker tactics. That is to say, they at least admitted they were selling cemetery lots. It was almost uncanny—unless you could figure out that they had a sucker list—how they headed, like ferrets, straight for the homes of the holders of the distressed certificates.

But why should anybody in Dayton want to buy cemetery lots 200 miles away, between Cleveland and Akron? The answers to that are what the salesmen had learned in class. The Building and Loan certificates were frozen and depreciated. Too bad. But here was a golden opportunity to realize the full value on them. All you had to do was to sign this contract, whereby you acquired burial rights in Crown Hill and authorized the Crown Hill Development Trust to resell them for you at double the price you paid—and maybe more. In the meantime the company would pay interest on your investment at the rate of 50¢ a month on each $100 lot—until they were resold. Certainly that showed how sure the company was of reselling within a couple of years, at the outside. Why, they'd be practically forced to sell at handsome profits! People had to die, didn't they?

And so the graves were sold, and the salesmen took the stock, and the buyers got impressive contracts with phrases like "Guarantee to Purchaser" and "Full Amount" in big letters. The contracts, sure enough, authorized the company as the sole reselling agency—

but didn't say anything about when, if ever, the reselling was to be accomplished.

Anyway, the salesmen got the Building and Loan certificates, and took them to local brokers to be converted into cash, at the market value; and if, as in the case of the Misses Palfrey, it had seemed wise to offer an immediate cash return, it was just a matter of mathematics to figure out the deal so that there would be a surplus over the regular price of the lots.

For two or three years, the 50¢ a month on each lot (amounting to 6% interest on the investment) came in; but the number of lots resold was only about big enough to supply the salesmen with a dossier of testimonial letters to show to other prospective customers. And then the owners of graves were notified that it would be impossible to pay interest any longer. (If the customers got the impression that this was because of some new state law, as many of them did, it made them all the more amenable.) And they were presented with new contracts to sign, which would relieve the company of continuing to pay the 50¢ a month on each lot. Instead, the company proposed to boost the reselling price 25%, thus getting the customer a "bonus"—*when* the reselling was accomplished.

Shortly after that, dissatisfied customers began bringing lawsuits, and a Grand Jury investigation got under way. That was bad for business, and the Crown Hill Development Trust quietly folded up, turning the cemetery over to another outfit. At the same time that the Crown Hill boys were working Dayton, salesmen for at least three other cemeteries, one in Cleveland and two in Cincinnati, were also mopping up. And the same thing is still happening with only minor variations in detail, all over the country.

Up to the early 1920's, the real estate sharks and the high-pressure promoters had overlooked God's Little Acre. Then somebody conceived a new kind of cemetery: a Memorial Park, with no old-fashioned monuments and gravestones, but with sedate bronze markers set flush with the ground in a landscaped setting. And then the promoters woke up to discover that out of the $500,000,000 spent every year in this country to dispose of the dead, 90% was going to undertakers, and only 10% to cemeteries. Despite that, they found that wherever cemeteries were operated for profit—most of them having been non-profit institutions—they rated second only to pawn-broking as a safe, profitable investment. Obviously, it was time to muscle in.

As a promotion, the Memorial Park was a natural. In the first place, being a cemetery for the motor age, it was situated out on a highway, where land was cheap. All you had to do was to buy options on an old cow pasture or woodlot, and instead of sub-dividing it into a few dozen house lots, you sub-divided it into thousands of grave lots. As the money came in, you paid off your mortgages and development expenses, and cleaned up. Accordingly, Memorial Parks began to blossom all over the land, complete with roadside billboards, neon lights and free public concerts to bring in the customers. A Detroit promoter installed an organ loud enough to justify his boast that "anyone driving within a radius of four or five miles of our Park hears this beautiful music floating through the air"; and as a result of this and other promotional activities he was able to boast further that the cemetery "has received more publicity, week after week, than any other Detroit institution with the exception of the Detroit Tigers."

But promoters are impatient fellows, as a class—much too impatient to rely on the old-fashioned method of selling graves only to people who are interested in a place to lay their weary bones. Not but what they are willing to sell them for Utility, as they delicately put it. Oh my, no! Obviously, if you are selling graves, families that have sick people in them, or people so old as to be contemplating eternity, are better prospects than those full of health. That's where the men known in the trade as "bird dogs" come in. They spot the about-to-be-stricken homes by various means: neighborhood conversation, contacting interns, nurses and doctors' receptionists. After the "bird dog" has reported to the Home Office, the salesmen lose no time in following up the tips.

The smart promoter, however, sees no reason why even the healthiest families shouldn't help put his project over. Or, as the beautifully illustrated brochure of Restland Memorial Park in Hanover, New Jersey, puts it: "A happy sense of peace and security comes to him who has provided thoughtfully and well for the future of his loved ones. The ownership of a burial plot, in advance of need, is as wise and thoughtful as the purchase of life insurance, the making of a will or other forms of family protection. Nothing can be gained by delay, and much may be lost."

If you have followed the signposts to the cemetery, from the big billboard advertising it on the highway, and gone in past the sign that says, with gross understatement, "Public Welcome," the salesman meets you at the little entrance cottage with "Information" over the door. He takes you over the grounds and to inspect the chapel —"inspired," as the brochure points out, "by the St. Giles Church at Stoke Pogis, England, immortalized by Thomas Gray's *Elegy Written in a Country Churchyard*." Inside the chapel, he points with particular pride at one modern touch which is absent in the Stoke Pogis church: a yawning grave in front of the altar, with "a special lowering device which permits one to have the entire funeral ceremony in the Chapel itself, even to commitment"; after which, of course, the corpse can be taken out and put in his own grave before the next one arrives. He shows you, outside, the formal garden, and the little fountain-statue of Pan, and shows you a picture of the Tower that is to be built. He expands on the theme of bronze markers versus gravestones, pointing out that in old-style graveyards "the rich are still rich and the poor are still poor," whereas "Restland Memorial Park with its uniform markers of imperishable bronze fully exemplified the 'democracy of death' and is more in keeping with the Christian philosophy of life and the hereafter"; and then hastens practically on to point out that: "These tablets make possible perpetual care at minimum cost because they lie flush with the lawn, permitting one man to cut 31 acres of lawn in a single week." If a funeral procession arrives while you are there, the salesman calls your attention (quite needlessly) to the funeral music flooding the Park, and explains that it comes from a loudspeaker in the studio, where a record is being played. But by the time the funeral party has settled down to burial exercises, and the loudspeaker is giving forth *Beautiful Isle of Somewhere,* the salesman is pretty sure to have you in a little office, with the door closed, and to be talking more and more in terms of finance, rather than sentiment. He is willing to admit that the cemetery business is just about the most lucrative business in the world, and that the company is in it to make money—but is willing to let you make some, too.

Then, with pencil and paper, he gets to the figures. Here's the way they go at Restland: "Four graves in an ordinary cemetery will cost you about $600. Then you'll have to pay around $500 for a modest monument. For perpetual care, you'll have to put down $300 more. Total, $1,400. Now the total cost of 16 graves in this Park, with perpetual care, and with no monuments allowed, at our

Pre-developed price, is $900. So you save $500 right off the bat. But you don't want all these graves. So you let us sell 12 of them. Now when this Park is completed, say in a couple of years, those graves in a beautiful spot like this are certainly going to be worth as much as graves in the old-style graveyards. So let's say $500 for each of the three four-grave plots you don't need. That's $1,500. Less $75 selling commission, $1,425. Subtract your original $900 from that, and you have made a profit of $525. And you have your own plot free."

The salesman is always conveniently ignorant about the actual number of lots that have been resold; but he has a sheaf of glowing testimonial letters. And he points out, persuasively, that when you invest in graves, your demand is assured by law—the law of nature that says people must die.

The only question seems to be: When will the demand catch up with all these magnificent new cemeteries? Around New York City, which Restland aims to serve, there is enough cemetery space so that the New York state legislature has put severe restrictions, amounting almost to a prohibition, against the establishment of any more cemeteries within a radius of 75 miles—which explains why Restland and several others have been built in nearby New Jersey, within the radius, but outside of New York jurisdiction. And out in Cleveland, which Crown Hill aims to serve, a banker put his statistical mind to work several years ago and figured out that the city had adequate grave space, in its established cemeteries, to take care of all the people who would die there in the next 200 years. It begins to be easy to see why so many smart promoters have preferred to sell their graves for Investment rather than for Utility—and let somebody else wait for the prospective tenants to die.

Mr. Christian William Beck, the smart man who promoted Crown Hill, is only one of many throughout the country, but he will serve as an example. Mr. Beck, before he turned his benevolent interest from the living to the dead, was the promoter of a huge home-building project in St. Louis, which failed, with losses of $242,000. As a result of this enterprise, Mr. Beck was obliged to spend considerable time in court, and was even ungratefully sentenced to three years in the federal penitentiary on a charge of using the mails to defraud; but the Court of Appeals upheld his contention that he had been misjudged, and acquitted him.

After this disillusioning experience with houses for the living,

Mr. Beck's imagination was caught by the possibilities of beautiful homes for the dead; and proceeding west, he created his first memorial park outside of Tulsa, Oklahoma. The next year, he moved on to Oklahoma City, and another mortuary garden spot took shape under his egis, with only minor legal run-ins.

Ready for bigger things, he headed east, settled on Cleveland and began to plan Crown Hill. He found his site on the Akron road, near the little town of Twinsburg. The 256 acres cost approximately $180,000. Then Mr. Beck proceeded to do some organizing. In Ohio, and many other states, cemeteries must be non-profit institutions, under the law. If you are a salesman, selling for Utility, you stress that point. But there is nothing in the law to prevent the cemetery from letting a separate corporation sell the lots—and make the profits. So Mr. Beck formed two corporations, Crown Hill, Inc., the cemetery, and Crown Hill Development Trust, the money-making organization. Mr. Beck started by selling his $180,000 property to the Development Trust for slightly more than $500,000. That made it, of course, $500,000 property. Then his Development Trust deeded the property to his cemetery corporation in return for an agreement whereby the Development Trust became sole selling agent for grave lots in the cemetery, and would receive 60% of the selling price of all lots sold. The other 40% was to go into development of the cemetery and a perpetual care fund. The cemetery was then laid out in 35,000 lots, marked at prices which would bring in a total of $4,375,000. But, of course, the Development Trust was to get a mere 60% of this, or $2,625,000. Out of that, it would have to get back the $500,000 that it had paid for the $180,000 property, and pay its salesmen, to say nothing of the expense of running classes in salesmanship, getting lists of likely prospects, and advertising for new salesmen whenever alumni got pinched, went over to other cemeteries, or otherwise faded.

Apparently the necessity of turning over 40% of the money received to the cemetery corporation was somewhat irksome, because when a lot owner brought suit a few years after the Park started, and the books had to be produced in court, it appeared that instead of putting cash into the perpetual care fund, the trustees had been putting in their own land contracts. The court decided this was not cricket, and ordered a full 40% in cash turned in, as advertised.

But there is more than one way to skin a cat. Shortly after the issuance of this court order, two new organizations came into being.

One was the First Commonwealth Trustees of Chicago, with one Mr. Ralph Stickney as head man. Mr. Stickney had formerly been one of Mr. Beck's associates in Crown Hill. The other was the First Refunding Company of Cleveland. Oddly enough, the chief business of both these high-sounding companies turned out to be the selling of graves in Crown Hill Burial Park. It seemed that they were able to buy the lots from the Crown Hill Development Trust at considerably reduced prices (which, of course, also considerably reduced the 40% to which the non-profit cemetery corporation was entitled and could then resell to the general public at the old scale of prices—and still hold out bright hopes of later resales at double-the-money, or better.

The First Commonwealth Trustees concentrated on the states west of Chicago; like the Crown Hill Development Trust, it aimed its efforts at people with depreciated bonds and other negotiable paper. Large numbers of bondholders in western states received this cheering letter to sign and return:

"Yes, Sir! I certainly would be interested in a plan designed to get me out without a loss on securities now selling at around 50% of what I paid for them.

"Since it does not obligate me in any way, you may send me full information about your plan.

"You may also furnish prices, and any other data you may have available, on the issues I am listing on the back of this letter."

A nice, compact letter, which had the virtue of coming right back to the writer, if his prospect was ripe, with a good and authoritative estimate of the prospect's ability to buy lots in Crown Hill.

Just to show how salesmen can sometimes muff sure things: out in Omaha, Salesman Albert Deutsch, got securities with a face value of $1,700 and a market value of $300 from a cook. He learned she had more money, went back to try again. But by then she had learned about cemetery sales; he got arrested for obtaining money on false pretenses, to which he pleaded guilty.

But when, in 1936, with lots amounting to about $2,500,000 in selling price having been sold, one of the customers brought suit against Mr. Beck and Crown Hill, charging fraud, the troublesome customer was promptly bought out. And when another litigant took up the torch, and was followed by a Grand Jury investigation, Mr. Beck quietly withdrew from the whole business, to take a try at oil. Crown Hill was taken over by one Emery Komlos, who had promoted the competing Sunset Memorial Park. Mr. Komlos also took over a third cemetery, Whitehaven Memorial Park, and welded them all together in the Metropolitan Memorial Parks. But, alas, Mr. Komlos soon ran into difficulties because of his Bond & Share Corporation, which had been selling stock in Sunset Memorial Park and which the Federal Securities & Exchange commission charged with fraudulent use of the mail. So Mr. Komlos discouragedly turned the whole business over to a Cleveland attorney for refinancing. A few months after that, Mr. Komlos jumped out his hotel window and killed himself. Fortunately, he had been thoughtful enough to provide himself with plenty of resting places.

(3)

I REFUSED TO BE A "POLIO" CRIPPLE *

What Courageous Effort Did After Her Self-Pity Nearly Made This Girl A Paralytic For Life

BY ELLEN SORGE

I am one of the 120,000 young persons in the United States who have been physically disabled by infantile paralysis. From an eager girl of eighteen, happily anticipating all of the good things in the life of a college sophomore, in a night, I became a broken invalid, unable to sit up without support, unable to lift my deadened right arm from my side where it dangled helplessly.

Awakened one autumn night, two years ago, by a hot agony at the base of my brain, I struggled to sit up in the darkness and found that I was unable to lift my shoulders from the pillow. Rolling on my side in an attempt to raise myself with my arm, I felt it crumple beneath me. As I lay there helpless, my voice strangled in my tightening throat, breaking out in a sweat as the hot, heavy darkness grew thicker, I did not need to wait for two specialists in the morning to diagnose my "case" as "polio." In numb terror I knew that I had caught that most dreaded of all children's diseases, infantile paralysis.

But in the morning, in spite of the throbbing, gnawing torment of my injured muscles, in spite of a staff of doctors who pried, poked, worried me with questions, and punctured my spine, I was powerless to understand what had happened to me. I couldn't be a

* Reprinted by permission of *Physical Culture Magazine,* A Macfadden Publication, and Miss Ellen Sorge.

cripple—why only yesterday I had been able to swim nearly a mile in Lake Mendota. It was other people, people whom I had unconsciously scorned, who were cripples—but not I—there were too many things I had to do for me to be crippled. It was all a black dream, from which I would awaken in a moment, and how relieved I was going to feel.

Not until, in an unguarded moment, I found my mother watching me with tearful aversion mingled with compassion, did the devastating significance of what had happened sweep over me in an engulfing wave. And in the throes of this awakening I sensed my changing status—my disability was the worst thing that had ever happened in our family. Before, I had been merely "big sister" to Betty, twelve, and Mickey, four, who managed to absorb the attention of our busy, rather undomestic mother so that she had had little time for me. Now suddenly all of her love and attention was centered on me; I was pitied and coddled, and my self-pity grew apace. I sobbed, writhed in my bed, refusing to lie as the doctors had placed me, and repeated to this overly sympathetic audience that I wanted only to die, that I was going to be a repulsive cripple whom they would be ashamed of, whom they would have to support even in their old age.

After such a spell, exhausted from crying, I would lie listless for hours in the depths of self-pity. In vain, would my people tearfully beg me to "eat just a little," to let them read to me, to talk about the trips we were going to take when I was well again, to listen to the radio. But I wanted only to lie and brood over the unfairness of a scheme of things which had made me what I was. Why had I been the only one in a community of 60,000 to get infantile paralysis that fall? I was convinced that I couldn't get well. How could a deadened arm come back to life, how could muscles which now were not even felt to move, ever become strong enough to support me? And I saw in the pitying glances of father, mother, grandmother that they too wondered. It is not surprising, therefore, that heat, massage, and under-water exercises which, after the first six weeks, I was taken to the hospital to receive each day were doing me little good.

Brooding over what I considered the shame of a weakened body, despite my family's efforts to gratify my every whim, I suffered constantly from hurt feelings and ideas of persecution at the hands of all who came in contact with me. I would let none of my friends come to see me, but preferred my moody solitude. I almost hated my sister for her arrogant healthiness, which made her condescendingly able to do things for me; and I saw with relish that she was impatiently pushed aside by father and mother.

Growing more despondent and tyrannical, day by day, if I were thwarted in the least, I would threaten to do the things which the doctors said would lessen my chance of recovery—sitting up, getting out of bed, trying to lift my arm. With these weapons I ruled the household. If grandmother, sister, brother, or parents didn't give in immediately, I would begin struggling futilely, awkwardly, to swing myself into a sitting position, and with my helplessness so cruelly demonstrated, they would capitulate. One day, in spite of my protests, my mother went down town to buy my sister a birthday gift; in helpless, jealous rage I actually rolled myself out of bed, and falling onto the floor, dragged myself beneath the bed where I refused to come out in response to my sister's and grandmother's hysterical entreaties, until my mother had returned.

Thoroughly alarmed by this demonstration, and alive at last to the danger of home love becoming, because not wisely directed in its expression, an influence worse in its effects than a physical handicap, my mother saw that pity and coddling had only resulted in developing a flabby morale; and she realized that now more than ever before I would need an ability to maintain an even temper, an alert intelligence, socially considered behavior and a happy disposition, if I hoped to take my place in the adult outside world again.

Thus it was that the next morning my mother casually announced that she had more shopping to do. When I protested and threatened in the usual manner she indifferently shrugged her shoulders and declared:

"You're eighteen years old, Ellen, and you're no longer sick enough for me to think that you aren't responsible for your actions; now if you want to wilfully injure yourself, it's up to you; I'm not going to worry about it any longer."

For three days I was left largely to myself while I sulked in hurt silence—but I didn't try to get up again. And how much fun the others appeared to be having! They were their normal, happy selves again as they enjoyed the pleasures which make winter evenings such fun—popping corn, pulling candy, sitting around the fireplace making plans for Thanksgiving, cracking nuts in the kitchen.

Then one November afternoon with the gathering darkness the first snow began to fall, and forgetting my unhappiness, I asked that my bed be moved so I might watch the storm from my window; and as I lay there while it quietly whitened the slope and the little icy creek below, I knew that after all I deeply enjoyed just being alive.

How well I remember the winter days that followed. In contrast to the preceding weeks, I was happy and content. I felt my parents' sympathetic understanding, but was given no opportunity to trade upon it. My hopeless dread of the future melted away as new interests filled the days. The ordinary person in our present-day society overlooks a wealth of values that could make a richer life for him. I discovered these values. I wonder how many of you have time to know and enjoy your family? I grew to lovingly appreciate mine in the weeks that followed. I had never had time to make the acquaintance of my small brother, and what a delightful friend he turned out to be with his solemn innocence and impish fun. What treasures were stored in my grandmother's mind of life in early Wisconsin. I saw pioneering as it really had been—the sordid mingled with its romantic glamour.

Books which in my sophisticated innocence I had considered too childish to read over at my age, I now read with a richer appreciation. Penrod's trials and tribulations were an unfailing source of delight. Sewell Ford's irresistible office boy, Torchy, could still make me laugh helplessly. I reveled in the adventures of that tough, ignorant, generous, pyrotechnically mendacious little vagabond, Huckleberry Finn, who in his nasal drawl naively supplies serious observation along with rich humor. To occupy my mornings I outlined a course of study which I rigidly adhered to. I listened over the radio to two lectures from the University of Chicago; trained myself to appreciate good music; read the books which everyone talks learnedly about but never reads.

Never did I enjoy the Christmas season so much. For hours I pored over long lists of presents for everyone. After my "treatment," stretched in a low bed in the back of the car, I would go along up town with my mother. As I waited for her to shop, how I loved to hear the holiday shoppers crunch by on the hard, snowy streets; how happy their voices sounded; how sadly cheerful were the bells of the Salvation Army Santa Claus. As Christmas drew closer, my room became a den of happy intrigue. In the evenings my bed was pulled around by the kitchen door so that I might watch all of the culinary preparations for the holidays.

Never had I been happier; my disability had brought me the poignant realization that one does not live long enough not to enjoy every detail of life; but that the details should never be allowed to become so important that they eclipse the enjoyment of the whole. So we did not awkwardly avoid talking of my defect, for it had become an incident and not the whole of life. One would do well to maintain this sustaining philosophy.

With this new mental lease on life, my attitude toward the medical treatment of my physical disability changed also. It seemed almost a game, after the warm, soothing heat and gentle massage, to see how well I could move my arm as I did my "exercises" in the hospital pool. How hard I would try to push my arm through the water to show them with what rapid strides I was improving.

Doctors usually say that the process of recovery from infantile paralysis is a slow and tedious one; and perhaps it is in most cases, but for me, with this changed mental attitude, my strength came back in leaps and bounds. Soon I was able to raise my arm above my head against resistance and sit up despite hands which pushed me back. In January I was allowed to get up—wearing an "airplane splint" and a heavy surgical corset to be sure. When the second semester at the University opened, already having recovered over 90 per cent of my strength and showing no traces of atrophy, I was ready to cast aside my splint and take up the burdens of an outside adult world.

Faintly reluctant to destroy this winter idyll, I went back to school. With a slight sense of inferiority serving as a spur to goad me on, I managed to get all A's for three semesters and consequently received the Fanny Lewis scholarship, which was given to two University women each year. But it was in sports that I was determined to excel. Because my own friends were too indolent for strenuous winter sports, I went skiing and skating with my sister and her friends. Asking no odds, I entered tennis and archery classes in the spring, and gained a passing skill in both of these sports; whereas the year before I had been given a condition in archery for "cutting" so many times. The next summer when my father bought a surfboard for our motor boat, I doggedly practised until I could do more tricks with it than the boys who went along with us.

At home I did my share of the household chores—wiping dishes, dusting, ironing, helping prepare meals, and in the summer I took over the care of our large yard. In my spare time, I typed a University professor's economics book; and last summer I did clerical work at one of the high schols. And to cap it all, last fall I was given a clean bill of health when the head doctor of the State of Wisconsin's Orthopedic Hospital told me that I was one of the few cases where an almost perfect recovery had been made. My handicap had proven an incentive and inspiration to make the most of my capacities; I found that there was no need to take a back seat in life.

So especially in orthopedic cases is the role of the mental hygienist becoming increasingly important. The handicapped child's feelings for himself are often borrowed for the most part from the attitude of others toward him. If only a child can have contact with adults whose attitudes are healthy and therefore healthgiving, his battle is three-fourths won. Playmates and friends may turn from him and shun him, but the sustaining influence of parental love and his acceptance within the family will mitigate the pain of many a bitter disappointment.

For this reason, however, parental love is apt to be too protective. The handicapped child is apt to come to regard his defect as one of his sources of strength as well as of weakness—particularly if on every hand he hears, "let me do that for you, you aren't able to." In a short time he will sink into babyish dependence or become a first class domestic tyrant, according to his temperament.

Because sooner or later the child must take his place in an adult world where allowances are not going to be made for handicaps, defects, and personality kinks, he must know from the beginning that he will have to face realities. He must learn to avoid the escape habit. Parents can do much to help the child in his emancipation. In the first place they themselves must find outside interests which will prevent their emotional life from centering too much about the unfortunate one. Then, too, they can plan to provide for the child satisfactory relations with persons and groups outside the family circle.

Emerson's law of compensation is not true in itself. As a well-known doctor has said, nature does not compensate a person with impaired hearing by giving him improved sight, nor does it compensate the person of limited vision by giving him better hearing. It is entirely possible, however, for the great majority of the handicapped to develop certain of their resources to the point where they can feel that what they lack in some aspects in life can be made up in others. The handicapped have lost certain definite provinces of life, but in the domain usually neglected by the average person they can acquire large regions which may prove an offset to them, and sometimes even more than an offset. Most children can be led to develop a deeper appreciation for nature, a greater enjoyment of music and art, a richer love for literature; and thus a vast field will be opened up for them which will go a long way toward assuring a rich experience in life.

Excellence in some of these fields also gives the child greater security in heightened self-esteem and opens a wide variety of possibilities for economic independence. In fact, gross handicaps of a physical nature frequently provide the basis or incentive for greatness and even genius in the highest types of human endeavor. Consider Confucius, Immanuel Kant, Schopenhauer, Ovid, Cervantes, Pope, Mozart, Lord Nelson and innumerable other examples. Thus it is a recognized principle of mental hygiene that child care and training is not the business of eliminating hurdles from the race, but rather the occupation of gaging the hurdles so that they will not be insurmountable; of shaving off a little here and there perhaps, but never completely removing the hurdles themselves.

(4)

CONFESSIONS OF A PROFESSIONAL LISTENER *

By Ellis O. Jones

To listen professionally is a new racket—well, not precisely a racket nor, indeed, exactly an occupation; rather let us say a new source of income and a new outlet for human ingenuity. That should be sufficiently euphemistical.

There are already quite a number of us here in Los Angeles, and the field threatens to become overcrowded unless something happens to stem the tide. I was not the originator of the idea—just among the early pioneers. It appealed to me right away as an interesting, perhaps useful, certainly not a criminal way of replenishing a much depleted exchequer. And of course I thought it would offer a swell chance to study human nature, that is, human nature in the raw—off guard, as it were.

* Reprinted by permission of *Forum and Century* and Mr. Ellis Jones.

As usual I was wrong about most of these conclusions. True, it was moderately interesting, for a time, but for so brief a time as hardly to be worth what one would call a formal effort. It would have been quite profitable if everyone who was anxious to talk was equally anxious to pay a reasonable sum for the privilege. As for its being useful, well, anybody who is in such a forlorn mental state that he or she is willing to pay out good coin of the realm just to pour his woes into the tired ear of a perfect stranger is perhaps beyond redemption or at least needs a vastly different and more rigorous form of treatment.

The "profession" of listener is at present very, very easy to get into. One doesn't need a diploma or a license or any special background or training—just a little gall and something of a flair for novelty and adventure. There may come a time in this rapidly changing world when my profession will become so important and well recognized that a National Association of Professional Listeners will draw up elaborate tables of ethics and regulations and urge our solons to drastic legislation in the interest of all concerned but chiefly of the National Association of Professional Listeners.

But just at present we listeners have nothing to guide us. We are in what might be called the formative period of our existence. There are no authorities, and no precedents, and the profession comes pretty close to being the only activity that one can take money for without government license or licenses. And of course a listener's initial investment is practically zero, as no fancy paraphernalia is required. All you have to do is to put an ad in the "personal" column of a newspaper saying that you are in the business of listening to all comers at so much per listen and at such and such a telephone number. The fact that a "reputable" paper will take money for an ad of that sort is, at the present stage of our development, a sufficient certificate of respectability.

"And are there people who are willing to pay just to have someone listen to them?" you ask incredulously.

Yes, good sir and madam, there are plenty of them. The woods are full of them, to say nothing of the mountains and the beaches and the deserts. Especially teeming with them are the streets and hotels and apartment houses of Eden, or Los Angeles as it is sometimes called. Los Angeles is full of lonesome people, and one of the best definitions of a lonesome person is one who has nobody to talk to. Los Angeles has a larger number of these per capita than any place in the world, I guess. They are mainly pensioners of all kinds, from industry, from the civil service, from the army and navy, on annuities—detached and nonfunctioning and lonesome. There are plenty, young and old, in the remittance class, whose well-to-do relatives north, east, and south have found them unbearable at home and are willing to pay them substantially for staying far, far away where they cannot nag or meddle or pester.

Then of course there is an uninspiring specimen of the human kind who is a natural for a thing of this sort anyway. He is found everywhere, in fairly predictable numbers. His sort includes the borderline cases, the cranks, the egotists, the reformers, the extreme introverts, and the maladjusted in general. These soon become well known and disrespected in their own relatively circumscribed communities, such as Terre Haute or Kankakee, where they receive scant courtesy; but as members of such a loose, disjointed, and amorphous society as Los Angeles, where everything goes and goes big while it lasts, there is no standard limit to the gamut of the physical and psychical peregrinations of these gentry.

Words, Words, Words

But, lest the reader get an utterly wrong impression of the kind of folk who made up my clientele during the short and not too bitter period of my professional career, let me add that really a surprising number and variety of persons manifested an interest in my services. They were all ages and about equally of both sexes, as far as original inquiries were concerned; but among repeats it was the women who predominated. From this I draw the simple conclusion that women prefer to talk to a man listener, while men also prefer a listener of the opposite sex. They were of all classes, the poor and the rich, the educated and the uneducated, the apparently intelligent, and the quite obviously unintelligent. Undoubtedly there were many out-and-out curiosity seekers among them who came just to have a squint at that strange animal called a professional listener, in about the same spirit in which they would go to look at the two-headed calf in the side show. There were many in the class of adventurers pure and simple, willing to "try anything once." And there were some who came for very special reasons, for serious investigation or research, and I will tell of one of these a little later. The majority of the people, however, were quite serious, even if bewildered, about the whole business. Mostly they wanted real help or they even wanted to be helpful in some way themselves. And there were plenty of those who were willing to assist me in listening—for a goodly share of the profits.

My fixed charges in the beginning were $2 for the first half-hour and $1 for each additional half-hour. But the theories on which this scale was formed were all wrong. In the first place, the charges were much too small. It is really much harder to listen than you can imagine if you haven't tried it, especially if you are at all conscientious about it. Then in the beginning I had the theory that the second half-hour, being easier, should be at a lower rate than the first. This is utterly erroneous. The first half-hour of anybody's line is the easiest to listen to, for almost anybody can be interesting for a brief period. But, oh, when it goes on and on and on, with endless repetitions of the same rigmarole, the pain of listening, even with calloused ears, is almost excruciating. So I had to revise my tariff. Beginning with a flat rate for the first half-hour, I then made arbitrary charges for additional time, in the same visit or for subsequent visits, in accordance with my idea of what the service was worth in each individual case, not neglecting, of course, to take into account the ability of the client to pay. For this there is the highest possible authority in the legal, medical, and other professions.

And what did the communicants talk about? About everything —their parents, their husbands, their children, their wives, their suitors, their fiancés, their neighbors; the president, the governor, the mayor, the councilman, the postman, the gold standard, the old-age pension, the unknowable; about God and the devil, about mind and matter and spirit and soul, about investments, about movies, about the cosmos, about the trend of events, about individualism and socialism and biology and sex and eugenics; about the fourth dimension, the precession of the equinoxes, the science of relativity, earthquakes, cyclones, dust storms, the future of Hitler, the latest spectacular crime—in short, everything under the sun, on both sides and beyond the sun.

People came to boast of their past exploits, to complain of present woes, to voice their dread of coming cataclysms, and to revel in dreams of a roseate future. Many came, no doubt, in the hope of finding a soul mate, as there is a great demand for soul mates, but when they found me a gray-haired old codger their ardor in this regard rapidly ebbed. There was, however, one bird of paradise, a lady of uncertain years, elaborately dolled up with paint and finery, to whom a few gray hairs and wrinkles offered no discouragement. When she spoke of a second visit, I said I should have to charge her $25 per half-hour. That didn't daunt her, and then she wanted to know how much I would charge for a private visit to her house. For that I put the charge at $50 per half-hour. That too seemed all right, and the appointment was fixed, but before the time arrived I notified her that I should have to cancel the appointment and I never saw her again.

All the Ills of Humanity

Many clients jumped to the conclusion that a professional listener was some new kind of cultist, a faith healer perhaps or maybe a fortuneteller. Such conclusions were of course wholly unwarranted. The contract of a professional listener is of the simplest. He promises nothing except to listen, and that doesn't mean he has to listen intelligently or understandingly or sympathetically. (On the contrary, it is natural to assume that anyone who would take up such a profession could hardly be expected to be intelligent.) He doesn't even promise to have an acute sense of hearing. In addition to listening, all he has to do, as a concession to elemental courtesy, is to remark, "Yes, yes," or, "Dear, dear," or, "How odd," from time to time—and this more than anything else to reassure the communicant that he is still alive.

And so I had to listen patiently to symptoms and then more symptoms. I never realized before how many different kinds of aches and pains and biological disturbances and irregularities and frustrations were afflicting the erring and vulnerable human race. And all the poor sufferers wanted me to play the miracle man and tell them what to do for relief. Of course I didn't know and, if I had, I couldn't have told them. If I so much as hinted that such and such a therapeutic device were "indicated" in any particular case, I should have been liable to prosecution for practicing medicine without a license.

Usually it was sufficient to explain simply that prescribing courses of treatment was entirely out of my province, but some clients were insistent. When I would tell them, "See a doctor," the answer too often was that they had tried many doctors of all schools in vain and had no faith in any. No faith in doctors, and yet they were showing a certain kind of faith in advice they might wheedle out of an entirely strange professional listener with no authenticated background! Some of these no doubt were not sincere but were trying to show me up and put me on the spot.

One man in particular, a rather gross type of individual, talked to me at great length about his symptoms and tried to get me to express a preference for a particular kind of laxative. Not content with my refusal, he tried me again on other aspects of his case but without success.

At length he gave it up, and I was quite astonished to hear him say: "Look here, you seem like a pretty good egg after all."

"That so? Thanks for the compliment."

"Yes, you do. They've got you all wrong."

"They? Who?" I inquired.

"Listen. I'm going to tell you something."

"Fire away. That's what you're paying me for," I told him.

"Well now, the people that sent me here—I won't say who, but maybe you can guess—are out to get you. They think you're a faker and, if they can only get you for practicing without a license, they'll give you the works."

"Well, you've got the low-down on me now, haven't you?"

"I sure have and I'll tell 'em you're O.K.," he replied fervently as he rose to go. "But say, man to man, all those things I told you about myself are true. Honest. Now, as man to man, what do you think I ought to do?"

"I think you ought to see a doctor, maybe several of them."

Listening to Death

I feel I was most useful in the cases of a relatively few young people who came to talk over their woes and their perplexities, their love affairs, their secret sins, their ambitions, their disappointments. All these were deadly in earnest, and I did my level best not only to listen sympathetically and understandingly but to offer real aid and comfort. Such a service is of vital importance to the orderly development of young people. They must have older people to whom they can go freely for counsel and guidance and to whom they can talk with the utmost intimacy and unrestraint.

Then too I have reason to believe that I was useful on several occasions in preventing suicides. Perhaps more than half my clients were of the despondent type, and many of them had sunk to the uttermost depths of despair through dire mental distress over something which to another in a more normal frame of mind would seem a trifle. It is a relatively easy matter to cheer these people up, at least for a time, maybe until they can survive the crisis and resume a more serene way of life. A cheering word at the right moment spells salvation. On the other hand, some are chronic and beyond redemption, and it is quite likely that, among the cases reported in the newspapers of Eden of unfortunates who committed the act of self-destruction, some had paid me to listen to their tribulations; but I kept no record of the names and addresses of my clients.

My strangest experience was one in which I was able to prevent murder—not one murder but two. One day there came a woman dressed severely in black and heavily veiled. After taking some pains to assure herself that I would not try to discover her identity, she proceeded to unfold a harrowing tale of how she had killed her husband by putting poison in his food. Though she went into considerable detail, still I did not take much stock in her story. That was why I didn't call the police at once, as was my plain duty. But I had grown rather accustomed to hearing people boast of both noble and ignoble exploits which they had not performed, and so the story of the veiled woman in black went in one ear and out the other, and then she was gone.

For the next day or two I was considerably troubled over the case, wondering what, if anything, should be done. Then she called me on the telephone to make another appointment. I was greatly relieved at this and more than half expected her to tell me that her former story was a harmless hoax, as there was nothing in her gentlewoman's voice or general bearing to suggest the murderess.

Instead of retracting her former story, however, she referred to it as an accomplished fact and then she proceeded to tell me that in the same manner she had also murdered her son, a high-school lad and her only child. Finally she left as calmly as she came, but this time I put on my hat and followed. It was my first experience as a shadow, but I was successful in finding out where she lived—an elaborate house in a good neighborhood. I then notified the police and advised an investigation.

It was a simple matter to check the main details of the woman's story and prove them false. In other words, both the husband and son were easily discovered to be alive. With that I was satisfied. At any rate, my duty was done. But the police were not willing to let it drop so easily, and further investigation convinced them that the woman undoubtedly intended to carry out the tragic deeds she had told me were already performed. In the end she was placed in a sanitarium.

Mostly, however, my contacts were commonplace and deadly dull, and the recitals just the stale, colorless palaver one hears among one's own relatives and casual acquaintances. To invest them with special interest and make them worth reporting would require the imagination and artistry of an O. Henry. And, if it is tiresome nothings you are looking for, you can get all you want free of charge by squatting on a bench in the park and conversing with the man next to you or by frequenting the more informal and friendly bars or other retreats where men and women of leisure are wont to do their loafing. And, by using this method, you don't have to do all the listening yourself. Now and then you can put in a spiel about your own symptoms, your pet theory, or your beloved hobby. That helps a lot.

Of course, if you want to become a professional listener, that is, at present, your privilege. We have shown how easy it is to enter the profession. It is just as easy to get out, for there is no investment to protect, and there are no assets to dispose of. If you stop advertising, that immediately cuts off the supply of new clients. The old ones are easily discouraged by high prices and poor service. If worst comes to worst, you can always move to a new location with a new telephone number.

Exercises

1. Turn through the magazine feature section of some newspaper and list the confession articles in chart form.
2. In the first column indicate whether the article reveals the writer's "sins" or is an exposé of conditions of life.
3. In the second column indicate the purpose the author had in writing the article.
4. Indicate in the third column the methods by which the writers gave a confidential tone to the articles.
5. In the fourth column list the number and types of illustrations used.
6. In the fifth column indicate whether the writers wrote anonymously or under their own by-lines.
7. Turn through three general magazines with which you are familiar and list in chart form the confession articles.

8. Indicate in the first column whether the confession is a revelation or an exposé.
9. List the purpose of each article in the second column.
10. List the methods by which the writers give a confidential tone in the third column.
11. In the fourth column indicate the devices by which the writers kept the articles from being didactic in tone.
12. In the fifth column indicate the probable readers of the articles as listed in this chapter.
13. Indicate in the sixth column the number and types of illustrations used with the magazine confessions.
14. Write not more than a 300-word discussion of the differences in content and method of confession articles in magazine newspaper sections and in general magazines.
15. Suggest a tip for a newspaper confession and one for a magazine and include a market for each.

Publication Analysis

Scribner's Commentator, Forum, and *American Mercury*

Do not spend more than two and a half hours on this report.

I. Identification: Name, publisher, editor, where published, price.

II. Make-up:
  1. What do you like and dislike about the make-up of each magazine?
  2. Point out briefly how they differ in make-up and indicate which you think has the best make-up.

III. Advertising:
  1. What appeals do you find in the advertising copy?
  2. Give a tip for a feature article suggested by the advertising in each publication.

IV. Appeals:
  1. To what class of reader do the features in each magazine appeal?
  2. Discuss briefly the kinds and variety of appeals in the feature articles in each publication.

V. Feature Articles:
  1. Classify the confession articles as to type.

2. List three points concerning the confession articles in each magazine that will help you in writing confessions.
3. What did you learn concerning the other types of features in reference to type, length, quality, and illustrations?
4. How many of the articles are written by well-known or "big" names?

VI. Two Tips: Source, authority, and three possible markets for each tip suggested by the study of this magazine.

7 THE PERSONALITY SKETCH

Deals with Achievements. Readers like to know the innermost details of personality and character of prominent and successful people, and even of some who are not in the limelight. The personality sketch, or success article (as it is termed in some newspaper offices), is therefore in great demand by editors of newspaper magazine sections, syndicates, trade publications, and general and class magazines.

The purpose of such an article is to portray the intimate details of a person's character and personality so vividly that the reader will feel he has not only met the subject of the sketch face to face, but knows him personally. This type of article has a strong reader appeal. Everyone desires to attain success, and he hopes that in reading about the eminent or near-eminent he will find the key to their success and be able to benefit thereby. Perhaps the interest in this type of feature is really due to the fact that the reader is interested, first of all, in himself and is constantly seeking guidance in the solution of his own problems and adjustments. He reads of the struggles of others and how they avoided failure, in the hope that he can find a way to overcome his own hardships and handicaps.

A personality or success sketch is a feature dealing with the achievements of men and women, prominent or otherwise, and how they surmounted obstacles to acquire fame or fortune. It serves to inspire, to instruct, and to guide the reader in seeking solutions to his problems or adjustments to life about him.

Although this type of article has elements in common with

those previously discussed, it differs from them in many ways. It gives interesting information about the interviewee's life rather than just his opinions, as the interview does. It may be like the utility article in that it aims to help the reader; but its major concern is to inspire the reader to improve his personality or character. It differs from the personal experience article in that the experiences, as a rule, are not unusual. It is similar to the confession article in so far as it reveals intimate experiences, but they are not so personal that the subject of the sketch wishes to keep his identity concealed. On the contrary, he probably is glad to share them with others who may be inspired and helped in overcoming difficulties, for the aim of the personality sketch is to give inspiration, instruction, or guidance.

Gathering Material Depends on Skill. In gathering material for the personality sketch, a beginner will attain success more quickly by interviewing and writing up little-known people who have attained some degree of success. Skill in interviewing and in drawing out information concerning character and personality of lesser celebrities should be acquired before interviewing those better known. That is why newspaper training is invaluable to one who aspires to become a writer of interview and personality sketches. It teaches him how to see sources of material, to interview skillfully, and to write quickly and accurately.

The novice's first sketch may be about an old gentleman who lost his job because of his age but who turned coppersmith and attained some financial success. It may concern the clever puppet show by which a young physician has become somewhat well known. Beginners will find that it is better to leave the great statesmen, theatrical, radio, and screen stars, and others already renowned, until they have improved their techniques for gathering material and writing it. It is not that the already well-known and prominent people are harder to interview, but the writer will obtain better sketches after he has developed more skill in drawing out the interviewee to relate incidents that have not appeared in previous articles.

Everywhere the writer looks he will see opportunities for success-angle personality sketches about people who overcame obstacles and achieved success, and whose experiences will serve as inspiration to readers.

As in writing all features, the markets should be fairly well determined before the article is too definitely planned or the interview obtained. The policies of publications should be studied: (1) to determine whether the aim of the article is to afford food for thought; (2) to inspire to action; (3) to give guidance; (4) to estimate the length of the publication's manuscripts; and (5) to see kinds and number of photographs or drawings the publication would be likely to use. Then, when the writer meets his interviewee, he will know what illustrative material he wants. He can arrange for the pictures and thus save time for the celebrity and for himself. He should secure informal snapshots rather than professional portraits; if possible, he should obtain pictures of the person as a child or youth, for they will add to the reader interest of the article.

Sources of Material. Material may be obtained: (1) by conversations with people who know intimately the subject of the sketch; (2) from an interview with the person to be described, supplemented by talks with others who can contribute information; (3) from printed sources, reference books (such as *Who's Who* and the *Who's Who* in the person's specialized field); and (4) from friends and associates of the subject of the sketch. It is easier for the beginner to write a straight personality sketch if he selects a subject whom he knows. Until he has had considerable practice, he should not attempt to write of those whom he does not know, or whom he knows but slightly. But he may, without any experience, attempt a personality sketch with a success angle, and, like thousands of beginning free-lance writers before him, receive an acceptance almost immediately.

After some experience, however, a writer will be able in a single interview to get impressions from which to write a satisfactory sketch, because he will have learned to observe carefully, to judge people quickly and accurately, and to know how to find additional material to weave in with his own impressions. Some publications combine the personality sketch with the interview by printing the sketch followed by the interview.

If one wishes to specialize in this type of writing, he will find additional prospects for his sketches by scanning memberships of clubs and organizations, particularly business and service clubs. Usually the secretaries are pleased to furnish suggestions about members who overcame obstacles and who are doing unusual and successful things. Newspaper stories and pictures will serve as tips for articles for syndicates, trade publications, and general or class magazines.

The writer must bear in mind that personality stories do not always deal with people who, because of fame or riches, are prominent in the day's news or the world's work. Many excellent stories are to be found in the personalities of those who have overcome physical handicaps and struggled to success. These stories are worthy of the time and attention of any writer. They have a wider human interest appeal than do the stories of the eminent and wealthy. On every college campus there are available achievement stories of talented young people who are educating themselves by their own efforts. Publications are always in the market for this type of success story because of the inspiration and help it will give their readers. Even newspaper files, previously published articles, and books are sources of ideas and material for personality sketches.

Persistence must be one of the qualifications of the writer of personality sketches. He will meet many people (1) who are indifferent to being written up; (2) who will not see the story in their own achievements; (3) who from a sense of false modesty will refuse to be interviewed; or (4) who will be afraid their rivals will profit if they reveal the methods by which they attained success. Occasionally a writer will meet someone who simply cannot talk in an interview but who, upon the request of the writer, is willing to write out a few notes and facts about his business or invention or whatever has been the foundation of his success. From these notes, a skillful, observant interviewer will be able to write a marketable feature.

Writing the Sketch. The easiest part of the personality sketch is the writing, if the writer has gathered all the material available and given careful thought to the selection of facts, data, and details. As he plans his outline, he must keep in mind the policy of the magazine at which he is "slanting." To sell success stories, the writer must learn to distinguish between the types suitable for the newspaper feature section, syndicates, trade publications, and general and class magazines. For the newspaper, syndicate, and magazine, the human interest angle should be emphasized, whereas for the trade publication the characteristics that made the person successful in his business or profession should be stressed.

Personality sketches should contain the following: (1) biographical data; (2) description of the person, the details of the setting, surroundings, and general atmosphere; (3) quotations from the interviewee, in which he gives his principles for attaining success and the advice or guidance to others; (4) a general account of success in the words of the interviewee, or friends, or of the writer; and (5) the person's philosophy of life.

To portray the subject of the sketch to the reader, the method of describing characters in fiction may well be adopted to avoid using general descriptive terms, but by: (1) actually describing the subject's personal appearance, demeanor, facial expressions, and dress; (2) telling of characteristic mannerisms and actions; (3) using direct quotations in a characteristic manner; (4) giving opinions of others about him; and (5) showing how his friends, associates, and employees react to him. Any combination of methods should be used that will enable the writer to make his readers feel they have met the person face to face, heard him speak, seen him act, and know his thoughts or opinions sufficiently to understand his past life and see how he attained success.

The reader may be enabled to visualize the subject through

a short opening paragraph of vivid sentences that (1) dramatize the hero before he attained success or renown, (2) describe the person as he is now, after he has become known, (3) answer the question of what is the secret of his success, (4) quote the motto or principle by which the subject has lived and to which he attributes his success, or (5) give the chronological beginning, if that is of sufficient interest. No matter how the story is written, it must be handled sympathetically. If the article concerns one who has overcome physical handicaps, it must be free from any suggestion of pity or it will thwart the very purpose for which it was written.

Personality sketches, more than any other kind of article, demand that the writer have a definite purpose, as well as market, in mind before beginning to write. If the article is about a person in some unique work, then its aim would be to inform. If it is about a character in a field of work that others could enter, it would instruct. If it is about someone in hazardous employment or work that requires unusual fortitude, or one who is victorious over illness or triumphs over old age, then it would inspire.

Aids in Humanizing Writer's Style. Many beginning writers overlook the advantage, both financial and inspirational, of writing personality or success stories. The field is wide and offers excellent material and well-paying markets. Such copy is eagerly sought by all kinds of publications and syndicates. Nothing brings the writer closer to humanity nor develops his understanding and sympathy (prime requisites of the writer) than does the writing of personality stories; and nothing can be more inspiring to him than to relate the achievements of men and women with the knowledge that others, too, will be inspired.

Examples of Success and Personality Sketches. How something new, even a book, may serve to suggest success and personality stories is shown by the first of the following examples. Taken from the Kansas City *Star,* the article relates how a small-town boy realized his ambition. The second, printed in the Milwaukee *Journal,* reveals character by citing incidents in the life of a man unknown outside his immediate community. The third, from *Scribner's Magazine,* emphasizes a man's success, but by so doing portrays his character also. The fourth, from the Kansas City *Star,* suggested by a name in the Hall of Fame, shows what a writer may do with historical sketches. Each was illustrated with an informal snapshot of the subject of the sketch.

(1)

A KANSAN IN STRIFE-TORN ASIA, WRITING HISTORY ON THE SCENE *

The Career of Miles W. Vaughn Is an Odyssey of Modern Newspaper Work, in Which a Native of Winfield Meets Revolutionary Figures and Army Leaders, Interprets Crises, Reports Battles and Has Personal Adventures That Make Good Copy in a New Book.

Toward the close of the horse and buggy era the chautauqua was a leading force for culture in the middle West. However much the sophisticates might sneer, these annual 2-week visits of preachers, lecturers and musicians brought a glimpse of the outside world unknown before the days of radio.

One of the leading chautauquas was at Winfield, known as "the Athens of Kansas." A permanent set of buildings dotted beautiful Island Park and under the great walnut trees tents were set up as quarters for the hundreds who flocked in from all the states around for the annual midsummer season.

From that background there emerged a group of young men who were to make their mark in the newspaper world. Starting out on one of the two papers then published in the town, these Winfield boys went afield to become widely known in the profession as news service or newspaper editors from New York to Portland, Ore., from Chicago to Dallas.

In that contemporary group grew up a short, stocky, pink-faced boy who secretly nourished an ambition to be a newspaper man. He had been known since infancy as "Peg" Vaughn. From the lec-

* Reprinted by permission of the Kansas City *Star.*

tures at the chautauqua and the Sunday school lessons at the Methodist church he gained particularly the desire to visit the orient and set down the strange habits and thoughts of the far eastern people.

Road to Outside World

Since he had started working in a drug store in his odd hours while attending high school, the beginner's class of newspaper instruction on the *Courier* or the *Free Press* appeared closed. But the day he graduated from high school—an event remembered after twenty years in Winfield, since it required almost a city ordinance to get him in long pants for the graduation exercise—he announced he was going to K. U. to study journalism.

That was along about 1911. After completing his course in the university, in which he worked on the Lawrence *Journal-World*, Vaughn went to the Salina *Journal* and, after that novitiate, to the Chicago office of the United Press. Two periods on The Kansas City *Star* before and after the war, a return to the news service, three years in South America prepared Vaughn for his big chance as far eastern manager for his service with headquarters in Tokio.

So Miles W. Vaughn, who dreamed of being a newspaper man in far places while drawing sodas at the Bird drug store, realized his ambition. Now he has written a book. After nine years in the far East, during which he became a first hand observer of stirring events and a personal acquaintance of most of the important actors, he has given his viewpoint of that vague politico-military mare's nest in "Covering the Far East," issued under the imprint of Covici-Friede, New York.

The Book Takes Form

Vaughn had not intended to write a book, although he had kept a diary. The decision to transform his notes into a history was made after he returned to an editorial post in the New York office of his association during one of the times when the Sino-Japanese situation was in another of its critical stages. So intimate was his knowledge of the orient that he was able to write lucid interpretations of the confusion of motives behind the attempted Japanese army coup without leaving his desk in New York. The secret lay in the fact that his ambition to know these people as people had caused him to live with the Chinese and Japanese as one of them. In fact, when he was in Pekin during a crisis he was almost ostracized by the European colony for associating with the natives on a basis of friendship.

Vaughn doesn't mention that incident in his book, but he does describe his European compatriots overseas:

"In all the years I lived in the orient it remained to me a mystery how much misinformation the average 'treaty port' occidental resident can acquire. . . . One cannot understand the blindness of many occidentals long resident in the orient who refuse steadfastly to use the common sense with which they were born or to see that which is in front of their eyes.

"The answer, I suppose, is that the average human is a creature of emotion; that he believes what he wants to believe and sees only what he wants to see."

Vaughn's expert analysis of eastern affairs caused publishers to seek him out and he finally agreed to a contract, took a month's vacation and turned out a book which will prove of interest to anyone desiring to know what the oriental trouble is all about and what kind of men the chief actors are.

Life of a Correspondent

"Covering the Far East" is not a travel book and neither is it an adventure volume, although naturally, in his travels through war-torn China, Vaughn had many experiences which appear the height of adventure to home-tied Americans. The book discloses, with no effort to stress the point, that the newspaper man who attends to his own business and treats with courtesy those he meets usually will get along even in strange ports.

Vaughn early picked up a philosophy which he enlarged as he went along. "When I began to travel the world after graduation from the university I found my hardest task was unlearning the history I had been taught in school," he writes. Then, after a hot experience covering race riots in St. Louis before he ever went overseas, he learned, "all men are brothers under their skins, brothers in that none of them is very far removed from the brute. And that difference in color is only an excuse for brutality—one of those 'reasons' for which even the most primitive of men seek before they do murder." And again:

"I have seen a dozen revolutions and all of them have been along entirely different lines; springing from different immediate causes; but the broad motivation behind each has been the same—the desire of mankind to improve, to gain more power and comfort, to create a better world for future generations.

"Rebellions that fail often are as important as those that succeed, for each is a part of a pattern which must be completed if the inevitable evolution of society is to go on.

The Run of Revolution

"I was to see revolution in China, the backwash of the Bolshevik revolution in Russia, the strange rebellion of the ultranationalists and military elements in Japan against what they believed to be an ineffective parliamentary government, the bloodless revolution in the Philippines which hastened the decision of the United States to grant independence to the islanders, ineffective movements in Java and Siam, and the edge of Gandhi's movement in India. And in all of them I was to see the same primary urge—for greater freedom, for a better life."

So he tells the story of the present day far East, the nationalist movement in China, the Russian effort to set up a Soviet state in the one-time celestial kingdom; the power, the jealousies and the cruelty of the war lords. Chang Chung-chang, the huge brute of a coolie who became commander of an army, springs to life at his great orgies where he drinks brandy in 8-ounce goblets and feasts hour after hour, and then booms with laughter when he shoots a cowering editor through the head with a pistol. Chiang Kai-shek, Feng Yu-hsiang, Chang Tso-lin, Gen. Sadi Araki, even the Emperor Hirohito are made human if not at all times understandable to the western mind. The chapter on the enthronement of Emperor Hirohito is a colorful description of a ceremony old as the ages but little understood outside Japan.

There are lighter moments; Vaughn's adventure with the little geisha who wanted to go to New York; the incident of the half caste young girl revolutionist, Mai Lin, part Chinese, part French; the glimpse of Rayna Prohme, the red-headed Jewess Vincent Sheean immortalized in "Personal History."

"Vincent saw Rayna as one of the remarkable women of all time," Vaughn writes. "To me she was merely a stubborn American girl filled with half digested revolutionary ideas and almost totally lacking in common sense."

Vaughn keeps that realistic attitude all through the book. In fact, after wading through most of the isms of the world, he ends up with the self-selected label of realist.

J. M. C.

(2)

'SO WE WALKED!' *

No Roads, Temperature Was 20 Below Zero, the Snow Two Feet Deep, and the Nearest Shelter Was 69 Miles Away, but We had to Get to Our Job, Says Norwegian Pioneer Who, With 40 Others, Survived the Ordeal; a Cobbler for 50 Years in One Town.

This should have been written by a Rolvaag or a Hamsun, or, better yet, by one of the old bards who sang of the deeds of men in the days of the Vikings. But they are not here; one of a softer breed must write of the strong.

At Prentice, in Price county, Wisconsin, a white haired, rather bulky shoemaker pounds and pegs every day, putting "lifts" on heels for young girls and nailing stout soles to heavy boots. To the town he is "S.T." At the postoffice his mail is addressed to S. T. Nelson. He has made and repaired shoes there for 50 years; this summer he will be 80 years old, though he seems no more than 60.

It was to talk of 50 years in the shoemaking trade that the call by the reporter was made. Fifty years seems a long time to work in one town at one job, but soon the question arose: "Why not." For "S.T." is one of the iron blood, a man of steel still under his deceptive padding. He once walked 69 miles through knee deep snow with the temperature far below zero, without food or water, in one 23-hour stretch! Why shouldn't he last, 50 years and more, at any trade?

* * *

"What? You want to put something about me in a paper?" A snort of derision as he picked up nails and kept on pounding. His mouth puckered under the bristling white mustache and his blue eyes peered sharply through his small gold-rimmed glasses.

"Put me in the paper! No, S-sir!"

There was just enough drag on some of the vowels, just enough

* Reprinted by permission of the Milwaukee *Journal*.

extra pressure behind the sibilants, to betray his Norwegian mother tongue. But the reporter knew something else about the old school Norwegians, about their ingrained modesty and manners of refusal. Many a hungry Norwegian has stayed hungry because American born hosts haven't understood that he was just being polite when he refused a meal two or three times in as many breaths. Here was the same hanging back, every sentence of an interview would have to be coaxed as a matter of etiquette.

Well, yes, he had learned the trade, learned it well, as they do in the old country. Two years at Kristiansund, two years at Trondhjem, a hitch in the king's army, then to America.

"Yes, they shipped me over all the lakes in God's country. I got to Milwaukee in 1880, by boat. There wasn't much there then, I tell you. The grand encampment of the G.A.R. was being held there that year. I saw Gen. Grant and Gen. Sherman and— Say! You're not putting that down, are you? Well, I never—hmmph!"

A stomp around the shop in mock indignation, then back to the standing bench. Well, it seemed funny that anyone should want to know, but after he came to this country he worked at his trade in several cities in Minnesota and even in Canada. That, he thought, was quite a joke.

"That makes me a Canadian and an American and a Norwegian," he laughed. The conversation was going better now.

And how had he got to Prentice? Walked, by God; walked from Cameron. A flash of pride behind the gold rims, the pride of the oldtimers in having been "good men."

"Yes, that I can tell you about, all right. Let me see. It was in 1886; there was a lot of snow that year. I had left Faribault, Minn., Jan. 7. We were snowbound for days at Ramsey. Maybe you know where that is. We got to La Crosse Jan. 11. Well, I stayed at La Crosse five or six weeks and then I hired out as a sort of foreman or straw boss to the Soo line to clear a right of way up in this country. They shipped 42 of us to Cameron in a box car, they called it Cameron Junction then, and eight miles east of there was the end of the tracks. We got there Feb. 20 at 8 o'clock at night. It was 69 miles to Millrue, just west of here. Boy, was it dark and cold! No place to stop and not a house between here and there. No Ladysmith, no Bruce, no Weyerhauser, nothing at all but a blazed trail. So we walked."

* * *

"So we walked." There it was in three words, the epitome of the courage and work of the Scandinavian immigrant of 50 and more years ago. No beating of drums, no heroics, no oratory on high purposes, no flame of adventure. Sixty-nine miles to the next place. "So we walked." Perhaps, romanticists to the contrary, that was the stolid, realistic spirit in which the Vikings spread over the western seas a thousand years ago—"so we sailed."

* * *

The shoe soles were getting Nelson's full attention again so he had to be started over.

"How cold was it?"

"Cold? At least 20 below, colder part of the time. Two or three feet of snow, and more in spots, all the way. But we made it, or most of us."

"Go ahead. How did you start out?"

"Well, there was no such thing as staying there. So I said, 'Well, boys, we better start hiking.' We were all big Swedes and big Norwegians except one little fellow. All tough. I mean physically tough, we weren't criminals, you know. Everybody had a pack on his back and a pint bottle of alcohol in his pocket.

"Everybody was feeling good then. Hollering and whooping. I didn't drink much in those days—I never have, just some beer now and then or something like that—and I thought to myself, 'You boys will get tired of that before long.' And sure enough. When they started they made so much noise it would scare a bear out of the country. A bear? You could scare a lion out with that noise. At 11 o'clock you couldn't hear a word.

"Well, we walked all night and all the next day. Not a bite to eat, not a bit of drinking water. Once in a while we'd take a little snow. We didn't see a soul, just that trail.

"The end of that day, at 7 o'clock, I and that little bit of a Norwegian got to Millrue. There a contractor had a big tent and we stopped. The others came in by twos and threes all during the night and the next day. No, not one of them was frostbitten. But I know there were two who never came through. We never found out what happened to them. Years later a fellow named Dixon out near Catawba told me they'd found a skeleton close to that trail. That must have been one of them; of course you can't tell."

"You must have been pretty weak and tired after that hike."

"Tired? No-o-o. In those days we didn't know what it meant to be tired. But I tell you, when we went into that tent I asked if we could get supper there and they said, 'yes, for 25 cents.' Well, that was all right, I had 35 cents in my pocket, and you can believe me, I got my money's worth!

"Then, you know, we had to walk 25 miles further to the place we worked, at McCord. We got there the next night; of course we'd had a good night's sleep."

The reporter couldn't help but think of his own puffing after a few blocks through last winter's worst.

"But how did you get through that first night? How did you keep to the trail?"

"Well, sir," and a meditative stare at something outside the door, "that's a conundrum to me to this day. I don't know how we kept the trail. But we did."

* * *

That's the end of the part about the walk. Shoemaking, by bare mention, seems an anti-climax. But shoemaking was strenuous in those hard days; "S.T." didn't enter a softer life when he quit his woods clearing work a few weeks later and dug his cobbling tools out of his pack. He started a shop in Prentice and then walked from lumber camp to lumber camp, measuring lumberjacks' feet for boots. Lumberjacks paid good money for leather, waterproof boots in those days. It was before the advent of the rubber bottom. Soon "S.T." had other shoemakers working for him, as many as four at some times.

"Shoemakers came around like lumberjacks in those days. Here was our shop—" picking up four or five tools in his big fist and motioning toward the last. "Some shoemakers had big shops. John Lundgren, at Fifield, had 13 men working the year 'round, but that didn't keep up.

"Look here," searching out a small four-page pamphlet, "I even had a catalog, running in competition to Montgomery Ward. We used to make the entire shoe. I still do sometimes; some of the old customers send for them. I make my own, too."

From under the bench he produced a partly completed shoe, ready for the sole. It was a neat job, as complete in all details as any machine made shoe.

"That will fit. These I've got on are store shoes, see how they run over. Now don't put that down. Oh, well, I guess it's all right.

"Buckskin? I never would have it. Lots of people wanted me to make moccasins but I said, 'Let the Indians do that. It isn't shoemaking.' Ladies' shoes? I can make them; I learned that in the old country. When I first came here the only women were—well, you know the kind of women there were in these towns. I had to make high top shoes for some of them. It was all snow in the winter and swamp in the summer, except on the railroad tracks. They had to have them."

The rubber bottoms brought the machines; the shoemakers couldn't stitch them tight to the leather tops by hand without tedious and hard work. Since that first machine "S.T." has worn out five sewing machines and four benches. He has been burned out more than once and started over. His sons are grown and departed. His old cronies and political friends—"S.T." has been in politics, too—have been replaced by new generations, but he endures and goes on. He stays alive with the new, kidding his young customers, taking an active part in the village which he has watched grow from a handful to a booming lumber town and then drop to fewer than 500. He is plugging for new paving on Highway 13 and is writing a continued history of the early days for the weekly paper.

Prentice goes to him for advice and is proud of him. It should be while it has the chance; they're not casting men in that mold these days.

W. L.

(3)

STEVE HANNAGAN *

By Stanley Jones

"According to Hannagan . . ."

Hardly a day passes without the printing of these three words in the paragraphs of some of the country's leading newspapermen. It is the three-note symbol—or sign-off—which accompanies fresh publicity on Steve Hannagan's clients.

It is also the tributary tagline of newspapermen who like Hannagan not only for his news, but for himself. Steve is a newspaperman's press agent. Reared in the newspaper business, he was writing signed articles for metropolitan dailies at seventeen, direct-

* Reprinted by permission of *Scribner's* and Mr. Stanley Jones.

ing publicity for the first event to attract 100,000 paid spectators at twenty. Now only thirty-eight, he has become a living myth, one of the most successful press agents in the country.

Most people accept Hollywood's portrait of a press agent as a stunt man, without realizing that he has come to be more potent, socially speaking, than a hundred Nicholas Murray Butlers all talking at once. Publicity grabbing may be part of his work, or none—his main task may be to keep his client *out* of the papers. The press agent affects the lives of millions of persons because he has a hand in the preparation of material for the newspapers, magazines, newsreels, movies, radio, and other avenues of attention. He influences in ways subtle and otherwise what we eat, where we go, what we think. And his most effective work is done, not among "the masses," but among the middle- and higher-income brackets where God is supposed to have distributed brains more plentifully. He is the motivating force in the spending of millions of dollars every year.

II

In an age of "public relations counselors" Hannagan calls himself a press agent, and he will admit, under severe grilling, that he is a good one. His record indicates that he is not talking through his hat, which he wears cocked on the side of his head in the oblique fashion of the late Odd McIntyre, an early idol.

Hannagan started out from Lafayette, Indiana, to write his way to fortune. His principal equipment consisted of a cap, a grin like a slashed cantaloupe, a nose for news, and a terrific amount of energy. He has today, as then, the sustained energy of a turbine with direct pipe line to a gusher. Words do not issue from Hannagan in streams; they explode in jets. Behind a shrewd Irish-American face, thoughts stampede for the exits of expression. When they burst forth, marshaled by quick gestures, no one within earshot is in any doubt as to where Hannagan stands.

Leaving the town of Lafayette, Hannagan paused briefly at Purdue University. To his logical mind, it seemed illogical that a student should be making more money than the professors who taught him. At the time, he was earning $28.50 a week as City Editor of the Lafayette *Morning Journal,* plus $25 a week as correspondent for metropolitan newspapers. At nineteen, then, he took a step which he was later to repeat. He accepted a decrease in income to write sports for a "bigger town" paper, the Indianapolis *Star*—salary $30 a week.

Hannagan next took a flier at advertising copy. The Russell M. Seeds Company hired him to extol "Pinex," a home cough syrup, Milk's Emulsion, and "Don Sung," a Chinese remedy which made hens lay . . . according to Hannagan. He also advertised the Stutz Motor Company's "Bearcat" car. So ran the road to the Indianapolis Motor Speedway, his first big-time promotion.

The first 500-Mile Race roared into America's motor consciousness in 1911. It attracted some thirty dare-devils, drew a crowd of 50,000. When it was resumed, after a lapse in 1917 and 1918 because the Speedway had been used as a flying field, directors became dissatisfied with the publicity. Carl G. Fisher, who had $5,000,000 in his pocket from the sale of his Prest-O-Lite Company, hired young Hannagan to step it up. Automobile reporting took a new turn. Hitherto concerned almost exclusively with motor parts and their workings, it lacked human interest. Not knowing a spark plug from a crankshaft, Steve did the only thing a good reporter could do—he wrote about the men who drove the cars. Tommy Milton, Ralph DePalma, Barney Oldfield, Roscoe Sarles, Joe Boyer, Howdy Wilcox. Hannagan's typewriter spilled their lives, their families, their superstitions, their "color" into columns from coast to coast.

Editors liked these faster paced stories. The Speedway got more publicity than it had ever had . . . crowds got bigger . . . and Hannagan became as much a part of the Indianapolis motor classic as the checkered finish flag. Last year 170,000 people paid to witness its thrills. Hannagan's outfit still supervises this promotion, but most of the work is now done by Joe Copps, one of Hannagan's associates.

In 1921, Hannagan flew all over the country with Captain Eddie Rickenbacker, who was then promoting the Rickenbacker motorcar. In this interim between Speedway races, he had touched fame in the persons of Ray Long, Jimmy Quirk, Roy Howard, and O. O. McIntyre—of whom only Howard now survives. These contacts fired him with an urge to go to New York. Howard sent him to Karl Bickel, then president of United Press, who hired him at $50 a week. Hannagan was willing, again, to slash his income to get to a larger field.

From United Press, in which he covered anything from Police to Features, he did a long stretch with N. E. A. Service. With this background, plus a flair for contacts and business, Hannagan was now ready for the job which made him best known.

III

Having watched his protégé vindicate his choice at the Indianapolis Speedway, Carl Fisher turned South, to build an incredible pleasure empire out of nothing. He pumped sand and soil from the floor of Biscayne Bay over the stumps of a mangrove thicket to make Miami Beach. In 1923 he called Hannagan to tell the unsuspecting world about it.

Hannagan drove straight to the heart of things. What did he have that California lacked? This: You could bathe here in January in a surf warmer than Los Angeles' in August. And what is the chief crowd come-on in surf bathing? "Why, LEGS, you damn fool!" said realist Hannagan. *Only* in Florida waters could hard-pressed newspaper editors find pictures of Gorgeous Girls with Lovely Legs in midwinter.

Riding this simple yet compelling sales theme, Steve Hannagan built publicity into an art and a big business at Miami Beach. In the doing, he created the Miami Beach News Bureau, a publicity service which has been the model for countless other resorts. His Florida staff consists of eleven old-time newspapermen, headed by competent Joe Copps, a placid native son. They are on the job five months a year, and the municipality esteems Hannagan's services to the tune of $25,000 a season.

How does the city estimate its dollars and cents return on this investment? In the past years many building permits have been issued for new construction in Miami Beach to a figure exceeding $30,-000,000. Yacht anchorage, another business barometer, continues to rise. If all the Miami Beach news developed by Hannagan had to be bought at space rates, it would probably run to more than a million dollars.

Hannagan refuses to estimate—or professes to refuse to estimate—publicity value by the number of clippings it draws. He has other ways. "At Miami Beach, we use garbage to check our attendance. All garbage is either scowed miles out into the ocean for dumping, or sent to Miami's incinerator. In either case it must be paid for by weight. So we keep a very accurate check on the 'Garbage Graph' at Miami Beach—its ups and downs tell us exactly how we're doin' in the number of visitors."

"Home-town paper please note" was another notable Hannagan origination. Credit Steve with the idea of sending pictures and write-ups to home-town papers. This stroke, a part of his fundamental merchandising at Miami Beach, was engendered purely by his own small-town heritage. *"Anybody,"* he says, "from *any* town, who went to Florida in the winter and could be pictured in a bathing suit, was important enough for a picture back home."

In pictorial news reporting, both static and newsreel, Hannagan relies a great deal on one thing—contrasts. Bathing girls on skis . . . Fur wraps over bathing suits in fashion shows . . . Ice hockey in tropic surroundings . . . Santa Claus in swimming. Along with his girls, however, Steve Hannagan developed some rather unusual rules for his press-agenting. He covers bad news in his territories, such as robberies, shootings, or hurricanes, with the same detail accorded the good. All he asks, blow fair or foul, is that MIAMI BEACH be mentioned.

One of his first wires to the United Press read: "FLASH—Julius Fleischmann just dropped dead on polo field here don't forget MIAMI BEACH date line." He reported the doings of Alphonse Capone, whose Palm Island home was just across the Bay from the Yacht estate of William K. Vanderbilt, with the same factual care devoted to visiting bluebloods, journeymen pugilists, or record swordfish.

This strange conduct on the part of a press agent won the press, traditionally suspicious of the free-space boys. Both businessmen and public relations counsels can sit at the knobby Hannagan knee and learn simple things of value from the way Miami Beach was promoted from a sand spit into a highly profitable pleasure resort. Hannagan himself might say:

"Be honest about your aims. If your clients have a real purpose for their product, their project, or themselves, you can be truthful and accurate. People will always go for your stuff—*if* it has news and is interestingly presented.

"When trouble crops up, don't run from it. No man in a jam ever hides if his conscience is clear and if he wants to remain in a business which *depends* on good will.

"Once you've won the confidence of people, don't ask too many favors."

Hannagan gets mad when anyone suggests that a few favors judiciously distributed among friends might give him an assist or two. He says, "I've got a lot of friends and if you'll show me the personal-service business that can be run without them, I'll buy the drinks. Every man past the panty-waist stage knows that the world revolves on a 'You kiss me and I'll kiss you axis.' I get help and I like to think I offer some in return."

Hannagan doesn't care much for any distinction between news that just happens and news that is created—"as long," he says, "as the event *actually* occurs. We do lots of crazy things in our pursuit of contrasts for our publicity releases. In one season at Miami Beach we had an Austrian nobleman sliding down a manufactured snow slide on skis, bang into a swimming pool with a background of palm trees. At the same time, with snow packed deep around the hot springs pool out at a Western winter resort, we had a girl in a bathing suit diving off a springboard covered with snow!

"These things were true—they happened. Hence, they are honest news."

IV

From 1924 on, Hannagan handled not only Miami Beach and the Indianapolis Speedway, but several interesting people. Let it be said here that he will attempt to build nobody into a name personality unless that person has a legitimate business reason. Socialites and similar fry find no welcome at Hannagan's house. A prize fighter, on the other hand, or a dance team (Veloz and Yolanda are clients)—they're "business" in themselves.

Hannigan spent part of every year from 1924 on with Gene Tunney, a type of pugilist new to the sports world. Hannagan took stock, recognized the paradox of genuiness and novelty, and exploited the fact that Tunney was "The prize fighter who read Shakespeare." He did this long before a match with Dempsey was projected and remained with Tunney until he retired. Thereafter, with Dempsey, Hannagan publicized the Sharkey-Stribling fight at Miami Beach in 1928, when Tex Rickard died. Their efforts resulted in a gross of $407,000—the second largest non-championship gate in boxing history.

The build-up of the fight wasn't easy, and Hannagan's friends liked to kid him about one incident. The news broke that Dempsey had been shot at by a night prowler. Reporters flocked to the scene, but not a bullet hole in the house could be found. This caused the Westbrook Peglers to begin raising their eyebrows, and the next day, according to some of the reporters, brought a nice, obvious bullet hole. Hannagan is still being kidded about this, but in his serious moments he claims he was framed.

Gar Wood is a sportsman who can thank Hannagan for righting his public relations speedboat after the Harmsworth Cup fiasco with English Kaye Don in 1931.

Before the race, reporters had heard Wood say that he was going to lead Don over the line. By so doing—"beating the gun" was what it amounted to—Don would have to turn with Wood and cross the starting line a second time, leaving Wood's *second* boat in the race (an inferior one) to go on to a hollow victory. So it worked out, with the added misfortune that the Englishman upset at high speed in Wood's wake during the race. The whole affair was a tragedy of misunderstanding, and Gar Wood was accused of very poor sportsmanship.

Hannagan induced Wood to come to New York. There Wood's pre-race remark was explained to the press: "Wood *had* stated that he intended to lead Don over the line. But by 'leading,' he meant to go over ahead of his rival, *not* ahead of the gun. He had intended to cut it close enough to stay within the rules, but to reach the first turn *first*. This was of vital importance, since the boats were evenly matched, and experts agreed that the strategy of victory lay in the race to the first turn."

In any event, Hannagan did a job. To wind things up, Wood came to New York the following year, when Don returned. He met him at the pier, posed with him for news shots, greeted him later at Detroit. In addition, he offered the Englishman all facilities for participation, such as boat lifts and mechanics. In every possible way, Gar Wood lived a denial that there had been any bad sportsmanship on his part in the past or could be in the future.

V

In March of 1936, Hannagan received a phone call in Hollywood from W. Averell Harriman, chairman of the board of the Union Pacific Railroad. Steve was handling publicity for the railroad then, and Harriman said: "I've had an Austrian ski expert named Count Felix Schaffgotsch combing the country for a winter-sports location. We want something that will match anything in Switzerland. The Count thinks he has it. It's a valley in Idaho, near a place called Ketchum. Please give me your impressions on it."

Hannagan flew to Pocatello, Idaho. There he transferred to train, went in to Shoshone, end of the U. P. junction line between Shoshone and Ketchum, and rose at 5. A.M. He was arrayed in a light tweed suit, a camel's-hair coat, and a pair of oversized galoshes borrowed from a trainman. With him was William M. Jeffers, now president of Union Pacific.

They made the bleak trip on a motorized handcar, proceeded from Ketchum as far as an automobile could go, and were thence conveyed to the Brass Ranch in a horse-drawn sleigh with a pot-bellied iron stove in the front of it. They then got out and walked the remaining distance—an excruciating ordeal for Hannagan, who rides a taxicab from one street corner to the next.

"I couldn't see," recalls Hannagan, "why any living thing except a St. Bernard on a rescue expedition should ever want to go there. I was convinced that the Count was nuts, and that Harriman himself was half-gone. Right at that moment, however, the sun wheeled up over the Sawtooth Mountains. Because the place is a natural amphitheater protected from wind, I had loosened my overcoat. Half an hour later I took it off. And one hour later I removed my suit coat and vest, and was perspiring at every step in the snow!"

"This is *different*!" said Hannagan. "Why a fellow could strip and take a sun bath right out here!"

Somebody else said, "There's a hot-water spring up the hill where you can take a bath, with deep snow all around."

"Let's see it," said Steve.

Falling and sprawling, they plodded up the valley to the spring. Then Hannagan really got the picture—the whole of it. "This *is* different!" he exclaimed. "I can see a fine hotel here. A skating rink there. An open-air, glass-walled, hot-water swimming pool with snow banked four feet deep around the rim and two feet of it on the springboards. Then a ski-lift with seats, to haul you up to the top of these mountains. Let's make this a modern *American* winter resort . . . such as the world has never seen. And for our theme song, 'winter sports in a summer climate.' "

A hundred names were discussed for the place. The directors wanted to call it "Ketchum." Hannagan opposed this violently. Harriman finally picked "Sun Valley"—just one day before the first story was released in August, 1936. On December 21 the hotel opened with terrific fanfare—and no snow—for the first time in fifty-four years!

Harriman wired all who had made reservations that there was no ski snow in the valley, but plenty of it within ten miles. If they would come, they would not only be transported to the snow, but would be *guests* of Sun Valley Lodge until there was skiing snow in the Valley. On December 26 ("St. Stephen's day," recalls Steve Hannagan) snow fell. And two days later, when a special train of Hollywood celebrities arrived under Tour Manager Hannagan, it was up to your hocks.

The rush never stopped. In the following summer—1937—a new hotel and complete village were built, including a modern movie theater and a night club. The winter of 1937 showed no slack-off. It is evident that the $2,500,000 which the Union Pacific has put into the project will prove one of the soundest of corporation investments. A cursory checkup of the publicity (which brought in the cash customers) reveals a dozen articles in magazines such as *Harper's Bazaar, Vogue, Cosmopolitan, Spur, Town and Country, The American, Collier's, Time, The New Yorker* (none of them for tabloid minds), nearly 3000 clippings in newspapers, two dozen newsreels, and a sequence in at least one photoplay, *She Met Him in Paris.* This does not include commercial tie-ups where other concerns plugged Sun Valley in their paid advertising.

Resort promotions of this character are the more remarkable when one knows that Hannagan wouldn't don a pair of skis himself for any amount of money, and that he swims only three or four times a year. He leaves those things to his partner, Larry Smits. When Hannagan wants exercise, he goes up to Bill Brown's farm for occasional two-week stretches, which include plenty of road work, handball, and exercises.

So successful has he been with Miami Beach and Sun Valley, however, that he has lately been given the publicizing of Puerto Rico. The place is to his liking; already he refers to it enthusiastically as "The Honolulu of the East."

VI

Hannagan is frank about some of his stunts that flopped. "For eleven years," he admits, "we tried to make a movie of roller-skate tennis on cement courts at Miami Beach. But we couldn't do it for the simple yet incredible reason that no one in Miami Beach could roller-skate! Then, when we had just about given it up, one of those

'Roller Derbies' rolled into town and made it easy." A current newsreel shot shows a Miami Beach basketball game on roller skates—with the costumes specially designed to bring out the beautiful legs of the girl players.

About the only big venture that failed to pan out as anticipated was 10,000-acre Montauk Manor, built by Carl Fisher at a cost of $12,000,000, on the tip of Long Island. But Hannagan still has the utmost confidence that Montauk, "last frontier on the Eastern Seaboard," will yet rise to rank as an outstanding summer resort. Designed by Fisher to be the Miami Beach of the North for summer pleasures, it was denied a real presentation to the public by two crippling factors: (1) the 1926 Florida hurricane which required much of Fisher's capital for repairs, and (2) the depression of 1929.

Another trick Hannagan admits he might have missed was that of an electric razor: "They told me to use it for a month, which I did. But I finally concluded that if a stupid guy like myself couldn't get anywhere with it, nobody else could. So I refused the account, and the sizable amount of money it involved.

Contrasted to the ones that didn't come off, Steve Hannagan undoubtedly could name a few which, while denied publicity themselves, were models of adroit handling of touchy situations. Associates in the business give Hannagan chief credit for the almost miraculous conversion of Sad Sam Insull, for instance, from a reprehensible fugitive into a gentle, misunderstood old man.

A glance at newspaper files of 1934 recalls the circumstances: The billion dollar Insull empire had fallen, and Mr. Insull had fled to Greece. He was finally brought back, after long legal palaverings which almost led to the use of the U. S. Navy as a means of persuasion. At the trial in Chicago a startling change in demeanor was noticeable. He hadn't a dollar in the world, he told reporters. Nothing save the pittance which his son saved out of his salary. He rode from his modest hotel to the trial in an omnibus where all the world could note the new humility induced by misfortune. Asked how one so poor could charter a ship, as he had done in Greece when trying to escape extradition, he said simply, "I had my friends. Thank God, I still have my friends."

Yet the friends who would charter a steamer now refused to shower down a dollar a day for cab fare. Equally stunning was the new Insull attitude toward the press. In the old days, reporters grew long beards in Insull's anteroom waiting to see him. Yet now he hobnobbed in court with one and all, posed for photographers, and apologized for not having met these splendid chaps before. He was even detected (by some surprising on-the-spot genius) giving up his seat in a cheap movie house to an old lady and a little child. All these things affected public opinion. Gradually the notion grew that no good would come from slapping a seventy-five-year-old man into the sneezer for doing what he had done, and Sam was acquitted.

Hannagan simply will not discuss the Insull affair. He won't talk, and that is that. Friends believe he regrets he ever handled the case. On his wall, among the pugilists and presidents and columnists, is a framed photograph of a friendly, smiling Insull in a gray Homburg and beautifully tailored overcoat. It is inscribed, with the simplicity of the truly sincere, "To Steve Hannagan, with appreciation, Samuel Insull. April 19, 1937." It is probably one of the most sincere of all the Hannagan inscriptions. . . .

Although Hannagan's fees, observers say, range from $10,000 to $50,000 a year, it is evident that his net earnings are not comparable to his fees. This is because of his investigations and groundwork, and the man power and travel demanded on his accounts. It is Hannagan's boast that for coverage he uses twice as many men on any job as competitors. And publicity for a Hannagan account is never enough in itself—he insists that his efforts be backed up by sound advertising. He would be very foolish if he didn't.

VII

His New York office overlooks Park Avenue. It reflects the glittering world of "names" with whom he works. Packed solidly around the walls, floor to ceiling, are signed photographs of celebrities. A glance confirms the nature of Hannagan's friendships: fighters, Presidents of the U. S., show girls, pilots, big businessmen, cartoonists, writers, columnists.

Dozens of phone calls pour in during the Hannagan work day, which generally touches sixteen hours. Motion-picture executives . . . (about 100 newsreels a year are devoted to Hannagan's ideas) . . . job-seekers . . . clients seeking qualified help . . . writers and composers requesting aid in publishing. Despite the enormity of the task, all receive attention. The Hannagan memory shames an elephant, and he remembers the insignificant things which cement friendships.

Hannagan arrives at the office at 9:30 A.M. every day. No night-before dallying with the wits and beauties ever cracks this rule. He is in business first of all; a hard-headed, demanding business, bristling with emergencies. Hannagan's friends respect him for the manner in which he swings this job, while retaining the common touch which is his chief charm.

Hannagan spends a lot of money on clothes and haberdashery, though his wardrobe will never attain the fantastic sartorial heights which distinguished his youthful idol, Odd McIntyre. Every item which will stand it is initialed or signed "Steve Hannagan." This passion for personalization soars to a mad peak in a robin's-egg blue monogrammed toilet seat—gift of an old friend in the business!

Hannagan is unmarried. His living quarters in the Hotel Delmonico are modest, comfortable, undistinguished—with a single notable exception. This is the bed, designed for him by Sport Ward and Rube Goldberg. Six feet square, its deep box springs set flush with the floor. The black built-in headboard extends some five feet past the sides—a masterpiece of cunningly designed cabinets, concealed reading lights, and bookshelves.

An extremely busy man, Steve can't spend much time in it, but when he does, the ideas spout forth as he lies there in its light-blue clutches—new ideas to cajole his fellow Americans into doing things they never did before.

Steve pats the bed fondly. "It's a honey," he says.

(4)

BRINGING EDUCATION TO WOMEN BROUGHT FAME TO EMMA WILLARD *

Back in 1814, When the Instruction of Girls Was in Small Favor, a Dauntless Woman Opened a School, Made Speeches, Wrote Pamphlets and Textbooks—Today She Is One of the Seven of Her Sex in the Hall of Fame.

Only seven of the seventy-two Americans in the National Hall of Fame at New York university are women; yet two of the seven are named Willard. Better known of the two perhaps is Frances Elizabeth Willard (1839–1898), supporter of equal suffrage and outstanding figure in the Women's Christian Temperance union. But

* Reprinted by permission of the Kansas City *Star*.

equally dynamic and colorful, probably more important, is Emma Hart Willard (1787–1870).

Emma Hart Willard was the inspired type who would have been a sensation in any age, and back in the nineteenth century when she was upsetting educational tradition in New England she was indeed a nine days' wonder. Picture a handsome, intelligent woman in her early 30s, with an outlook almost as modern as that of a present-day dean of women students at the University of Missouri or Kansas; picture her moving about among the frosty masculine educators of her day, a group of professional men as stiff as their own black hats and as wooden as their cloth-covered buttons; picture her winning gradual concessions and grudging admiration from them, and you begin to appreciate the measure of genius animating the woman.

Emma Hart undoubtedly was fired by nature with talents and enthusiasms. After her marriage, in 1809, to Dr. John Willard, her hunger for knowledge drove her, in spare time from her household duties, to read his medical books, to study geometry with her nephew, to read Locke's "Essay on the Human Understanding" and Paley's "Moral Philosophy." When financial reverses struck her husband, she made the event an occasion to recoup the family fortunes and at the same time attempt the improvement of women's education. She opened a boarding school for girls, in 1814.

At that time the educating of girls was in small favor—in how small favor is indicated by Willystine Goodsell's book, "Pioneers of Women's Education in the United States" (McGraw-Hill, 1931), "Of what use book learning to women?" most parents asked. "Would it make them better cooks and seamstresses, better nurses of the sick and caretakers of children? Would not the higher education tend to make them ambitious, upset the established order?"

Famous Educational Plan

Mrs. Willard had spent several years working on her famous "Plan for Improving Female Education," and after receiving the warm approval of Governor De Witt Clinton of New York upon the manuscript, she had it published in pamphlet form at her own expense. The clarity and logic of her appeal, its freedom from bitterness, won for it a favorable hearing from many liberal-minded men. President Monroe and Thomas Jefferson are said to have approved it and John Adams, who had always encouraged his talented wife Abigail in her studies, wrote Mrs. Willard a letter of commendation.

But the plan was too "radical" for the great majority, from whom it drew jeers and ridicule.

In 1819 Mrs. Willard removed her school from Middlebury, Vt., to Waterford, N. Y., where interested citizens leased a large 3-story building to house the academy. With Governor Clinton backing her, Mrs. Willard hoped for financial aid from the New York legislature. But the prejudice of the legislators could not be overcome. A bill granting $2,000 to the school passed the senate but was voted down in the assembly. And the regents of the university of the state of New York withheld assistance from the state "literary fund."

This was a bitter disappointment to the pioneer educator. She said she felt the humilating defeat of her hopes "almost to a frenzy" and years afterward could not recall it "without agitation." But it only spurred her to more intensive effort. She brought her cause directly before the people with the expectation of thus influencing the legislators. Encouragement came sooner than she expected. Prominent citizens of Troy, N. Y., invited her to move her school to that city. In 1821 the common council of Troy adopted a resolution to raise $4,000 for purchase of a building for a female academy. Moulton's Coffee house was purchased and repaired. A board of trustees was appointed by the council, and these men in turn appointed an advisory committee of women to confer with Mrs. Willard from time to time on important matters concerning the school. Thus the active interest of a body of influential women was secured for the new experiment.

An Enrollment of Ninety

So the school was moved from Waterford to Troy. When it threw open its doors that September, ninety young women entered, representing seven states. Gradually its popularity grew. In spite of the continued refusal of state aid, the seminary eventually was placed on a sound economic basis.

Freed from financial anxiety, Mrs. Willard turned her attention to the course of study. Little by little she added courses in algebra and geometry, history, geography and natural philosophy (physics). No other girls' school in the country could boast all these "advanced" courses in the early twenties of the nineteenth century. In the teaching of geography by an appeal to the eye through charts and maps, Mrs. Willard was peculiarly successful. With little knowledge of psychology but with intelligence and zeal for the improvement of teaching, she hit upon objective methods of imparting knowledge which, in modified form, are esteemed today.

Mrs. Willard wrote a book upon the improved method of teaching geography and published it in combination with a similar work by William C. Woodbridge. The book appeared under the name of both authors in 1822 as "A System of Universal Geography on the Principles of Comparison and Classification." It was favorably received and widely circulated. This was the first of a long list of publications by Mrs. Willard designed to improve methods of teaching, not only geography, but universal history, history of the United States, and morals. Among her widely known books were "History of the United States or Republic of America" (1829), "Willard's Historic Guide to the Temple of Time and Universal History for Schools" (1849) and "Morals for the Young" (1857). Mrs. Willard was also facile at writing verse; she wrote an ode to Lafayette, and she is remembered today for her song, "Rocked in the Cradle of the Deep."

Visit of Lafayette

In 1824 when Lafayette made a triumphal tour of the country he helped to free, he accepted Mrs. Willard's invitation to visit the seminary. An arbor of evergreen was constructed for the occasion in front of the school bearing the motto in flowers: "We owe our school to freedom; freedom to Lafayette." Through this arbor came the distinguished visitor and was welcomed by Mrs. Willard and her teachers, while the girl students, in white dresses and blue sashes, sang the ode Mrs. Willard had written to the national idol. Lafayette seemed impressed both by the ode and by the school. When Mrs. Willard visited France some years later, she was invited to court balls, visited the chamber of deputies and was shown through the most noted French schools for girls.

One of Mrs. Willard's greatest services was in training and sending out to the nation's newly established schools a corps of efficient teachers. Realizing early in her career the need for trained teachers, she set out to supply it by encouraging her girls to take up teaching as a profession. She gave free tuition as a loan to promising young women too poor to meet their own expenses. During the seventeen years of her principalship of Troy seminary she is said to have lent about $75,000 to needy girls fitting themselves to teach. Each signed a contract to repay the money in time, so that other girls might have similar opportunity. However, only about half ever repaid the loan.

In 1832, after Greece had freed itself from Turkey, Mrs. Willard became interested in the improvement of the educational opportunities of the young women of Greece. She sought by organizing meetings and preparing addresses to arouse public interest in her plan for establishing a seminary. By her single-handed efforts she raised $3,000 which was applied to the founding of a school in Athens for training women teachers.

Retired but Went on Working

In 1838, when Mrs. Willard was 51 years old, she retired from active management of the school at Troy, leaving its supervision to her son, John Willard, and his wife, one of the teachers. Withdrawing to Kensington, Conn., she did not abate her work for the promotion and modernization of education. She helped Henry Barnard in his improvement of the public schools of Connecticut, organizing housewives of Kensington into the Female Common School association.

By 1845 she was carrying on a fresh campaign in New York state. Setting out in her own carriage, with a former pupil at Troy as companion, she went from town to town, speaking at institutes for teachers and pointing out ways of educational reform. Particularly, she urged the organization in every community of a committee of women to collaborate with the men in improving the training of teachers and methods of instruction. She is said to have traveled 700 miles in this crusade, instructing 500 teachers, men and women. The following year she made an 8,000-mile journey by stagecoach through states of the West and South, addressing groups of teachers and citizens interested in education.

Mrs. Willard's second trip to Europe was made in 1854 on the occasion of the World's Educational conference in London. Her fame had preceded her, and she received conspicuous attention, including a peeress's ticket to the House of Lords. Upon her return to America she made her home in a pleasant little house in the grounds of Troy seminary. She spent her time revising her textbooks, influencing by her extraordinary personality the students who came to visit and drink tea with her. Busy with congenial literary work, she lived quietly near her son and daughter-in-law, in close touch with the famous school she had founded. She died April 15, 1870, at the age of 83.

L. M.

EXERCISES

1. How many personality sketches did you find in the magazine section of your favorite newspaper?
2. Of that number, how many were concerned with unknown or comparatively unknown persons?
3. In chart form, list each personality sketch in your favorite newspaper and indicate what appeal was made to the reader in each one.
4. By adding a second column to the chart in Exercise 3, list the purpose of each sketch.
5. In a third column, list the number of pictures, charts, maps, or other illustrative material used with each article.
6. List five ideas for personality sketches for Sunday features that you could write about persons in your community, and tell briefly why you think each would make a good feature article.
7. List one idea for a story about some person who has overcome a physical handicap and list three possible markets for it.
8. In chart form, list each personality sketch in your favorite magazine and indicate the appeal to reader interest made in each.
9. In a second column to the chart in Exercise 8, indicate which one of the five methods of portraying the subject of the sketch to the reader was used for each personality sketch.
10. In a third column to the chart indicate the purpose of each article.
11. List three ideas for personality sketches that you could write about persons in your community. Indicate which you would submit to magazines or trade publications to inform, instruct, or inspire the reader. Tell briefly why you think each would make a good feature article.
12. List a series of six personality sketches that you might write for a syndicate and indicate to which syndicate you would submit the series.
13. List four possible success stories for trade publications and tell why the persons would make good subjects for articles.
14. Indicate a possible market for each of the above success stories.

Publication Analysis

Country Gentleman, Business Week, and *Hobbies*

Do not spend more than two hours on this report.

I. Identification for each magazine: Name, publishers, editors, where published, price.

II. Make-up: What to you, as a future magazine editor, are the interesting things about the make-up of the three magazines? Give reasons for your answers.

III. Advertising:

1. From the point of view of what you know about advertising, do you think the copy in each publication will appeal to the reader?
2. What did you like about the advertising in each publication and give reason?
3. What did you *not* like about the advertising in each publication and give reason?
4. What tips were suggested to you by the advertising?

IV. General policy:

1. To what types of readers do the three publications appeal?
2. Why should you as a free-lance writer know these magazines?
3. What features might you have written?
4. Anything of special interest in either publication?

V. Features: Read a personality sketch or a success story in each magazine and list five suggestions for each feature read that will enable you to write better personality sketches or success features. (Fifteen suggestions in all.)

VI. Slogans: Write a slogan for each magazine.

VII. Four tips: Source, authority, and three possible markets suggested by this study.

8 THE NARRATIVE ARTICLE

Uses Devices of Short Story. Readers like rapid action, thrilling adventure, and vivid description along with facts. The narrative article, like the short story, is therefore extremely popular with magazine readers in America. Its purpose is not only to instruct or guide the reader but to entertain him by the same devices that the short-story writer uses, except that the feature writer never uses fictitious nor exaggerated details.

A narrative article is defined as one used to present facts by using devices of the short story—conversation, rapid action, vivid description, thrilling adventure, and sustaining suspense—to heighten the effect and to entertain as well as to inform the reader.

Although similar to the interview, the personal experience, and the confession article, in that they all contain narrative, the "narrative article" is always written in the third person, whereas the others may not be. It may be somewhat like the utility article by aiming to help the reader with definite directions or advice, but it is written in a narrative-descriptive style to appeal to the reader's imagination. Its purpose is to entertain as well as to inform. It differs from the personality sketch in so far as it is not concerned with achievement from the personal point of view; nor is its purpose to inspire.

The writer will find it advantageous to present material in narrative form, if it can be so treated. It is easier, in many ways, to interest the reader and to hold his interest by presenting facts along with action and adventure. Suggestions for gathering material for the other types of articles may be applied in planning the narrative. Travel, historical, and biographical data, material presenting processes, and the results of scientific research can be presented effectively by the devices used in fiction writing.

Narrative Affords Variety in Form. In writing the article, one must remember that narrative affords variety and action and that description must be vivid enough to make the reader hear, smell, taste, feel, or see as the writer desires. The writer must, however, guard against overdoing the description in his attempt to produce dynamic impressions. The clever writer may frequently find opportunity to inject humor into his narratives, but the beginner, unless he is particularly gifted, should avoid making too great use of it. If humor is overdone, the article may be ridiculous instead of funny. Later, when one has attained skill and ease in his writing, he should attempt writing humorous narratives or adding a humorous tone to narrative articles whenever his material lends itself to such treatment. Editors pay well for articles with a humorous slant, and they find it difficult to obtain clever ones.

Large Demand Due to Popularity. By developing his ability to write narrative articles, a writer will acquire variety in style and type. He will be rewarded by facility in marketing his manuscripts, and he will be rewarded well financially. Editors constantly need well-written narratives since the popularity of feature articles written in fiction style has increased so rapidly.

Examples of Narrative Articles. Clever writers often write narratives humorously, as is the first of the following articles, which was printed in the Chicago *Daily News.* The historical narrative is well illustrated by the second article, from the Indianapolis *News.* The third, which appeared in the New York *Times* magazine section with excellent photographs, is descriptive. The fourth, from *Outdoor Life,* shows how adventure may be written with zest. The fifth, from the *Woman's Home Companion,* shows how travel lends itself to narrative treatment. Each article was illustrated with at least two photographs, and most of them had five or six.

(1)

MANY A HOP AND A SKIP FROM THE MARSH TO THE FRYING PAN FOR MR. FROG *

By William H. Fort

It probably would never occur to the casual frog-leg muncher to wonder, as he nibbles his golden brown saddle nubbin, where that delicacy came from or how much trouble it had been for somebody to get it to Chicago for him. Or Milwaukee, for that matter—or Peoria or an other town within a few hundred miles of Lake Michigan.

Frogs is frogs, no? They live in marshy meadows, don't they? And they start to croak around sundown and they're much more expensive than round steak or lamb chops. So what more is there to know?

Much more, my dear fellow. Much more. They don't make any hop, skip and a jump from their lily pad into the frying pan. Not by any means. And those terrapins, now, that are translated into soup and broiled breast of baby turtle with a fancy French title —they don't walk a thousand miles or more to meet the chef. They're stupid, but not that silly.

Have Booking Agent

No, sir, they all have a booking agent, so to speak, and if you buy turtles or frogs the chances are exactly ten to one they were "booked" for you by Messrs. E. R. Neuenfeldt and E. G. Hoffman, who run the only frog-and-turtle ranch in the middle west, so they say. The odds are ten to one because 90 per cent of all the frogs and turtles sold to Chicagoans come from their ranch, which isn't a ranch at all, and is located not in the wild and woolly of the west, but in Chicago. It consists of huge galvanized iron tanks, with barrels for the turtles, in the basement at 625 West Randolph street.

Usually there are anywhere from two to five tons of frogs croaking around in the tanks, according to John McCrorie, "foreman of

* Reprinted by permission of the Chicago *Daily News*.

the ranch," who rides herd on the frogs and who swings a 200-pound turtle by the tail with as easy nonchalance as the average person waves a flag.

Mr. Neuenfeldt got the idea for a frog ranch thirty-eight years ago, and Mr. Hoffman had the same idea around the same time, so they came to town with it and have been running ever since.

Those days, as all students of the bottle will remember, were long before prohibition was ever thought of seriously, and the frog-and-turtle market was very brisk indeed. Somehow, as Foreman McCrorie explained today, a good cocktail or a fine glass of wine just naturally seems to suggest a partnership with frog legs and turtle soup.

Eating Places Flourished

The luxurious little Richelieu hotel was still famous then, and Rector's tables were glittering their brightest, and Batcheller's, with its three stories of private dining rooms, and Billy Boyle's chop house and Kinsley's and Mike Burke's, which later became the Chicago Oyster House, and all the other oldtime eating houses for which Chicago was noted from coast to coast and back again, were operating.

"Some of our first customers," Mr. Neuenfeldt will tell you.

Demand for frog legs dropped off quite a lot during prohibition, but the business has picked up steadily and speedily since repeal. An average of a half-ton of frog legs is eaten every day now in Chicago. Some of the restaurants have their frogs sent in direct from down south, where the big jumbos are most plentiful, but that takes quite a lot of "contacting" for the average person and so most chefs find it much simpler to call Mr. Neuenfeldt on the telephone and have them delivered.

Barney's, for instance, almost next door to the "ranch"—the nearest approach to a modern counterpart of Billy Boyle's famous old chop house of the '90s and known among senators and others who have time to be expert gourmands as one of Chicago's "choice spots" —uses an average of 100 pounds a day.

Guided by Moon

Whether you can get big jumbo frogs alive depends on the moon. If there isn't any moon, or, well, maybe just a sliver or two, the supply of live ones arrives in plenty. But during the time of the month when there's a lot of moon showing—and especially in full moon time—there's nothing doing. Frogs just naturally don't like the sight of a full moon and won't show their noses from under their lily pads. During such times the customers have to be satisfied with frozen legs that arrive in iced blocks. There is always plenty of terrapin, which seem to have no inhibitions about the moon. It comes in all varieties and sizes, from five-pound diamond backs and snappers to huge deep-sea galapagos that tip the scales up to 1,000 pounds.

Besides the table variety, Mr. Neuenfeldt and Mr. Hoffman also have almost a monopoly on frogs among schools and colleges, medical schools and various dissecting laboratories. Thousands are supplied every season to both Northwestern and Chicago universities. Other thousands are pickled and jarred in formaldehyde for the convenience of fishermen.

Fussy About Types

Both Northwestern and the University of Chicago are very snooty about the type of frogs they get, Mr. Hoffman says. Northwestern wants the kind that measure around four inches from nose to toe tip. Chicago insists on frogs two sizes larger. There are also salamanders of various ages and size, to say nothing of tons of fresh-water clams on supply for either dissecting or table purposes.

There is no way of gauging in advance just how many frogs the public will eat on a certain day. There are certain regular customers, of course. Some so-called high-class bars, for instance, cook up a large supply every day to serve as a constant "free lunch" for their patrons. To the universities, high schools and other dissecting parlors go an average of another half-ton a day. Frogs are sold by the pound, like flour and sugar and potatoes and fish. And housewives can buy them for the papa's supper, if they want to, right off the farm.

Don't Grow Tame

Contrary to popular belief, it's impossible to grow tame frogs. They are all wild, and are shipped in from almost every state where they have ponds and marshes.

Wisconsin, Michigan, Illinois, Vermont, Maine, North Dakota, Mississippi, Florida and Louisiana are among the biggest "shippers." They're shipped in by subagents who hire small boys to catch them.

Among the turtles a lot of the "snappers" come from Wisconsin, but most of the diamond backs and other terrapin are sent from Florida.

(2)

BEAUTIFUL INDIANAPOLIS BRIDGES MARK PASSING OF FERRY DAYS*

By Griffith Niblack

It seems a little strange that Indianapolis—the largest city in the world not on navigable waters—can be described as a city of beautiful bridges.

The Hoosier capital has been termed "the city of beautiful homes," while various other phrases, each suitable to some characteristic quality, also have been coined.

No one, however, seems to have paid much attention to the numerous bridges that span the streams. But if all these viaducts were suddenly torn down some night, a large part of the population would be unable to get to work the next morning!

White river, Fall creek, Eagle creek, Pleasant run, Pogues run and the canal all stretch watery barriers to communication between one part of the city and another, and in an early day, these streams served to delay the transportation which already was leisurely enough.

How different from the first, crude wooden bridges are the graceful arching stone and concrete structures that now carry the traffic across the streams, but how different, too, is the traffic which is carried!

There is now a chain of approximately thirty stone and concrete bridges, many of which were planned and designed by one man, Henry W. Klaussman, a citizen of Indianapolis, now dead.

The original one, probably was the bridge in Washington street, over White river. This completely Hoosier stream was a natural barrier to the cavalcade of pioneers traveling endlessly from east to west, over the route of the national highway, which always has been one of the great east-west thoroughfares.

Ferry First Used

A ferry was first used and only a little more than a century ago, four years before the straggling little settlement on the west side of

* Reprinted by permission of the Indianapolis *News*.

the river had received a charter, the first effort was made to span the stream. The bridge, a crude, clumsy affair, was completed a year later.

It was a covered, wooden bridge, timber at that time being so plentiful it was a nuisance, and for many years it stood there, echoing to the history-making rumble of the wheels of the pioneers. And perhaps the echo was a little more triumphant when the wheels of the stage coach, brilliantly painted, clattered on the wooden floor. An east-west transportation line had been established.

A historian wrote of that time: "From morning till night there was the continual rumble of wheels, and when the rush was the greatest there was never a moment when wagons were not in sight."

Referring to the stage coaches, he said: "I think there has never been a more graceful turnout than one of those fine old stage coaches, filled inside and out with well-dressed people. We could hear the driver play his bugle as he approached the little town."

This bridge weathered the years well, but with the advent of the automobile it became outdated. Its successor was a steel bridge whose history was short lived, as a flood destroyed it.

A bridge of steel girders replaced it and this, too, met destruction in the swirling waters of the 1913 flood. An arched concrete and steel bridge, now standing, then was built. It contained twice as much material as any of the preceding structures and five times the difficulty was involved in the foundation work.

Another bridge which has had an interesting history is the Michigan road bridge. The Michigan road was an important north and south highway in the early days, traveled by stage coaches and transport wagons. Its route had been fixed by the legislature as the land had been ceded by the Potawtami tribe of Indians for road building.

At the southern end of the White river bridge was a cycle path and this intersection was a popular resting place when cycling was popular.

As the road dips down rather steep hills on either approach to the bridge, the site became used as a place to test the early automobiles, especially as to their hill climbing ability. Many demonstrations were given over the hill at the north end, and if one of these early machines could struggle up the incline, it was regarded a remarkable feat, the more so if there were four or five passengers.

The Kentucky avenue bridge over the river was a key-link in the chain of roadways that led to the important industrial part of the city. The iron structure built there in 1904 was regarded the last word in bridge construction. A few years later interurban cars sought a passage across the bridge and a short time after that it was found that the days of the structure were numbered. Signs had to be placed limiting the load and heavy traffic was detoured.

A novel bridge was built here, dedicated December 22, 1925. The structure is V-shaped, with one leg in Oliver avenue and the other in Kentucky avenue. Each leg serves a different part of the city.

The old iron or steel bridges were universally popular at one time, believed to be the best type, but they are out of the picture now. A few of them are still standing over the streams but they are largely condemned as unsafe.

When Indianapolis, growing steadily, spread across Fall creek, it marked the inauguration of a new style in bridge construction and design. The first of these was in Central avenue, completed in 1900. Now Fall creek is spanned by many of these graceful arches. The beauty of their architectural design adds a distinctive touch to the appearance of the north side.

Floods have played havoc with Indianapolis's bridge building program. In 1904, high waters swept over the canal levee northwest of the city and destroyed most of the bridges over White river. The city was in no financial condition to stand this added burden, so the county assumed the responsibility, appropriating nearly $1,000,000 for the purpose. A systematic program was adopted and work progressed rapidly until the city again was connected with the west side.

The west side was isolated in 1913, when the most disastrous flood of the city's history swept down Fall creek and White river. Many bridges were washed out. Since that time, however, the levees have been raised and strengthened and it would take a flood of unimagined proportions to break the several strong links that now connect the two parts of the city.

The canal, originally planned as a water highway and now used as a source of supply by the Indianapolis Water Company, likewise is crossed by many beautiful and sturdy concrete structures which add to the attractiveness of the city.

One of the most novel and architecturally beautiful viaducts is the Emrichsville bridge over the river at Sixteenth street. A heavy stone archway crosses the road at one end. The archway is surmounted by a tower at one corner and one gets a sudden illusion of approaching a medieval city when nearing Indianapolis through this gateway.

Likewise, one should not omit mentioning the X-shaped bridge which crosses the canal at Northwestern avenue and Sixteenth street. It was built two years ago when Sixteenth street was widened and extended to the west.

There are numerous handsome little bridges spanning Pogues run. The city solved the bridge problem for Pogues run in the downtown district when the railroad tracks were elevated several years ago. The run was a tempestuous stream, overflowing often and causing much damage. So the engineers decided the way to get rid of it was to bury it. This they did, and now Pogues run is an underground sewer through the downtown district.

(3)

WHEN FARMLAND IS SEARED BY THE DROUGHT *

A Picture of The Midwest, Its Fields and Folk When The Rain Holds Off and Even Hope Is Dimmed

By Harlan Miller

Over American farmland broods the feverish, piteous atmosphere of a sick room where a crisis impends. For half a year the indifferent heavens have sent down little more than half their customary rains. Last Winter the heavy snows covered the fields with moisture in abeyance, a promise of abundant water for the roots of the new crops. But sudden thaws sent the melted water racing down to torture the lowlands. And now, in the first weeks of Summer, growth pauses and waits for rain.

Next year's bread stands immature in the fields. Kernels of grain that should be waist high now form sparsely a few inches above the parched earth. Cows with dry udders nuzzle the scorched pastures vainly and wander hungrily among the weeds in the roadside ditches. From sorely stricken ranges caravans of trucks laden with bony cattle rumble over dusty roads toward green meadows somewhere else.

Food, in the cities, is something that men snatch from trays at shining counters of metal and glass or that is brought smoothly to their tables by waiters in restaurants, or that grocers deliver with

* Reprinted by permisson of the New York *Times*, and Mr. Harlan Miller.

clocklike regularity to the kitchens of their wives. In the farmland food is the precious booty of endless skirmishes and sieges, wrested from a capricious and implacable nature, without any certainty. To the city the farmer is invisible and his battles inaudible. But meat will be scarcer next Winter in the city, and bread dearer, if the rains do not pour down over the farmlands within thirty days.

* * *

Inexplicable are the caprices of nature, the vagaries of rain and soil. In one field the corn stands waist-high, in the next it scarcely reaches the knee, in the field beyond the tassels are level with your head. One valley is lush and fertile, the next is gaunt and sere. One State ripens normal crops which will be worth millions more because of lean harvests in three adjoining States plagued by the drought. Fertility deploys itself with the illogical swirls of a weather map.

Vacationists embark after breakfast in a fat, lucky State, and before lunchtime they are motoring through a rainless desolation where in better years cattle grazed knee-deep in grass. They drive past what was once a pleasant lake ten miles long and three miles wide. Now it has dried up to the proportions of a stagnant pond, and they see cottages with docks where boats were once tied up, high and dry, with half a mile of caked mud to the water's edge.

They pass on the highways trucks and wagons laden with casks of water. At a farmhouse where they stop for water the well is dry. The farmwife gives them a pitcherful brought for several miles. Occasionally they reach a village where the water supply is exhausted, the tank or reservoir empty. On the railroad siding is a tank car with water transported from a more fortunate town. A restaurant which has its own well 200 feet deep is famous for miles around, its delicious water a topic of discussion at tourist camps.

Some of the towns are rationing their water. Sprinkling the lawn is forbidden, and there is a limit on baths. On the side porch of every farmhouse is a row of tubs, buckets and cans, filled with water and covered with wet sacks. They drive for miles without seeing a drop of water in any creek-bed, and when they reach a great river that is often as broad as the Hudson it is a waste of dry sand shoals with a thin trickle in its bottommost channel.

The tourists from the fat, lucky States shrug their shoulders and look at one another in wonderment. They remember their own green fields left behind that morning. "It's like going from the Garden of Eden into a desert," they say, "a regular Sahara, isn't it?"

* * *

After days of implacable blue skies brassy with pitiless sunlight, a ragged mob of clouds tumbles over the saucer rim of the horizon. The farmer stands in his barnyard as one in a beleaguered city might stand on the ramparts searching the distance for succor. The sun is veiled, the animals stir, a little wind rustles the thirsty cottonwoods. The farmer's wife comes out of her kitchen and stands beside him. They set out empty vessels to catch the rainfall, and roll an empty barrel over beside the empty barrel that stands under the downspout of the eave-troughs. The children strip down to their impromptu swimming suits, ready to frolic under the first drops of rain.

But the clouds hurry on as if intent on a more important mission beyond the opposite horizon. The farmer mops his brow, climbs into his truck and sets off to haul some water from the filling station on the edge of the nearest town which offers a barrelful to its gasoline customers.

One day the sky is completely overcast. This time it is rain, and no mistake. The clouds mobilize in earnest, as if prepared at last to perform with special diligence a task too long forgotten. Low black clouds scurry across the sky at tangents against a loftier background of gray. For interminable minutes the thunder crashes, the wind assails the trees, a filtered yellow light tints the subdued gray with unreality, rolling up to a Wagnerian climax.

Then the rain lashes down in torrents for twenty minutes against the earth baked as hard as a cinder running track, and the water rolls off the ground and away as on an asphalt street, unabsorbed; flows in small rivulets to the gullies and vanishes. In an hour the sun blazes again and the earth is dry. Where the farmer has dammed the brook that empties his pond, with sticks and earth, enough water remains to form a temporary wallow for his animals. Once Conrad described a small gunboat standing off the coast of Africa and bombarding the Dark Continent with its guns. Also valiant and futile is the farmer in a drought, with his acres and his barrel of water.

Through the land echo the voices of leaders in the political campaign. The voices ring with indignation or pride, with blame and praise; they attack and they defend. Few listen more attentively than the farmer, judicial in his blue denim overalls, a newspaper on his lap and a pitcher of water at his side, the freest of individualists in a treadmill, one hand on the plow and the other on the wheel of State, his feet on his parched land and his head in Washington, alone in the no-man's land between nature and economics.

* * *

He hears splendid plans for his salvation, but his mind turns anon to the prospect of rain. He reads the weather forecast as the speeches grow dull and repetitious; he studies a weather map. Some of the honest plans of his friends, the generous plans of his wooers, seem genuinely helpful, whether calculated to win his vote or to help him produce food for himself and for the cities. Others seem as exigent and temporary as the repair of one of his machines with a piece of wire where a bolt, a nut and a cotter pin are needed. Fundamentally and eternally his faith is still in abundant harvests. If his bins and cribs were only full! Then there would be food enough and, with wise management and financing, money too.

"Here's a piece in the paper," he says to his wife, "that says they're digging down in Nebraska, and they think they're going to prove that some of the droughts in North America have lasted hundreds of years. What if this one lasted for years?"

But as an elderly husband looks at his elderly wife and sees only the blooming girl he married long ago, so he thinks of his withered fields and remembers only the luxuriant greens, the fat kernels and the abundant bushels of the last bumper crop. This is fruitful land, as good as any—with a little luck, a little rain, a little loan to bridge the lean times. He does not want to be resettled, to be moved to other acres, any more than he wants to divorce his wife. These crop-control plans, these economic contraceptives—they work sometimes, they have seemed to do some good, but they fly in the face of Providence, they defy the whims of nature, they leave him dubious.

He has heard more than a score of speeches—will they do as much good as a score of prayers for rain? Why wasn't there—at the party conventions—a prayer for rain? He rises stiffly from his chair—he has been cultivating all day—and goes outdoors to look at the stars. Maybe it will rain tomorrow.

* * *

In the fields the stunted crops are acrawl with insects. When the land produces the least for man, the insect pests flourish, grow most numerous, hungrier and most destructive. Hordes of grasshoppers, caterpillars, crickets, fray beetles, cutworms and chinch bugs have hatched in their dry nests and grown to maturity. They assail the frail dwarfed stalks with a light-hearted, idiotic malevolence that adds exasperation to impotence. They eat and reproduce and die, leaving the crops devastated in the luckless counties, leaving the crops in the fatter counties untouched to sell for higher prices.

But fury harvests no crops, and the farmers grimly dig ditches to halt the onward march of the pests; they spread poisoned bran. This seems the darkest hour. The farmer looks upward for compassion, and there is no compassion, only thicker swarms of insects. The vertical lines on his brow deepen and criss-cross the horizontal lines.

He thinks of Job, and then he thinks of the government, which cannot enrich him, but will not let him perish. This is a national emergency like a war, and the government must help him and rescue him and save him to sow another crop next year. The sudan grass is so dry that its stalks are saturated with prussic acid, and the cattle that eat it moan in agony and some of them die. Fantastic thoughts crowd into the farmer's mind, little wispy odds and ends of memories. He stops at the grocery, where cans of food cost a few pennies more.

"I see by the almanac," he says, "that they have an inch of rain every day down at that town in South America. As much in a week as we have had all year. We could use a little of that here."

"How many billions of gallons of water flow past our farms toward the ocean each year! How many millions of people are idle and must be fed! The government can help us feed them; they can dam up the rivers and the creeks and the brooks and save the water. Yes, the government is powerful enough to pipe water to every farm, and we could sprinkle our fields with tank carts." Then he feels sheepish at his own preposterous day dream. Water, of course, cannot be piped to farms; it can only be piped to great lawns and golf courses, and mighty expensive, too. In a burst of indomitable energy he begins to dig a new well; and he rakes the dead grasshoppers and chinch bugs and locusts into great glistening heaps, higher than a man's head.

"I guess I'll use 'em for fertilizer for next year," he says.

* * *

And now in the luckless States the drought is more protracted and devastating than the great drought of 1934. The statistics of disaster are plain; they bring a preview of doom while there is still plenty of time for nature with a whim to save the crops. All that moisture that has evaporated from the land must be somewhere; it cannot wander in the skies forever; soon it must fall somewhere, and not all of it will fall in the ocean. It is incredible that this drought can continue; it has been so long.

Yet the myth of security is shaken, and the theory of cycles. This cycle seems to be flat on one side. Dimly the farmer remembers that once his ancestors followed the grass with their herds, and the weak and the luckless perished, with no government to save them, only their own pluck and toughness. They matched their indomitable spirits against an implacable Providence.

At the village club to which his wife belongs the banker's wife reads passages from a little book by Rose Wilder Lane. It is about a pioneer man and woman, and how she saved their baby in a sod lean-to on the great plains during a Winter of blizzards, while a broken leg kept her husband away. Yes, she actually brought a milch cow into the shack and tumbled through the drifts and brought hay to feed it and got milk for her baby. This book is being passed around a great deal to revive individualism. It is especially popular among the people of the small towns.

* * *

Meanwhile, though neither politician nor statesman can make it rain, there is a great scurying about to prove that to a certain degree security is no myth, and that the government can help round out the flat segments in the weather cycles. The farmer, at the nadir of his despair, is heartened by this, like a castaway on a raft who discovers he is not so far from the steamer lanes after all.

There are conferences at the White House, consultations in the Washington bureaus. Committees are appointed; the Secretary of Agriculture will go to see the drought with his own eyes; allotments of funds are made, experts are called in, there are reconnaissances at the drought front. Famished cattle will be bought, half-starved cattle shipped at low rates to better pastures, feed will be shipped in, families on ruined land moved out, farmers paid for the day labor of their own salvation, on the idealistic theory that the country must eat in the future.

* * *

More sensitive to ideas in the crisis, the farmer accepts new-fangled tutelage more docilely. He learns to rely more on grass crops, especially in the marginal desert lands. He will plow his land around the contours to husband the moisture on tiny terraces, instead of plowing straight furrows uphill and downhill where the water races away. All this bustle of "paternalism" will mitigate his losses, but if the drought continues it will by no means leave him unscathed. His farm, with an invested capital greater than that in many a Fifth Avenue or Broadway shop, will have deteriorated; important improvements will be deferred; he will be in debt, after a year of loss instead of profit; another year of his life will have passed without any progress toward accumulation of a competence for his old age.

In adversity as in affluence, the farmer is at heart a conservative, a capitalist and a rugged individualist. The "paternalism" on which he relies in such emergencies as drought does not "regiment" him. It serves rather as a yardstick by which to measure the extent and virtues of his self-sufficiency. Emergency aid of this sort borders closely on the police function of the State, which hardly dares neglect its food supply.

Still the clouds roll by without dropping any rain. The drought enters the last act of a great drama for which the shrill alarms of politics and economics are only incidental music, a drama which may end as tragedy, but for which a happy ending is still possible. In the sickroom atmosphere of the dry farmlands, the crisis is now at hand. The next few days, perhaps the next few hours, will bring doom or reprieve to the fever-stricken crops.

Only one or two States in the land have had normal rainfall. Of the thirteen States which form the bread basket of the Republic, two or three are in acute distress, five or six may lose a dangerously high portion of their crops; only Iowa and Ohio, Wisconsin and Minnesota seem likely to emerge with nearly normal harvests to sell at enhanced prices.

It is a piteous thing to see strong men down on their knees to pray for rain and fruitfulness. But such prayer has been the backbone of scores of religions for thousands of years. The farmer stoops low to pick a head of grain. The kernels are dwarfed and meager; there will be only a few bushels to the acre; it will scarcely be worth while to take the harvest machinery out of the sheds—unless it rains. Soon. Or bread will be dearer, meat will be scarcer, in the cities.

* * *

With no undue flourishes, the skies are clouded over. The farmer awakes as from a nightmare. A gentle rain has been falling most of the night. The hard crust of the earth has been softened, the thirsty earth absorbs every drop, the tiny deep-searching roots drink up the water, send it climbing up into the plants. In a few hours the acres have been tinted an almost unnatural green.

The farmer stands bareheaded in the rain, his bosom swelling, his throat tight with joy and thanksgiving. His wife bakes a cake. The children scamper in the puddles. The animals, too, understand. It is that highly improbable, always inevitable day, the day the drought was broken. (The wheat pit is an uproar of selling orders.) All day the rain falls gently to complete the miracle of growth. There is, after all, compassion. Perhaps there is security, too. Could the farmer ever have doubted it?

(4)

MOUNTAIN CLIMBERS—TRY AMERICA FIRST! *

By Arthur Hawthorne Carhart

The slashing attack of a tiger, the lumbering charge of an elephant, the furious leap of a great swordfish all have their thrill, but that fact doesn't make bare-handed wrestling with a mountain any less exciting.

For instance, there were three men, well-seasoned in the sport of climbing high peaks, who were fighting their way one blustery day toward the top of Longs Peak. Their hobnails bit into the ice, their bodies bent, as two of them, Bill Ervin and Carl Blaurock, gazed up to where Roger Toll clung to a crumbling edge. Below was nothing but 1,000 feet of almost vertical rock, lacquered with ice. Toll was cutting inadequate footholds in the fragile ice. One treacherous hold gave way. He slipped, then caught himself. A move might take him to safety, or it might plunge him down to carry three climbers to their death.

Toll gropingly dug hobnails into a crevice, and slowly, painfully straightened up against the cliff. With new caution, the three men continued their climb to the top.

Yes, mountain climbing holds thrills.

"I prayed in those few moments," admitted Ervin as he told me

* Reprinted by permission of *Outdoor Life*.

of this brush with death, "just as I had done on two or three other occasions when I thought everything was over. For the most part, you can do something to pull yourself out if you get in a jam. You know the hazards, measure them, and meet them. It's when something beyond your individual control happens that the danger comes."

You can take Ervin's word for it, scaling a 14,000-foot peak in the American Rockies carries its excitement, but it entails no more risk than any other equally stirring outdoor sport. For Ervin and Blaurock, both of Denver, have climbed every 14,000-foot elevation in Colorado. They have mastered the Wind Rivers in Wyoming, the Tetons and Moran, and together made a trip to Switzerland to compare the roughest climbs of Europe with those of our own Rockies. Their experience, together with the lore accumulated over the years by the Colorado Mountain Club, makes a dependable guide for any outdoorsman who wishes to tackle this fast-growing field of adventurous sport.

Switzerland long has been the Mecca of mountain climbers, and the peaks of the Alps are world-famous. Few know that the Rockies challenge the hardihood of a climber to as great an extent as any Swiss peak.

The Rockies are particularly appealing in Colorado. In the State are 1,029 peaks which exceed 10,000 feet in height, eighteen times as many as are found in Switzerland. There are sixty-four peaks in continental United States that reach 14,000 feet. One peak is in Washington, twelve in California, and fifty-one in Colorado.

There are several marked differences between climbing in the Alps and in the Rockies. A large percentage of Swiss mishaps occur when melting ice releases rock slides which thunder down upon parties caught helpless in their path. During the summer, the Rockies hold no such risks. The most difficult climbing there is rock work. Few ropes are used in American climbing, and, because he is not roped to other climbers and a guide, a man can depend less on others to get him out of ticklish situations. Where ropes are used, they usually serve to speed the descent. A fifty-foot rope, dropped over a solid finger of rock, will let the climber down over a twenty-five-foot drop, and save a mile of roundabout climbing. The rope is then pulled free by one of its ends.

Weather conditions present another difference. In the Alps, parties are sometimes forced to wait several days before clouds clear the summit. During his years of American climbing, Bill Ervin has been held up only twice because of bad weather.

The point of starting is more quickly accessible in the Rockies. In scaling the higher Alps, it often is necessary to start the day before, pack your back grub, bedding, and fuel across ice to a cabin some distance above timber line, then start from there before dawn to get back before sundown. Many of the climbs in the Rockies can be started from an automobile highway, and a round trip to the top completed before dark.

The high timber line of the Rockies is in strong contrast to Switzerland where there is no fuel or forest shelter above 7,000 feet. In Colorado, timber line ranges between 10,000 and 12,500 feet. If bad weather comes, it is possible to drop down from the crest, find sheltering pines, fuel, and a place to weather a bad night.

If you wish to attempt the more hazardous snow climb, you will find that the Rockies in winter offer big drifts, ice work, and the extra danger of the avalanche. There is a rapidly growing group of experienced climbers now making the winter ascents. Except in the most difficult climbs, skiis are used, which permit the climbers to make a swift, exhilarating return to the base camp.

Equipment for climbing in the Rockies is far from elaborate. Clothing consists of a light, woolen undersuit, woolen socks, ordinary high-laced shoes similar to the army dress shoe, close-woven wool pants, a light shirt of the same material, an old felt hat, light, tough gloves, and a rainproof jacket such as fishermen tote in a creel to slip on in case of sudden showers. Shoes are lightly hobnailed, and, where rock work is ahead, they are edged with Swiss edging nails. A party may carry a light ice ax, and fifty feet of medium rope.

The food carried leans heavily to sugars. Climbing burns up energy, and hunger for sugars becomes a craving. Candy, raisins, and similar snacks meet this need. Crackers, a piece of salami, or similar cooked meat, and a can of grapefruit or fruit salad complete the usual rations for a climb. It is better not to eat bulky foods during the hike. Only occasionally are the concentrated and evaporated foods, standard in Europe, taken on a climb in the Rockies.

A Geological Survey or Forest Service map, cameras, a first-aid kit, and perhaps a pair of binoculars are distributed among the climbers in a party. The objective is a light load, a fast ascent, and a swifter return to the base camp in the evening.

Through experience, Western climbers have been able to work out a few simple rules for planning a climb. The Mountain Club advises that a party consist of four climbers. In case of injury to one member, two may go for aid, while one stays with the injured person. In the majority of cases where loss of life has occurred in climbing the Rockies, there have been less than four persons in the party.

Another simple rule enables climbers to estimate time required to reach the top. The elevation from which the climb will start usually is known. A geological map will give it exactly, and will indicate the routes that are feasible. The difference in elevation between starting point and the top will, of course, give the vertical feet to be climbed. Where climbing is normal, the time required for the ascent is determined by adding the number of miles to be traveled to thousands of feet of elevation, then dividing by two. Take, for example, a climb which requires six miles of travel, and a climb of 4,000 feet. Adding six and four gives ten, which, divided by two, gives five. Five, therefore, is the number of hours required to reach the top. The descent takes half that time. Novices usually go at it too hard at the start, and wind themselves before they are well on their way. This rule gives them something by which to gauge their speed, and adjust their pace to the gait followed by experienced climbers. For a large party, since it moves more slowly than a small one, the total of miles and thousands of feet should be divided by one and one half instead of by two.

A Geological Survey quadrangle is the best map for a climber if one has been published covering the district. These maps cost but a few cents a sheet. Second best is a map of the national forest in which the peak is located. These, as a rule, are available without cost. Those on which the mile-square sections are shown in quarter-inch squares allow the climber to locate himself more readily. Another helpful guide for the prospective climber is a handbook issued a few years ago by the Colorado Mountain Club. It contains "A Climber's Guide to the High Colorado Peaks," compiled by Elinor Kingery. On this list, the peaks are grouped by the ranges in which they occur. The nearest town is listed, together with directions for reaching the base camp, the length of the route, specific directions for following it, the elevation of the peak, and an estimate of the hours required for the climb.

However, the man undertaking a climb for the first time is wise to talk with some one who has made the ascent before. Your chances of making a climb safely increase with every scrap of information you can pick up. For instance, the route to the top of Pyramid takes you at one point along a knifelike ridge, so narrow you must sit down, and straddle it, with 1,000 feet or so of air under each shoe, and hitch the length of the ridge by hand. Knowing that, you might prefer some other climb!

Among the climbs which require only good physical condition, good sense, and the will to go to the top, are Mount Elbert, second highest peak in the United States; Mount Massive, second highest in Colorado; Mount Harvard; Uncompahgre Peak; Grays and Torreys peaks; Mount Evans; and a host of others. Grays and Torreys, easily reached from a motor highway, are regarded as suitable for the beginner.

Peaks that require a reasonable familiarity with climbing include Sierra Blanca, Kit Carson, the American Wetterhorn, Castle, Shavano, and Tabeguache. For success in climbing peaks in this group, a little knowledge of mountains and their peculiarities is essential.

Pikes Peak, not, as many believe, the highest in the State, but only twenty-eighth, formerly was the most-climbed peak. Since the trip to the summit has been reduced to an automobile ride by a good highway, Longs Peak, in the Rocky Mountain National Park, attracts the most climbers. It offers several degrees of difficulty, depending on the route selected. The route most often used is moderately challenging. Climbers who have sought the best Longs Peak could offer have found that scaling it from the east side is downright dangerous. This route goes up sheer cliffs a ledge at a time, the last cliff tilting out several degrees over the climber's head. The last few rods of the climb is through a "chimney," a smooth-walled cleft in solid rock. Up through this, the climber inches by bracing elbows and knees against the sides. Just outside the chimney yawns 2,000 feet of nothing.

It was on the east face of Longs Peak that Bill Ervin had one of his prayerful moments. With a companion, he was climbing the face of the cliff toward the chimney. The two of them halted on a solid ledge some four inches wide, and hugged the granite. A party of tourists, having climbed the regular route, had already gained the top. Neither party knew the other was on the peak. One tourist could not resist the urge to toss a rock over the edge.

"The momentum picked up by the big rock carried it out into the air beyond us," Ervin said, "but it knocked loose others as it fell. All we could do was yell, flatten ourselves against the rock, and hope that the big ones all would miss us. Fortunately only little pieces hit us, but they raised welts on our scalps despite our heavy hats. If a rock the size of a pullet egg had struck us, we'd have ended our climb right there. I'll bet I left the print of my body in that granite that day!"

"Bill," I said, "you and Carl have climbed them all. What are the really tough climbs in the Rockies?"

"Pyramid first," replied Bill.

Carl Blaurock had made the same assertion some time before.

"There's loose rock over Pyramid," said Bill. "That makes it as risky as any you'll encounter. Crestone Needles is another tough one, but its rock is solid, sheer, and steep. Moran is known as a top-rate climb, probably the stiffest in Wyoming. In Colorado, the two Wilsons, in the southwestern part of the State, are terrors. Lizard's Head is another."

Although it does not approach 14,000 feet, the loose shale of the Lizard's Head shaft defied climbers for years. Hanging on by ropes, toenail, and eyelash, several at last reached the top. Climbers are like that. Let them hear of an unscaled peak, hidden away in the Rockies, and a little party slips quietly out of town, and comes back a few days later with a new climbing scalp.

Other peaks rated as hazardous are Capitol, the Maroon Bells, Snowmass, Handies, and El Diente. Climbing them involves rock work. That is where American climbing differs basically from the Swiss. In the Alps, the danger lies in the treacherous ice, and a guide who has studied local weather is indispensable. In the Rockies, the ice-walled passage is replaced by a rock chimney, and the conditions a climber must face are always in plain sight, so that any sensible person can see how to tackle it. The masked dangers found in rotting glacial ice do not exist.

As in all sports, lives are occasionally lost in mountain climbing. Just as an unloaded gun in the hands of a nitwit, or a canoe in charge of a greenhorn, spells danger, a foolhardy climber can endanger the lives of experienced climbers. Sound judgment and cool nerve are vital above timber line. From start to finish, mountain climbing is a test of a man's stamina and courage—or of a woman's, for there are scores of outdoor girls who climb the higher peaks. One girl, Mary Cunin, has climbed all of Colorado's 14,000-foot mountains.

"It's the fellow who loses his head that is the real danger," remarks Ervin.

And Carl Blaurock adds, "Keep cool. Don't stampede. If you get into a tight spot, you can get out if you use your head."

So, any time you think you've wrung all the thrills from outdoor sports, just remember there's a mountain out West waiting to tell you whether you've got the stuff it takes.

(5)

TWO MONTHS IN MEXICO *

By Wallace Biggs

My wife and I sat one night last May and tabulated the cost of holding our apartment over the summer.

Our living expenses were about seventy-five dollars monthly—thirty for rent, forty-five for groceries, meats and incidentals. With a will to travel, we had to ask the age-old question, "Can we afford a summer of traveling?"

We had had many fine vacations in the States and after our fling at seeing America first we were anxious for a change. Finally we decided to drive to Mexico City over the Pan-American Highway, into a country we had always imagined strangely barbaric and wild, but a country where the rate of exchange on American money was highly favorable.

After sharpening pencils and using up scratch pads, we decided that we could travel four thousand miles from Missouri to Mexico City and back, and live for six weeks in the Mexican capital on one hundred and fifty dollars—the cost of living for two months in our apartment, wishing we were somewhere else.

We bought sufficient canned goods to last a month, deciding that if we got stuck somewhere on the highway from Laredo to Mexico City by washouts, high water or car trouble, we would camp out until we could move on. Our best information was that several hundred men were working during the summer rainy season on the bad stretches from Tamazunchale to Jacala, two hundred miles north of Mexico City; and we concluded that if misery came our way, we should have company—and perhaps a push if we needed it.

* Reprinted by permission of *Woman's Home Companion*, and Mr. Wallace Biggs.

Our canned goods were the convenient kind: sardines, mackerel, potted ham, baked beans, marmalade and soup. A large jar of mayonnaise substituted for butter; and a jar of mustard was added to use with the mackerel and potted ham. A large box of crackers was stored away for emergency; and two gallon thermos jars were added for water supply.

We left the Missouri Ozarks the last day of May. Through Oklahoma and Texas we slept on the stagger system, one night in the car and the next night in a tourist camp.

In Nuevo Laredo, across the Rio Grande in Mexico, three Mexican porters tore all of our excellently packed boxes and suitcases out of the rumble seat; and charged us a peso a package for the privilege. After an hour's red tape, with our pockets full of pesos (thirty-five for ten American dollars) we were off down a long black-surfaced road that sent a slight shiver up our spinal columns when we realized we were taking a long shot, traveling "on the margin" in a foreign country.

It was an easy day's drive from the border to Monterrey, where we stopped at the Hotel Bridges across from the railway station; we were charged three pesos for the night for a large tile-floored room with a shower bath (the hot water was only lukewarm).

In Monterrey one should take in one of the tent street shows—rowdy and a little tin-panny, but entirely safe. Tickets are good for four acts; at the end of each session an usher tears off a section, until the *boleto* is completely used up.

Monterrey is a fine city to walk in—compressed and centralized, hemmed in by beautiful mountains. During our two-day stay we lived on oranges at ten cents a dozen, pumpkin rolls and cream puffs filled with mango fruit—a little heavy, but digestible with sufficient exercise. Street urchins in Monterrey, coached to beg from Americans, are constantly hanging on your heels, selling chicle or offering to keep someone from stealing your hub caps while your car is parked; but it is fatal to become generous. Mexican corn on the cob (cooked in the shuck and kept warm), sold by street-corner venders at five centavos an ear, is both excellent and economical.

Leaving Monterrey, over an excellent road, we crossed the orange belt of Nuevo León. At Montemorelos the last good oranges are to be bought. For four hundred miles out of Monterrey, the beautiful Sierra Madre range lies to the right as the highway winds and dips its way southward. In Victoria, one hundred and seventy-five miles south of Monterrey, there is little to do except take a casual walk around the town, inspect its market, get advice about the road from any of its garages and proceed southward. Unwilling to pay four pesos for a hotel room in Victoria, we parked just off the highway on a high mesa twenty-five miles south.

Over excellent hard-surfaced road we passed through Villa Juarez and into the palm country below the Tropic of Cancer, two hundred and seventy-five miles south of Monterrey. Two lessons we had learned by this time about traveling in Mexico: to buy gas every time we saw a filling station, and save all metal money possible by getting a bill broken with every purchase. Silver and copper money are good throughout Mexico, even in the remotest village, but natives generally are skeptical about paper.

About three hundred and sixty-five miles south of Monterrey we stayed our third night in Mexico in a tiny Indian coffee-buying village, Huichihauhan (Witch's Flower), probably so named because of the wild orchids which grow in the valley of the Rio Axtla close by. In Huichihauhan live an American, Sam Brown, and his Indian wife, Secorra. A lanky Texan, he always welcomes Americans and his quarters are yours for the asking. Well worth a day's stay-over, Huichihauhan is a typical Mexican-Indian village with two stores, a dozen thatched shacks, innumerable pantsless native children and a pack of barking noisy dogs.

To the Rio Axtla every summer evening the entire village goes; petticoated women pound their clothes clean in the cold mountain water, and one hundred yards above, the men and boys strip to cool off in the clear waters. Crossing the stream at intervals through the day come pack-mule trains out of the hills loaded with coffee to be sold in the village.

We slept that night in a common sleeping-room with Sam and his wife, several servants, a parrot and two dogs; and to add to the strangeness, the roof was kept intact during a night-storm only by saddling the apex with several small tree-trunks tied together. The next morning we left Huichihauhan somewhat reluctantly to begin the treacherous sixty-mile climb from Tamazunchale (pronounced Thomas and Charlie) to Jacala. We went through the country of the Huastecan Indians, who plant their corn on hillsides so steep that they have to lower themselves by ropes to bury the seed-corn in perpendicularly sloped fields. At the end of the most dangerous piece on the Pan-American Highway, requiring from four to eight hours for driving, lies beautiful white-housed Jacala against a green background and blue sky-drop, nestling one thousand feet below in the valley. This is an end to bad road: Mexico City lies one hundred and sixty miles to the south over an excellent highway.

Two types of travelers enter Mexico: those who try to live in Mexico as they live in the States; and a second group who, curious to get beneath the skin of Mexico, take rooms in the homes of Spanish or German residents of Mexico City at from ten to thirty dollars rent monthly, or rent furnished apartments at from twenty to thirty-five dollars monthly for four rooms, bath and kitchenette.

We decided to throw our lot with the latter group.

Once in Mexico City, the newcomer should get settled as soon as possible—preferably at Servicio Shirley, a modern tourist camp in the heart of Mexico City on Manuel Villalongin, or at the American-patronized Hotel Geneve. The next step is to find more economical lodgings, for which several sources are open: rental agencies on Cinco de Mayo and Madero Avenues; newspapers, particularly the American Weekly News; or the offices of the University of Mexico summer school.

Interested primarily in economy, we passed up comfortably furnished three-room kitchenette-and-bath apartments near the summer school, with a sixty-five-peso monthly rental (twenty dollars), and took a single room apartment on Independence Avenue, a block from Mexico City's busiest corner, Madero and San Juan de Letran, at thirty-five pesos a month (ten dollars). Our landlady spoke no English; but the porter had lived for two years in New York City and spoke a jargon that we could understand. A garage for our car was rented four blocks away at three pesos weekly.

We budgeted ourselves for a six weeks' stay on an eating allowance of two pesos daily for the two of us (fifty-six cents). Now an excellent eight-course meal in Mexico City costs only a peso (twenty-eight cents), a good meal eighty centavos (about twenty-four cents); and meals may be purchased for as low as fifty and sixty centavos.

Our daily menu consisted of fruit for breakfast, purchased from street markets and eaten in our room; *comida,* our chief meal, at one o'clock; and rolls, pastry or more fruit in the evening. We found Mexican meals elaborate affairs, usually composed of soup, two eggs, a fish course, meat (pork, beef, rabbit), potatoes, a vegetable, rolls, the inevitable *frijoles refritos* (fried beans), dessert and coffee or tea. One can thus satisfy a normal appetite in Mexico City on one meal a day, supplemented with fruit and rolls.

Enchiladas, tacos, fresh-fruit drinks (*refrescos*), and candied fruits can be bought safely from refreshment stands over the city if the stroller gets hungry.

Our one-room apartment served two purposes: a place to sleep at night, and a reading and lounging room during the almost daily afternoon showers in Mexico City during the summer. We literally lived on the streets of the city except to steal a few hours' sleep each night and the two hours' rest during siesta time when all the stores close.

Probably our greatest luxury was our camera. Mexican officials object to the photographing of beggers, squads of soldiers or sordid scenes, but Mexican markets, street scenes, fiestas, bullfights, and never-ending beautiful landscape provide a gold mine of photographic material.

Seeing Mexico at the Mexican level is very inexpensive. A seat high on the sunny side of the bull ring for instance costs three pesos —and one on the shady side costs ten pesos. Theater seats on the lower floor, center, cost three pesos; seats in the gallery, twenty-five centavos, with the privilege of staying through several shows if desired. For everything you wish to buy in Mexico, ask *"Cuanto* (how much)?" It always pays, whether the transaction be a shoe shine or a hundred-mile taxi trip. Mexicans believe all gringos rich. A little good-natured haggling over prices, however, is always in order when dealing with Mexicans, especially in the markets. They expect it.

Guide-prices range from fifty centavos to two pesos an hour, according to whether you inquire about the price at the beginning or at the end of a tour.

Every Mexican village has its market day once a week or oftener. Baskets and sombreros at Tuluca, forty miles from Mexico City, over an excellent road; exquisite candles at Guadalupe, five miles north of Mexico City; hammocks, shoes, *chinas poblanas* at Cuernavaca; zarapes and woolens at Oaxaca; pottery at Puebla.

Dozens of interesting spots are within half a day's drive from Mexico City: Cholula, with a cathedral dome for every week in the year; Puebla, conservative and reactionary, military key to Mexico; Toluca, forty miles south, with its excellent vegetable markets, streets swarming with dark interesting faces; Texcoco, from where Cortez launched his boats to defeat the Aztecs in 1521. Mileage expenses in Mexico are about the same as in the United States, with gasoline at twenty cents a gallon and oil at thirty.

In early August we prepared with considerable regret to leave Mexico after sixty days of a perfect "gringo holiday." A week later, back in Missouri, we put the trip down in black and white.

Our food in Mexico had come to approximately thirty-five dollars; lodging, twenty dollars; garage rent, five; gas and oil for the four-thousand-mile trip, fifty; groceries consumed on the trip, ten; tourist camp charges, ten; and presents and incidentals bought in Mexico, twenty—making a total of one hundred and fifty dollars, the amount we had allowed.

Exercises

1. How many narrative articles did you find in the magazine section of your favorite newspaper?
2. By referring back to your previous exercises, tabulate the number of each kind of articles found to show which type seems to be most favored by the feature editor.
3. In chart form, list the narrative articles, and in the first column indicate in what way each feature is similar to the short story.
4. In a second column in the chart indicate the purpose of each article.
5. In a third column indicate from what sources the writers obtained their material.
6. In a fourth column enumerate the appeal to the reader's senses which the writers have used.
7. After summing up your findings by means of the chart, write a paragraph of not more than 200 words pointing out why your favorite newspaper is, or is not, a good market for narrative articles.
8. How many narrative articles did you find in your favorite magazine?
9. In chart form list the names of the articles, and indicate: (1) the elements in the article that are similar to the short story; (2) the purpose of the article; (3) the sources of the material; and (4) appeal to the reader's senses.
10. After totalling up your findings, write a paragraph of not more

than 200 words pointing out why your favorite magazine is, or is not, a market for narrative articles.

11. List two ideas for narrative articles for a newspaper section and two ideas for narratives for a magazine, and indicate a market for each "tip."
12. List one "tip" for a narrative that could be treated humorously and indicate a market to which you might send it.

Publication Analysis

Collier's, Esquire, and *Ladies' Home Journal*

Do not spend more than two hours on this report.

I. Identification for each magazine: Name, publishers, editors, where published, price.

II. Make-up: What to you, as a future magazine editor, are the most interesting make-up devices used in each publication. Give reasons for your answers.

III. Advertising:
1. To what class is the appeal made in the advertising of each magazine?
2. What novel ideas in advertising make-up did you find in each publication?
3. From which one of the three magazines do you think the advertisers get the best returns?
4. Suggest one "tip" for a feature article suggested by the advertising in each magazine.

IV. General Policy:
1. Make a comparative summary of the three magazines as to content and appeal.
2. Make a brief comment on the fiction as to type, titles, appeal, writers, and the amount of space devoted to it.
3. What did you learn of each publication's policy by reading its editorials?

V. Features:
1. Make a comparative summary of the features, as to style, subject matter, content, length, and writers (whether they are, or are not, well known).
2. Make a comparative comment on the illustrative matter

(pictures, charts, graphs, maps) used in each magazine.

3. Read a narrative article in each publication and list two suggestions for each feature read that will enable you to write interesting narratives.

VI. Slogans: Write a slogan for each magazine.

VII. Three tips: Source, authority, and three possible markets for each, suggested by this publication analysis.

9

SLANTING ARTICLES TO PUBLICATIONS

Magazine Growth Makes Slanting Necessary. Although feature writers are fortunate to be writing in this period—which might well be known as the golden age of the magazine, at least as far as numbers are concerned—they have to have a keener knowledge of markets today than did their predecessors. Never in the history of journalism have there been so many publications as there now are. Writers must ever be alert to the constant change in periodicals. Seldom a week passes that a new magazine does not appear on the newsstands; or another disappears because it has failed financially; or two combine and change the editorial policy and the appeal to reader interest in an attempt to meet tremendous competition.

Until the last two decades, few publications existed, and they all had similar conservative policies. Today there are 2,056 daily newspapers, of which 593 have Sunday editions, according to N. W. Ayer and Son's Directory.* It lists 6,155 periodicals. However, the directories of Standard Rate and Data Service list a total of 6,428 general, business, religious, and farm magazines. The magazines publish 253,516 issues annually, each carrying from one to twenty feature articles. Each magazine makes a different appeal to its readers. Each offers to

* Ayer, N. W., and Son, *Directory of Newspapers and Periodicals,* 1939.

the writer an opportunity to market his manuscripts if he will study its issues and learn its needs.

Slanting Defined. When beginners in feature writing classes sell their articles, it is because they study the markets assiduously. They avoid rejection slips and returned manuscripts by being ever alert to opportunities to sell. One often thinks of salesmen as people who travel with samples. Feature writers, too, are salesmen. Their sample kits, or manuscripts, are not exhibited personally, as are the traveling salesman's. The articles are sent direct to the middleman, or editor, the writer thinks most likely to be interested in buying for resale, as a merchant, to his customer-consumers, who are the readers of the magazine. There is a place in some publication at some time for every well-planned and well-written feature. It is the writer's job to be extremely businesslike and to see that his manuscript is at the right place at the right time.

A slanted article is one written to the editorial requirements of a particular publication. The writer's problem is to find the particular policy for each publication before he even outlines his article. Some writers, who like to think of themselves as "literary artists," object to deciding beforehand where they will send their manuscripts. But they never become known as authors, since their works seldom are printed. The practical, businesslike person determines his markets before he writes. He sells if he writes, or "slants," to suit a certain publication or type of publication. The formula of any publication may be found by analyzing not only the articles but the entire contents, and by studying the style of other contributors in recent issues.

Problems in Slanting. Writers with something worth writing do not have to go begging for a market if they apply the same intelligence and study to the salesmanship of the article as they did to the technique of gathering and writing the material. Markets are as numerous as feature writers. But the majority of beginners are not competitors. They refuse to study periodicals; and their copy, sent out hit or miss, is rejected. Novices will find slanting an insurance against rejections instead of a baffling problem. Of two writers, otherwise equally experienced and versatile, the one who is practical and prepares in advance to aim at definite markets will get acceptances instead of rejections.

Qualifications for Slanting. A businesslike attitude toward the selling of his copy is the author's first requisite in slanting an article. He must be familiar with all kinds of publications and observe closely the type of article and the subject matter most favored by the editor of each. After a writer selects his subject, he should have the ability to visualize his readers or market and seek a publication that goes to such subscribers.

It is important that the writer be a close newspaper reader and a keen observer, in order to see the trends of current news and to detect the undercurrents of thought before it is too late to gather, write, and submit material while interest is high. If he is determined to know the markets, his determination will make the business of publication analysis interesting. He will not be bored or think he is wasting time in studying the markets before beginning to write his articles.

Finding Specific Buyers. Ambitious beginners hope to have their articles appear in the "slick paper," or class, magazines. If their articles are accurately gathered, carefully planned, skillfully written, and wisely slanted, the writers need only stamps and envelopes. Although the big magazines receive from 2,000 to 3,000 articles a week, they do look at every manuscript. One can assume that every successful magazine is satisfying its readers, at least to some degree. The surest way to determine the interests of its readers is to study carefully the contents of the entire publication to which one is submitting a manuscript, and then to plan and outline the material to fit it. It is a waste of postage, effort, and time to send articles out to the first market that comes to mind. The manuscript is sure to be returned so promptly that the writer will marvel at the speed of the mails.

An unskilled writer is inclined to offer his manuscript indiscriminately and frequently. This practice tends to prejudice the editor against future contributions and, in addition, wastes the writer's time and postage. Nothing labels one as an amateur more quickly than sending his manuscript to the wrong type of publication, as did the junior journalist who sent an article on student health to the *Christian Science Monitor*. After being carefully slanted and rewritten, it later sold to *Hygeia*. But if an editor receives a feature showing that the writer senses the reader-appeal of his magazine, even though the particular article is not acceptable for some reason, he will often suggest in a personal note that he would be pleased to see more of the writer's work. If beginners would only be willing to study the magazines thoroughly before attempting to write articles, they would have little difficulty in marketing.

Though there may be obvious defects in a manuscript, if it has some merit and is well pointed to a specific publication, it may be salable. Finding buyers for one's manuscript may be likened to finding a position. It takes a lot of searching, and sometimes a bit of luck, but in the long run most worthy people do find work if they apply where their services can be used. A manuscript, like any merchandise, is marketable when the right buyer is found. Editor-buyers can be found easily if the salesman-writer will display only the wares that will appeal to the middleman-editor because he knows his customer-readers will be interested.

Feature Article Is a Commodity to Be Sold. Not many beginners sell, because only a few are willing to learn: (1) of market requirements; (2) of editors' methods of handling manuscripts; (3) of ways of impressing the editor favorably; (4) of price scales for features; or (5) of the great number of possible markets for their articles. The result is that a small number of nationally known magazines receive almost the entire output of the multitude of novices.

It is not surprising that relatively few attain success; proportionately, only a few are willing to recognize their manuscripts as a commodity that must be designed for definite markets. Manufacturers of furniture do not let their product remain in their warehouses; they see that it is sold. Many writers, however, feel that when they have struck the last period on their manuscripts, their work as writers is done. They refuse to be salesmen. They are too lazy or too indifferent to study the magazines in detail in order to manufacture a commodity that the middleman-editor and his public will want. Such an analysis would increase their chances to sell at least 500 per cent.

Usually they complete their final drafts and mail them out to the first market that strikes their fancies. They shoot in the dark, trusting to luck instead of devoting (1) considerable time to the study of thousands of opportunities and (2) serious thought to marketing the articles.

Two Ways of Marketing. From the commercial point of view, there are two ways in which creative writers may approach their work. First, they may write what they feel like writing, in whatever way they wish to write it, and then, if they feel like it, see what they can do about selling. One beginner, in spite of being advised to study markets, wrote what he "felt like" writing. He thought his "self-expression" was nearer to "real art." He did not sell the article. Meanwhile, his classmates, who had analyzed the markets before outlining and writing, received checks. He changed his plan of work, and since then has sold many articles. He admits now that it is much more fun to have readers and checks than to write as he "feels." He found that writing to a plan was much more enjoyable and successful than writing in a haphazard manner. Those writers who yearn to "express themselves" generally send out what they do write to the best-paying of the class publications. They do not realize that thousands of other beginners are sending to the same markets because they, too, do not know or will not learn of the existence of thousands of other publications where there is but little competition. They receive rejections and become greatly discouraged. There are exceptions, of course. Occasionally someone does sell the first time he sends out his article, without giving the marketing any thought.

The second way is for the beginners to learn everything they can about the needs of all the current newspapers, syndicates, trade and business publications, and magazines. After they have learned of the existing demands of the markets, they attempt to supply it: (1) by selecting subjects that they hope will be suitable; (2) by writing articles in a style similar to that of articles already published, in order to fill the needs of the editors in the way that they seem to want them filled; and (3) by obtaining photographs and other illustrations of the type the editors seem to want. They succeed where the would-be "artistic" novices fail.

Adapting Professional's Technique Is Helpful. These beginners who attain success do so by incorporating the devices of the professionals already writing for the publication to which they are slanting. Concrete incidents and instances, people, direct quotations, and interviews with authorities whose names may interest the reader are devices that most editors like. Each may have his own notions about what his readers like, but frequently they change their ideas. A semi-professional who, over a period of time, had sold a number of articles to a well-known magazine, neglected to continue his study of the publication. He had an article returned with a personal note suggesting that if he would take out the expert's name and quotations, rewrite the manuscript to conform to the new policy, and return it, the magazine would accept it. In making a study of the publication, he found to his surprise that the editor, several months previously, had discontinued the use of interview articles.

Learning Editor's Desires and Needs. To insure acceptance, a manuscript must fit a particular magazine, as previously pointed out. In reality, it must appeal to the editor who buys what he believes his subscribers want. As the middleman, he buys from the producers what he thinks he can sell to his customers. Unless his customer-readers are satisfied, they will shop elsewhere for their reading matter.

Editors buy those articles in which the reader can visualize himself, or herself. Human beings are interested, first of all, in themselves. People go to movies and read current magazines and best sellers to escape from their prosaic lives and live for a brief time in a world of their own, in which they see themselves as the hero, or the heroine, of the film, article, or story. Why do people look at the advertising in publications? Psychologists say it is not that they are interested entirely in the commodity, but that the readers like to see themselves—consciously or unconsciously—in the illustrations and in the copy. The women like to think they look like the radiant girl in the swimming suit advertisement; the men see themselves as the handsome young chap in the collar advertisement. It is only human nature for readers to identify themselves in everything. If writers base their work on that principle of psychology, they are more successful in interesting editors.

Another principle upon which editors base their selections is appeal to subscribers. Most magazine readers are from the great middle class. They have grade-school and high-school educations. They read little else than their newspapers and the magazines. They look to them for their entertainment and their information. They go to the movies, play bridge, and tune in on their radios. They are buying their homes or they have borrowed money in order to build homes. They drive "popular-priced" cars. They like romance, adventure, and the things close to their own lives. They want to be healthier, wealthier, and wiser. They are the average American families.

This is the kind of reading audience the average editor has to consider. With them in mind, he attacks his daily pile of manuscripts, but always with the hope that he will discover a new writer whose work will lend distinction to his publication, or at least will compare favorably with the work of his staff writers or those who write articles "on order" from the editor. But no matter how well written the manuscripts are, he cannot accept any of them unless they are what the readers want. Readers are interested in accounts of what someone has done more efficiently, more satisfactorily, or more profitably than they have.

Amateurs and semi-professionals long have had a wrong conception of editors because of the rejection slips they receive.

They do not stop to think that had they sent in well-written articles containing something new to inform, guide, or entertain the reader, and written for the editor's particular subscribers, that he would have been only too happy to have sent a check instead of a rejection slip. All editors are constantly on the lookout for new contributors. After analyzing a publication and before even outlining his article, a writer should imagine himself in that editor's place in order better to keep the readers in mind as he works. Just as the editor, were he writing the article, would (1) make himself master of the subject before beginning to write, or (2) interview an authority whose expert opinions would add to the reader's faith in the content of the feature, so must the beginner do if he would satisfy the editor's wants and needs. Editors are easy to please if the writer will apply himself to learning what they want. Beginners should remember that duck hunters do not load their guns, shut their eyes, and shoot into a duckless sky when they wish to bag game. But the feature writer who does not slant is doing just that.

Factors Determining Editorial Selection. Every magazine's success depends upon the ability of the editors to visualize their readers—their incomes, their expenses, their problems, their likes and dislikes, their entertainment, their ambitions, and their aspirations—in order to publish the kind of periodical that will please them. A great editor producing a home magazine to appeal to the middle class saw in his mind a typical community of 1,500 inhabitants, somewhere in the Mississippi valley. He selected everything that went into that publication—editorials, articles, fiction, and poems—with a view to satisfying an average American family—a father, mother, and three children, aged 14, 9, and 6. For two other magazines that he published, he employed editors who as accurately visualized their readers. The subscribers in one case were country gentlemen; in the other, business people. The owner of these three magazines became one of the outstanding editors and millionaires of his time. He attributed his success to visualizing his readers. If an editor can attain great success on that principle, so may feature writers if they will visualize their readers when planning and writing their articles.

Distinguishing Factors as Markets. To determine where to sell an article, a writer must decide whom the article will interest and where will he find a ready market. Both factors are dependent upon the subject matter. However, if it would interest the newspaper reader as well as the magazine reader, or would interest only the former, the writer will find it is easier and quicker, perhaps, to sell to the newspaper magazine sections. Their editors buy from three to six weeks in advance, while the magazine editors buy from four to six months before publication. Although Sunday newspaper sections are not so numerous now as magazines, many papers run daily features on their editorial pages in addition to those in the large Sunday, or Saturday night, feature sections. Newspapers are broader in reader appeal as well as more varied in style of writing and the type of features they use, and the author's name does not need to be well known, as it must be with some of the class magazines. But whichever publication one writes for, he must know the reader's interests.

If one is slanting for the newspaper, he should learn to know the people who read that newspaper; he must talk to the elevator boy, the judge, the waiter, the minister, the janitor, the teacher, the laborer, the banker, and all the other kinds of readers. Newspaper reporting experience affords excellent background for anyone who desires to write features. The reporter is writing regularly, whether or not he "feels" like it; he writes under the constant criticism of the city editor; and he is continually coming in contact with all kinds of people. If one cannot work on a newspaper, he should write every day and he should attempt to know as many kinds of people as he can.

Diversity in Publication Appeals and Policies. It is the purpose of every publication, magazine or newspaper, to have a definite appeal to a particular reader; it is the writer's task to learn the appeals of the publication. The magazine differs from the newspaper in that its appeal must be national, while the newspaper's is local or sectional. Newspaper readers living in the same community or in the same section of the country have similar interests, but national magazines cannot appeal to people throughout the country in a single issue. To satisfy the demand of a widely varied appeal, editors developed the class magazine, to attract readers of certain types throughout the nation. Timeliness is more important in the newspaper, because its very name signifies giving the news. If an article has a news angle, it has twice the chance of being accepted in the Sunday section.

The newspaper and the magazine are business enterprises. As they must sell their products and they must retain their reputations, they buy only those manuscripts that help them to carry their business policies of dependability and reliability. The newspaper and the magazine are constantly changing, but the latter is a greater follower of fads and fashions than the former, and it is easier for the beginner to slant to the newspaper than to the magazine.

Knowledge of Circulation Aids Slanting. Since publications are business ventures, they are dependent upon circulation. In this phase, more than in any other, lies the greatest difference between newspapers and magazines. Most popular magazines have nation-wide circulation to people of many classes. Some agricultural and trade journals are published for a distinctly sectional circulation because climatic conditions or geographical locations present different problems and give rise to different interests in different sections of the country. Others are published for subscribers interested in the same profession, business, or industry who live in all parts of North America.

It is essential, in selling, that the writer know, as does the advertising agency buying space in publications, just what the circulation is and who the subscribers are. By knowing the variances, the writer will be able to slant his articles accurately.

High Standards of Writing Are Required. Some beginners believe that it is easier to write for the newspapers than for the magazines, and that the former will buy poorly written and carelessly constructed articles. They are mistaken. Newspaper feature editors have an abundance of material from which to choose, and competition is keener today than it ever has been before. Therefore, writers must turn out good manuscripts for the newspapers as well as for the magazines. In writing for the former, the free-lance has to compete with other free-lance writers, regular staff members, and syndicate writers, many of whom are well known in the world of letters. No writing is ever too good to appear in the Sunday sections. The articles of the best writers appear in both types of publications.

Slanting to the Newspapers. The newspaper is an excellent field for the beginner if he slants his article to it. In every city there are daily newspapers publishing feature articles. Even in the smaller city there is at least one daily, and it, like the metropolitan paper, will use articles on local subjects that are right at the beginner's door. Since only local writers, as a rule, submit manuscripts to the smaller papers, the novice does not have as much competition in free-lancing. In addition to giving the news of the locality, a newspaper also prints the important news of the world. So, too, does it publish, in addition to its local features, articles of a broader scope, and herein lies the beginner's opportunity. His financial remuneration will be smaller, but he will gain in experience and will learn how to write for print. Small city dailies have offered apprenticeships to hundreds of writers who later moved on to larger opportunities.

Because of their broad appeal, metropolitan newspapers offer a ready market for articles, or "special feature stories" as newspaper workers term them. Some newspapers, such as the Kansas City *Star* and the Milwaukee *Journal,* publish articles daily on the editorial page, and others print them elsewhere in the paper. Five hundred and ninety-three of them have Saturday or Sunday magazine sections containing features similar to those found in general magazines. Newspapers obtain the articles they publish from: (1) members of the newspaper staff—reporters, correspondents, special writers, or editors—who are employed for the purpose or who, on some papers, are paid for the features they write in addition to their routine work; (2) syndicates, which are companies that buy articles from writers and sell them to a number of newspaper feature editors in different cities for release on the same dates; and (3) from free-lance writers, either amateurs or professionals, who submit their stories to the feature editor. Staff workers on smaller papers frequently submit articles to the larger ones, as do news correspondents, if the paper upon which they are employed does not desire them. Through their feature writing, they develop a sideline that adds to their regular income and affords them the opportunity of seeing their by-lines in papers other than those upon which they are employed.

Analyzing Newspapers to Detect Differences. Each newspaper should be studied to learn the differences in reader appeal. Some papers, such as the New York *World-Telegram,* may stress local color and atmosphere; the Chicago *Daily News* may emphasize human interest; the New York *Times* may require scholarliness and timeliness; the *Christian Science Monitor* may demand accuracy; the New York *Herald Tribune* may use features of national and international importance; and the great majority, such as the Kansas City *Star,* the Milwaukee *Journal,* and the Indianapolis *News,* publish anything of general interest if it is unusually well written. Newspapers, like persons, may appear to be alike; yet upon analysis one finds that they have as varied personalities and as many dissimilarities as do individuals. The character of the readers of a newspaper determines the character of its features, just as the readers influence the presentation of the news.

It is not a waste of time to study publications. If tailors or dressmakers made up suits or dresses in different styles and different sizes than their customers could wear—because they "felt like expressing themselves in that way"—or if they made the garments several inches too long, or too short—because they did not take the measurements accurately—their customers would refuse to accept them. The editor feels just that way when unsolicited manuscripts are not cut accurately to fit the pattern of his publication.

Kinds of Features Wanted by Newspapers. Current topics, because timeliness is the keynote of the newspaper, furnish the basis of the majority of daily feature stories. They may contain elaborated details of past news or they may anticipate coming events.

To satisfy the reader's curiosity concerning the details of the concise announcements of news events, by interviews and research a writer may elaborate them into features. They may be concerned with: accounts of scientific discoveries or inventions; sketches of personalities and successful persons; reports of industrial, social, economic, or political conditions; narratives of seasonal occasions, such as holidays, vacations, opening and closing of schools, and the fishing and hunting seasons; synopses of local, state, national, and international affairs; and reviews of historical events that may be timely because of some news angle or because of some approaching anniversary. The daily news columns are provocative sources of "tips" for features, for either Sunday sections or for magazines. When in doubt as to a market, one may slant to the newspaper. Its readers are interested in all kinds of subjects.

To entertain subscribers by giving them reading matter with which to occupy their leisure, or to serve as "literature of escape" from their workaday worlds, newspapers often print articles on subjects of little or no value, simply because they are written in an amusing and entertaining style. Sensational newspapers devote considerable space to topics that lend themselves to melodramatic treatment in features. The sensational paper is about the only market for highly dramatized features, with the exception of a few recent periodicals. Most periodicals generally do not attempt to attract readers by that means.

Sunday Magazine Features. The magazine sections of the Sunday newspapers, like the daily editions, contain features concerning: (1) rare, unusual, novel, romantic, tragic, and adventurous things in life everywhere; (2) the outstanding achievements in the arts and sciences; and (3) authoritative opinions on current issues and events. The articles in the sections devoted to features are similar in subject matter to those used daily. They are much longer than those used in the week-day issues, and frequently they are as long as those in general magazines. The Sunday feature sections use more pictures and other illustrations than the daily does, and often equal in number those in the magazines.

By noting the subjects of the articles, the types most used, the point of view from which they are written, the form, the length, and the appeal to the reader, a writer will soon discover what the feature-section editors desire. The newspaper and periodical studies at the end of each chapter in this book indicate the points to keep in mind in studying publications in order to slant material to the newspapers.

Syndicated Features. Newspaper syndicates buy series of articles from free-lance writers, but they seldom buy the work of a novice. They obtain most of their material from writers of already recognized prominence, because professionals are better judges of reader interest, they have "big" names, and they have the ability to produce a series of articles. Occasionally a beginner will be able to sell a series to a syndicate, but as a rule he is wasting his time and stamps to attempt it before he has become an authority, or at least recognized as an outstanding and reliable writer.

Slanting to the Magazines. Most beginners are familiar with the magazines of big circulations, the majority of which use articles only by well-known names. But they are not acquainted with the thousands of lesser-known periodicals that have achieved such success in their fields that advertising agencies consider them excellent media for their clients. Each has an appeal to a certain class of reader, and each has its special field. Each is like a store on Main Street: it has something definite to "sell" to its readers.

The personality of a magazine is the result of its editorial policy or program, developed over a period of years. It portrays the purpose behind the magazine, its motives, and something of the personality of the staff and writers. A magazine's identity is measured and its worth evaluated by the extent to which it serves its readers by understanding their problems and seeking and finding practical solutions. Every editorial staff attempts to develop its publication into a personality that its readers will like and of which the staff may be proud. If free-lance writers would learn something of the personalities of publications before outlining their articles, they could help editorial staffs to be of greater service to the subscribers as well as to insure the sale of their manuscripts.

Slanting Requires Thorough Study. In learning the personalities of magazines, one should try to know all the publications that cover the same field and what distinguishes one from another. If an article does not sell to the first periodical to which it is submitted, it may then be sent out again, with but minor changes, to one with a similar personality. As a writer becomes more experienced in the art of slanting, he will develop a sixth sense, or instinct, for discovering publications to suit the things about which he desires to write.

A novice should analyze several publications each week, in order to acquire a knowledge of the markets. Because of the great number of publications and the constant change in their policies, a writer probably will never know all of them thoroughly; but he should know every publication in each of the fields for which he is writing. If possible, three or more issues of a newspaper or magazine should be studied in order to see what the editor avoids and in what he specializes.

Magazines Vary in Appeal. Unlike newspapers, which interest persons of all classes, each magazine has its own particular group of readers. Since appeals are not in the same proportion to all persons, the class magazines were developed. Some appeal to a limited class group with similar ideas, while others interest a number of classes. Still others are directed toward the business man, the housewife, the home-owner, or the farm family. For every group, no matter how it is classified, there is a magazine skillfully edited to consider the readers' problems, interests, and pleasures. The editors are in the market for articles that will fit their particular publications. The feature writer has an advantage in that he can select his audience to make the right appeal. This point is discussed in the next chapter.

Classification of Magazines. Magazines are divided into two classes, the "slicks" and the "pulps," according to the quality of paper upon which they are printed. The former are printed on "slick paper," or high grade stock. Their contents include all types of writing—fiction, features, poems—in which the editor thinks his readers will be interested. The "pulps," or action magazines, as they are sometimes termed, are usually all fiction and are printed on pulp, a rough heavy paper. Since they seldom use fact articles, the feature writer is not usually concerned with them.

The "slick" periodicals consist of class, general, business, religious, and farm magazines. Standard Rate and Data Service lists a total 6,428 publications, with 253,516 issues annually. Each is a possible market for unsolicited manuscripts.

The class and general magazines number 632, with 10,807 issues a year. They each print from one to fifteen or twenty feature articles covering a wide range of subjects.

Business papers—trade journals and house organs—are listed as numbering 1,585, and publish 31,736 issues a year. Some of the journals consist entirely of features, while others carry one or more in each issue. They make up a class of periodicals that, for the most part, pays a lower rate than the class and general publications, but their editors buy more articles, not only because there are more of them but also because they receive relatively few unsolicited manuscripts. The majority of free-lance writers are not aware of their existence. They are edited to appeal to people in the professions, businesses, industries, and trades. They are concerned largely with aiding the subscribers to overcome their problems, inspiring them to greater effort in attaining success in their work, and pointing out occasions to widen their services or to increase their opportunities.

House organs are published by commercial organizations and business houses to appeal to limited groups. Their purpose differs from that of the trade journal in that they aim to serve as a means of establishing feelings of good fellowship and friendly relations among the subscribers, their staffs, or their customers. Railroad companies, shipping lines, and commercial concerns of all types issue such publications. Many of them have circulations that compare favorably with the trade papers. They afford markets for novices, because the editors do not have many manuscripts submitted to them and because writers are not aware of them. Many of them feature hobbies, amusements, sports, success stories, and guidance articles of all types. They offer advice or suggestions on everything of interest to the readers, who are members of the organization, employees, or customers of the firm issuing the organ.

Religious periodicals listed in the Standard Rate and Data Service directory number 237, totaling 8,311 issues annually. Their editors, like those of the business papers, do not have as many manuscripts submitted to them; and so they, too, are in the market for articles. The majority of the religious journals contain shorter features than do the general and business magazines, and as a rule they do not require as many illustrations. Although their rates are lower than those of other types of magazines, writers find them profitable. Sales are quicker and, if the articles are aptly slanted, sales are easier.

Farm publications are listed as numbering 3,974, with a total of 202,622 issues annually. This group, along with the business papers, offers the novice an excellent market for all types of practical articles of interest to the rural reader. Successful farm men and women, county agents, extension division leaders, and professors and research workers in agricultural colleges are excellent sources for articles for farm publications. They have knowledge and experience that will enable the beginner, by means of the interview, to write articles helpful to farm dwellers with problems.

When the beginner realizes the great variety of markets in all classes of magazines, he can look about him—no matter whether he lives in the heart of a great city or on a remote farm—and find numerous subjects that may be used by the five classes of "slick" paper magazines.

Manuscripts Are Submitted by the Thousands. The beginner need not be discouraged when he learns that such magazines as the *Saturday Evening Post* receives about 6,000 manuscripts a month and that *Good Housekeeping* gets more than 2,000 during the same period. The larger publications buy very few unsolicited manuscripts. Most of their articles are written "on assignment" or by special contract with well-known writers. But when the beginner recalls that there are 9,293 newspapers and magazines that publish from one to twenty articles in each of the 1,111,360 issues, and that a great majority of these periodicals receive only a few unsolicited manuscripts, he will realize that opportunities are about him everywhere if he will slant his articles.

Surveying the Contents of a Publication. Editors have said that 95 per cent of the failures to sell are due to the writers' lack of market knowledge. Many novices write the article and then consider where they can sell it. It behooves the writer to make thoughtful surveys of all classes of publications. The wider his market knowledge the greater will be his sales. As soon as one decides definitely on an idea for an article, he should select three or more markets to which he believes he could slant the material to fit the publications' policies. Strange as this method may seem to a beginner—determining the possible markets before doing the "research," or background reading, interviewing the interviewee, outlining the material, or starting the actual writing—it is the secret to success.

The survey of the publication should include a thorough analysis of the (1) reading matter, (2) photographs and illustrations, and (3) advertisements.

Analyzing the Reading Matter. Sending articles to magazines to have them rejected is not only costly in time and postage, but the delay in finding a market may make the article out of date, since newspaper feature editors plan their sections from three to six weeks, and magazine editors from four to six months, in advance. The professional as well as the beginner must study the markets constantly. Publications change policies by varying the appeal, the purpose, or the content. As soon as one becomes a free-lance writer, he becomes a perpetual student of publications if he wants to see his articles in print.

In examining the content and policy of a publication to which one is planning to submit a manuscript, he should: (1) study the table of contents, to see whether the by-lines are "big" names, the names of well-known writers, or names entirely unknown, in order to get an idea of the editor's attitude toward accepting manuscripts from beginners; (2) note the number of pages of features as compared with fiction, to perceive why the subscriber buys the magazine; and (3) scan the editorials, to ascertain the editor's point of view on topics that he discusses in addressing the reader, which may be a key to the policy of the publication.

The feature articles should be examined carefully to note: (1) the subject matter; (2) the types of articles that are used, particularly those that predominate and those that are used sparingly or not at all, in order to submit only the kinds that the editor uses; (3) the writers' general approach and point of view, in order to learn the editor's point of view; (4) the appeal and the kinds of persons to whom it is made; (5) whether the article contains the opinions of the writer or whether he interviewed an expert whose name or experience gave an authoritative tone; (6) the interest-arousing qualities of the paragraph beginnings; (7) the literary style, including figures of speech, and the vocabulary, to see if the publication has any preferred or standardized presentation; (8) the average length of the sentences, paragraphs, and the articles, in order to have a measuring stick for his own manuscripts; and (9) the style and length of the captions, or headlines, in order to "pattern" his after them, because if the editor uses sprightly and short ones, so should the writer.

Consideration should be given to the fiction, poetry, and special departments. The fiction and poetry indicate the editor's appeal to the subscribers' interests in reading for entertainment and relaxation, particularly if the former predominates. The special departments reveal the practical interests of the reader and the publication's policy of helping and guiding him. In addition, one may find possibilities and opportunities of submitting manuscripts to the departments.

Planning Pictures to Fit the Publication's Policy. Never have pictures been so important as they are today. Because "a picture is worth ten thousand words," as Confucius said, beginners and professionals alike must give considerable thought to the illustrations of their articles. Writers must learn to think in terms of pictures. As a nation, we have become picture-minded. By means of pictures, editors hope to create an even greater demand for their publications. If the editor "sells" his publication to his readers on the appeal of pictures, the writer, in turn, must "sell" the editor his manuscript on the same basis.

Snapshots generally are preferred to the formally posed photographs taken in a photographer's studio, although some editors use both. One, however, must know which kind the editor prefers before he arranges for the illustration of his manuscript. Other kinds of illustrations, such as drawings, charts, graphs, and maps, should be noted, because some newspapers and magazines have the policy of using them, although others would reject them.

Advertising Analysis Is Clue to Reader Interest. A feature writer must develop the habit of investigating the advertising to gain an insight into the reader's income and interests and to know the manuscript markets better. Advertising agencies spend thousands of dollars annually to learn all they can about the readers of each magazine that they use as a medium for their clients' copy. By means of surveying the subscriber, they know the source and range of his income, of his buying power, his living standard, his education, his class standing, his recreational interests, and his likes and dislikes. They know where the magazine's readers live and how they live. They know the number of readers who buy the publication by subscription and the number who buy it on the newsstands. They know whether they are professional, business, industrial, or agricultural people. The agencies know how much the readers spend on necessities and how much on luxuries. They know whether they are single or married; the size of their families; and whether they own their homes or rent them. They know whether they go to church or to the golf course on Sunday.

On the basis of these tabulations, made from questionnaires and surveys, the agencies place their clients' advertisements. Because the advertising agency must know where it can get the best returns, it must know everything it possibly can about the readers to whom the appeal is made in the advertising copy. Thus, one sees that the advertising is a safe guide for the writer if he would know all about the readers. A knowledge of a publication's advertising will enable a writer better to interest the reader in his article. Agencies do not buy space at anywhere from $50 to $15,000 or more a page without knowing who will read and be influenced by the advertising copy. For his purposes, the writer does not have to spend thousands of dollars, nor even a single dollar, to learn about the readers, if he will use the agencies' knowledge. He can profit by their studies by simply familiarizing himself with the advertising.

By noticing whether or not the magazine carries advertising for servant's uniforms, vacuum cleaners, carpet sweepers, or brooms, the writer will learn a great deal about the reader. Or it may be the kinds of floor coverings, kinds of refrigeration, kinds of automobiles, or prices and brands of wearing apparel advertised that may serve as a guide to knowing the subscribers. For example, if a brand of shoes is advertised for $1.95, or one for $22.50, the writer will know a great deal about the reader's income, spending power, and his interests. Immediately in his mind he will picture an average person in whichever group the appeal is made. With this definite picture of the reader in mind, he will be able to slant his article to appeal to him better.

The percentages of reading matter and advertising copy

should be compared to indicate something of the probable income of the publication. A comparison with other magazines that are similar in appeal also should be made, in order to determine which publication is regarded by the advertising agencies as having the greatest reader interest.

Because the income from advertising and from subscriptions is so closely related, one may profit in slanting by knowing the circulation figures of a publication. This may be obtained by looking in one of the publication yearbooks or directories listed under the "Free-Lance Writers' Library" in the Appendix. The appeal of the advertising and the subscription price are clues to the kind of reader a publication has. Careful and thoughtful analysis of advertising and circulation will repay the writer manyfold, because it will lessen his opportunities to receive rejections.

Examining the Advertising Tie-up. In modern publication production, the business and advertising departments influence the editorial department either consciously or unconsciously. Successful periodicals must have an editorial policy that harmonizes with the salesmanship aims of the agencies that place the national advertising. The readers of the magazine also read the advertisements, and this means that the two policies must necessarily consider the same reader. If the magazine is to obtain subscribers and the advertising copy is to sell the goods displayed in the advertising, the two divisions must cooperate with each other.

A recent study of seven of the largest women's monthly magazines, made by the author over a six-months' period, revealed a decided "tie-up" of the editorial copy, or reading matter, with the advertising copy of each of the periodicals analyzed. For example, an article on cosmetics either described the container or pictured it so distinctly that the brand name showed or that the reader-consumer could recognize the brand by the shape of the jar or carton. In some instances the advertised brands were mentioned in the article. The survey disclosed a range from 36 definite advertising "tie-ups" in the *Ladies' Home Journal* to 147 in the *Woman's Home Compan-*

ion. The remaining five women's magazines over the same period averaged 85 "tie-ups" for each publication. In sixteen outstanding monthly farm publications for the same six months, the advertising "tie-ups" varied from 2 in *Country Home* to 66 in the *California Cultivator,* with the other fourteen magazines averaging 28 apiece. The percentage for the two classes of magazines was practically the same, because the farm publications, on the whole, are much smaller in size and have a lower number of advertising accounts. Because of the nature of the appeal in both reading matter and advertising copy, it is easier to plan advertising "tie-ups" in these types of magazines. But even a scanning of other publications will show that almost every magazine makes use of the opportunity when it is offered. Even if the "tie-up" is not obvious, the article may begin where the advertising leaves off, because the policy of magazines is to help both the reader and the advertiser as much as possible.

From analyses that writers will make, they will find that they should give heed to opportunities to write articles for farm and women magazines that lend themselves to possible "tie-ups" with advertising copy. A young writer observed that a farm magazine did not carry advertising copy of washing machines or other laundry equipment. She interviewed an authority on household management and several housewives, and then wrote an article on "Short Cuts to an Easy Washday." In the note to the editor she called his attention to the opportunity to solicit laundry equipment advertising. The editor of *Capper's Farmer* bought the article for $25. The advertising staff contacted manufacturers of washing machines, mangles, and soap (or the agencies placing their advertising copy), and increased the magazine's advertising lineage and revenue. Another writer, basing her material on an uncopyrighted government bulletin for authority, used the same approach in her note to the editor and sold an article on "Canned Meat That Keeps" for $30 to a woman's editor. The article was used to contact national advertisers of pressure cookers and resulted in added advertising lineage for that publication.

Antagonizing advertisers in manuscripts should be avoided. Editors will not purchase articles that will offend their financial supporters. A novice wrote an article on "Making Your Own Face Creams," in which he pointed out the money that women could save by not buying commercial products. He insisted on sending it to a well-known woman's magazine that carries a great amount of "copy" advertising high-priced cosmetics. He could have saved time and his postage on the manuscript had he given thought to the attitude of the publication's advertisers toward such an article. Eventually he sold the article to a periodical that did not carry cosmetic advertising. In writing for the "slick" magazines that take advantage of advertising "tie-ups," one writes to the advertisers as well as to the readers, while the fiction writer slanting to the "pulps" writes only to the readers, because that class of publications depends on support from subscriptions and newsstand sales rather than from advertising.

Developing a Selling Technique. A card file, even a small one that costs only a dime, will be convenient for recording for future reference the market information one acquires from his publication studies. Since magazines are changing constantly, one must keep up to date and add the changes to the card as he notes them. By analyzing the articles that have been accepted and by slanting material to the editor's needs, beginners and semi-professionals will soon have prospective feature writers examining *their* articles as they appear in print, to see how they attained their acceptances.

From this five-pointed plan, the prospective writer realizes that success is not due to being a good writer entirely. He must also be a good judge of markets. Like the aviator, he must have a sixth sense; but instead of a sense of balance, the writer has the sense of slant that enables him to plan and write his manuscripts to appeal to a definite editor of a definite publication.

Beginners Should Aim at Small Markets. Novices frequently are torn between the urge to submit their manuscripts to the better-known class publications, in order to satisfy their hope for renown, and the desire to submit to the less familiar ones and receive acceptances instead of rejections. This problem can be solved in their minds before it is formulated if they stop to realize that the bigger and better known the magazine is, the greater and keener the competition. Most amateurs are astonished when they learn of the number of publications for which they could write. Because they are lazy or indifferent, they continue submitting manuscripts to a few well-known magazines—with the result that the articles are returned in an astonishingly short time.

Amateurs often feel that they are handicapped if they do not live in one or the other of the two great publishing centers, New York or Chicago. The experience, however, of many professionals proves the fallacy of their desire. The advice that successful writers and editors give to the beginner is to stay in the community that he knows and where he can find marketable material to interest readers. Since the great majority of subscribers do not live in the publishing centers, the editors, in order to interest their readers, desire manuscripts concerning things close to the readers' lives—another point that the writer must keep in mind as he writes.

The Use of Manuscript Market Guides. Guides to the manuscript markets are available for writers who wish to learn more about opportunities for selling. Their greatest value lies in acquainting the writer with the fact that such markets exist. If possible, he should examine copies of the publication suggested in the market books before writing the article. The market books are suggestive in supplying ideas for "tips." Upon learning that there is such a market, one may think of subjects that he quickly may turn into salable features. A young man turned through a market book and noticed a trade journal for barbers. He wrote up the experiences of a student who became a barber in order to earn his way through college. He received $25 for the manuscript. Another saw listed a magazine for shoe-repair men, and that reminded him that the manager of the shoe-repair shop where he had just had his shoes mended would make a good success article. He sent in the story and received $20. Used with intelligence and ingenuity, the market lists may be of real value not only in suggesting markets but ideas for articles. A number of the market books are listed in the Appendix.

Querying the Editor. A beginner does not need to be concerned about querying an editor in order to get approval before writing an article. Editors do not buy manuscripts unseen, except from professionals with whose work they are familiar. In that case, there are times when the professional might save his time, energy, or expense by querying the editor. As a rule, however, the best plan is to write the article and submit it. The editor might accept it because of the way it is written, the clever style, or its unique point of view, which, of course, he would not discern in a note of query.

The Use of Literary Agents. The feature writer wastes his time in depending upon literary agents to market his manuscripts. (1) They are interested only in selling articles for professionals who write regularly and whose manuscripts demand high prices. (2) One may have more difficulty in persuading an agent to accept him as a client than he would have in marketing his material himself. (3) If the article is timely, it may get out of date while it is on the agent's desk waiting until he has the time or inclination to try to place it.

By having the services of an agent, the writer is less likely to keep up his analyses of magazines. As a consequence, he is not as familiar with reader interests and is not as adept in slanting his material as he would be if he marketed his own articles. Then, too, he has to pay a fee to the agent.

If a writer finds it necessary to employ an agent after he has become well known, he should make careful investigation as to the agent's reliability before contacting him. One should avoid making any agreement with an agent who makes extravagant claims and promises and who requires a fee in advance. The writer who receives offers from unknown agents should resist the alluring contract. Reliable agents who have the confidence and respect of the big magazines do not have to solicit clients. If an article has merit, any editor to whom it is submitted will recognize it without the influence of an agent. In fiction writing, however, a reliable agent may save even the beginner hundreds of rejections. Marketing unsolicited stories or serials presents a more difficult problem to the author than does selling features.

One Sale Leads to Another. Just as experience is most valuable in applying for a position, so is success in selling. The acceptance of a manuscript gives the beginner confidence because he has learned to study the markets with an eye for slanting his material. With the success of selling just one article he loses his fear of a rejection slip. Because the editor is generally more willing to trust a writer whom he has tried once and found competent, it is a good plan to try to follow up one sale with another. Personal contacts with an editor means nothing unless one can prove to him his unfaltering dependability as a writer.

Contacts Resulting from Sales. If a writer sells regularly to a publication, particularly to those in the trade field, he may be offered an associate editorship or he may be offered a position as a staff writer. If the publication is a monthly one, it is not difficult for the writer to produce the required articles in addition to his regular work. If an editor finds a free-lance writer dependable, he may ask him to do articles on assignment, or on order. If a writer wants a position on the staff of a particular publication, he may attract the attention of the editor by submitting unsolicited manuscripts. Strong friendships often spring up between editors and contributors who submit manuscripts regularly over a period of time.

Basis of Payment. Financial compensation varies with publications, because they pay upon the basis of their incomes. The income of most periodicals is dependent entirely upon the circulation and the advertising, with the latter contributing the largest percentage. A magazine like the *Saturday Evening Post,* which at the end of 1937 carried 1,880,932 lines of advertising at $8,000 a page, surpassed all records by earning a gross revenue of $26,575,599, according to *Time* magazine. It also broke all circulation records in magazine history. Its 50,000 boy salesmen totaled a weekly circulation of 157,456,000 copies. The magazine broke its own record by buying twenty-three unsolicited manuscripts from the 70,000 submitted by free-lance writers (until 1937 the publication had never bought more than ten in a year). It specializes in new writers, and last year it used 147 on assignment; but an analysis of the by-lines showed that although their names were new in the *Post,* they were professional writers who contributed to other publications. From this sketch of the magazine one may sense at a glance that the *Saturday Evening Post* should be able to pay generously when it does accept an unsolicited article.

Naturally a less-popular periodical with a smaller income from advertising and subscriptions could not pay as much for a free-lance article as the *Post* does. On the other hand, the smaller magazine, in comparison with the *Post,* does not receive many manuscripts from free-lance writers and, because it cannot pay professional writers big sums, it depends more on the unsolicited manuscripts of the beginners and semi-professionals than on those written "on assignment." Until his name becomes well known, the beginner will fare better if he slants to the smaller markets.

It is a tradition in free-lancing that no matter how much time, energy, and expense the writer may have put on his manuscript, he does not set a price on his work but accepts what the editor offers. If he feels the price is not sufficient, he may refuse it; and when the manuscript is returned to him, he may submit it elsewhere. As a rule, the wise beginner accepts what he is offered, because he cannot set a price until he has become established in free-lancing. Professional writers, whose by-lines are known, may benefit by shopping about for a better price. One writer, who had been having his manuscripts accepted for years, was offered $75 for one that he felt was worth more. He refused the offer and later sold the article to a larger publication for $300. Such instances, however, are the exception even for the professional.

In writing for the newspapers, one may expect anywhere from $2.50 to $10 per column; from the magazines one may expect anywhere from $3.50 up to $1,000, the price depending upon the publication's ability to pay, the importance of the article, and the name of the writer.

Slanting Has Its Rewards. A good writer likes to think of himself as a literary artist, but he must also consider himself a practical business person. He must be a good salesman. And like the salesmen in other lines of business, he must know where to sell his wares. A writer's ability to slant his manuscripts, or the lack of it, either lifts him into the rank of the professional or dooms him to failure. The first law of free-lancing is that the manuscript must be slanted to fit the publication to which it is submitted. Slanting not only enables the writer to sell, but it also provides him with ideas for more articles.

An ambitious, enthusiastic student, in spite of her instructor's advice, did not wait to study the markets in order to slant her material. She wrote the article, and, like a blind hunter, shot hit or miss at the magazines. The result was that the article always came back. By the end of the course, she had sold all the other articles she had written because she slanted them carefully. After analyzing a publication that she was confident would take the material if it were slanted for it, she rewrote the first article. A couple of weeks later she sought out her instructor to report a check for $65, which completely converted her to the doctrine that "it pays to slant."

When a writer has an article in print, he should always obtain a copy of that issue, not only to serve as a source of gratification but to keep in his files for future reference. He may wish to present it in applying for a staff position on a publication; or, if the articles are along a certain line, he may want to publish them later in book form. Whether or not he ever makes use of his file of published articles, it will be a satisfaction to see his printed articles increase as he becomes more adept in slanting and has greater success in selling.

EXERCISES

1. From observation of your favorite newsstand or from talking with its owner, how many new magazines have come out during the past year?
2. How many have ceased publication in that same period?
3. What magazines with which you are familiar have changed their policy during the last year? What change or changes were made?
4. Have any of the big magazines changed ownership during the last year? If so, what ones?
5. List all the publications with which you are really familiar and list their appeals to the reader as you recall them from having read the publications for some time.
6. Select four from the list and enumerate the feature articles and short stories.
7. In recalling the appeal of the advertising copy, do you believe the editors have planned the publication for the lower, middle, or upper class?
8. What item in the current news suggests to you an idea for a feature that might be hung on a "news peg" for one of the magazines that you already know?
9. Select a feature story in the magazine section of your Sunday newspaper and one in your favorite magazine and list all the differences that you can find.
10. After looking up the circulation of the four magazines on your list in Exercise 6, jot down the ideas you have about what kind of appeals you should incorporate into articles if you were writing for them.
11. Make a chart for the material in your favorite metropolitan newspaper by listing the feature articles in the feature section in one column. In the second column indicate the probable sources from which the editor obtained each.
12. Add to your chart the information concerning: (1) the classification of the articles; (2) the points of view from which they are written; (3) the form; (4) the style; (5) the length; and (6) the kind of reader to whom they would appeal, to judge from the advertising appeal; e.g., vacuum cleaner or carpet sweeper advertising, etc.

13. In a sentence, tell what kind of feature articles you think the Sunday feature editor wants for his readers.
14. For what departments, other than the feature section, do you think you could write features that the department editor would buy?
15. How many of the features listed in Exercise 11 concerned current, timely topics?
16. Indicate in your chart for Exercise 11 the features that are local, state, national, and international in appeal.
17. From your chart in Exercise 11, what did you find was the length of the shortest feature and of the longest? When you slant an article to this newspaper, how long should it be?
18. Add to the chart in Exercise 11 the number of pictures that each feature had. What does this tell you in reference to the policy concerning pictures?
19. Write a definition for editorial policy of a newspaper and for a magazine and point out how each varies.
20. What is the subscription price by the year and by the single issue of your favorite general magazine? From this, can you tell whether it is a magazine to which people take yearly subscriptions, or do they depend upon getting it at the newsstand?
21. How many advertisements does it carry?
22. Using as the basis the goods advertised, to what income level do you think the magazine appeals? What kind of subject matter would a free-lance writer send the publication?
23. List the names of one magazine of each of the five types of "slicks."
24. List four ideas, or "tips," for features that you could write for each publication you listed in Exercise 23.
25. Work out a chart for your favorite magazine as you did in Exercise 11 for the newspaper. Include the information suggested on page 272, on Analyzing the Reading Matter. Include the three points concerning the content and policy of the publication.
26. In analyzing each of the feature articles, list the nine points suggested in this chapter, on page 272.
27. In analyzing the fiction, list the two points suggested in this chapter, on pages 272, 273.
28. Are formal or informal photographs used to illustrate the

features, and how many pictures of each type does each article have?

29. Does the publication use any other type of illustration besides photographs? If so, list them on your chart.
30. Analyze the magazine advertising to see whether it appeals to the readers in the home equipped with a broom, a carpet sweeper, a vacuum cleaner, or with servants in uniforms? Or take any other commodity advertised as a basis for your judgment in studying the appeal of the advertising copy.
31. What percentage (by page) of the publication is devoted to advertising? How do you think the advertising agencies regard it as a media for their clients?
32. Look in one of the periodical directories (N. W. Ayer & Son's *Directory of Newspapers and Periodicals,* the International Year Book Number of *Editor and Publisher,* or the magazine and farm section of Standard Rate and Data Service) and find the circulation of your favorite magazine.
33. Scan the articles again to see in how many there are any evident "tie-ups" with the commodities advertised. What were they?
34. From a brief survey of the market books to which you have access (see list in Appendix), indicate the individual purpose of each book in addition to that of listing the markets.
35. Suggest a "tip" for an article that came to you while you were examining the market books.

Publication Analysis

Saturday Evening Post and *American Magazine*

Do not spend more than two hours on preparation of this report.

I. Identification: Name of magazine, name of editor, where published, price. Do single sales or yearly subscription attract the purchaser?

II. Make-up: What do you like or not like about the size and make-up of these magazines? If you were the editor, what changes would you make in them?

III. Advertising: To what classes and types of purchasers does the advertising appeal (broom, carpet-sweeper, or vacuum-cleaner class)? Did you notice any advertising that appealed to a particular class? Judging from the advertising, what types of features do you think these magazines would buy?

IV. General Policy:

1. Do these magazines have editorials? What is the content and appeal of editorials?
2. What percentage (rough estimate) is devoted to fiction in each, and to whom does it appeal?
3. What is the circulation of each magazine? (See one of the directories.)
4. What are the chances for selling, to judge from the names of the writers?

V. Feature Articles:

1. What types of feature articles and what subject did you find in these magazines?
2. What devices were used to make the feature articles attractive to the reader?
3. List the thing that you liked about one feature.
4. List the things that you did not like about it.
5. List the things that you learned about "how to write features" or to "slant" to these magazines.
6. Did you find any announcement of "clubs" or contests? What is the purpose of a contest? Do you have any "tips" you could write to submit?

VI. Slogan: Make a slogan for these magazines.

VII. Four Tips: Source, authority, and three possible markets suggested by this study.

10 PLANNING AND OUTLINING THE ARTICLE

The Purpose of a Plan. Planning the feature article has been likened by some writers to architecture. The architect cannot build without a plan; neither can the writer "build," or write, without one. Others have compared the work of the artist with that of the writer. Like the artist, the writer must get all the details, in order to enable the reader to see the article and understand it as the writer wishes. The writer uses words rather than a brush, but the purposes and the results are the same. Still others have compared writing to public speaking. The writer, like the speaker, must catch the attention of the reader. But the writer has to hold his reader-audience after he gets his attention. If he does not, the reader will go on to the next column or page, while the speaker's audience will not often be so rude as to walk out of the meeting. The work of the writer is more similar, in that respect, to that of the person who speaks via the radio. If the person before the microphone does not hold his audience's attention, his audience will turn the dial to another station. Neither the broadcaster nor the writer can expect to hold attention if he attempts to work without a plan.

The writer of a feature article is much like the pioneer who crossed the frontier and blazed a trail in order to start a new life in a new place under new conditions. Although the pioneer had definite ideas of the kind of place to which he hoped he was going to establish a home and occupation or business, he had to adjust those plans to meet the actual physical conditions of the new land, the living standards of his fellow settlers, and the opportunities or the hardships as he found them. The true pioneer always knew what he wanted to do and why he wanted to do it, and he never became discouraged. No matter how much writing one may have done, each article offers new frontiers, like the pioneer's trail into a new and unknown land. The writer, like the pioneer, must have a purpose, a definite goal, and he must plan his trail, or outline, just as carefully and as enthusiastically.

Writers Write to Help the Reader. The newspaper feature section or magazine that helps the readers is the most successful. As previously pointed out, in order to help the reader, one must think of him constantly—that is, not of readers in a mass, but of a particular reader. If one would write successfully, he should think in terms of a person whom he knows. But he must remember that instead of talking to one person he is talking to hundreds, or even millions, of people who are like the one person or the several persons he knows.

Writer Writes to Please Readers. The writer who receives checks for his manuscripts, rather than rejections, never writes to please himself, but always to please the readers of a particular publication to which he wishes to sell his manuscript. He does not outline the material nor write the article until he has given those readers a great deal of thought as to: (1) who will be interested; (2) why he will be interested; and (3) how much he will be interested. Not until the writer has answered these three questions can he successfully plan his article.

In order to please his readers, the writer must visualize them. Only the businesslike writer is able to do this. One cannot visualize readers unless he knows who the readers are. By careful analysis of the advertising in the publication to which one is slanting, one may visualize the subscribers accurately. Not until then can the writer plan and write the article interestingly and sincerely.

Timeliness Is Important. Because the contents of magazines must be timely when they are published and on the newsstands, writers must plan their articles long in advance. For magazines, a writer should plan his material six months in advance, because many editors plan the contents of their magazines that far ahead. If the article is returned the first time it is mailed, there is then still time to send it to one or two other publications. In submitting to newspaper feature editors, the writer should plan his material six, or at least three, weeks in advance, if possible. Even newspaper feature editors must plan their make-up, art layouts, and engravings some time ahead. Exceptions may be made in magazines and newspapers only when the material is particularly timely. Sometimes the editor of the newspaper feature section will pass a particularly current article that is too late for his section on to one of the departmental news editors, who may use part of the article as news, at a much smaller rate than the feature editor pays.

Catching the Attention of the Reader. In the planning of the article, much thought must be given to the devices of obtaining the reader's attention. The feature writer, like the advertising writer, must (1) catch the reader's attention, (2) arouse his interest, and (3) hold his interest throughout the article, by making the body of it so interesting that the reader cannot lay down his newspaper or magazine until he has finished reading the article.

When one visualizes hundreds or millions of readers intensely interested in an article, the amateur may think that it will be difficult to catch and hold reader interest for his own work. In reality, however, it is very simple if the writer gives a great deal of thought to planning. Before beginning to write, he should have a definite idea of: (1) the title, or caption, or heading; (2) the lead, or beginning of the article; (3) the plan of development of the body of the article; (4) the conclusion; and (5) the illustrative material, including photographs, snapshots, drawings, maps, charts, and graphs. In the planning of the outline, one frequently may determine the caption last, or he may plan the illustrations before he outlines his material. The order of planning is not important, but the five elements of the tentative outline, or plan, are essential to success.

Determining the Aim of the Article. There may be so many interesting phases of an article that the writer may attempt to include all of them, with the result that the article will be aimless and uninteresting because it does not make a definite impression on the reader's mind. An amateur interviewed an authority in home economics concerning vitamins in foods. Before completing his material, he had talked to several experts and, when he came to outline the article, found that his notes included not only the nutritive value of foods, but the canning, storage, and preparation. He felt that all these phases were important, and he included them, forgetting that the magazine to which he was slanting the article was concerned with only the health value. After class criticism of his article, he eliminated all material except that which pertained to the health value for the health magazine. From the remainder of his notes he wrote an article on canning and storage of vegetables for a farm publication. A third one, on food preparation, he slanted to a home magazine. In due time he received three checks, which made him feel well repaid for the thought and time he had given to re-planning the three aims for three articles instead of crowding them all into one manuscript without a definite aim.

The writer, whether amateur or professional, before planning his outline should always ask himself "Whom am I trying to help or please and how am I going to do so?" In other words, one must determine the aim or purpose of the article before selecting from his notes the material that he wishes to include. After having selected the aim, the writer must never fail to stick to that aim or angle of the subject that pertains to it.

Articles Have Three Aims. In turning through magazines and newspapers, one finds that each article has one of three purposes. It aims to (1) inform, (2) give practical help, or (3) entertain the reader. A clever writer frequently can treat the same subject and the same material to accomplish two or more of the aims. If his purpose is to give facts to inform or add to the reader's scope of information and knowledge, he will present them in a manner that will impress and stimulate the reader's mind. If he desires to help or guide the reader in his practical pursuits, work, or recreation, he may include all the details that will enable anyone to use the suggestions in a practical way. But if one step of the process is omitted, the reader's efforts will result in failure. If the article's aim is to entertain, the writer will select a style and the aspects of the topic that will provide amusement, diversion, or recreation for the reader. An amateur found that in gathering material for an article on trout fishing he had accumulated notes that would inform, instruct, and entertain the reader. His good judgment told him that he could not catch and hold the reader-attention if he tried to accomplish all three aims in one article. He sent the informative one to a general outdoor magazine, where it was purchased after the writer had revised it to meet the editor's suggestions. A helpful lesson in trout fishing under the caption "Beginners Can Catch 'Em Too" was sold on its second trip in the mail. The third, "Trout and Mosquitoes Are a Lot of Fun," was purchased by an adventure magazine to amuse its subscribers. Had the writer tried to incorporate the three aims in one article he would have failed to interest any one reader for any length of time.

Informative Articles. Every free-lance writer has unlimited opportunities to write articles containing interesting and significant information. Nearly everyone who desires to be better informed depends on features in newspapers and magazines for latest news and opinions concerning current affairs, as well as biography and history with which the current events may be concerned. The average reader, after graduation from high school or grade school, turns to newspapers and magazines for his further education. Only a small proportion of the 130,000,000 people living in the United States go on to college. In planning the informative type of article, the writer must select only those facts that are worth remembering or that will stimulate the reader to think about the subject. By keeping the purpose firmly in mind, the writer will be able to select the material intelligently and to determine the point of view from which he should write the article in order to attract and hold the reader's interest.

Practical Guidance Features. Articles giving the reader practical help, suggestions, or guidance have not only increased in number during the past decade, but whole magazines are now devoted to such features. People want to get more pleasure out of living, to advance, to be more successful, or to do for themselves what others have done successfully. Therefore, their interest is easily attracted and held with articles of this type. The simplest guidance articles are found in the recipe features in women's magazines.

Utility articles may be written as simple how-to-do articles in which definite directions are given. Or they may be written so that the utilitarian purpose is not obvious to the readers, because the detail of carrying out the processes is presented so interestingly that the readers are not bored with all the information necessary to accomplish a similar enterprise. They will be interested because the narration and description appeal to their imagination.

In writing articles of this type, the author must consider carefully the class of readers whom he hopes will be reading the article, and must give thought to their ability to carry out directions. A device that will often serve to hold the reader's interest is that of the writer who confides in the reader that he has made mistakes. Such a device can be used only in a personal experience article written in the first person. If the third person is used, the writer may relate how the interviewee made some mistakes because he tried some short cut or did not follow directions accurately. If the reader feels that the writer or the interviewee was not perfect the first time he undertook to do or to make the thing described, the reader not only will have more interest but more confidence in attempting the undertaking. This device also softens the egotistical or "preachy" tone that is so easily given to guidance articles.

Leads must be particularly attractive in this type of article.

The writer has to make the article appeal to the reader by means of a clever beginning. Dialogue makes an effective beginning if it is handled well; or direct address is a good beginning by which to attract the reader's eye.

Entertaining Articles. The supply of entertaining articles has never exceeded the demand. Not every free-lance writer seems to have the ability to write features containing humor, pathos, adventure, or romance in a style that will hold the reader's interest to the end. But to the writer who can see the comedy and tragedy or the adventure and romance in life about him, the opportunities are unlimited for writing entertaining features. Because the reader's desire for this type of feature article is never satisfied, he turns to fiction, drama, and the moving pictures.

To prepare such articles is not difficult if the writer has a sense of humor, a sympathetic point of view, an understanding of human nature, and can express himself cleverly by means of an apt vocabulary. The larger part of the success of an article aimed to entertain depends upon the way in which the writer stimulates the reader to see what he wants him to see. This is done by avoiding general terms and using specific words. Every verb should be scrutinized to see that it is a colorful, suggestive word. Use of figures of speech, if original and clever, adds much to the style of this type of article.

Articles aiming to entertain are the most difficult to write before the writer has acquired considerable experience, unless he is particularly gifted or has practiced writing this type of article in his spare moments. Just because editors have difficulty in supplying the demand for good entertainment articles, a writer—amateur or professional—need not think that it is useless for him to attempt such features. On the contrary, he should practice writing them—even short pointed paragraphs—until he finds he has developed a skill to write in an entertaining style.

Young beginners frequently have the mistaken notion that in order to write in an entertaining style they must stoop beneath the best journalistic standards and write articles that, if printed, would have a pernicious influence. No matter what the editor's personal standard of ethics may be, he will not buy articles that will result in adverse criticism of his publication and in cancellation of subscriptions. To sell entertaining features, one must always write in a constructive vein and never stoop to gratifying a reader's taste for the morbid.

Formulating the Purpose. In order to write marketable features, the writer must obviously have a definite purpose—not only when he gathers his material, but when he outlines and writes his article. To avoid drifting away from the purpose as he outlines or writes, the free-lance will do well always to write down in one sentence at the top of the first page of his outline a statement of the aim and purpose of the article. When the writer cannot decide which of his notes do or do not pertain to the article's purpose, a glance at the statement at the top of the outline may aid him in sticking to his aim and subject. With the purpose clearly defined, it is easier to devote the proper amount of space to each division of the outline, and thus avoid too much detail in some parts of the article and too little in others. If the purpose is not clear as the writer plans his outline, the finished article may lack coherence and unity, which lack may necessitate the rewriting of the article.

A definite objective in outlining and writing each article will result in sales; without it the writer will have rejections rather than acceptances to show for his efforts at the typewriter.

Planning the Reader Appeal. The millions of people who read fact articles in newspapers and magazines differ in their interests because of differences in race, temperament, environment, education, society, occupations, professions, recreation, health, and wealth. There are, consequently, thousands of publications, to appeal to those particular interests. In planning the appeal to make in an article to catch and hold the reader interest, the writer must realize that keen competition faces him. But if he has the spirit of the pioneer toward his writing, this very competition in appealing to the reader will afford the writer a great deal of pleasure and satisfaction.

Appeals Are Based on Psychology. No matter what appeals the writer uses, he must base them on common sense and the principles of psychology. In every article he must assume that he is addressing people who are uninformed and uninterested and who need their attention not only pricked, but stabbed, to catch and hold their interest. A writer does not need to be sensational, but he must know how he can get and keep the reader's attention. The various psychological devices by which this may be done are: (1) an emphatic caption and lead, to catch the reader's attention; (2) emphatic paragraph leads throughout the article, so that as the reader's eye wanders down the column he will retain his interest and will read on to the end; (3) association, by means of reference to people, places, or things with which the reader is familiar; (4) recall of things the reader has experienced at some previous time; and (5) using the point of view of the reader, in order to aid him in seeing himself in the article.

In addition to knowing the devices by which one may appeal to the reader, one must know: (1) how widespread the reader-interest in the subject is; (2) just how much it will appeal to the reader of the publication for which the article is being slanted; and (3) what phases of the appeal will have the greatest interest for the greatest number of readers. These things one cannot determine without knowing and liking people, or without knowing the likes and dislikes of the publication's readers. The things that a reader likes to see, hear, and do are the things that in his reading will give him pleasure and satisfaction.

Every human being wants to be healthy, wealthy, and wise to at least some degree. In appealing to readers, remember that magazines are based upon this principle. If the writer succeeds in showing the reader the way to health, wealth, and wisdom, the editors will buy what he writes.

Select Appeals with Wide Interest. Eight out of ten articles that come to an editor's desk cannot be used because the interest does not have an appeal to his particular readers. If the writer observes closely, he will find some appeal in every experience. "What I Think of My Boss," which appeared in *Harpers Magazine,* had an appeal to each boss. When he read the article, he immediately wondered what his workers thought of him. It had equal appeal to every employee, because as he read the feature he compared his superior with that of the writer's. The article had wide appeal. It caught the attention of every employer and every employee. Consequently, the article had practically 100 per cent interest for that particular magazine's readers. After the writer had selected her subject, she visualized her audience and sought a publication whose readers she knew would be receptive to the topic.

When a writer is tempted to give but little attention to the development of the article's appeals, he should imagine that he along with 100,000 others are at a football game where he is called upon to make a speech between halves. He sees the packed stadium, the press box with its alert reporters from the metropolitan newspapers and press associations, and the amplifiers to carry his voice to all parts of the huge structure. In the seats are people from all walks of life with all kinds of interests. What subject will the speaker select. If he knows how to appeal to his audience, he will not attempt to discuss the Einstein theory—for two reasons perhaps. He will choose a simple subject with a wide appeal, the one thing in which every one of the 100,000 would be interested—football. Editors of magazines and newspaper feature sections must find articles that will appeal to even larger crowds, since some of them have ten million subscribers.

Subjects that Have Reader Appeal. If a writer studies the features in newspapers and magazines, he finds a wide variety of subjects to attract readers. They have been selected by editors because they appealed to the readers. For convenience, the subjects may be divided into the following classes, but, as in any grouping one might arrange, there is bound to be considerable overlapping: (1) current topics; (2) the unusual and extraordinary; (3) mysteries and catastrophes; (4) romance and sex; (5) adventure and exploits; (6) competitive contests; (7) child and adult life; (8) animal life; (9) recreations and hobbies; (10) the familiar and well known; (11) business, professional, and home interests; (12) social welfare; and (13) success and happiness.

Current Topics. Human beings are instinctively curious about what goes on around them. Therefore, timeliness of subjects is an important factor in writing features. Readers like to be the first to know the news, to get the latest and most recent facts, and to know the details of most recent developments. It is easier to sell features that are current, and a writer will profit by finding a timely angle in any subject about which he is writing. Current topics have such a wide appeal that entire magazines are devoted to articles that depend on the appeal of timeliness to interest the reader.

The Unusual and the Extraordinary. The alert writer finds articles everywhere in which he can make use of the appeal of the unusual, unique, extraordinary, or novel. Readers are ever curious about the things that are not commonplace and familiar in their own lives. The biggest, the smallest, the greatest, or the first of anything—all have appeals. For this reason, the extraordinary and novel in the physical, industrial, commercial, and social life about us provide subjects to interest subscribers.

Mysteries and Catastrophes. People are fascinated by anything they cannot understand or by events producing subversion of the usual order of things. Fiction abounds with these appeals. They are the basis for the ever-popular mystery story in which readers from all walks of life find relaxation. The journalist will find in life all about him events that will furnish subject matter sufficiently mysterious or startling to appeal to this type of reader, who is curious or superstitious about the unnatural and the calamitous.

Romance and Sex. Of the elemental instincts, that of love is one of the strongest, according to psychologists. The romance in the life about him is more interesting to the reader than that in fiction. It has been said, "All the world loves a lover." If that is true, all the world loves a romantic feature. Never before has there been so much space devoted to the discussion of sex, but to sell, the articles must be based upon expert authority and avoid an appeal to the morbid.

Adventure and Exploits. New and hazardous enterprises and heroic acts have a wider reader appeal. There are few subscribers who do not enjoy escaping from their monotonous lives for even a few minutes by reading daring tales concerning their fellow men. Many fiction writers capitalize on this method of appeal, and the feature writer could do well to pattern after the novelist. The thrilling tales of the aviator, the radio operator, the explorer, the seaman, the engineer, or the pioneer in any field offers an opportunity to catch and hold the reader's interest.

Competitive Contests. Any struggle for superiority, victory, or defense—whether friendly or hostile—has a strong appeal. Human beings have an inborn love, or competitive instinct, for a good fight, whether it is a battle between prize fighters or contestants in a recreation room, or at the bridge table. Everywhere the writer will find material for an article based upon man's inward impulse to fight to win. Business, politics, sports, strikes, revolutions, conquering the air, the water, and communication are but a few of the topics that people read because they give a zest to their humdrum existences.

Child and Adult Life. Living beings, whether children or adults, attract the reader. All types of articles concerning child and adult life are of interest. Love for children and for life is instinctive to all mankind. A child, even the most unattractive urchin, is given sympathy and admiration. Every person recalls his own childhood and sees in the youngster before him the image of his former self. Articles on the education and welfare of children are in great demand, because of parent interest in them.

The appeal of association is the basis for reader interest concerning adult life. In each article concerning a person or persons, the reader finds interest because he, too, is a human being. It is instinctive to want to know more about that with which we may be familiar to at least some degree.

Animal Life. Features about animals have a perennial

charm for readers of newspapers and magazines. The readers are attracted by the animals' traits—those similar to as well as those dissimilar to human beings. Love for pets is almost as universal as love for children. Interest in animals of all kinds is the reason that the zoos are crowded by young and old, and that many Sunday editors regularly assign a "zoo story" for their sections. In addition to attention given to animals in captivity, there is keen interest in wild-animal life. Fishing, hunting, and trapping have an appeal to many as a sport, while to others it affords an occupation. The care and breeding of all types of domesticated animals on the farm supplies subject matter, not only for articles but for entire publications that are in the market for free-lance articles.

Recreation and Hobbies. Diversions, amusements, and pastime pursuits pertaining to all sorts of interests are always popular with readers. The instinct to play is one that even adults never lose entirely. The writer will find an easy market for articles with the recreation appeal, since editors buy them to intersperse between the more serious types, to use in special departments in both newspapers and magazines, and to use in magazines which contain only recreation features or hobby articles.

The Familiar and the Well Known. It has been said that the most thoroughly read publication is one's home-town newspaper. If the statement is true, it is because the news concerns people and places familiar to the subscriber. Alert news editors always try to find a "local end" to add to the appeal to news accounts that happen elsewhere. Just because a person, place, or object is well known in one community is no reason for it not to be known in another. All the citizens in a county may have known for years about the druggist who has been in business in the same building for fifty years. They may know something of his policies, which have made his business a success for half a century. But druggists all over the country do not know about him unless a free-lance submits it to a trade publication for druggists.

Well-known persons, places, and objects that readers have

never seen may be as familiar to them as those that they see daily. Each person has an instinct to know the prominent persons, places, or objects. Royalty, statesmen, cities, parks, planes, boats, and trains are well known to many readers, because editors are constantly in the market for such articles that have wide reader interest. Some of the people best informed about far-away places have never set foot on plane, boat, train, or foreign shore, but they are avid readers of travel articles and of the travel magazines.

Business, Professional, and Home Interests. Whether one's business, professional, or financial interests are in the business district or in the home, there are articles and publications to appeal to all. There was a time when magazines designed to appeal to the business or professional reader contained articles to interest only men, but since women have entered many fields hitherto monopolized by men, many publications have widened their appeals to include the business and professional women. Special writers for the business and professional magazines are eager students of all matters pertaining to their readers, such as labor disputes, tariffs, taxes, price fixing, consumer relationships, co-operatives, and legislation concerning the fields for which they write.

Home-making is still the chief business of the majority of urban as well as rural women readers, whether they "live alone and like it," or live with their own families. A sufficient number of men, however, have turned to keeping their own homes or apartments and magazines and newspapers, ever alert for new subscribers and an opportunity to serve, have installed departments to guide and help the men homekeepers, just as a half a century ago they developed departments and publications for the housewife. If writers have not had personal experience with the various phases of home-making, there are unlimited opportunities to interview those who have had. Reader-interest surveys have shown that articles pertaining to the home and welfare of the family in the women's magazines are still in greatest demand. In addition, women's interests outside the home are being appealed to by features pertaining to the civic, political, and cultural life. In fact, the women's magazines are in the market for any article that will catch and hold, not only the women readers, but men, too.

Social Welfare. Sympathy for and extensive interest in others are instinctive with practically all mankind and, because of this widespread "human interest," the demand for articles concerning all types of social, educational, and religious welfare is never filled. The subject matter may concern aid for those in distress, better hygiene, improved health and living standards, self-improvement along educational and religious lines, increased recreation, and legislation for better working conditions. These are but a few of the appeals that a writer may use to secure wide reader interest.

Success and Happiness. Each human being is born with the protective instinct that makes him interested in himself first, above all others. Consequently, articles concerning success, prosperity, and happiness are in such great demand by the public that whole magazines are devoted to this appeal. The reader hopes to attain happiness by means of his success or prosperity, and he is interested in reading how to make or save more money, how to do his work more easily and more efficiently, how to improve his physical well-being or his mental capacities, and how to find more pleasure. Because he wants to be wealthy, healthy, wise, and happy, he subscribes to publications that will give him the information he desires.

Using Appeals Effectively. To make the articles interesting, the writer must make it possible for the reader to see himself in everything he reads. It is because an individual wants to see himself that he and millions of others go to the movies. He wants to hear himself—and so he and millions of others turn on their radios. He wants to read about situations in which, in his imagination, he is the center of interest—therefore he and millions of others buy publications containing articles in which they can see themselves, or how they think they would look, speak, or act under the same circumstances as those of the heroes.

The same instinct that compels people to look into mirrors

compels them to wish to see themselves in everything they see, hear, and do. It is that same instinct that compels magazine subscribers to turn through the advertising. The men like to think that if they only had that brand of collar, they would look like that handsome young chap. The women like to think that if they had that swimming suit they could look like the bathing beauty pictured there.

To make the reader see himself in every article is not difficult if the writer gives vigorous thought to the appeals he can use most effectively with the subject matter. In many articles it is possible to use several of the appeals, either simultaneously or successively. A student writer, relating the discovery of a simple preventive for pellagra and its cause, for instance, combined nine of the appeals enumerated. If a number of appeals can be combined at the beginning of the article, it will have interest for a greater number of readers. This is the key to success for the writer who plans his article thoughtfully.

Outline Is Essential Part of Plan. Since a writer is an artist in much the same sense as an architect is, he must, to accomplish his goal, work much as the master builder does. While the latter uses building material, the writer uses facts, thoughts, and words. Like the artist, if the writer is to make his finished product a work of art, he too, must first make sketches and draw plans of what he desires to accomplish. He should make two outlines: first a tentative one, later a final one. If the final one is well planned before the actual work of writing is begun, the article will have a style that will add greatly to its value. The manner in which the article is written determines to a marked degree the price the writer will receive. The better the style, other things being equal, the greater the value each word in the manuscript will have. Therefore, it is good business to make the article in every way just as nearly perfect as is possible, by giving careful thought to its construction.

The more carefully one thinks out the outline, the more quickly he can write the article and the more easily he can sell it. A good outline saves time, produces more money, and enables the writer to turn out more, rather than less, work in the course of a year. The time the beginner or the professional spends on outlines will be time well spent. As a matter of fact, the person who begins writing articles without first making outlines is taking a great risk. Unless he is a genius, the articles he writes without plans will be badly written and will create a poor impression upon the editors. This, in turn, will make it more difficult to sell future articles. A well-written feature often leads to an opportunity to become a regular contributor.

The well-planned outline compels the writer to keep in mind the purpose of the article and aids in avoiding digressions and overlapping of material. It helps to evaluate the space to be given to the various divisions, and it calls attention to omissions of necessary information. It reduces time and energy spent in revision.

Three Rings of Interest. In predetermining the construction

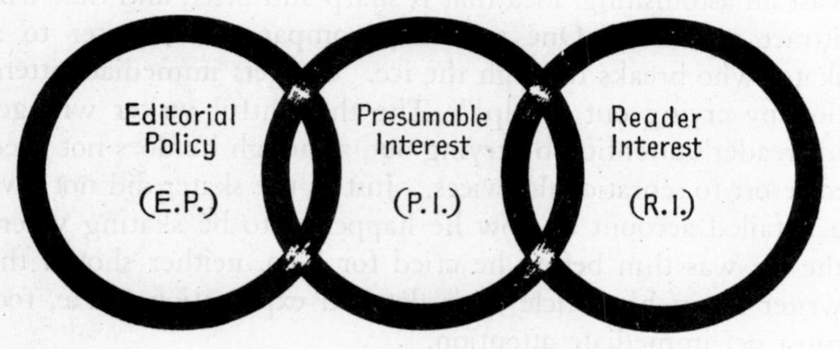

FIG. 2. THREE RINGS OF INTEREST.

of an article, a successful writer will pre-establish the three rings of interest. The point of the reader's presumable interest in the article is represented by the center ring. It is determined by the editorial policy and the advertising appeal. The reader's actual interest in the subject matter is embodied in the second ring. The editorial policy, which is in reality the editor's interest, is shown by the third ring. The writer's problem is to link the three rings together briefly and effectively by giving consideration in the outline to the three elements in such a way that the editorial policy, or the editor's interest, the reader's presumable interest, and the actual interest will not only be attracted but held to the very end.

Features Are Built on Pyramid-like Structures. In reporting courses, journalism students are frequently taught to outline and write their news story to the "inverted pyramid," as the story form required of Associated Press correspondents is termed in the classroom. Some writers construct their feature articles like a pyramid, but they do not invert it as does the correspondent writing his news story. They use an upright pyramid, large at its base, and its apex at the top.

The apex, or the first section, represents the point of presumable interest between the reader and the editorial policy, with its one or more appeals. Since this point of contact between the reader and the periodical is often slight, the writer must plan in his outline some sort of a lead that will immediately get the reader's attention. It should contain a startling, or at least an astonishing, idea that is sharp and brief, and that will attract attention. One authority compares the writer to a skater who breaks through the ice. He gets immediate attention by crying out "Help!" The thoughtful writer will get his reader's attention by crying out, although he does not need to resort to sensational devices. Just as the skater did not give a detailed account of how he happened to be skating where the ice was thin before he cried for help, neither should the writer begin his article with detailed explanations. He, too, must get immediate attention.

A writer used such a device when he began an informative article on insurance with: "You who begin this sentence may not live to read its close. There is a chance, one in three or four billions, that you will die in a second, by the tick of the watch." That writer found an immediate point of presumable interest, or contact, whether or not the reader was interested in insurance as an investment. Death has an appeal, although not an attractive one, since it is mysterious and familiar.

Even after the point of presumable interest (P.I.) is established in the first section of the pyramid, the writer must plan to carry it into the second, or third, or possibly the fourth and fifth paragraphs in order to establish in an interesting way the purpose of the article, which is really the publication's editorial

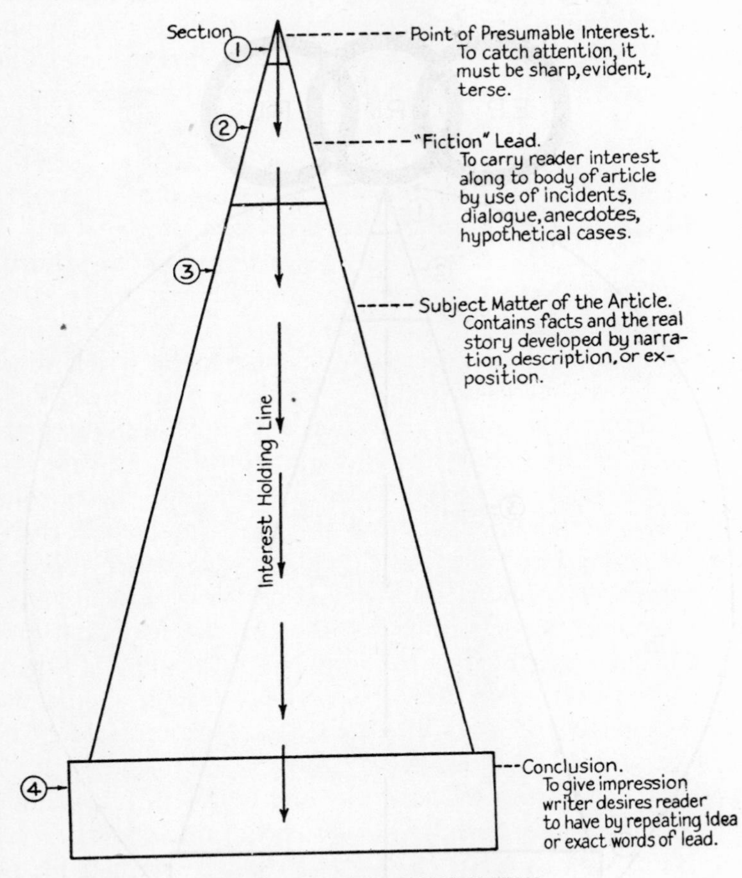

FIG. 3. PYRAMID CONSTRUCTION.

policy (E.P.), and to hold the reader's interest (R.I.). This "fiction lead," or "second lead," or "light opening," as the device is spoken of in editorial offices, is represented by the second section. It may approximate the beginning of a short story in an effort to appeal to the imagination, or it may be concerned with relating an incident, or an anecdote, or with dialogue—imaginary or real. The writer of the insurance article carried his reader's interest along and appealed to his imagination by pointing out that the very chair in which he sat read-

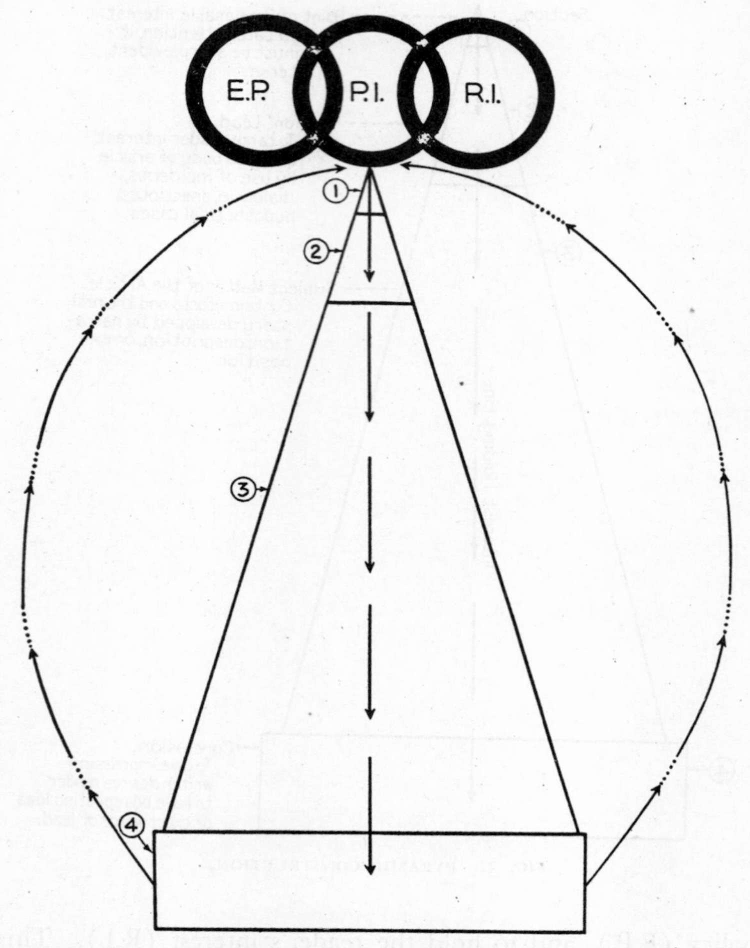

FIG. 4. ENTIRE PLAN OF CONSTRUCTION OF A FEATURE.

ing might collapse, or that he might have an automobile collision, or that his heart might suddenly cease to function.

The third section of the pyramid, following the "fiction

lead," is the real subject matter of the article. It contains facts, opinions, and figures to inform, guide, or entertain the reader. It is presented by means of narration, description, or exposition. The real story in the insurance article told why insurance companies are willing to seem "to bet" on the span of life of their policyholders because they gamble on a sure thing: the average death rate.

The fourth section of the pyramid is the base upon which the story rests, or the conclusion of the feature. It contains the impression that the writer desires the reader to have when he has finished the article.

Whether the presumable interest lead, or the "fiction lead," or both, are used, the writer must plan in his outline a conclusion that will be forceful, yet artistic. This is easily done by repeating either the exact words or the main idea of the lead paragraph in the concluding paragraph, in order to clinch the idea of the entire article in the reader's mind. In the diagram this is illustrated by drawing an extended semi-circle around the pyramid in such a way that its middle touches the apex of the pyramid and the ends touch the base. This device indicates that the writer will take the reader by the hand, as it were, back to the beginning, or apex, in order to leave the reader with the impression the writer planned when he wrote out the purpose of the article before starting his tentative outline.

General Outline Is Similar to Advertising Copy Writer's. Courses in advertising teach the students that there are definite steps that the copy writer must take if he would write forceful copy. The same principles may well be applied to outlining the feature article. They are:

1. *Catch the eye.*
   Use a short picture-making title that will make the reader begin to read the article.
2. *Hold the attention.*
   Make statements in the first sentence and the first paragraph that will grip the reader sufficiently to cause him to read on.

3. *Arouse interest.*
   Follow the first paragraph with statements of an interesting nature and with which the reader will agree, or at least that will continue to hold his interest.
4. *Gain confidence.*
   Continue holding reader interest in the body of the article by making comparisons, drawing analogies, or using hypothetical examples; or in other ways show that the ideas set forth are informative, helpful, or entertaining and that they add to the reader's knowledge, wealth, health, or amusement.
5. *Convince the reader.*
   Conclude the article by showing the reader in a subtle or suggestive way how much the ideas set forth will inform, guide, or entertain him if he acts upon them or adopts them.
6. *Test the outline.*
   Test the plan of the article to see that the reader will be left with the impression that you, as the writer, wish him to have.

Factors Determining Points in Outline. The architect keeps in mind the width, length, and location of the lot, the roll of the land, the relation of the lot to others in the block, and the structure and color of the neighboring houses. So must the feature writer give thought to the publication and its readers when he outlines the article.

Before the outline is started, the length of the article must be determined for the publication to which one is slanting. Editors frequently return articles that do not fit their publication's length. A young man wrote an article of the length and in the style used by *Country Gentleman,* for which he received a check for $100. In the row ahead of him in his class sat another student who received his manuscript back from the same publication on the same day. A personal letter said that because the article was "mid-length," the editor was forced to return it. It added that if the author would write a 300-word digest, the editor could still use it in the crops department.

The second young man, as well as the entire class, profited by his mistake.

To write out in a brief sentence the statement of the purpose of the article before making even the tentative outline will save time and energy. It will prevent the writer's getting off the subject by eliminating those portions that will not contribute to the reader's grasp of the content or to the purpose of the article.

The amount and the nature of the subject matter selected from the notes, and the order of their presentation, must be planned before one can determine even roughly the main points, parts, or divisions of the outline. Again, the writer must work like the architect, who has to determine the size of the house that can be built on the lot before he can plan the number of rooms. Just as the master builder sketches the floor plans, so must the writer think through his material and sketch out the points or blocks of material in order to find the best arrangement and relationship of paragraphs. Thought must be given to the outline as a whole, to see that the parts are all in relation to one another. Care and thought given to this phase of the outline will result in the best possible arrangement of material, because there will be simplicity of effect and harmony throughout the article.

Details Must Be Planned before Outlining. The successful writer has every detail worked out both in his mind and on paper, in a tentative outline, before he even starts to make his permanent outline. Changes are difficult to make after the article is written, if it has been carefully thought out, because things will not be in a right proportion. Before starting the final outline, the writer will have transcribed everything—notes from the interviewee, notes from his research, ideas from books, bulletins, or publications, ideas gained from talking with others —to writing. Some journalists put their notes on little cards, as do the historians, but the majority of professional writers prefer sheets of typewriter paper; they transcribe their notes on the machine, and paper is easier to handle. Another advantage of the latter method is ease of cutting the paragraphs into separate blocks, or of pasting or pinning the various parts together to make a unified whole. Such a plan will prevent an article from being a mere juggling of ideas.

Organizing the Material for the Outline. After all material has been transcribed to typewriter paper, the writer spreads the sheets—much as if they were parts of a puzzle—out on a long table or series of tables, and arranges the material in order of the outline. Such a process gives him the opportunity to view the material as a whole and to make the necessary shifting of pages or paragraphs to give the article emphasis, coherence, unity, and interest. It also enables him to see what space he should give to the various points, and this aids him in planning the lead and the conclusion of the article.

By checking the material with the outline—or checking the outline with the material, as the case may be—the writer cuts, rearranges, pastes, or pins the transcribed notes into whatever order he desires. By this process of double checking, the outline is modified or revised where necessary or where greater effectiveness will result. However good one's outline may be, he should never let himself be dominated by the first arrangement. As he organizes his notes, a better arrangement of parts may suggest itself.

The writer checks and rechecks the material with the outline, or vice versa, and satisfies himself that: (1) the plan is as effective as he can make it; (2) the purpose of the article has been adhered to throughout; (3) all possible appeals have been used to catch and hold the interest; (4) the parts of the outline fit together naturally and readily; (5) the reader will get the impression the writer wishes him to have; and (6) a close relation exists between the article and the magazine for which it is being slanted. He may then determine the style of treatment to which the various divisions of the outline lend themselves.

The writer may find it profitable to save time by writing in the margins of the outline whether to use dramatic incidents, anecdotes, typical instances, hypothetical cases, description, narration, or exposition to keep the reader interested to the end.

He then determines the style in which he will write the article and sits down to his typewriter, ready to start the actual writing. By this time the writer has become so enthusiastic about the subject that unless he writes very poorly, he cannot help writing an interesting article.

Sales Are Results of Planning and Outlining. For the amateurs who are willing to give vigorous thought to planning and organizing material, success will come as it did to the young man who made the tentative plan as follows:

Tentative Outline for Article on Grass Juice.

I. *Purpose*
 1. To inform dairymen of result of research that will enable them to increase the quality of their dairy products.

II. *Source*
 1. Background reading of printed material in library and in bulletins pertaining to differences between summer and winter milk.
 2. Interviewing laboratory assistants for background information.
 3. Interviews with Dr. Harry Steenbock and Dr. Conrad A. Elvehjem, professors of biochemistry.

III. *Experiments*
 1. How experiments came to be undertaken.
 2. What previous experiments were made.
 3. What experiments are being conducted on this campus.
 4. What experiments are being conducted elsewhere.

IV. *Results*
 1. What results have been obtained and from what methods.
 2. What progress has been made.

V. *Conclusion*
 1. May be retrospection.
 2. May be introspection.

VI. *Possible Markets*
Hoard's Dairymen
Capper's Farmer
Farm Journal

After the young writer had gathered, evaluated, and organized his material, he made his final outline as follows:

There's Gold in the Grass.

I. *Purpose*
1. To inform dairymen, poultrymen, and farmers of the result of research that will enable them to increase the quality of their dairy and poultry products.

II. *Rings of Interest*
1. P.I.: Show farmers' future when new product is on market.
2. R.I.: Farmers who are interested in improving herds and flocks.
3. E.P.: Only those publications that appeal to readers who desire to be better informed and who have some scientific background.

III. *Plan of Development*
1. Presumable interest: Appeal to farmers of the future by picturing bossie getting her grass juice daily.
2. Fiction lead: Future farmers mixing winter drinks for bossie and biddy.
3. Body of article:
Story of work of the three pioneers in dairy science.
Experiments to know why summer milk was more nutritious than winter milk.
Discovery of the vitamin.
Experiments with pasteurized milk and with winter milk.
Problem to produce milk of high quality the year around.
Further search for growth-promoting factor in summer milk.

Experiments with juice pressed from fresh grass.
Result: grass juice is the vitamin-like substance essential to growth and to better nutrition.
Expense of manufacture of product is prohibitive.
Commercial firm hopes to market product that will enable farmers to produce better milk and eggs.
Problems facing scientists and manufacturers.

4. Conclusion (Base upon which the triangle rests.):
Farmers will hear more of "grass-juice factor" because it has been proven a success.
Need for better name.
Bossies all over dairyland having their daily juice.

IV. *Markets*
The Farm Journal
Capper's Farmer
Country Gentlemen

After the final outline was completed, the amateur spent considerable thought on developing the various parts of the outline in an interesting way to appeal to as many readers as possible. He knew that if he could interest readers who did not have herds of cattle or flocks of poultry, he certainly would be able to appeal to those who did. The completed article follows.

THERE'S GOLD IN THE GRASS! *

BY

WADE H. MOSBY

Can you dairymen and farmers imagine yourselves carefully conserving every blade of grass, crushing the juice out of them, and then presenting the resultant meadowland cocktail to bossie with fond hopes that she'll drink it all and moo for more? Or can you picture yourself painstakingly stirring the same concoction into the raw winter milk? In the light of recent knowledge shed by scientists of the dairying industry, such may well be the design for living for the

* Reprinted by special permission from *Country Gentleman* and Mr. Wade H. Mosby.

farmer of the not-so-distant future. And the discoveries, the pioneering scientists assert, are not at all limited to bovine diets. Poultrymen may some day be performing a similar chore—feeding grass juice to their chickens!

The story of grass-juice research doesn't begin with a brewing vat of tender nodules, but rather with three University of Wisconsin scientists, Profs. G. O. Kohler, C. A. Elvehjem, and E. B. Hart, who some years ago were experimenting with the comparative nutritive values of different types of milk, particularly pasteurized milk as compared with raw milk. These men, all experts in biochemistry and agricultural chemistry, early established to their own satisfaction the fact that summer milk is far more nutritive than winter milk; but along these same lines, they found that while pasteurization does not materially decrease the nutritive content of summer milk, it does produce some negative change in the winter milk. With curiosity born to scientists, they asked,

"Why can that be?"

Let us imagine that we have been silent witnesses to the deeds of the comrades of the microscope.

An idea of the superiority of summer milk was gleaned from a series of experiments conducted several years ago. It was found that rats, fed on milk produced in February and March, grew on an average of 2.5 grams per day. Those fed on summer milk, on the other hand, produced in September and November, showed an average daily gain of 4.2 grams—nearly twice as much. The milk produced during December and January was intermediate in its growth-promoting properties.

"During the past three years," Dr. Elvehjem declares, "all samples of commercial milk obtained in midwinter have shown reduced growth-promoting properties. Feeding experiments involving evaporated milks have given the same results."

The latter statement was also borne out by experiments with rats, which proved that summer evaporated milk produced a daily gain of 3.6 grams, while winter evaporated milk gave only 1.7 grams—less than half the gain procured by feeding with summer evaporated milk.

"The results for the pasteurized milk showed that the growth on pasteurized summer milk was identical with that on raw summer milk," Dr. Elvehjem explained. "However, the gain in weight for pasteurized winter milk was inferior to that for raw winter milk."

These experiments gave our scientists their first inklings of a factor in milk which is present in great enough quantities in summer milk, so that heating during pasteurization does negligible damage, but is not sufficiently present in winter milk to remain unaffected by the pasteurization process.

"Thus, the *kind* of milk which is used for pasteurization is more important than the changes which may occur during the process," Dr. Elvehjem holds.

It became evident that one of the major problems facing dairymen today is that of producing a milk of high nutritive quality the year around. Research indicated, though, that a milk superior to ordinary winter milk can be produced by feeding of either artificially dried alfalfa or A.I.V. and molasses alfalfa silage.

"We knew from these experiments," Dr. Elvehjem says, "that fresh green forage contains a factor or factors which ordinary roughage does not supply. These factors may be preserved (at least to a considerable extent) by improved methods of handling green forage."

Scientific Proof

As true scientists, our research men were not willing to let the matter drop at this point. If there was some growth-promoting factor in summer milk, what was that factor, and mightn't it be isolated to a sufficient degree for application to practical dairying and farming? Those were the problems next tackled by the men of science. It was clear, now, that the cows producing the superior summer milk were getting the growth-stimulating factor from their summer diet of fresh, green grass.

The next step was to see if the green grass had any important role to play in the source of the interesting factor. Immediate results indicated that it had. Male rats, fed mineralized milk produced by a cow that had been on dry feed for one year, grew from 40 to 130 grams in six weeks, while males from the same litter grew from 40 to 200 grams on the same diet with the addition of a *small amount of juice pressed from fresh grass.*

Now the investigators knew that the elusive factor was present in grass juice. For want of a better name, it was dubbed "the grass-juice factor." Similar experiments conducted with guinea pigs resulted in the death of the pigs that had been fed the ordinary mineralized winter milk, the diet which had only reduced the rate of normal growth in the rats. When a small amount of grass was added to the guinea pig's diet, it was found that it grew at a normal rate. Our scientists assumed that it might have been the increased bulk furnished by grass that was vital to the guinea pig's normal growth. But when fresh grass juice was added to the milk diet, the guinea pigs still grew at a normal rate. The *grass-juice factor*, then, was the vitamin-like substance essential to growth and so important to good milk.

Of interest to poultry raisers, too, the grass-juice factor has been found to aid in egg production. Grass juice added to buttermilk, "green buttermilk," causes poultry to grow faster and lay better.

Practical application of this near-vitamin is not yet in sight because the expense of manufacturing a usable farm product is still prohibitive. But a Kansas City company, now in possession of the secrets of several grass-juice factor products, is working at the problem and may soon market a method for producing better milk. (Although the Kansas City company made most of its discoveries independently, it is now co-operating with the Wisconsin scientists.)

One of the questions facing such experimentors at the present is, should the grass juice be added to the raw milk, or should it be included in the cow's diet? The former method, in the light of most experiments, has proved to be the more practical. There is a certain loss of efficiency when the grass juice is added to the cow's meal, since her bovine constitution absorbs some of it.

But whether it's added to the raw materials or mixed with the finished product, dairymen, farmers and poultrymen of the future are sure to hear a great deal more about the grass-juice factor.

Perhaps by the time that the bossies all over dairyland are mooing for their daily cocktails, the vitamin-like substance will have a shorter name.

Writer Receives Check. The article, which was the author's third feature, was written in an unusually attractive style and to the length that *Country Gentleman* was using at the time. Since it contained new facts, the instructor advised the writer to send it there rather than to the first market he had indicated. Three weeks later the student writer received a check for $100.

The Value of the Outline. The amateur who has never bothered to make an outline for any writing may be tempted to start his first feature without making a tentative and, later, final one. Professional writers who have attained national success say that they cannot urge too strongly the use of the outline, whether one is a beginner or a writer of experience. It is true that the writer who makes free-lancing his career and who sells perhaps hundreds of articles during a year may not make as detailed an outline as he did during his earlier writing years, but no matter how many decades one may have written, he will outline his material, consciously or unconsciously.

Although the careful planning and outlining of every article does take time, in the end it: (1) saves a great deal of time and energy; (2) enables one to write an attractive, interesting style, because his mind is free from planning and arranging; (3) permits him to write rapidly, and at the same time effectively; (4) results in but little revision, except perhaps the improvement of vocabulary and the correction of minor errors and the final retyping of the manuscript to give it a professional appearance; (5) aids in making an almost 100 per cent aim in slanting; (6) brings a check to the writer instead of a rejection; and (7) increases the writer's earning power, because publications pay more for well-written articles.

The majority of writers admit freely that writing is difficult because it requires thinking, and for most persons thinking is difficult. A beginner must not have the notion that he can sit down to the typewriter and dash off an article. Even most professional writers cannot do that. But it is true that if one has given thought and care to planning and outlining his material, he will be so inspired that he will find great fun and satisfaction in the actual writing, even though it is hard work. With practice, the beginner will acquire spontaneity and alacrity. These qualities—which will make the writer feel that he is inspired—will come with a suddenness, as did the ability to play the piano or to learn to use the typewriter. Then even the embryo will write with confidence and skill.

Just as the advertising copy writer cannot write effective copy with strong sales appeal unless he firmly believes in the product about which he is writing—or, as advertising writers say, unless they are "sold" on it themselves—neither can the feature writer write an article effectively. But one cannot give careful thought, make a tentative outline, and then make a final one without becoming enthusiastic about the subject matter. By the time he has completed his final outline, one could not keep the beginner from writing his article.

Exercises

1. In your favorite newspaper select three features. Jot down in chart form the captions. Indicate in the first column what purpose each author had in writing the article.
2. Select three articles in your favorite magazine. In chart form indicate the purpose each of those authors had in writing the features.
3. In the second column of your newspaper chart indicate who the probable readers are.
4. In the second column of your magazine chart make the same indication as in Exercise 3.
5. In the third column of the newspaper chart indicate why they will be interested in the article.
6. In the third column of the magazine chart indicate why those readers will be interested in each of the three features.
7. In the fourth column indicate, by a rough estimate of the number of words, just how much the reader will be interested according to each editor's judgment in selecting the length of the article.
8. For the magazine chart indicate in the fourth column, by making a rough estimate of the word length, just how much the readers will be interested.
9. Enumerate in the fifth column the devices that each writer used in catching and holding the newspaper reader's attention.
10. In the fifth column of the magazine chart list the attention devices for each article.
11. In the sixth column list the aims of the three newspaper articles.
12. List the aims of the magazine features in the sixth column of the magazine chart.
13. Select one of the newspaper features and list in the seventh column any psychological principles that you find.
14. Select one of the magazine articles and in the seventh column list psychological principles that you find.

15. After classifying the reader-appeals for each newspaper feature, list them in the eighth column.
16. In the ninth column of the magazine chart, list the reader-appeals for each of the three articles.
17. Underneath the chart for each type of publication write down the word "Outline," and the title of the feature you select to outline. Beneath that write a short, concise statement of the purpose of the article. Then outline each of the two articles as you think the writers must have done before they wrote the articles.
18. For each article outlined, draw a construction pyramid similar to Fig. 4 in this chapter. Apply its four sections or parts to each of the features you outlined. Does the treatment of material permit you to put an extended semi-circle around the pyramid, or did the writer fail to bring the reader back to the beginning of the article?
19. Test the article outlined and "pyramided" to see if the writer failed to apply the principles listed under the general feature outline.
20. List any suggestions for the improvement of the outline, or, in other words, the rearrangement of the article as it is written.

Publication Analysis

American Home, Better Homes and Gardens, and *House Beautiful*

Do not spend more than two hours on this report.

I. Identification: Name, publisher, editor, where published, price.

II. Make-up:
1. What do you like about the make-up of the magazines?
2. What do you dislike about them?
3. What changes would you make if you were the editors?

III. Advertising:
1. If you were placing advertising, what appeals would your copy have to have?
2. After glancing through the advertising, do you think that the advertiser gets returns from his copy?
3. Give reason for your conclusion.
4. A tip suggested by the advertising in each magazine.

5. If you were advertising manager, what changes would you make?

IV. Feature Articles:

1. What types of articles do you find and to whom does each one appeal?
2. Analyze any article that you wish and in any way that you wish, but also include the pyramid form of analysis.
3. What do you think are your chances of selling to these magazines?

V. Three Tips: Source, authority for the article suggested, and three possible markets for each one that was suggested by the study of this magazine.

11

WRITING THE ARTICLE

Plan of Writing. When the amateur starts his first article, he thinks he must first write the caption, or heading. He is surprised to find that the title is generally written after the completion of the first draft—sometimes not until after the copy has been revised. The idea for the caption frequently comes to the writer like a flash if he has given much thought to the planning and outlining. The best advice to the tyro is not to be concerned about the caption at the beginning of his writing. He may not write it until just before he mails the article to a market. For this reason, the discussion of writing the title is left until Chapter 12.

Some authorities advocate writing the body of the article and then going back to the first part and writing the beginning. If the writer, however, has followed carefully the plan suggested in the previous chapter, and has constructed his article on the pyramid form, he will have the idea for the lead transcribed into his notes, or at least have it definitely in his mind. The beginning is an integral part of the article. It must be written so that the reader is never conscious of where the lead ends and the body of the article begins. Both time and energy are saved if the writer composes the lead first.

The novice who has given thought to his article does not wait until he starts writing to ask himself, "How shall I start?" He not only asked but answered that question when he developed the plan. At that time he selected the most interesting fact or anecdote to be used as the point of presumable interest.

The Function of the Lead. The beginning of the article, like the advertisement, should: (1) catch the eye and lure or guide the reader on into the article; (2) give the reader an idea of the content of the feature and the movement and spirit of the article; and (3) provide the point of presumable reader interest.

The Importance of the Lead. The beginning is the critical point. The article is dependent upon it to obtain and hold readers. The first few paragraphs are the determining factor in whether the reader will read on or turn the page over to the next article. One realizes the importance of the lead if he stops to consider the competition an article has with the many others, even in a single publication. Just as the "cub" reporter learns that the lead of a news story is similar to the merchant's show window, in which the most attractive merchandise is displayed, so may the feature writer compare his lead to the show window of the ultra-exclusive shop that displays but one suit or one dress. By its very interest, individuality, or style it will attract the attention of hurried pedestrians, who stop to "window shop." The feature lead attracts attention, although it, like the exclusive shop on Fifth Avenue or Michigan Boulevard, has hundreds of others with which to compete.

Ease of Writing Lead. The article writer has a greater freedom in drawing on his imagination and his originality than the news reporter does. Thus, the writing of the lead is not so difficult as one may think. After all, it is just an introductory paragraph that is appropriate to the content and that will appeal to the reader.

If one has thought out the plan and outline carefully, he will be so enthusiastic that he will write with a spontaneity that will cause him to type hard and fast. If, as he types, he pictures in his imagination not only the reader but the printed article in the publication, with its art layout of photographs, drawings, or charts, he will write with inspiration.

It is always difficult to begin any project with which one is not familiar. Starting the feature is not an exception. But if the novice will take time to examine a number of leads in any publications at hand, or those at the library, he will find he has stimulated his own enthusiasm until he can hardly wait to get to his typewriter to begin his lead. Of course, he will save time and will attain success more quickly if he will analyze carefully the leads in six or more issues of the publication to which he is slanting. Even the professional writers study leads constantly to find out how other writers challenge and hold readers' attention. The more one thinks about and analyzes beginnings, the easier it will be to write them.

Constructing the Lead. Upon the basis of the three rings of interest and the pyramid construction, one realizes that although the lead is a unit by itself (serving to catch the reader interest and to link it to the policy of the publication), in reality, it consists of two parts. The first serves as the point of contact between the reader's presumable interest and the article in such a way that he will follow on down the interest-holding line to the conclusion. The presumable interest lead is the most vital part of the article, since it strikes the keynote of interest and holds it—or should.

The second part of the lead, the "fiction" lead, carries the reader interest along to the body of the article. It may consist of one paragraph of one sentence, or a long paragraph of several sentences, or of several paragraphs, as diagrammed in Fig. 3. Whatever type is used as the lead—summary, striking statement, narration, description, quotation, question, or direct address—it should be a complete unit in itself and give the reader a unified impression.

The point of presumable interest must be sharp, evident, and terse, and yet be a structural part of the article, else it will fail in its purpose. Its connection with the "fiction" lead and the body of the article must be logical as well as enticing. The transitions must be accomplished so skillfully that the reader is not conscious that the point of presumable interest and the "fiction" lead are separate units. Above all, both must be brief, not longer than 5 to 10 per cent of the whole article.

Faults to Be Avoided. In writing the lead, eight faults to be avoided are: (1) packing the lead with too many details that will prevent the reader from getting the unified impression the writer desires him to have; (2) neglecting to make the lead a significant part of the article by uniting it with the body of the article; (3) developing the details of the beginning to a length out of proportion to the body of the article; (4) failing to make a skillful transition from the lead to the body of the article; (5) exaggerating incidents; (6) making the dialogue stiff and unnatural; (7) using pointless or inapplicable anecdotes; and (8) resorting to dissociated and irrelevant hypothetical cases.

Classification of Types of Leads. The entire article is dependent upon an effective lead. Much thought, therefore, should be given to the type as well as to the way it is written.

Each writer has his own classification, but for convenience the types used in the majority of publication offices are: (1) summary; (2) striking statement; (3) narrative; (4) descriptive; (5) quotation; (6) question; and (7) direct address.

The novice will find many suggestive examples in his weekly or biweekly Publication Analysis and in his continual study of current periodicals. Styles in features, particularly in leads and captions, change as rapidly as fashions in wearing apparel. It behooves the writer, amateur or professional, to keep posted on feature fashions.

Summary Lead. Material for a beginning often lends itself to a bird's-eye view, or summary, treatment. As the news reporter groups the important facts in the first paragraph for the hurried reader, so may the feature writer. The average news reader has become accustomed to finding the happening, the persons or things concerned, the cause, the result, the place, and the time all assembled in the first paragraph in answer to the questions, What? Who? Why? How? Where? and When? This type of lead will attract reader interest if the most striking element is "played up" in the first sentence, or the first part of it. If the writer is in doubt as to which of the types of leads enumerated to use, he will do well to select the summary to emphasize the most salient facts.

Striking Statement. An unusual idea, or one that is expressed in an unusual way, commands attention. Because of its brevity and its force, it may be similar to the reporter's "snapper" lead, which is aimed to make the reader jump—at least, mentally. Its purpose is to lead the reader on by arousing his interest or curiosity. It is used with other types as much as it is used by itself.

In turning through feature sections and magazines one finds many articles where the striking statement concerns numerical figures or things of enormous size, or pertains to startling discoveries. If the size of the revelation is of such magnitude that the reader will not comprehend it, the writer should interpret it into terms that may be readily understood.

Subject matter that is unique, predicts the unusual, is paradoxical, or is novel may be made all the more effective if this type of lead is used. Forceful figures of speech, startling words, or gripping phrases may be employed to attract the reader's attention, but the writer must resist the temptation to exaggerate or to make false statements.

Narrative Lead. A fiction-like tone may be given to the lead by beginning with narrative. This lead is popular because Americans are great fiction readers. Practically all devices common to the narrative fiction story may be incorporated in this type. It is best suited to personal experience, adventure, and narrative articles. Incidents, anecdotes, conversation, and definite examples may be used. They may be developed by means of dialogue as well as by active narration.

Descriptive Lead. Dealing with images rather than ideas, and appealing to the senses, the descriptive lead may be used artistically for those articles where the aim is to stir the reader's emotion. It must be suggestive rather than detailed, because the former is easier to grasp. Words that have an emotional connotation or an association for the reader, or that are picture making, are essential for this type of lead. If the description is forceful and vivid, the reader is impelled to read on.

Quotation Beginning. Although quotation leads are out of style because of overuse, they are still effective when they have pointed or unusual application to the article. If the quoted portion is one with which the reader is familiar, however slightly, it will serve as an attention-arresting device. Not only actual quotations, but any unique form—such as an advertisement, a menu, a sign, a budget, or a bit of prose—will appeal to the reader. Even though the source of material is unlimited, particularly if one resorts to the quotation books as sources, a quotation lead should never be used unless it has a close association with the subject matter and body of the article.

The various typographical forms in which quoted material may be arranged adds to the attention value. If the writer desires a verse printed in smaller type, he may indicate on his manuscript by setting the quoted lines single space. Quoted slogans and phrases may be set as separate paragraphs. Advertisements may be set off in "boxes," made by placing around the quoted portion a box-like structure. Reproductions of telegrams, menus, price lists, invitations, or clippings are used, as in fiction, to attract the reader.

Question Lead. Although the question beginning has waned in popularity, as has the quotation, there are times when it is the most advantageous. If the writer desires to arouse the reader's curiosity, the form is occasionally excellent. The lead may consist of a single question, or a series of them. Or each of the questions of the series may be used separately in a series of paragraphs if the writer's purpose is to give greater emphasis to each question. This type is often combined with direct address.

Direct Address Beginning. Used occasionally and appropriately, the direct address makes a strong reader appeal. The reader feels that the writer is speaking to him personally rather than to the thousands or millions of other subscribers. Utility articles are often built on this type of lead, but the writer must be constantly on his guard to keep the article from having a dictatorial, or "preachy," tone. He must remember that the reader has been preached at all his life—at home, at school, and at church, and by his associates and friends—and he certainly does not want to be preached at in his reading. The use of the second person makes the reader feel that he has been "button-holed," and he resents that, unless it is done unobtrusively. Since the imperative verb is the most forceful form of direct address, it is effective; but one must use it tactfully and with caution in the lead.

It is true that the use of "you," or "yours," or "Mr. Reader," or "Mrs. Citizen," and other similar forms aid in personally appealing to the reader, but one must avoid overuse of the device; it soon becomes monotonous. Indirect address may be employed, although, of course, it does not have such strong appeal.

Methods of Using the Types. From studying features in current publications, it is apparent that many of the most effective leads are not used singly, but that two or more types are combined. Because the types overlap, no hard and fast rule can be laid down for their use. The only rule that is applicable in selection of the type of lead is to choose one, or combinations, that will be appropriate and that will attract the attention and hold it to the end.

The two methods in the use of the type of the leads are: the deductive, in which the writer begins with the general and goes to the particular or the specific (although this is the oldest method, it is less interesting); and the inductive, which opens with the particular and concrete and then takes the reader to the general. The second has the greater attention-getting value.

Writing the Body of the Article. After the lead is completed, the main part of the article almost writes itself, if the novice has made his final outline thoughtfully. The feature is in his mind, and all that remains to be done is to write it.

The possible markets have been selected, the reader interest in the subject has been deduced, the amount of material has been ascertained, and the approximate length has been adjudged. The style has been determined, either consciously or unconsciously, as a number of articles in the same field have been analyzed, in order to slant accurately. The beginner knows just how he plans to develop the units that he blocked out on the construction pyramid, because he indicated on the outline which are to be narration, description, and exposition, and where dialogue, anecdotes, and incidents are to be used. The transition from the lead to the article itself will follow smoothly, as will the changes from one paragraph to another. Thus, the reader's curiosity is carried down the interest-holding line enthusiastically to the end.

With a wealth of material on a promising subject, a well-organized outline, and the creative zeal of the artist, the beginner is ready to put the units together to make an interesting article that he hopes will appeal to an editor's eye and checkbook.

Determining Factors. With the problems of how to begin and where to begin solved when the outline was made, the writer must consider in what person he will write the main part of the article. It is a common fault of most novices to write their features in either the first or second person, whether or not it is a confession, personal experience, or a utility article. The personal pronoun becomes extremely monotonous and should be avoided unless the feature cannot be written effectively in any other person. As a rule, a writer will be much more successful if he keeps himself out of the article, except in the types noted. The second person becomes wearisome to the reader unless the writer softens the "preachy" tone by relating his own mistakes, as pointed out previously, to show the reader that he, too, is not perfect, or that results may not be successful if one attempts short cuts. When in doubt, the amateur or professional will do well to write in the third person. Then the reader will not be so conscious of the writer. This style is not as emphatic as writing in the first or second person, but the clever writer will find other devices to hold the reader's attention without running the risk of seeming to "talk down" or to "preach" to him.

In writing the story, the beginner must keep in mind: (1) the reader and his interests; and (2) the interest-holding line, which is the most direct approach from the point of presumable interest to the conclusion. By keeping the reader in mind, the writer will constantly think, "What will the reader want to know about this?" He will be less inclined to miss or bury important facts. Neither should he lose sight of the reader's interest in himself. The psychological devices of recall and association will bring the reader into the article and keep him on the interest line. One should put himself in the reader's place as he writes, to see how he will react to the article. If he, as the possible reader, finds breaks in the interest line, he will do well to incorporate a few of the appropriate appeals listed in the preceding chapter. If the writer would meet the reader upon a common ground, he must bear in mind the latter's limitations. These he will have learned by an analysis of the advertising.

Qualities Characterizing Writing. The first characteristic of a good article is the ease with which it may be read. This is dependent upon simplicity of style and repetition of thought—in different ways, of course—to stress the points. Spontaneity and enthusiasm result from sincerity of purpose. The content should be presented so that the reader may discover ideas for himself, or think that he has. A beginner is inclined either to underestimate or to overestimate the reader's knowledge and ability. Facts with which the reader may, or may not, be familiar should be presented tactfully by such phrases as "one recalls," or "one remembers." One should resist the temptation to moralize, to preach, or to advise: readers resent it. But if it is done by means of adequate reference to authority, it will give weight and credence as well as aid in taking away the dictatorial tone. Facts must be presented, but there is no reason why they cannot be presented interestingly. By inference and by appeal to the reader's imagination, the writer can make dull facts sparkle.

Even though the novice has made a well-planned outline, he constantly will be confronted with decisions. He must have several times the amount of material he will need. From this he must select with precision. Too much detail destroys clarity and emphasis; a lack of it prevents adequate treatment that will result in loss of interest.

Length of Feature Articles. The fact that feature sections and magazines are not static in their policies makes them interesting to the subscribers but makes a problem for the free-lance writer. Just when he has discovered by analysis that a publication uses articles of from 2,000 to 3,000 words, he may find in the current issue on the newsstands that it has changed its style of make-up and is now using 1,000 to 1,500 word articles, or perhaps it is not using anything less than 5,000 words. Why the professional, as well as the amateur, must study the individual periodicals is obvious.

The beginner should not attempt long articles. The structural problems will be more complicated and more difficult, and he will be inclined to become discouraged with resultant loss of interest. He will find that articles of from 1,200 to 2,000 or 2,500 words offer good practice and that the demand is large for medium-length articles. Thus, selling will be easier.

Structural Units Must Have Variety. The study of articles in the Publication Analysis at the end of each chapter shows how articles are built out of blocks, or units, such as (1) incidents, (2) examples, (3) hypothetical cases, (4) statistics and (5) processes.

Incidents and Anecdotes. The use of incidents, anecdotes, and episodes helps to entertain, to make the reading more interesting, to illustrate points, and to drive home facts in the development of personal experience, narrative, and confession articles. In studying the articles in Part II or in current publications, one finds that most features contains one or more of the devices. They offer opportunities to make use of description and dialogue that gives variety to the subject matter and the form.

Specific Examples. Concrete cases give a realistic tone and appeal to the reader's imagination. At the same time, they enable him to comprehend the facts that the writer is presenting. For instance, one might be writing an article on taxation, which would consist of factual material. The reader, at first glance, might think he was not interested, because it looked as though it would be dull reading. But if the writer takes his tax receipts, or those of his friends, and shows how the citizen's tax dollar is distributed, and how he is benefited by the services his tax dollar helps to finance, the reader will be interested immediately. He will realize that the facts touch his own life. The writer must remember always that the reader is interested in himself first of all.

Humorous matter may be incorporated into articles by use of examples of that type. Such material will make a dull article entertaining. An alert writer will find such aspects in most subjects, but they should be used only when relevant.

Hypothetical Cases. Suppositional incidents may be resorted to when the writer does not have an appropriate concrete example with which to illustrate his point. They must be typical and plausible, or they will fail to add to the reader's interest. One should avoid the overuse of this type of unit. It may result in monotony and a feeling of lack of confidence. Such cases may be introduced by such phrases as, "Suppose, for instance that," or "If, for example."

Statistical Material. Any systematic computation of facts is generally avoided by young writers. They do not realize that there are various ways in which such material may be presented interestingly for the reader to grasp the information readily. To find ways of making units of statistics appeal to the reader is like playing a game with oneself, a young writer exclaimed after he had overcome his dread of using sheets of figures that his interviewee had given him.

The first principle in using statistical units is to translate the figures into terms that the reader can comprehend. This may be done by reducing large figures to smaller ones with which the reader is familiar, in order that he will understand them at a glance. A student wrote a story explaining how railroads know at every minute where each one of their thousands of freight cars are. He impressed the reader with the huge number of cars on the tracks of railroads in the United States by explaining that if they were in one long train they would extend around the circumference of the earth three times. Realizing that the comparison would not mean much to the average reader, he explained the terms in how many rows of cars there would be if placed side by side extending from New York to San Francisco. Since he was writing it for a state newspaper feature section, he broke the figures down even further by showing how many rows of freight cars there would be side by side if they were placed on tracks between Chicago and Minneapolis.

Scientific Processes. The average individual avoids scientific and technical information just as he does statistics, unless the writer makes the terms sufficiently simple for the reader to understand them. Narration and description are the best methods of presentation for technical and scientific procedure. Utility articles based on processes and techniques may be given variety by presenting the material through interviews, dialogue, quotations, charts, or tabular form.

Methods of Presenting Units. The articles in Part II and in current publications illustrate how units may be presented to the reader in such a manner that they will be varied yet forceful. The methods of presentation of the five units may be done by means of (1) narration, (2) description, (3) exposition, and (4), occasionally, by argumentation, or the elements of it.

To give variety to the forms of discourse the writer may employ (1) dialogue, (2) interview, (3) quotations, direct and indirect, and (4) tabular forms, graphs, or charts for statistics and recipes. By frequent checking with the notations made on the outline opposite the various units, and their methods of treatment, the writer will avoid unconscious repetition and will attain variety in presentation of material.

Paragraph Is Flexible. Although form is second in importance to content in fact writing, yet knowledge of its technicalities enables one to progress more rapidly out of the amateur class. The paragraph is pliant and affords the writer the opportunity to employ individuality in its development. In many respects each one is a distinct unit and offers a separate problem of composition, but, of course, each must have unity and coherence. In planning one paragraph, consideration must be given to the manner in which it may be linked to the one following. Although it is developed as a unit, it cannot stand as one by itself, because the outline was designed upon the theory that each paragraph is dependent, more or less, on the preceding one.

Paragraph Development. The connective idea between paragraphs should be in the first sentence of each to make a smooth transition. These word-links give variety throughout the article. A few methods by which they may be used, selected at random, are as follows: hypothetical instances; illustrations; questions; analogies; descriptions; figures of speech; reasons; causes; effects; and phrases such as, "to continue," "to put it another way," and the like. Natural ability, observation, and practiced skill will enable the tyro to include in each paragraph word links appropriate to the content and the style of the subdivision.

After the selection of suitable word links, the writer states the paragraph topic, and then gives attention to the expansion and amplification of the paragraph subject. He presents the facts he wishes to use by means of anecdotes, figures of speech, and examples. These are followed by the paragraph conclusion, which emphasizes the idea of the paragraph, either by giving a new angle, or by repetition for emphasis.

Like the feature article, every paragraph consists of a beginning, the paragraph itself, and an ending; or, as rhetoricians say, the connective link, the developed topic, and the conclusion.

Factors Determining Paragraph Length. Just as the advertising copy writer plans sufficient white space for the display of his advertisement, so does the feature writer when he makes the outline, with its numerous paragraphs. Short pithy paragraphs make for variety and for easy, rapid reading. They break the solid appearance of the column, and the prominent display of the paragraph topic aids in catching and holding the reader's interest.

Paragraph length is determined by the magazine to which one is slanting rather than by the nature of the subject, although that is secondary in importance. The average paragraph for feature sections or for magazines with mid-length lines is from two to five sentences. One successful writer said he never had less than two paragraphs on a typed page, double spaced; but he found that usually three or four paragraphs were better and were more attractive to the eye. If he were writing for a newspaper section, with its shorter line, he made his paragraphs even shorter. The magazine with a wider line can use longer paragraphs, since the width makes the paragraph appear shorter and easier to read.

Sentence Structure Must Be Evident. Sentences—particularly paragraph lead sentences—are important. They serve to get the reader's attention as his eye glances down the page and to convey ideas to a more or less hurried reader. The first requisite of a good sentence, whether it is the lead or not, is that its grammatical structure should be obvious. If the reader cannot see at a glance the relation of the parts, he cannot read rapidly. Then he will lose interest.

Sentence lengths vary in features for the same reasons that paragraph lengths do. Short ones contain fifteen words or less, while long ones have thirty words or more. Because the meaning is easily grasped, short sentences are more emphatic than longer ones and they serve better as transitions between paragraphs. Variety in sentence length is necessary to prevent monotony.

Importance of Words. As the beginner trains himself for his career or avocation, he should develop skill in selecting the right word while he writes. He should not leave the task entirely until revision of the article, as some novices are inclined to do; because they dislike to think, they defer it as long as possible. One should choose words that: (1) are familiar to the reader for whom he is writing; (2) are concrete, to stir the imagination and to paint vivid word pictures; and (3) are likely to have associated ideas and feelings that will enable the reader to recall literature that he has read or experiences that he has had. An up-to-date dictionary and a thesaurus are the writer's best friends.

Arrangement of Material. Fortunately for people with a creative instinct, the actual arrangement of material is flexible. There are very few rules for the development, other than to arrange the content of the article logically, in order that it will be interesting. Beginners as well as professional writers enjoy freedom in their writing. An article should be written in any way that will be effective and that will keep the reader on the interest-holding line (Fig. 3) to the end.

Because of the many varied arrangements, due to the initiative and originality of writers, it would be difficult to plan an elaborate classification. There are four methods, which, in general, apply to most plans. They are: (1) the logical order, which consists of a systematic arrangement of the related ideas and events in which the relating of one thing suggests another; (2) chronological order, which as the name indicates, follows the time elements in which the events happened, so that the article is developed as the events occurred; (3) general news story order, in which the most important points are placed at the beginning, with the less important material following; and (4) the "snapper" news story order, in which the point of presumable interest is a brief paragraph, consisting of an anecdote or a hypothetical case, that fairly reaches out and grabs the reader's eye. The main part of the article following the "snapper" lead may be developed in logical or chronological order. The order of development in most well-written articles may include elements of one or more of the several methods listed.

Formula for Writing. The conventional method for writing features is not a very set form. The writer writes what he has to write; he writes it interestingly, and with a purpose. He employs the writer's artifice wherever it is needed, and thus pleasantly surprises the reader just when he was about to become bored. He sustains the interest throughout by withholding some of the best units until the end.

Many professional writers take a week, or even a month, to prepare an article of 5,000 or more words. They know that editors wish literary workmanship in the features they buy.

Therefore, they regard the writing of the article as of first importance.

From the preceding paragraphs the amateur has learned how to avoid tiring the reader's mind by giving him too many weighty facts at a time, or too-ponderous paragraphs of narration, description, or exposition. He knows how to incorporate the various units in order to relieve dullness and to give variety. He understands the technique of making his style vigorous by means of colorful description, lively narrative, and lucid exposition. He knows that his vocabulary must be vivid and his figures of speech appropriate and effective to aid in making the article appeal to the reader.

He has learned the formula, if there is one, for writing features. He is ready to start the first copy of the article.

Putting the Units Together. In the writing of the first draft, the novice checks the various parts of his pyramid-like outline as he writes, in order to ascertain that he has all the units and their elements in their proper relationship. He aims at clearness in every sentence, although he does not devote too much attention to the English mechanics until revision (which will be discussed in Chapter 13).

As the beginner writes, he should imagine that he is speaking his article to a friend. His diction will then be fresh and vital. He will find that it is not difficult to dramatize the facts by means of the varied units, since all he has to do is to put them together. He will give attention to making the paragraph transitions smooth. But his main purpose at this stage of writing the article is to get the article, as he had perceived it, on paper as rapidly and as enthusiastically as possible.

If, as he is writing, he finds that some of the methods of presenting the various units are not as effective as he had anticipated, he should change his outline as well as his first draft. He should check his outline to see whether that change will necessitate additional ones.

Writing the Conclusion. A good lead requires a good ending. Its function is: (1) to leave the reader with the impression that the writer wishes him to have; (2) to give the reader a feeling of satisfaction, or even gratification; and (3) to make an artistic conclusion, for finish, to the article.

No matter which type of ending one uses—summary or general statement—the writer should keep one or more interesting facts for it. It may be an application of the facts, or an astonishing result, that proves the statement in the lead. Regardless of what facts the conclusion contains, the writer must take the reader back to the point of presumable interest, as illustrated in Fig. 4. By so doing, the semicircle is completed around the apex of the pyramid and makes the conclusion unified and artistic.

With the exception of writing the caption, the amateur finds that the first draft is completed. He should give it an immediate reading, checking with the outline carefully to see that the paragraphs are in the best order and that nothing has been omitted. Some professional writers say that the revision comes easiest immediately after the writing of the first draft. The majority, however, prefer to put the article aside and revise it after they have had time to look at it from a detached point of view. No matter which method the writer finds best, he should give thought to his caption and write it, if possible, before typing the final draft. Ideas expressed in the caption may necessitate changes in the article.

Best Writing Conditions. With the completion of the first draft, the amateur will realize that he, like the professional, can write easier and better under certain conditions. Half of the difficulty of writing is overcome when the amateur has firmly made up his mind that he will start his first draft at a set time, regardless of what distractions there may be. No matter when he starts, or under what conditions, he probably will increase the business of the paper manufacturers by filling up his waste basket until he gets his brain cells and fingers limbered up. One will never be inspired to write until he has worked up an inspiration by writing. If possible, one should at least start his writing in a room free from distractions, to enable him to think clearly and concentrate earnestly. Some persons write better at night; some in the morning. Some cannot get started at their article until they have had a brisk walk in the fresh air; others until they have had a short nap.

If one does not use the touch system on the typewriter, he will save time and energy by learning it immediately. Practicing an hour a day for three weeks, he will acquire skill and speed. He should train himself from the beginning to compose on the typewriter as he writes. It is only the newest novice who writes out the article in longhand and copies it on the typewriter.

Professionals are divided upon the question as to whether it is better to outline the article and write the first draft immediately after the interview, when their enthusiasm is high, or to transcribe their notes and wait to outline and write until they have had sufficient time to think through the material and the methods of development. The majority of writers combine the two methods. They transcribe their notes in any order that they may interpret later. By this method they retain the ideas, expressions, and quotations that they acquired in their first zeal. The material is put aside and forgotten temporarily, but the subconscious mind is working away on the article. This results in clearer ideas of methods of presentation and of development. This, after a little experience, makes for easier writing—and a first draft that will need but little revision.

If one has difficulty in making the passages clear or determining how to develop one of the outlined units, he may find that talking it off to himself will solve the problem. It will increase his enthusiasm and will aid his creative instincts immeasurably.

A young home economics teacher, after the completion of her first feature, exclaimed with considerable emotion, "Writing is hard work. I never worked so hard in my life. If I have to work like that, I am going to return to teaching, much as I hate it."

She was astonished to find that very few people "dash off"

their articles. Most writers admit they work and struggle over every paragraph, every sentence, and every word. Of course, with experience one writes much more easily and smoothly, but even so, writing *is* work. However, it is fun, as the home economics teacher found out before the end of the semester. By that time her checks totaled $683. She also found that there is no satisfaction that equals that of creative work and the pleasure of seeing one's writing in print.

Analyzing Articles Aids Novice. For the beginner's convenience in studying the techniques of feature writing, a number of articles written by novices, and sold to periodicals of all kinds, have been reprinted in Part II. It is suggested that the tyro examine these student-written features to study the sources, the manner of presentation, and the style. The writer, amateur or professional, should include in his study current publications of the type for which he plans his feature, because fashions in features are ever changing. What was the vogue with an editor a year ago may be passé with him the next month or week.

Exercises

1. List three ideas that you could use for possible leads for your next feature article.
2. In which articles in your favorite magazine did the beginnings fail to meet the functions of a lead?
3. In chart form list the appeals used in the leads in the articles in the magazine of your choice.
4. Which lead is suggestive to you for ideas in the development for the lead for your next feature?
5. In three paragraphs of not more than fifty words each, describe the kinds of leads that each of the three possible markets, to which you are slanting your next feature, seem to wish.
6. In the second row of the chart started for Exercise 3, indicate any faults that you found in the lead that the writer should have avoided.
7. In the third column of the chart, classify the types of leads that you analyzed for the sixth exercise.

8. In the fourth column of the chart, indicate the person in which each of the articles is written.
9. Hurriedly read one of the articles to ascertain the devices the writer used to keep the reader's attention on the interest-holding line, and list them.
10. Estimate the length of each article and record the result in the fifth column of the chart.
11. In the sixth row, indicate which structural units were used in each article.
12. Indicate in the seventh column the methods used in presenting the structural units.
13. For each article tabulated, make a rough estimate of the number of words in the average paragraph and place the figures in the eighth column opposite the article.
14. Estimate the average sentence length used in each article and record in the ninth column.
15. In the tenth column, write "yes" or "no" after each article listed, according to whether or not you think the vocabulary met the three requirements of words as listed in this chapter.
16. In the eleventh column, indicate which type of arrangement of material was used by each writer.
17. Indicate by "yes" or "no" in the twelfth column whether the endings meet the requirements of the function of a conclusion.
18. Make a diagram, similar to Fig. 4, in the previous chapter, of one of the feature articles.
19. Read through the leads of the articles in Part II and classify each according to the types listed in this chapter.
20. What structural units did you note in the articles in Part II that are suggestive to you for use in your next feature article?

Publication Analysis

Popular Mechanics, Good Housekeeping, and *McCall's*

Do not spend more than one hour and a half on the preparation of this report.

I. Identification: Name, publisher, editor, where published, price of each magazine.

II. Make-up:
   1. What do you like about each magazine?
   2. What do you dislike about each magazine?

III. Advertising:

1. What is the difference in the appeal in the advertising of the magazines?
2. From the advertising, what kind of a reader do you visualize for each publication?
3. One tip from the advertising of each magazine (three tips in all).

IV. General Policy:

1. If you were editor, would you change either of these magazines in any way?
2. Give reason for your answer to the preceding question.
3. What types of articles could you submit to each magazine?

V. Feature Articles:

1. What types of articles do you find in each publication, and to whom do they appeal?
2. Analyze an article from each magazine, using Fig. 4, in Chapter 10, as a basis for the analysis.
3. List five suggestions for improving the writing of your own feature articles, and in finding markets for them.

VI. Four Tips—two from each magazine: Source, authority for the article suggested, and three possible markets for each one that were suggested by the study of this magazine.

12

COMPOSING THE TITLE

The Purpose of the Title. When the reader opens the newspaper feature section or the magazine, his eye is drawn to a particular article by the title or the headline, the illustrative material, or the name in the by-line. If the writer's name is unfamiliar to the reader, then only the caption and the pictures or other illustrative matter will attract. The purpose of the title is to make the reader want to read the article immediately. His first impression of the article is obtained from the heading, which gives him an idea of the content and arouses his curiosity. Its function is not only to catch the reader's attention but to advertise the content of the article.

The writer gives thought to composing the caption of a feature as the copy writer does when he is planning a title for an advertisement. A challenging heading not only adds to the appeal of the article, but it frequently aids in "selling" the editor the idea that his magazine should have the article in a future issue. The novice must not be tempted to make it simply decorative. The purpose of the title is to attract the reader and to take him on down the interest-holding line to the lead. As the manuscript reader looks over the copy, his eye will be attracted by a good title and his favorable opinion will be carried to the lead and into the article. It is essential to give thought to the writing of the caption because the writer hopes not only to attract the reader, but the editor. Many writers consider captions as important as the article itself, or even more so.

Factors Influencing Form and Style. From the weekly or semi-weekly Publication Analysis one sees the great variety of form and style in which titles are written. The influencing factors are the size of the printed page and its "make-up" as well as the editorial policy. The tendency of the newspaper to use shorter headlines with fewer "banks" or "decks" has extended, with a few exceptions, to the feature section and to the magazine. Conciseness and terseness are required in almost any publication's captions because of the restrictions of the size of the page and the limitations of type. The beginner should analyze the form and length of the titles of the publication to which he is slanting, in order that his will fit the publication "style sheet." He will find that captions follow the fads of the time. Some are written all in capital letters, or with no capitals at all, while others are a combination of capitals and small letters (or, as the headline writer says, "upper and lower case").

In examining the titles of the articles in Part II and in current periodicals, one finds a great variety in style and in form. Alliteration, figures of speech, verbal balance, rhyme, jingles, quotations, parodies, and puns are all used by clever writers when, by so doing, they make the caption more effective and more attractive. Humor, if in keeping with the tone of the article, frequently can be used to advantage. The allure of alliteration, if not overused, is pleasing. The writer may use any device that will aid in making the title clear, stimulating, and appealing.

Elements of the Good Title. Since the purpose of a good title is to get the attention of the reader, it should be (1) attractive, (2) accurate, (3) terse, and (4) concrete. Since the title is a concise, accurate statement of the content of the article, it makes the same appeal as the article does. But in the caption, not only the idea that is expressed, but also the way in which it is written, is important.

One must avoid sensationalism and exaggeration as well as misleading statement of fact. The title should be honest; it should portray the same spirit and tone as that expressed in the lead and throughout the body of the article; and it should be adapted to the taste of the reader. If the tone of the article is serious, so should the title be; if it is humorous, so should its caption be.

Some persons seem to be born with an aptitude for writing clever captions, as was a young woman who sold everything she wrote. Her features were not particularly outstanding, but the headings were. She had a way of giving a simple declarative sentence an unexpected twist that lifted it above the ordinary class. The ability to write a clever caption that will attract the reader is an art, but it is one that anybody may learn. Editors appreciate clever titles if they are informative and give the reader an idea of the content.

There can be no rule as to when one should write the title. An idea for a caption has probably been under consideration in the writer's subconscious mind ever since he selected the tip for the article. If a clever one has not occurred by the time he has completed the first draft, he should attempt to write it then, in order to get a detached point of view about it by the time he starts revision.

Space Limitations and Mechanics. Since the size of the headline type, the width of the column, and the size of the page of any periodical are fixed, the caption must be planned to fit the available space. Careful study should be given to the typographical style and to the space limitations of the captions in the particular publication to which one is slanting. Should the article return, it is a simple matter to retype the caption to fit the second periodical to which one may be sending an article.

Any type of mechanical arrangement that will add to the interest should be adopted. The novice will find that paradoxical, figurative, interrogative, or alliterative forms will aid in the attention-getting value, as will verbal balance or rhyme.

Word Selection Is Important. An attention-arresting vocabulary, which aids in giving a vivid picture to the reader, is important. One should not be satisfied until he has found colorful words that will call forth mental images and recall associations to the reader's mind. Concrete words are essential in the caption if the reader is to comprehend the meaning quickly. Because specific words are necessary to give the reader a clear-cut mental image, abstract words are to be avoided. The novice will find that picture-making nouns and action verbs used in declarative sentences will entice alike the editor's and the reader's eye. A verb, or an implied one, should be used in every caption to give it life.

An analysis of titles will show that they generally contain three or four important words, with the additional particles and connectives to complete the idea. The majority of titles, or "top decks," do not exceed at most seven words. Short, pithy words, rather than long ones, are to be preferred. They enable the reader to grasp the idea at a glance.

The Sub-title. Many publications use a second title to amplify the first, which must be in sufficiently large type to attract the reader. This limitation makes it difficult to give an idea of the content in the few words alloted to it. The sub-title's purpose is: (1) to give supplementary information, to explain the short compact caption; (2) to increase the reader's interest; and (3) to serve as a connecting link between the short caption and the lead.

In a well-written sub-title, the same tone is retained as in the title, but repetition of words is avoided. In some publications the title and the sub-title are combined to make a continuous statement. The average sub-title consists of from nine to twelve words, or even more if one includes the articles and conjunctions. As in planning the caption, one will write a more accurate and interesting second "deck" if he analyzes several sub-titles in the publication to which he plans to mail his manuscript. The nearer the style of one's headings approximate those of the possible market, the more confidence the editor will have in the manuscript and the more inclined he will be to think that the writer is a professional.

Classifications of Titles. In classifying types of captions, one encounters the same difficulties of overlapping that he did in grouping the leads. This probably explains why many editorial offices classify the titles under the same names as they do the beginnings. Although publications may vary in the arrangement of the types, many offices, to distinguish between the kinds, use the following terms: (1) summary, (2) striking statement, (3) narrative, (4) descriptive, (5) quotation, (6) question, and (7) direct address.

Summary Title. This type of caption includes (1) the label, (2) the simple statement of fact, and (3) "W" titles. The first type, which is most popular in trade and class publications, may consist of a single word or a few simple ones and may, or may not, have a sub-title to explain the first caption. The second consists of simple statement of facts. The third group contains the words *who, what, where, when, why,* and *how* in declarative form. The following are examples of the various kinds of summary captions:

(1)

(*Harpers Magazine*)

NEW ENGLAND HURRICANE

(2)

(*The Model Craftsman*)

SCENIC MODELING

(3)

(*House & Garden*)

SELECTING A HOME

How to insure that your choice of a home will be the wisest possible investment is explained by C. W. Moody, builder and developer

(4)

(*Atlantic Monthly*)

THE COÖPERATIVES—AN EXPERIMENT IN CIVILIZATION

(5)

(*Arts and Decorations*)

GARDEN FOR A MAPLE TREE

(6)

(*Country Life*)

BROCADE GARDENS

(7)

(*Mademoiselle*)

PACK TRIP

Buffalo Bill's Country, Boots and Saddles, Murmuring Pines and Eternal Snow for Your Dude-Ranch Vacation

(8)

(*Cosmopolitan*)

PEACE AND QUIET

It takes all kinds of people to make a world, and you'll meet them all at a trailer camp

(9)

(*Ladies' Home Journal*)

FEAR IN CHILDREN

(10)

(*Esquire*)

THE LIBEL RACKET

Maintaining that the loud silence of newspapers concerning libel actions is a big help to crooks and shysters

(11)

(*Capper's Farmer*)

$50,000 a Year

TURKEY BUSINESS

(12)

(Milwaukee *Journal*)

FISHING CHAMPION—THE GREAT BLUE HERON

More Than 200 Pairs of These Beautiful, Long Legged, Tireless, Eternally Hungry Birds Are Raising Families in Rookery Near Palmyra, Wis., in Jefferson County; Nests as Large as Bushel Baskets

(13)

(*Forum and Century*)

ADJUSTING YOURSELF TO YOURSELF

(14)

(*Better Homes & Gardens*)

BOOKS FOR LOOKS

Frame a door with bookshelves and you can get a substantial feeling of depth to your walls, as well as a charming decorative effect

(15)

(*Scientific American*)

NEW AIDS FOR CRIMINOLOGY

Finger Prints "Raised" with Iodine . . . Spectrographic Analysis of Materials . . . Tiny Traces Yield Evidence . . . Contribute to Conviction

(16)

(*National Geographic Magazine*)

NEW SAFEGUARDS FOR SHIPS IN FOG AND STORM

(17)

(*Woman's Home Companion*)

SHOES THAT GO TO SCHOOL

(18)

(*Ladies' Home Journal*)

A HOUSE FOR THE TWO-DAY WEEK

(19)

(New York *Times* Magazine)

SACRED BEAN OF CHINA LENDS US ITS MAGIC

Brought From the Orient Long Ago but Only Recently Discovered By Industry, It now Links Farms and Factories of America

(20)

(Portland *Oregonian*)

CANINE FRIENDS FOLLOW POSTMAN

Carrier for 23 Years Has Daily Dog Escort

(21)

(*Good Housekeeping*)

WOMEN WHO WORK

(22)

(*Field & Stream*)

ON THE IVORY TRAIL

Thrills, action and drama a-plenty in hunting the dangerous African elephant

(23)

(*Ken*)

WHERE LEPROSY BREEDS

The Hawaiian lepers' island of Molokai is an unsanitary pest-hole of infection. Father Damien and like martyrs bring pity-publicity, and bands to play, while garbage continues to be dumped on the beach, and no sewers are laid. Lepers handle mail that goes out over the world; visitors come and go—perhaps carrying the disease. Patients in need of sanitarium food live on a bare subsistence diet.

(24)

(*Flower Grower*)

WHEN THE CHILDREN ARRANGE FLOWERS

(25)

(*American Home*)

WHY BOYS STAY HOME

(26)

(*Popular Science Monthly*)

HOW SCIENCE MEASURES "AUTO-FATIGUE"

Striking Statement Title. A novel idea expressed in an unique way in the caption to arouse in the mind of the reader wonder, surprise, or astonishment is classified as striking statement heading. It is effective because it is a departure from the ordinary, but it must be brief in order to have the reader grasp the idea. All sorts of figures of speech are adaptable to this classification. Of such a type are the following:

(27)

(*The American Magazine*)

THIS TOWN HAS JUST BECOME A FATHER!

Banker, grocer, doctor, blacksmith—they open their doors to Carmel's school boys and girls and give them a chance to try their wings. Is your community giving its youth a break like this?

(28)

(Kansas City *Star*)

Now on a Big Gambling Spree

AMERICA BETS 5 BILLION DOLLARS ANNUALLY

(29)

(*Review of Reviews*)

GAMES—OR GANGS

(30)

(*Field & Stream*)

MORE WATER—MORE DUCKS

(31)

(*Physical Culture*)

COLD FEET, COLD SKIN
ARE DEADLY

(32)

(*Country Gentlemen*)

NEW FEET FOR OLD

(33)

(*Flower Grower*)

A Weekly Spray Keeps Insects Away!

(34)

(*Mademoiselle*)

GUESTS ARE PESTS

—And Vice Versa

(35)

(*Outdoor Life*)

LIONS ARE FRIENDLY

Except, Of Course, When They're Not

(36)

(*Popular Science*)

HUNTING LITTLE BIG GAME
WITH YOUR MICROSCOPE

(37)

(*Ladies' Home Journal*)

MULTIPLYING IRIS BY DIVISION

(38)

(New York *Post*)

SO! IT'S THE MALE WHO BUYS BEAUTY!

*Veteran Face Lifter Breaks Down and
Confesses That Men Are Plastic
Surgeon's Best Customers*

(39)

(*Popular Science*)

NEW NOSES
IN 40 MINUTES

(40)

(*Scribner's Magazine*)

ONE EVERY MINUTE

Picture magazines—the problem publications of the decade —selling 16,000,000 copies a month, making and losing millions of dollars

Narrative Title. To tell the reader something in the caption by means of action words or any of their forms, or by words which imply action, is effective. As with the lead, any techniques used in fiction are appealing to the majority of the readers. Narrative titles are as follows:

(41)

(*The American Magazine*)

I Used to be an I-Man

Limelight is heady stuff—like moonlight. Can you take it? Here's the honest confession of an ambitious businessman who tried it

(42)

(*Redbook*)

O. HENRY AS I KNEW HIM

(43)

(*Good Housekeeping*)

I TRAVEL TO SEE PEOPLE

They're More Enlightening Than Museums And Mosques—And More Fun

(44)

(*Christian Science Monitor*)

ROLLING DOWN TO MEXICO CITY

New Horizons Are Opened to the American Motorist Through the Completion of the National Highway South from the Texas Border, and the 776 Miles All Are Easy Driving

(45)

(*Scribner's Magazine*)

FIGHTING THE CENSOR

It's a struggle between American correspondents, intent on giving their readers unbiased news, and censors who suppress unfavorable reports

(46)

(*Better Homes & Gardens*)

COMES THE CROCHETING SEASON

(47)

(*Arts and Decorations*)

LIMITED SPACE
ENLARGED

(48)

(*Esquire*)

THE ART OF MUG-MENDING

Thanks to plastic surgery, close-ups of the mellower movie queens can be viewed without blinking

(49)

(Brooklyn Daily *Eagle*)

ONE OF FEW MASTER SILVERSMITHS
LEFT IN COUNTRY FOLLOWS CRAFT
OF PAUL REVERE IN BROOKLYN SHOP

(50)

(*Christian Science Monitor*)

SOUTH OF THE FROST-LINE

Key West, Most Tropical Point in the United States, Presently Will Become Accessible to Motorists as a New Road Is Completed Linking the Colorful Island.

(51)

(*Collier's*)

GIRLS GO FOR MASSACRES

Don't be misled by that ecstatic look on your girl friend's face. It's not enthusiasm for sport.

Descriptive Title. Just as the descriptive lead deals with producing images in the reader's mind, so does the caption. The purpose of the descriptive heading is to enable the writer to make the appeal to the reader by means of words with an emotional connotation. Figures of speech with vivid adjectives or implied ones predominate in this type of caption. Humor also is used to advantage. Here are some examples.

(52)

(*Travel*)

PAINTED MEADOWS IN SAN JOAQUIN

(53)

(Baltimore Evening *Sun*)

PAINTS POOCHES' TOENAILS
AT FOUR-PAW RATE OF $1

Park Avenue Dog Valet Doing Big Business.
Charges 50 Cents A Head To Pluck
Their Pretty Eyebrows

(54)

(*Arts and Decorations*)

THE OUTDOORS INDOORS

In A Week-end House

(55)

(*Good Housekeeping*)

TRANSIENTS IN THE GARDEN

(56)

(*Better Homes & Gardens*)

STURDINESS IN STONE

A distinguished small home in the oldest of building materials

(57)

(Dallas *News*)

LAST OF COWGIRL NOMADS
FORCED TO LEAVE THE RANGE

(58)

(*Travel*)

WHITE NIGHTS AT HERSCHEL ISLAND

(59)

(Milwaukee *Journal*)

WARMING GLOW OF CRANBERRIES IS
BACK TO BRIGHTEN AUTUMN MENUS

Quotation Title. That fashion in features is as inconsistent as fashion in costumes is shown by the lack of quotations used as leads, although they are in abundance used as titles. A quotation with which the reader is probably familiar makes an appealing title, but if the application to the article is not evident, it will require a sub-title or might better be discarded for a new one. Well-known quotations paraphrased in a novel way are effective because of the psychological principles of recall and association of ideas. A title that "plays on" or assumes the form or likeness of a familiar quotation has strong attention value, because its familiarity and strangeness arouses the reader's interest. Examples of such titles are these:

(60)

(*Saturday Evening Post*)

"NO JOBS IN CALIFORNIA"

(61)

(*Hygeia*)

"THE VITAMIN FOLLIES"

(62)

(*House & Garden*)

TIME FOR TEA

(63)

(*Atlantic Monthly*)

AN APPLE A DAY

(64)

(Chicago Daily *News*)

FROM CRADLE TO THE GRAVE
DOGS NOW GET ALL LUXURIES

(65)

(*McCall's*)

"A PLACE FOR EVERYTHING . . .

(66)

(*Better Homes & Gardens*)

COOK'S EYE VIEW
OF POTS AND PANS

(67)

(*Arts and Decorations*)

DESIGN FOR
COOL WINDOWS

(68)

(*Country Life*)

EAST meets WEST at SANTA MONICA

(69)

(*Capper's Farmer*)

HER PHANTOM MAID

Electrical Equipment Eases Labor and Reduces the Number of Hours That Must Be Spent in the Kitchen

(70)

(*House & Garden*)

A garden of flowers in the crannied wall

(71)

(The New York *Sun*)

MAYOR HAS TWO PAUL REVERES

They Ride Motor Cycles Instead of Horses
and Have No News of the British

(72)

(*Christian Science Monitor*)

ALL IS GRIST TO THE MAKER
OF BUTTONS AND BUCKLES

(73)

(*American Home*)

MIRROR WISE
and other whys

(74)

(*Forum and Century*)

DIET BEGINS AT FORTY

(75)

(*Better Homes & Gardens*)

SEVEN LITTLE SPICES
TURNED THE TRICK

(76)

(*Survey*)

Little 'Dobe Homes in the West

(77)

(*The American Magazine*)

MAN of the MIST

For twenty years Captain Hardy Smith piloted great liners through the tortuous channels of New York Harbor, and then . . . But here's his story, as thrilling as fiction

(78)

(*Capper's Farmer*)

As a Man Thinketh

SO DOES
HE FARM

(79)

(*Cooperative Merchandiser*)

PEPPER

The "*spice*" of Trade

(80)

(Indianapolis *News*)

ANCIENTS MAY HAVE HAD THEIR LOTUS-LAND, BUT INDIANA NOW IS LETTUCE-LAND, PRODUCING CARLOADS OF LETTUCE THAT REACH WINTER MARKETS IN MANY CITIES

(81)

(New York *Herald Tribune*)

SUN NEVER SETS ON EXTENT OF G.M. RESEARCH

Laboratory Facilities in Detroit
Are Being Increased by
300,000 Square Feet

(82)

(New York *Times*)

REUNION ON THE PIER

Liners, With Home-Coming Crowds, Give
New Atmosphere to the Waterfront

Question Title. The interrogation attracts some readers because they are curious or they desire to be informed. It may be used as a challenge to the reader's knowledge. If a subtitle is used, it may consist of a second question, but the writer must avoid using it as an answer to the why or how of the question asked in the title. Because of overuse, it is not so popular now as it was a few years ago. The following are typical:

(83)

(*American Magazine*)

What Becomes of
ALL-AMERICAN stars?

Here's the answer from 150 of football's immortals

(84)

(*Cooperative Merchandiser*)

ARE YOU GETTING YOUR SHARE
OF THE
CANDY BUSINESS?

(85)

(*American Home*)

Is your room piano conscious?

(86)

(*Better Homes & Gardens*)

How Does Your Garden
CLIMB?

(87)

(*Outdoor Life*)

HOW SMART IS A DUCK?

(88)

(*Capper's Farmer*)

PROFIT IN OATS?

(89)

(*Hygeia*)

DO YOUR SINUSES
TROUBLE YOU?

(90)

(*Forum and Century*)

IS INSTALLMENT BUYING SOUND?

(91)

(*American Magazine*)

Do You Believe
in a Future Life?

(92)

(*The Open Road*)

Got A Hobby? Don't Overlook Its
Picture Possibilities

(93)

(*Better Homes & Gardens*)

HOW DOES YOUR HOUSE SIT?

Does it blend into the landscape, or does it perch like a trick rider on a one-wheel cycle, insecure and grotesque?

Direct Address Title. Direct address may be used or implied in captions as well as in leads, but it likewise should not be overused and it should be employed only when the writer can avoid a dictatorial tone. A test of when it may be used is to ask oneself the question, "Is there any other type that may be used effectively?" If the answer is negative, then the writer may use it, as, for example, in the following:

(94)

(*Hygeia*)

WHAT YOU SHOULD KNOW ABOUT CANCER

(95)

(*American Home*)

Picnic in Your Garden

(96)

(*Physical Culture*)

STRAIGHTEN
YOUR
Round Shoulders

(97)

(*American Magazine*)

YOUR CHANCE IN THE MOVIES

If you want to be a Clark Gable or a Carole Lombard don't look for a job as an extra. Nowadays Hollywood has all it wants and the Central Casting Bureau has locked its doors. Here's how it is from the inside looking out

(98)

(*Model Airplane News*)

DESIGNING YOUR MODEL FOR DISTANCE

How the Twin Tractor Rates As a Distance Model and What the Proportions of Your Twin Pusher Model Should Be

(99)

(Kansas City *Star*)

WITH MICROFILM YOU CAN CARRY A LIBRARY IN YOUR VEST POCKET

Development of a New Marvel in Publishing Promises to Revolutionize an Industry

(100)

(*American Business and System*)

YOUR CREDIT ISN'T GOOD IF YOUR ACCOUNTING IS OBSOLETE

Writing the Title. After the novice has analyzed the titles in the publication to which he plans to send his manuscript, he should jot down, as a first step, a number of "sample" headlines. From these he may ascertain the number of letters, or units as they are termed journalistically, that can be accommodated in the title and the sub-title. He should keep these "samples" before him as a "pattern." Accurateness in writing a title of the correct length and style will impress the editor with the writer's ability as much as by writing a clever caption in tone with both the publication and the article.

A reference to the purpose of the article, which was written as a declarative sentence at the top of the final outline, is the second step. It will refresh the memory as to its aim, and it may be suggestive of a good caption. Before determining the content of the heading, the writer should ask himself, "What is the biggest thing in my story?" Further checking with the final outline will yield at a glance the high spots of the article. Any one of these may be suggestive for a title that will attract the reader and "advertise" the content of the article. These points should be written down as declarative sentences. A reading of the manuscript may suggest ideas for making the declarative sentences more vivid or alluring to the reader. If so, these should be added to the sentences.

With the idea, or ideas, for the content of the title on the paper before him, the beginner, in doing the third step, will analyze each caption-sentence that he jotted down, to see: (1) if it will serve as a connecting link between the policy of the periodical and the presumable reader interest as outlined in Fig. 2; and (2) that it is in harmony with the interest-holding line in Fig. 3.

The fourth and final step is to juggle the ideas by taking part of one of the declarative sentences and combining it with another, in order to adapt it to the style and length of those in the proposed market. When a combination is found that meets the requirements of a good title, the novice condenses the declarative sentence selected by finding shorter or more vivid or more colorful words. He should be sure that the title contains picture-making words that will enable the reader to know the content of the article as well as words that will have an association or that will recall something in his experiences. If the content of the article lends itself best to an interrogative type of heading, then the declarative sentence should be changed into a question to meet the requirements.

Constructing the Sub-title. In writing the sub-caption, the same steps are taken, except that one may have to amplify the declarative sentence instead of condensing it. One must remember that the purpose of the secondary title is to explain the first and to aid in the transition between the title and the lead.

Value of a Good Caption. The writer will be well repaid for his time and efforts in writing a clever title. It is a sort of tactful compliment to the editor that one knows just how his captions are written. Painstaking accuracy in trying to slant the article 100 per cent to his publication gives the editor confidence in the writer's manuscript. A clever heading serves as an ace salesman in "selling" the manuscript reader and the editor the article.

A careful writer may have ten or thirty possible captions jotted down if he has approached it from as many different angles as possible. From a large number, there may be one or more that the writer feels have attention values. If so, he should submit them all and let the editor choose the one to be printed.

If one is unable to obtain a copy of the publication to which he is slanting, he should keep his title short but see that it has a vivid verb to give it action. It is a good policy in writing a caption without a "pattern" to include a sub-title, for it aids in giving the manuscript reader a definite idea of the content even if the form of the titles and sub-title may not fit the publication's style.

The experienced writer generally does not set about in any formulated way to write the caption. Somewhere in the procedure of gathering, planning, outlining, and writing the article, one or several excellent ideas will flash across the mind. The professional jots it down immediately, wherever he is, lest it be lost to memory by the time he has revised the manuscript and typed the final copy of the article. But of course the novice may have to have considerable experience in writing before he will be able to have a clever and appropriate title pop into his mind.

Exercises

1. Turn through an issue of a magazine that you have not even glanced at heretofore. Look at each feature article. Jot down the caption and indicate which did, or did not, attract you.
2. List any unusual fads that you find in the titles.
3. Turn through the issue of a newspaper feature section that you have not seen. Note the headlines and what did, or did not, attract you.
4. Compare the form, length, and style of the titles in the two periodicals.
5. Write down the titles that did not contain all the elements of a good caption.
6. Make a list from the two publications of the words that you consider good title words.
7. What differences did you find between the sub-titles of the two publications?
8. Write down an example for each of the seven classifications of titles from the magazine and also from the feature section. What differences did you find for each type in the two publications?
9. List ten titles included in this chapter that you think will be suggestive in writing the caption for the article that you are working on now.
10. List the "pattern" titles from the publication to which you are slanting the article that you are now writing.
11. Copy the declarative sentence, from your final outline, that contains the purpose of your article.
12. Condense or amplify it to meet the requirements of your "pattern" title.

Publication Analysis

Coronet, Country Life and *The Sportsman, Travel,* or *The Magazine Antiques*

Do not spend more than an hour and a quarter on the preparation of this report.

I. Identification: Name, publisher, editor, where published, price.

II. Make-up: Including typography, size, style, etc. What do you like about the magazines?

III. Advertising: To whom does the advertising appeal? Is there anything different about it from that in the other magazines studied? From the advertising, what type of material would you expect to find in the magazines? List at least one tip suggested to you by some advertisement in *each* magazine

IV. General Policy:

1. From the table of contents, estimate roughly the amount of different material used.
2. What do you think are your chances of selling to these publications?
3. What do you like about the magazines?
4. If you were editor, what would you change in the magazines?

V. Titles:

1. Why did, or did not, the titles in each publication attract you?
2. Enumerate any novel ideas that you found in the captions.
3. Distinguish the policies of each publication toward its titles in reference to style, form, and length.
4. List the words that you thought were good headline words.
5. What variances did you find in the use of sub-titles?
6. Which one of the classifications of titles did you find used most often? Which least? Which not at all?
7. What suggestions did you get for writing captions that will aid you in your own writing?

VI. Features:

1. What feature articles could you have written for each of the publications?
2. Which types of features seem to predominate?
3. What ideas did you get for your own article for photographs or other illustrative devices used in the publications?
4. Analyze one feature article in each magazine in any way you wish, but do it from the point of view of what you can learn about writing your own articles. (Devote not more than thirty words to each article.)

VII. Slogan: Make a slogan for each magazine.

VIII. Four Tips: Source, authority, and three possible markets suggested by this study (six tips in all, including tips suggested by advertisements).

13

REVISING THE MANUSCRIPT

Necessity of Revision. The majority of authors will agree that revision of the first draft is necessary, even for the professional. If anyone is to write freely and enthusiastically, he must write rapidly; and rapid writing does not permit time to think through the structure and simultaneously to polish up every sentence as it is formed. Amateur and professsional alike will save time and energy in the long run if the amplification, correction, and deletion is done after the first draft is out of the typewriter. Literary excellence demands something more of the author than the bald recitation of facts. It is the difference between doing a thing and doing it artistically, in a way that will please the reader's aesthetic taste.

A novice may expect to make several drafts of his article before it is ready to be submitted. In feature writing, however, the beginner who has had training or daily practice in writing for print and who follows accurately the suggestions in planning, outlining, and writing the article, as given in the three preceding chapters, may find little revision necessary, except to give attention to the elements of style and the touching up and the tightening of sentences and paragraphs.

Style of Writing Is Important. Style may be summarized roughly as the way in which a writer does his work, or the manner in which thought or emotion is expressed in words. Each person's thought differs from any other's, and a writer must transfer the feelings of his own mind, mood, or emotion to the mind of the reader. Style is as essential in fact writing as in any other type of composition. It is an organic, integral part, and is written into the article. The elements of it may be improved by revision of diction and phraseology. But style cannot be used as a woman's compact to touch up the shiny or the bald places; it is fundamentally as much a part of the article as the facts are. It is the way the article is written that enables the writer to convey what he thinks, what he sees, or what he or others do in such a way that the reader grasps the author's thoughts and emotions.

Factors of Style. The market, the subject matter, its purpose, and the writer's point of view influence the style in which an article is written. Because of its importance, it should be given as much thought as the gathering, planning, and writing of the article.

Style affects the reader intellectually, emotionally, and aesthetically and is dependent upon the qualities of clearness, force, and good taste. The best style consists of transferring to the reader the exact words or the exact feeling that one has, in order to give him the exact idea. To do so, the writer (1) must see exactly in his own mind what he thinks, or sees, or feels, and (2) must have the words to express the shade of feeling or thought that he desires to express. The first requisite of style is its readability. Therefore, the writer must select words that will appeal not only to the reader's sight, but to his senses of sound, taste, smell, and touch as well.

It is not the purpose here to discuss the theories of style in detail. The interested student will find several excellent books listed in the Appendix, under the "Free-Lance Writer's Library," that will be informative and stimulating. It is suggested that the articles in Part II and those in current periodicals be analyzed in order to ascertain the elements of style used by the authors.

Growing Vocabulary Is Aid to Style. The writer's solution to the problem of style is to have a large and ever-growing vocabulary. Authorities have estimated that a minimum of from five to fourteen thousand words is required to read a newspaper, although the journalists use words that everyone will understand.* People with a high-school education or its equivalent are known to have a reading vocabulary of between nine and ten thousand words, sometimes even more. The effective vocabulary, it has been said, is one that is large enough to permit wise discarding.

Whether one is making writing an avocation or a career, he should strive to have the best diction possible. Anyone writing regularly can easily use words over and over again. Constant reference to dictionaries and a thesaurus for specific words will enable a writer to get into the habit of using them in place of abstract ones. Thus may he inject life into his articles and lift himself above the amateur class.

As the rhetoric books explain, the elements of style are (1) words, (2) sentences, (3) paragraphs, and (4) figures of speech. The theory of style is an old subject to anyone who has had a composition course; yet it takes on new interest to the novice about ready to revise the initial draft of his first feature.

Function of Words. The word-tools used by the writer to bring forth the reader's images and emotions depend, for their efficacy, upon the nature and experience of the reader. If he cannot comprehend, he will not respond. The novice should choose: (1) only those words with which the average reader is familiar; (2) concrete words, to aid in giving the reader definite ideas; and (3) words that will have an association for the reader, or that will enable him to recall ideas out of his own experiences.

The beginner should select usual words—but not commonplace ones—and combine them to give the reader a vivid picture, to stir the reader's imagination, or to take him back to his own experiences. When it is necessary to use an unfamiliar term, it should be explained the first time it is used. The most forceful words are short ones. If it is necessary to use trite, antique words, the writer may give them new life by using them in phrases or clauses with little-used ones.

Language is a vital force in writing. Some words that are

* Smith, S. Stephenson, *The Command of Words,* p. 1. New York: Thomas Y. Crowell Company, 1935.

full of life and meaning to us may carry no significance whatever to others, and vice versa. On the other hand, certain words and phrases have the power of stirring everyone. Success as a writer depends not only upon ability to say what one wishes to say, but to transmit to the reader the impression the writer desires him to have.

Advantage of Specific Words. To make the phraseology specific, avoid excessive use of adjectives and adverbs by substituting active verbs that will take the office of the modifier and at the same time denote action. Beginners usually feel that an adjective adds something to a noun; but it may also cut off some of its possible meanings. When one writes of the *placid sea,* he may decrease the reader's possible impressions conveyed by the single word *sea.*

In narrative and descriptive sentences particularly, the words should not only produce pictures in the reader's mind but should enable him to have all the sense impressions of taste, sight, sound, touch, and smell as well. Active verbs should replace passive ones, in order to make the reader feel that the event he is reading has just happened.

By analyzing published features, the writer observes how the professional constantly creates concrete pictures in the reader's mind by using active verbs that call forth vivid images. When one writes the sun "came" in the window, the reader does not know what time of day it is; if the writer says the sun "is creeping" in the window, the reader not only feels that the article is about the present, but he knows that the writer refers to the early morning sun. The word "broncho" yields a different meaning to the reader, as contrasted with the abstract word "horse." As one revises his manuscript, he should strive to substitute specific words for abstract ones, and active verbs for passive ones. By giving thought to the fine distinction between words as well as their emotional value, the novice will improve his style. Words have dynamic force only when used correctly and skillfully to convey to the reader the suggestion of the pictures they paint, or of the memories they revive.

Word Position Is Important. In revising the manuscript,

the writer is able to survey the position of the words in the sentence, to see whether the style could be improved by changing the word order. The rapid reader's eye is attracted by the first group of words at the beginning of the sentence. Sentences may be made more effective by rearranging the words to have the important ideas near the beginning.

Improving the Diction. In order to add to the effectiveness of the phraseology, the writer should exclude (1) unnecessary words, (2) general words (by substituting specific, colorful ones), (3) unfamiliar terms (unless he explains them), (4) words not in keeping with the tone or pace of the article, and (5) words used in hackneyed phrases and figures of speech.

By constant reference to a thesaurus and the dictionary, a writer not only develops his vocabulary but clarifies his meaning and stirs the reader's imagination.

Skillful Use of Sentences. If the hurried reader is to grasp the meaning of the sentence, the relation of each part to every other should be clear and definite. Grammatical structure must be evident to enable one to grasp the meaning immediately, even in the short sentence.

The structure of the sentences determines the tempo of an article even more than the choice of words. It also effects the harmony between the movement of style and the ideas advanced. Whatever the rate of movement, it should be appropriate to the content. Thus, the writer is enabled to adjust the tempo to the nature of the material. Although the tone of the article is produced more by word selection than sentence structure, it is influenced by the latter. Both tone and tempo may vary according to the material.

Sentence Variety. Next in importance to vocabulary is sentence variety. It is attained by diversity in sentence length, structure, and form.

The length of the sentence is influenced by the short line in the newspaper and magazine column, as pointed out in Chapter 10. The narrow measure makes sentences and paragraphs appear longer than they are and suggests that the novice should guard against too-long sentences, which are a handicap to clearness. In revising, he must check to see that the sentence length is varied. He should see that a short sentence contains fifteen words or less; a medium length one from fifteen to thirty; and a long sentence thirty or more words. All lengths should be used to attain variety and contrast. A short sentence should be used to give clearness and emphasis to a passage. It also speeds up action and serves as an excellent means of transition. The mid-length sentence should be used to present average thought. A writer should avoid excessive use of it, because it tends to become monotonous. Because of its length, the long sentence is excellent to present a series of details or a summary. It offers contrast to the short, rapid sentence, because its structure impels it to move slowly and deliberately.

A variety of the various types of structure will prevent sameness and will aid in holding reader-interest. The periodic, the balanced, and the parallel sentences are aids to easier reading and to arresting attention.

The form of the sentence gives opportunity for variance. A simple sentence may be used for emphasis, to attract attention, or to serve in making transition from one paragraph to another. The compound sentence aids in making contrast; the complex in summarizing details. In revising the manuscript, the writer will give variety to his style if he makes use of the three forms.

Revising Paragraphs. The novice must keep in mind, in his task of correcting his manuscript, that paragraphs are to a sentence what the latter is to a word. Before revising them, the novice should refresh his memory on paragraph requirements by reference to Chapter 11. If paragraphs run the same length consistently, they should be amplified or pruned down to give variety. To attract the reader, the average newspaper or magazine paragraph runs from two to five sentences. Some should be longer; others should be shorter. Attention should be given to coherent connectives to see that they fit their tasks.

The reader may often glance over an article before beginning to read it. If he sees long solid paragraphs, the chances are that he will not bother to read the article. The beginning of the subdivision, like the beginning of the sentence, should be emphatic. If it is not, it should be revised to arrest the reader's attention as his eye goes down the page. Each paragraph should be scrutinized to see whether it can be improved —whether it sounds natural and logical.

Figures of Speech. Derived from feeding thought with imagination, figures of speech have been called the romance of composition. One author says figures of speech are devices, both comparative and mechanical, used for the purpose of beautifying, clarifying, vivifying, energizing, and picturizing language.* They serve: (1) as a departure from the ordinary way of writing, for the sake of greater effect in phraseology; (2) to arrest attention; (3) to stimulate the imagination; and (4) to appeal to the emotions. In improving the style of a manuscript, the novice should use only such figures as the reader can best understand. Although the feature article lends itself to literary treatment, just as the short story does, the writer should never use a figure unless it contributes to the effectiveness of expression. Figurative language cannot be used as an adornment nor as a jewelry of literary style.

The psychological devices of association and recall may be adapted to figurative phraseology. The author may make it easier for the reader to comprehend the new by comparing it with the familiar by means of a simile, or by implying the likeness by use of a metaphor. Often references to literature and to language will give the reader the effect, even if he does not know the story to which the writer refers. For further discussion of this particular aid to style, the novice should examine some of the books on the subject referred to in the "Free-Lance Writer's Library," in the Appendix.

The Novice Revises His Manuscript. Desired results in any form of art depend as much upon leaving out as upon putting in. Sometimes skillful trimming or cutting counts for more than perfect technique. To put in too much is bound to result in confusion and lack of reader-interest; to leave out every

* Opdycke, John Baker, *Get It Right,* p. 78. New York: Funk Wagnalls Company, 1935.

nonessential increases clarity and heightens interest. Cutting is more of a problem than padding—and it is more necessary, because the beginner must make every word work. Editors pay by the word, and every word should be worth its price. If one writes anything of which he is particularly proud, he should delete it—or at least cut it in half. Learning what to leave out is learning how to write what will sell.

As psychology points out, an individual can think effectively of only one thing at a time. For that reason, the beginner should go through his manuscript several times, each time seeking to improve a different element of style. He will save time if he gives attention to: (1) the general organization, to see that the relation of paragraphs is effective and that the first six words of each contain a striking idea; (2) the grammatical structure of each sentence, to see that the modifiers are related to one another in just the right way to clarify the meaning at a glance; (3) the length and type of sentences, to see that they are varied; (4) the length of the paragraphs, to see that they give variety in appearance; (5) a scrutiny of every sentence, word by word, to see if better words may be substituted, and if clauses may be reduced to phrases, and phrases reduced to single words; (6) elimination of errors of grammar, spelling, punctuation, and capitalization; (7) the tempo and tone, to see that they are harmonious throughout the article; (8) the lead and conclusion, to see that the reader is left with the impression the writer desires by repetition in the ending of the words or the idea expressed in the beginning; and (9) the title, to see that it has an active verb, or an implied one, to give it life, and that its tone and tempo are harmonious with that of the article.

Good magazine writers work in the cleverness of their articles by revising several times. Many of them prefer not to revise until a period of time has elapsed after the completion of the first draft. They feel that the interim enables them to look at their manuscripts with a detached point of view and to become keener self-critics. Every minute spent in revision will increase the opportunities for sales, as will constant study of the articles of other writers to learn the secret of the success of their style.

With experience, the beginner, like the copy reader on the news copy desk, will be able to detect several or more faults at one reading and will then find it necessary to go over the manuscript only once or twice instead of nine times to find the specific faults.

Errors Common to Beginners. In the course of handling many manuscripts written by amateurs, editors find a number of mistakes that they all have in common and that crop up constantly. Generally they are due to (1) neglect of checking the outline for omissions and (2) failure to punctuate accurately.

Articles may have to be revised because the beginner fails to fulfill the purpose he had in writing it. In others, the young writer could not resist the temptation to "preach" or editorialize, forgetting that the reader is not interested in his opinions and that he should leave himself out of the article. Or he may fail to keep the article addressed to the same reader. Frequently the authoritative sources that would give confidence to the statements are omitted, as may be proof to back up drastic statements. Statistics may be given in terms too large, or too many at a time, for the reader to grasp them clearly and quickly.

Failure to make use of opportunities to refer to events in history or literature, or to use appropriate figures of speech, keeps the articles in the mediocre class that editors return "with regrets." Important information may be omitted and sentences may be incomplete in meaning because the tyro has not learned to see his own shortcomings in writing. Too often a beginner fails to keep in mind that the subject matter must be timely six months in advance for magazines and from three to six weeks for newspaper feature sections. Or he may write and revise the manuscript without checking to see if the length falls short or is beyond the limits of the publication to which he is slanting.

Typographical style presents a problem to the amateur who is inclined to be careless. Capitalization, punctuation, and spelling may not be uniform. He may have failed to follow the typographical style of the publication for which he is slanting, either through his own carelessness or through his failure to examine an issue to ascertain the style. Many first manuscripts abound with punctuation, particularly dashes, parentheses, and exclamation marks. This fault is most commonly found in articles written by young women, although young men have it too. Dashes should be used instead of commas only when the expression so set off is thrust into the sentence and does not have a close grammatical connection. Printers object to the use of dashes, except when necessary, because they break up the artistic appearance of the printed page. Many neglect to start a new paragraph for each new and separate quotation, while others fail to put end quotation marks at the end of quotations. Thought and care in checking the manuscript before typing the final draft may prevent a rejection slip. To read the article aloud enables a beginner to hear mistakes that his eye fails to catch.

Determination Will Bring Success. If one is sincere in his desire to write, if he wants to write more than anything else in the world, he will not find the details of revision discouraging. Determination to succeed is an important factor in writing. Probably more than half of the well-known writers of today would never have succeeded had they not been filled with dauntless resolution. It is quite true that many are born with the happy faculty of adapting themselves readily and naturally to a smooth, narrative style of writing. But the beginner may be assured that even they have had to work hard to attain it, however shorn of major difficulties their efforts may have been. They, too, had to give much attention to the details of revision before they were able to take their place with other successful magazine writers.

Those who follow the suggestions in these chapters will learn to write successfully, as have thousands of beginners before them who have followed this so-called "formula" for writing and selling articles. In the process they developed the true writing instincts, by means of which they learned to command words, phrases, and sentences to do their bidding, and to marshal the elements of style in such a way that readers across the land were guided, informed, and entertained by their articles. Beginners who fail are those who feel that what they write is too good to change in any particular. They refuse to revise their manuscripts. "Writing, revising, and keeping at it" supply the secret of successful free-lance writing.

Many beginners who have been painstaking with their revisions have been rewarded not only with checks but with letters from editors commending their writing. Such a letter is shown here:

Mr. Harry E. Wood,
Madison, Wis.
Dear Mr. Wood:

In preparing our August schedule, which is to contain your article on how to make a sea horse, I have just read over the manuscript again and cannot refrain from expressing my congratulations upon the skill displayed in its wording. It is a vivid, lively piece of writing and a remarkable demonstration of what can be done with a subject which in most hands would be tepid and matter of fact.

Sincerely yours,
Arthur Wakeling,
Home Workshop, Editor
Popular Science Monthly.

A careful survey of published articles will reveal that originality in the presentation has been the winning point, rather than anything particularly new in the content. "It is the way it is written," the results of thoughtful revision, that has influenced many editors to buy articles from writers they did not know were beginners. If the novice will give the editor and the reader something out of the ordinary, a check will be forthcoming.

Exercises

1. Select some piece of writing, preferably your first feature article, that you did some time in the past and list suggestions for its amplification, correction, and deletion.
2. Which factor do you believe will be the most important in influencing the style of your next article?
3. Make a list of ten words and their synonyms that you think you will find it necessary to use in your next article.
4. Write a 100-word summary of your reading in one of the books pertaining to words, writing, or style, as listed in the "Free-Lance Writer's Library" in the Appendix.
5. Write a summary paragraph of 100-words for each of five books listed under Vocabulary Aids in the "Free-Lance Writer's Library." Include in each paragraph the help that a writer should expect to find in the book, according to the preface.
6. Select an article in a current issue of a newspaper feature section and one in a current magazine and make a table listing the average number of words in a short, medium, and long sentence in each of the two articles.
7. Write down an example of periodic, balanced, and parallel sentences taken from each of the two articles. Analyze them to see why they are, or are not, effective to the style of these particular features.
8. Which of the three forms of a sentence predominate in each of the two articles?
9. What is the average length of the paragraphs in the two articles?
10. Which length predominates?
11. Do you find any paragraph lead sentences in either article that are not emphatic and attention-arresting? If so, copy them down to read in class.
12. List the most effective figures of speech that you found in each article. (A list of the figures of speech will be found in any of the books on style listed in the "Free-Lance Writer's Library.")
13. Did you find any paragraphs, sentences, or words that could be deleted in either of the articles? If so, list them.
14. Select one of your own manuscripts and read over the first five pages seeking to improve the style in the nine ways suggested.
15. Check the first five pages selected for Exercise 14, to see if there are any errors that are common to beginners.

Publication Analysis

Harpers Magazine and *The Atlantic Monthly*

Do not spend more than one hour and a quarter on the preparation of this report.

I. Identification: Name, publisher, editor, where published, price of each magazine.

II. Make-up:
1. What do you like about each magazine?
2. What do you dislike about each magazine?

III. Advertising:
1. What is the difference in the appeal in the advertising of the magazines?
2. From the advertising what kind of a reader do you visualize for each publication?
3. One tip from the advertising of each magazine (two tips in all).

IV. General Policy:
1. If you were editor, would you change either of these magazines in any way?
2. Give reason for the foregoing answer.
3. What types of articles could you submit to each magazine?

V. Feature Articles:
1. What types of articles do you find in each publication and to whom do they appeal?
2. Analyze an article from each magazine, using the pyramid as a basis for the analysis.
3. From the articles make a list of ten words that you feel give distinction to the style of writing.
4. List three figures of speech from the features in each publication and discuss their effectiveness.
5. Did you notice in any article a lack of completeness, or did the writer anticipate the answers to your questions?
6. List five suggestions for improving the writing of your own feature articles.

VI. Four Tips (two from each magazine): Source, authority for the article suggested, and three possible markets for each one that were suggested by the study of this magazine.

14

PREPARATION OF THE MANUSCRIPT

Professional Appearance Aids Sales. After the free-lance writer has carefully revised the manuscript, he is ready to start copying the final draft to send to the editor, his prospective purchaser. As has been pointed out in earlier chapters, one's manuscript competes with hundreds, or even thousands, of others in the editorial offices of a large publication. Therefore, the article must be submitted in a neat form that will attract the manuscript reader's eye immediately as the work of a professional. The reader detects the work of the amateur at first glance by the manner in which it is prepared. Naturally, he will have more confidence in the manuscript that obviously is written by an experienced writer. He will be inclined to give more consideration to an article that is carefully and neatly prepared in the professional manner.

The way in which a manuscript is submitted may mean the difference between an acceptance and a rejection. The novice must take great care to prepare the copy carefully, just as he would give thought to the details of his dress and manner if he were applying for a position. The editor's first impression of the writer's accuracy and dependability is formed when he looks at the manuscript for the first time. Many beginners fail to sell because they lack pride in the "physical" appearance of their articles. Editors say that Americans are more careless than foreign writers in the preparation of their manuscripts.

A well-prepared manuscript will make for an immediate friendly feeling toward the author on the part of the manuscript reader or editor.

Method of Preparation Is Uniform. A writer should give every possible consideration to the manuscript reader or editor who has to read his article and determine whether it will be accepted or rejected. Professional writers follow, on the whole, a uniform style in drafting the final copy. They are anxious to prepare it in the editor's accustomed way and to do everything that will make the reading of the article easier.

If a manuscript is typed on paper that is too thin, or is written on both sides, or is single spaced, or is written in longhand, or is without page numbers, the editor will classify the novice with others whose manuscripts are physically unattractive to him. Some authors submit well-prepared thick manuscripts on first-class bond paper, but instead of sending them flat, they fold them twice and mail them in business-letter envelopes. The editor has to take time to straighten out each page —which is most annoying. Others use the same typewriter ribbon for years, with the result that the letters are blurred and difficult to read, and this will exasperate any editor.

Before beginning to type the final copy, one should plan to include: (1) a cover sheet; (2) the typed article; (3) a back cover sheet; (4) pictures or drawings (the preparation of which will be discussed in the following chapter); (5) cardboard for packing; (6) a self-addressed postal card to acknowledge receipt of the manuscript; (7) a large manila envelope for returning the manuscript; (8) adequate postage stamps, attached by means of a wire clip for the return of the manuscript; (9) a still larger manila envelope in which to mail the manuscript, and (10) sufficient postage for first-class mail.

Every person who writes for publication should check his manuscript with the following points to see that he has not omitted any of the requirements of a professional manuscript.

Manuscripts Must Be Typed. Every person who writes, even as an avocation, should learn to use a typewriter. Until the writer has learned to type accurately he will have to have a typist copy his manuscripts.

A good typewriter with type kept clean and with a black ribbon in good condition will produce neat, legible copy. An editor will usually read such a manuscript with some degree of interest and will feel kindly disposed toward the writer.

Unruled white bond paper of good quality (not too heavy) in standard typewriting size, 8½ by 11 inches, should be used. Good paper not only looks well but stands more handling and saves retyping of manuscripts when they are returned, because it will be less worn and "dog-eared." A good quality of paper may be had for seventy-five cents or a dollar a box, and it is cheaper to buy it that way than in smaller quantities.

The professionally prepared manuscript is typed on only one side of the paper. It has a margin of at least an inch on the left-hand side, at the top, and at the bottom of all pages except the first page, which should have a margin of three or four inches at the top. The copy is double spaced to allow room for editorial corrections, changes, or subheads between the lines.

A businesslike writer makes a carbon of everything he writes for print: one copy for the editor, the other for his own files. If the original is lost in the mail or in the editorial office, the writer may replace it easily by retyping the carbon copy. If the article is accepted, the carbon also serves as a check to see how the printed copy was changed; or it may be of further service to the writer at some later date, even after the article is printed. One should have a sufficient supply of good carbon paper to insure clear copy.

Preparing the Cover Sheets. If a writer wants to sell articles, he should have a front cover sheet to serve as an introductory salesman in meeting the buyer—that is, the editor. If it is properly prepared, it tells the editor (1) the purpose of the article, (2) the identity of the writer, (3) the source of the material, (4) the number of words, and (5) the kind and number of illustrations.

In the upper left-hand corner the writer should type the

statement: "to be paid for at usual rates," etc., as shown in Fig. 5.

The author should type the title on the cover sheet about one-third of the way down the page, in order to leave sufficient space for the editor to change the caption if he wishes to. If the publication to which the article is slanted uses all capital letters, so should the author. If capitals and small letters are used—or, as a journalist would say, "upper and lower case" letters—the author should do the same. If the publication uses a second deck, or subtitle, underneath the caption to further explain the content of the article, so should the writer.

Two spaces beneath the title the writer should type his name, or "by-line." If he has "ghosted" the article, he should use the name of the celebrity on the "by-line" and, two spaces lower down, type his own name on a second "by-line," preceded by the words "as told to."

The note to the editor should be started three or four spaces below the "by-line," as shown in Fig. 5. It contains the salesmanship points and guarantees the goods, or, in other words, assures the editor of the authority for the content. One or more plausible reasons should be listed why a given article has reader interest, and it should convince the editor that he ought to read all of the manuscript. The name and identification of the interviewee or other sources that will aid in "selling" the manuscript to the editor should be included.

However, the note does not serve as a means of telling the editor how to run his publication or what his readers want to read. The youthful amateur in his enthusiasm and in his desire to "sell" the editor often offends rather than convinces. It is important that one give thought and care to writing the note. A tactless note is worse than no note at all.

The number of words in the article should be listed at the end of the note. That is where the editor is accustomed to finding such information. A quick and fairly accurate estimate may be made by counting all the letters, or "units," in one average typed line and dividing by 7 (the number of letters in the average word). The result is the number of average, or seven-letter, words to a line. By counting the lines on an average page and multiplying by the average number of words to a line, one knows the average number of words to the page.

To be paid for at usual
rates, or to be returned
with the eighteen (18)
cents in stamps enclosed, to

Written for Hygeia

Robert E. Neprud,
740 Langdon Street,
Madison, Wisconsin.

MILK--FROM DAIRY TO DINNER TABLE

By

Robert E. Neprud

(Note. This article is based on an interview with
Dr. L. C. Thomsen, an associate professor of
Dairy Industry, College of Agriculture,
University of Wisconsin, and on material
from government bulletins concerning milk
consumption. It contains 1,850 words.)

Two (2) photographs are enclosed, as follows:

1. Rinsing the Milk Bottle Under the Faucet
2. A Clean Cold Place for the Milk

Two (2) drawings are enclosed, as follows:

1. The Housewife Should Know Her Dairyman
2. Milk Ranks at the Top As a Food

FIG. 5. A COVER SHEET FOR A MANUSCRIPT

Multiplying the number of average words to the page by the number of pages in the manuscript gives a fairly accurate estimate of the total number of words.

In the note to the editor the author may explain his reason for writing under a pseudonym by saying "that for obvious

Place
Date

To Whom It May Concern:

I have read this article and it is scientifically (or technically) accurate. The quotations are just as I made them.

Yours respectfully,

(signed) ______________________

FIG. 6. APPROVAL SHEET TO BE SIGNED BY INTERVIEWEE

reasons I am writing under an assumed name." Or an author may not want to use his own name because the interviewee may be a member of his family. Or the article, particularly if it is a confession, might be too personal. If a nom de plume is used, it should be written in parentheses after the real name in the upper left-hand corner of all the pages, in order to insure mail delivery of the acceptance or of the rejected article. If the article is accepted, this practice enables the business office to write the check out in the writer's own name rather than in his assumed one.

The number of photographs, drawings, or other illustrations should be listed three spaces below the end of the note. The captions, or "cut-lines," of the illustrations should be listed as well as the number, as shown in Fig. 5.

Before inserting the completed manuscript in the envelope for mailing, a blank sheet of typing paper should be placed at the end to serve as a "back" cover sheet. It, like the front cover sheet, will aid in keeping the manuscript from becoming grimy and soiled as it is passed about from one manuscript reader to another in the publication office.

At least the cover sheet and the first page is read in most offices. From those pages the manuscript reader judges whether or not the article will have enough interest for the publication's subscribers for him to read all of it. A writer can see how important it is to prepare the cover sheet and the first pages with extreme care if he would impress the manuscript reader favorably.

Approval Sheet May Aid in Selling. If an article is of an extremely scientific or technical nature, or contains facts that the editor may doubt, the writer should ask the interviewee to sign a statement that he has read the article and that it is accurate or scientifically correct, whichever the case. The writer should type on a separate piece of paper the form as illustrated in Fig. 6. The signed approval sheet is placed just under the front cover sheet when the article is assembled for mailing.

Summaries Are "Boxed" on Separate Page. Some publications have a policy of occasionally using a summary, a list of directions, recipes, or a check list by "boxing" or indenting the material and placing it at the beginning of the article, or at the end, or perhaps in the center of the printed page. Since the writer does not know where the make-up editor would like it placed or whether he will want to use it at all, it is advisable to type such material on a separate page.

Lines may be drawn about it to form a "box," or the word "box" enclosed in a circle may be written at the upper left-hand corner of the page. If the writer knows that the publication's policy is to indent rather than box such material, he should write the word "indent" enclosed in a circle at the upper left-hand corner.

In arranging the manuscript for mailing, the sheet containing the boxed or indented material should precede the first page of the article. It follows the cover page and approval sheet (if there is one).

Typing the Final Draft of the Manuscript. The upper half of the first page of the article should be left blank, in order that the editor may write a new title and subtitle if he so desires. The title, subtitle, and author's name should be repeated on the first page exactly as they are on the cover sheet. The article should begin three spaces below the "by-line," as shown in Fig. 7.

At the left-hand side and as close as possible to the top of each page after the first should be placed the author's name, followed by a dash and the title of the article. The pages should be numbered clearly and consecutively in the upper right-hand corner, thus:

Neprud—MILK—FROM THE DAIRY TO THE DINNER TABLE —2—

Unnumbered pages may be dropped, scattered by a breeze, or even lost in the editorial office. Pages without numbers may cause the reader trouble and annoyance, which will not make him any more appreciative of the manuscript than he is compelled to be.

Each paragraph should be indented five spaces on the typewriter. A sentence should be started two spaces after the period of the preceding one. An end mark, or double cross

(#), should be put at the end of the manuscript to indicate that there are no more pages.

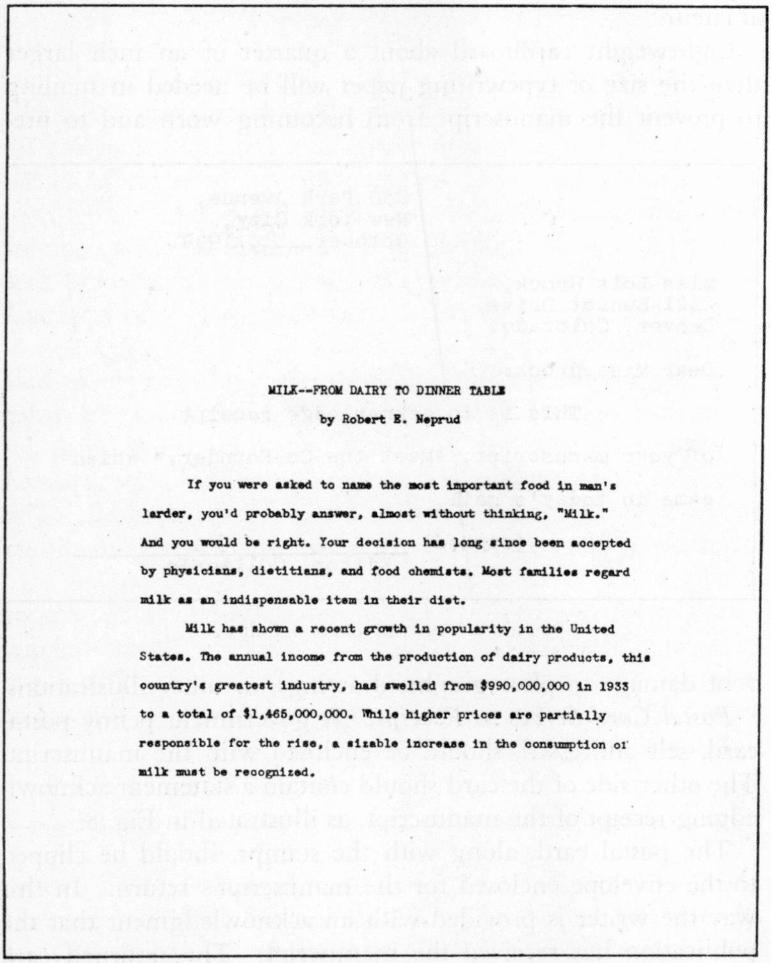

MILK--FROM DAIRY TO DINNER TABLE

by Robert E. Neprud

If you were asked to name the most important food in man's larder, you'd probably answer, almost without thinking, "Milk." And you would be right. Your decision has long since been accepted by physicians, dietitians, and food chemists. Most families regard milk as an indispensable item in their diet.

Milk has shown a recent growth in popularity in the United States. The annual income from the production of dairy products, this country's greatest industry, has swelled from $990,000,000 in 1933 to a total of $1,465,000,000. While higher prices are partially responsible for the rise, a sizable increase in the consumption of milk must be recognized.

FIG. 7. THE FIRST PAGE OF THE MANUSCRIPT

Any last minute corrections that cannot be made neatly on the typewriter should be made legibly in ink. Every omission or error in the typing should be corrected either on the typewriter or with a pen. A writer cannot expect an editor to think well of a manuscript if he himself does not respect it enough to make it as nearly letter perfect as is possible. One should remember that carelessness is the earmark of the amateur.

Lightweight cardboard about a quarter of an inch larger than the size of typewriting paper will be needed in mailing to prevent the manuscript from becoming worn and to pre-

```
                              250 Park Avenue,
                              New York City,
                              October ____, 1939.

Miss Lois Brock,
2421 Sunset Drive,
Denver, Colorado.

Dear Miss Brock:

          This is to acknowledge receipt

of your manuscript, "Meet the Co-Founder," which

came in today's mail.

               (signed) _________________________
                          Editor, Collier's
```

FIG. 8. POSTAL CARD RECEIPT

vent damage to photographs, drawings, or other illustrations.

Postal Card Serves as Receipt. A government penny postal card, self addressed, should be enclosed with the manuscript. The other side of the card should contain a statement acknowledging receipt of the manuscript, as illustrated in Fig. 8.

The postal card, along with the stamps, should be clipped to the envelope enclosed for the manuscript's return. In this way the writer is provided with an acknowledgment that the publication has received the manuscript. The returned card should not be destroyed until the manuscript has been accepted or returned. In many offices the envelopes are opened by a clerk or an office boy, and the card may not come to the immediate attention of anyone with the authority or interest to mail it. Since the idea of the postal card receipt originated in a journalism class room, a few publications have adopted the practice of mailing out their own cards acknowledging receipt of the article.

Manila Envelopes for Mailing Manuscripts. Two sizes of manila envelopes are needed. They must be large enough to contain all manuscript material without folding the paper or breaking the pictures. The larger envelope, in which the article is sent to the publication, should be 13 by 10 inches. The smaller one, for the return of the manuscript, should be 12½ by 9½ inches. If one cannot obtain the two sizes, he will have to fold the envelope that he encloses for the return of the article. The author should check to see that the smaller return envelope has his correct self address and that his return address is written in the upper left-hand corner of the large envelope, which is sent to the editor. In case the publication no longer exists, the manuscript will be returned.

Postage Stamps. Before one writes in the amount of postage on the cover sheet, he should include all material to be mailed—manuscript, pictures, drawings, return manila envelope, and return postal card—and it all should be weighed on a postal scales. Stamps should be attached, along with the postal card, to the return envelope with a wire clip. Stamps should not be pasted on the return envelope. If the editor buys the article, he buys the stamps along with it. If they are pasted on the envelope they will be useless.

Following the Accepted Typographical Style. Before typing the final draft of the article, a writer should analyze several issues of the publication to which he is slanting to ascertain the typographical style. He should list the publication's peculiarities of typographical form and follow them. However, if the style is extremely different or freakish, it is better to write the final copy according to the commonly accepted rules of capitalization, abbreviation, punctuation, hyphenation, and the use of figures. If the manuscript is returned, it will not then need to be rewritten because of its unusual typographical style before it is mailed out to another publication.

In typing the article, the writer should remember that each

page should end with a complete sentence—if possible, a complete paragraph. The copy then can be divided between several operators to set the copy in type. If the page ends in the middle of a sentence or paragraph, it is more difficult to break up the manuscript.

Correcting Typographical Errors. Manuscripts should be typed as nearly perfect as possible. If errors slip in here or there, the novice could correct them in ink. Copy-reading marks accepted by all editors and printers are the following:

Three lines under a letter or word indicate that it is to be set in capital letters; thus, united states = United States.

Two lines under a letter or word indicate that it is to be set in small capital letters; thus, Kansas City Star = KANSAS CITY STAR.

One line under a word indicates that it is to be set in italics; thus, Gone with the Wind = *Gone with the Wind.*

An oblique line drawn from right to left through a capital letter indicates that it is to be set in lower case; thus, Feature Article = feature article.

A circle around a numerical figure or abbreviation indicates that it is to be spelled out; thus, (5) feet and three (in.) = five feet and three inches.

A circle around a word or figure spelled out indicates that it is to be abbreviated or that numerical figures are to be used; thus, (President) J. D. Jones is (six) feet in height = Pres. Jones is 6 feet in height.

A caret is placed at the point in the typed line where letters or words written above the line are to be inserted; thus, One should never write ^ (a letter) to the editor = One should never write a letter to the editor.

Short curved lines indicate that two words or two parts of a word are to be run together without space between them, in order to make one word; thus, cran berry = cranberry.

A vertical line between two words indicates that they are to be separated by a space; thus, An amateur should neverquery an editor = An amateur should never query an editor.

A small cross or dot within a circle indicates a period; thus, U S or U S = U. S.

Small half-circles around single or double quotations indicate whether they are beginning or end marks; thus, "Ten cents a quart is much too high," he said.

A curved line under one word and over the next indicates that they are to be transposed; thus, article feature = feature article.

A paragraph mark is used to indicate a new paragraph; thus, They are as follows; or ¶ They are as follows:

A line is used to connect the end of one line with the beginning of another when both are to form a continuous line of copy; thus, The check came in an envelope—a long one—with nothing else in it.

Sending the Manuscript. Postal regulations require that all written matter must be sent as first-class mail at the same rates as letters. The envelope, containing the article with the pages clipped together, should be sealed and marked "First Class—Handle With Care." Delay in the delivery of the article because of insufficient postage may be prevented by weighing the article on an accurate postal scales. Stamps to cover the postage for the article's return, in case it is rejected, should be attached along with the post card receipt to the return envelope with a wire clip.

Even though one knows the editor's name, it is advisable to address the outer envelope containing the manuscript simply to "The Editor." If the article is going to a newspaper, it should be addressed to the "Sunday Editor" or to the "Sunday Feature Editor." If one addresses the outer envelope by using the editor's name, it may reach his desk when he is away, and his secretary may think it is personal and not open it. Unnecessary delay would result.

Manuscripts, even those of a few pages, should be mailed flat with a sheet of cardboard a little larger than the paper, to prevent the article from becoming crumpled and the photographs bent or broken. If large photographs or drawings are sent, two pieces of cardboard should be enclosed to assure protection. As previously pointed out, a manuscript is an article of merchandise to be sold to a customer—the editor. Needless to say, he will not be interested in buying one that is not neat and professional in appearance any more than he would want to buy a suit of clothes that was wrinkled and shopworn. It is important then that careful attention be given to "packing" the manuscript, in order to have it arrive on the editor's desk in the best possible condition.

A careful writer, before putting the manuscript in the mail, will check again to see that he has included all the material to be mailed: manuscript, pictures, drawings, and the return manila envelope, with postal card receipt and sufficient return postage clipped to it.

If the manuscript is a bulky one or the photographs so large that the package cannot go as first-class mail, it should be sent by express.

Mailing Manuscripts to British Markets. The English publications offer a wide variety of opportunities to all writers. But before submitting to publications there, it is best to write to the publications in which one is interested and obtain sample copies if they are not available on newsstands or in the local library. Many authors could add to their revenue by selling second rights to manuscripts that they have already sold in this country.

Often writers do not know how to obtain English stamps for return postage if the article is not accepted, and they defer the day of mailing manuscripts to English publications for that reason. Return postage may be secured by writing to the Postmaster, London (no further address is necessary), who will send English stamps in exchange for an international money order. Or one may obtain at his local post office an international postage coupon, which may be sent with the manuscript for return postage. Though more expensive than English stamps, it has the advantage of being obtainable at one's local post office, and it therefore saves time.

The Manuscript in the Editorial Office. Although editorial offices vary in their methods of handling manuscripts, most of them have systems that are similar. For that reason, it is important that the author be systematic in the preparation of his manuscript.

A record is made of the manuscript by most publications as soon as the huge mail sacks are opened in the mailing room and the manuscripts are sorted and delivered to the various editors. Some offices make the record on a card, others use ledger-like books. The name and address of the author, the title, the type of article, the number and nature of illustrations, and the time of its receipt are entered. The amount of postage on the envelope and the amount clipped to the return, or "inner," envelope is noted on a card. The estimated number of words is also recorded. If the photographs or drawings are damaged, that, too, is noted.

The manuscript and illustrations, with the record, is sent to the editor's or the assistant editor's secretary. She sorts the manuscripts as to assistant editors, records on the card the name of the department or the assistant editor to whom the article is to be given, and files the record card under "Manuscripts Received."

If the editor or manuscript reader to whom the article was delivered rejects it, he clips a rejection slip to it. If he "almost accepted" it, he may write a letter to the author. The secretary takes the card from the manuscript received file, stamps the date on it, and places the card in the case marked "Manuscripts Returned." The secretary or the office boy puts the manuscript with the rejection slip and photographs in the envelope, and, if sufficient postage was enclosed, sends the manuscript to the mailing department. However, if the writer did not send an adequate amount of postage, as many amateurs do not, the manuscript is held in the publication office. Some offices send a postcard to the author asking for postage sufficient for the return of the article; others destroy the rejected article if it lacks return postage.

Some publications send out a form letter explaining to the contributor why the article was rejected. Others send a personal letter of rejection and may suggest another market to which the manuscript might be acceptable. Or an editor may suggest revision of an article with merit, and ask that it be submitted again.

If the manuscript is accepted, the associate editor notes on the card the suggested payment for the manuscript and for the illustrations and sends it to the editor. If he approves of the article, he may raise or lower the price indicated on the card, his action depending upon the author's rating or ability, the authority contained in the article, and the probable reader interest in the subject. He approves of the associate editor's judgment by endorsing the card. It, along with the manuscript, is returned to the reader who recommended the purchase. The card then goes to the secretary, who stamps it paid, and it is then filed under "Manuscripts Paid." In some offices from four to six associate editors must approve of an article before it is accepted.

A few publications submit galley proofs to the author for correction and for any necessary changes he desires to make. Only necessary alterations should be made, however, in order to avoid delay and expense of resetting type. The author should return the proofs promptly.

The Length of Time for a Reply Varies. The efficiency and the size of the editorial staff determines the length of time it takes to inform an author concerning the fate of his manuscript. Some offices reply within a week; other within a year or even longer. However, the better established offices do not hold a manuscript longer than three or four weeks and they pay promptly. They realize that the free-lance writer has to pay his bills and that prompt consideration and prompt payment wins friends. The result is that they have a larger number of manuscripts submitted by free-lance writers, which enables them to choose their manuscripts rather than to take what they can get.

Plans and Methods of Payment Differ. Publications vary in their systems of payment as well as in their methods of handling a manuscript. Some pay once a month, whereas others pay once a week. A few pay upon acceptance, but the majority pay upon publication. And a few pay only when the author threatens exposure of the publication's inability or lack of interest in paying.

Some publications pay as little as $1.50 for an article, whereas others pay from $100 to $500. If the contributor is well known, he may be paid several times that amount.

In the majority of publication offices, rates of payment are based upon a certain amount per word. Others pay so much per article, regardless of the number of words. Rates per word vary from a quarter of a cent to five cents per word to unknown writers, whereas established authors are paid more than the minimum rate by most publications. Some editors require a statement that a manuscript is original, or that by accepting the check the writer gives certain rights to the publication. These rights will be discussed in Chapter 16. The present tendency is toward prompt payment and also toward payment on acceptance.

Successful Writer Keeps a Manuscript Record. Keeping a record of one's manuscripts is most important, because it enables one to know: (1) where his articles are, (2) where they have been, (3) how long it takes the editor to make a decision, (4) the rate of payment, (5) the time of payment, (6) the cost of photographs, art work, paper, envelopes, and postage, (7) the total cost, (8) the hours spent in gathering the material and in writing it, and (9) the profit. The form for such a record is shown in Fig. 9.

The professional writer, by examining his manuscript rec-

Article No. *9.* Title *Taming Wild Pasture*

No. of Photographs *3.* No. of Drawings *2.* Date Written *October 3, 1941.*

	Publication	Date Sent	Date Ret'd	Date Accpt'd	Amount Paid	Photo Cost	Art Cost	Paper Cost	Envel. Cost	Post-age	Total Cost	Hrs. Spent	Profit
1.	*Country Gent*	*10/ 5*	*11/ 2*	.....	.....	*1.60*	*.40*	*.05*	*.07*	*.18*	*2.30*	*8*	.....
2.	*Success. Farm*	*11/ 3*	*11/25*	.....	.....	.....	.....	.....	.....	.....	.....	.....	.....
3.	*Capper's Farm*	*11/26*	.....	*12/18*	*35.00*	.....	.....	.....	.....	.....	.....	.....	*32.70*
4.													
5.													
6.													

FIG. 9. FORM FOR MANUSCRIPT RECORD

ord sheets, or cards, knows how soon he may expect a decision from most publications to which he submits articles. If an article depends upon timeliness for its interest, he cannot risk sending it to an editor who takes several months to consider a manuscript; otherwise, if it is rejected, it will be too late to send elsewhere. By surveying his manuscript record, he will note the publications that give prompt decisions; and by sending his article to one of those, his chances of selling will be infinitely better.

Checking Up on Unheard-from Manuscripts. Manuscript records should be filed by the dates upon which a manuscript was mailed out last. A check-up then can be made easily to ascertain the articles that have been out a month or more. The writer should send a note or postal card of inquiry as to the manuscript's whereabouts. He should phrase his note tactfully by insinuating that he is afraid the manuscript has been lost in the mails, since he sent it on the date a month previous and has heard nothing concerning it. He should suggest that if the manuscript has not been received, he will be glad to send another copy. If the editor ignores the inquiry, the writer should follow it up with another every week until he does get a reply.

Some professional writers use a "top front" cover sheet of salmon, pink, or red paper, which is placed on top of the regular front cover sheet to call the manuscript reader's attention to the immediate timeliness of an article. If the writer does not hear within ten days about a timely manuscript so prepared, he should send a postal card inquiry to the editor to call his attention to the fact that he has not taken any action. If nothing is heard within a week thereafter, a letter to the same effect, asking for the return of the manuscript or its definite acceptance for publication, should be sent. The writer can explain tactfully that because of the very timeliness of the article, his work in gathering and writing it will be lost if the article becomes outdated. Needless to say, the red cover sheet and the ten-day follow up should never be used except for extremely timely articles. If the red cover sheet is overdone, it will fail to catch the manuscript reader's eye, just as the cry of "wolf" by the boy in the fable failed to get attention when he really needed it.

Writers deplore the long time it takes editors to make a decision concerning a manuscript. But the fault often is with the writers themselves for not following up manuscripts systematically and periodically. Of course, the follow-up notes must be phrased tactfully. One should type a sympathetic and understanding letter that will go right to the editor's heart and make him say to himself: "What a cad I am." But never write an abusive letter. Many editors are overworked and are even more aware of the delay in replying than the contributor is. Remember that the editor is the free-lance writer's best friend and should be so treated.

Resending Manuscripts to Market. Many writers have received rejected manuscripts in the mail only to realize that they must be retyped before they could be sent to other prospective purchasers. The pages were battered and wrinkled from careless handling in the editorial office or by hurried mail clerks. Much as an author may begrudge the time spent in retyping, it is time well spent. A fresh, crisp, unwrinkled manuscript that bears no traces of prior journeys to other publication offices invariably will be given the editor's first attention.

Retyping is slow and costly in time, and to a person with creative instincts it is apt to be boring and monotonous. An electric iron and a soft gum eraser will save hours of time for the free-lance writer. Many have finally sold articles that have been out four or five times by ironing page by page over a thick magazine placed on an ironing board until the entire manuscript looked fresh and crisp. One must take good care that the iron is not too hot or the paper will be yellowed or scorched. If it is necessary to retype a few pages, they, too, should be pressed, in order that they will have the same yellowed appearance as the other pages.

If the edges of the sheets are soiled, they may be cleaned with a soft gum eraser. The pages should be straightened, until they all are even, and then they should be "riffled" in order to spread them apart at the edges. The manuscript—with the pages still a little apart or offset at the edges—should be put on a flat hard surface so that the edges of the pages will project like miniature stair-steps. The gum eraser may be rubbed over the page edges that project, and they will thus be cleaned in surprisingly quick time. By treating the four edges of each page—both front and back—with the eraser, a manuscript can be made to present a fresh and untraveled appearance with very little effort.

New cover sheets—front and back—should replace the old ones each time an article is remailed. But remember to press the fresh pages, in order that the color will match the rest of the manuscript. The time saved by not retyping the article may be spent in gathering material and writing another. The more one writes, the more he sells.

Writer May Syndicate Articles. A writer may add to his earnings by sending copies of an article to several newspapers for simultaneous publication. This method is termed "syndication" in newspaper parlance. Newspapers circulate only in certain areas or localities. For example, Kansas City papers are not read in Detroit or Minneapolis, thus, the feature sections of these papers could publish the same article on the same day.

One cannot syndicate his articles to a number of magazines, however, because their circulations overlap, and magazine editors buy only exclusive articles. A subject may be written in two or more ways, to make entirely different articles, which may then be submitted to different magazines. Different pictures should be obtained for each article for a magazine, but in syndicating to a newspaper one would need only duplicate sets of the same pictures. Unless one knows absolutely that a publication's circulation is sectional, he should never send the same material or illustrations to two or more publications simultaneously.

In syndicating feature articles one must: (1) ascertain that the newspapers' circulations do not overlap; (2) make as many clear copies as he intends to submit; (3) obtain separate sets of photographs for each copy; (4) indicate that the article is syndicated by writing in the upper right-hand corner of the

To be paid for at usual
rates, or to be returned
with the twelve (12) cents
in stamps enclosed, to

Robert Anderson,
Shorewood Hills,
Madison, Wisconsin.

Written for Milwaukee Journal
(Exclusive for the Journal's
circulation territory. This
article is also being submitted
to the Boston Transcript,
The Kansas City Star, and the
Los Angeles Times.)

Release for publication,
Sunday, November 8.

MANY PUPILS IN WISCONSIN TAUGHT
TO TUNE OF RADIO SPEAKERS

Instruction in Music, Drawing, Conservation, and Geography
Given to 50,000 School Children

By

Robert Anderson

(Note. This article is based on interviews with Harold B. McCarty, director of Station WHA, Prof. E. B. Gordon of the School of Music, University of Wisconsin, and Wakelin McNeel, 4-H club leader, all of Madison, Wis.
It explains the methods and relates the results of class room radio instruction as conducted by this educational radio station. It contains 2800 words.)

Three (3) photographs are enclosed, as follows:

1. Education Is in the Air for Wisconsin Pupils
2. Professor Gordon Instructs His Unseen Pupils
3. Wakelin McNeel, Known to His Radio Classes as Ranger Mac.

One (1) drawing is enclosed, as follows:

1. A Radio Student Draws Rip Van Winkle

FIG. 10. COVER SHEET FOR A SYNDICATED NEWSPAPER ARTICLE

cover sheet that "This article is exclusive for your circulation territory. It is also being submitted to . . ." and then name the other publications to which it is being sent; (5) indicate the date upon which the article may be published, by writing, for example, "Release for Publication, Sunday, Oct. 4"; and (6) mail the articles out at least three weeks in advance of the release date, to enable all Sunday editors to arrange for engravings for the pictures and for publication of the articles on the release date.

It is almost futile for the beginner to attempt to submit articles to a syndicate company, as pointed out in Chapter 9. However, he may be quite successful in "syndicating" his articles directly to several newspapers. A student wrote a feature concerning a student equestrian club. He sent copies of the same feature to ten different newspapers in ten different sections of the United States and Canada, because the home cities of the students were in the circulation territory of the ten newspapers to which the articles were submitted. He received ten checks from the newspapers in addition to the original feature, which he had written for a national equestrian publication. His sales for the original article and ten syndicated ones totaled $140.

Understanding the Editor's Problems. Novices are continually protesting against ill-treatment by magazines. They forget that the editors did not ask them to offer their manuscripts. They entered the most highly competitive market in the world of their own free will. They must realize that they are the sellers and that they must accept the buyer's offer. If the editors mess up the script, they should not complain. He did not ask them to send their articles to him.

Editors are not disagreeable. With marketing experience, the beginner will find editors very human and willing to help those who show promise in mastering the craft. They are the best friends a writer can have, if one will work with them instead of against them. Treat your editors as friends and they will treat you the same way.

If one would attain success in writing, he must not be discouraged every time an article does not sell. A young woman who tried writing features was discouraged every time an article was returned. But she often rejects all of the many dresses that she tries on in the shops without ever thinking that the saleswomen might feel hurt because she did not buy. Shopkeepers cannot afford to take offense when their customers do not buy; neither can free-lance writers. The shopkeeper does not throw the dresses in an old trunk just because they did not sell the first time they were shown to a customer. But the young woman is so hurt when a manuscript returns that she tosses it into an old trunk. The free-lance writer must take the attitude of the merchant who, when he does not make a sale, consoles himself that there are others who will buy. No one is likely to succeed at writing unless he is fair-minded, patient, tactful, and willing to meet editors half way in an effort to gain mutual advantage.

Membership in a writers' club, subscriptions to writers' magazines, and a review of textbooks on feature writing will aid the novice who is easily discouraged or irritated at rejection slips to adopt a cheerful friendly attitude toward the editors to whom he hopes to sell. By these means he will acquire an understanding of the editor's problems.

Exercises

1. After checking your supplies for writing features, make a list of additional ones you need before starting to write your final draft.
2. Make a tentative headline schedule for your first article by analyzing the "style" of captions used in the publication to which you are slanting your first article.
3. Make a tentative "style sheet" by listing all unusual style usages found in analyzing three features in the publication to which you are slanting.
4. Make a tentative "style sheet" for the cut-lines used in the publication.
5. What is the average number of pictures used for each article in the publication?
6. What is the average number of drawings used for each article in the publication?
7. What is the average wordage of articles in the publication?

8. How long are the short ones? The long ones? The mid-length ones?
9. Is the content of your article of such a nature that you will need an approval sheet?
10. Is there any material in your article that would lend itself effectively to being "boxed" or indented?
11. Would the content of your article lend itself to syndication?
12. If so, to what newspapers would you submit copies of it?
13. To which of the writer's magazines listed in the appendix--"The Free-Lance Writer's Library"—do you plan to send a subscription? Give reason for your choice.
14. Which market book listed in "The Free-Lance Writer's Library" do you plan to buy with money earned by writing feature articles?
15. Before submitting your article to your instructor or before mailing your article, check it with all the points enumerated in this chapter in reference to preparation of a manuscript. List the points that you had failed to include in the preparation of your article for market.

Publication Analysis

Country Home, Capper's Farmer, and *Successful Farming*

Do not spend more than one hour on the preparation of this report.

I. Identification for each magazine: name, publishers, editors, where published, price.

II. Make-up: What to you, as a future magazine editor, are the interesting things about the make-up of the three magazines? Give reasons for your answers.

III. Advertising:
1. From the point of view of what you know about advertising, do you think the copy in each publication will appeal to the reader?
2. What did you like about the advertising in each publication and give reason?
3. What did you find different about the advertising appeal in each publication?
4. What tips were suggested to you by the advertising?

IV. General Policy:
1. To what types of readers do the three publications appeal?
2. Why should you as a free-lance writer know these magazines?
3. What features might you have written?
4. Do you find any difference in the appeals here than in your last study of magazines? What ones?

V. Features: Read a feature in each magazine and list five suggestions for each feature read that will enable you to write better features (15 suggestions in all).

VI. Slogans: Write a slogan for each magazine.

VII. Four Tips: source, authority, and three possible markets suggested by this study.

15

ILLUSTRATING THE FEATURE ARTICLE

Writer's Hobby Will Bring Profits. Since many psychologists are advising everyone to have a hobby, the feature writer finds himself in a fortunate situation. He may select a hobby that not only will be interesting but will add to his success in his avocation or career. It will help him to sell his manuscripts, it will pay its own expenses, and it will bring in profits. The hobby is photography. The development of engraving and photography, and the increasing popularity of the camera, have been important factors in the growth of magazines and the use of illustrations.

With a little study and practice, writers can take photographs that will aid in telling the stories of the articles and that will reproduce for printing as well as those taken by professionals. The writer-photographer may take pictures how and when he wishes. He will decrease his expense account and will increase his sales. Unconventional pictures add to the reader interest of an article and are in much greater demand by editors than are stiff, formal photographs.

The processes of developing films and making prints and enlargements are even more interesting than taking pictures. They, too, will serve as a means of reducing expenses on the manuscript record. However, it is advisable not to attempt taking or making pictures until one has had some photographic experience.

The Value of Illustrations. The modern writer has learned to think in terms of pictures because the nation, as readers, has become picture minded. Editors desire illustrations in their publications. Pictures show graphically what otherwise would require description in hundreds of words or even pages of type. They convey facts so effectively that in the last decade entire sections of newspapers and magazines have been devoted to pictures. Now entire publications are given over to them.

Readers are attracted by illustrations and frequently, because of them, are lured into reading the article. They give an authoritative tone to the written word and add to the attractiveness of the page make-up. They serve as a universal language and thereby aid in sales of manuscripts. An editor of a well-known trade publication says that if a contributor, for example, sends him an article on how to paint a house, he probably rejects it. But if the writer also sends pictures to illustrate the article, he generally buys both. Another editor finds that approximately one writer in forty submits an illustrated manuscript; the other thirty-nine articles go back promptly.

Photographs Must Be Twice Slanted. Photographs add to the value of the manuscript only when they are twice slanted. In preparing the article, as described in Chapter 9, a writer should consider carefully the number and character of photographs or drawings necessary to add to the interest of the manuscript, as well as the kinds of photographs that fit the publication's art policy. One publication may desire the artistic variety, with shadows and bright high lights; another may prefer the straight news picture, without any pretense at artistic photography. The successful writer will increase his sales by studying the art in the publication as diligently as he studied the features and advertising.

Sources from Which Photographs May Be Obtained. One of the most difficult things for the amateur to overcome, in his attempt to become a free-lance writer, is his lack of willingness to learn about and to obtain illustrations for his articles. Many novices fail to sell because they do not realize that purchasing illustrations, hiring photographs, or having drawings made is a part of their necessary expense and their stock in the business of writing. They willingly pay large fees to take courses in writing, or they buy expensive typewriters, but they begrudge spending a cent for pictures or investing in a camera. They do not realize that editors reject articles because illustrations are lacking.

Photographs may be secured from photographers who have suitable negatives taken for other purposes. For a small charge—25 cents to $1—they will sell prints from negatives. If a writer desires a picture of something in a distant community, he may contact a photographer there by addressing a letter to "Photographer" at that place. If the postmaster does not wish to deliver the letter, it will be returned, provided the writer has requested a "return in three days" (the minimum allowed by postal regulations). If a reply does not come in a few days, one might refer to a newspaper directory for the name of a newspaper in that community, and ask its art editor or news editor to recommend a photographer to whom one could write. Perhaps the newspaper art department might be willing to sell a print if it had a suitable negative.

A writer unable to obtain prints from photographers should not hesitate to have pictures made if there is no other source from which he may obtain them more cheaply. The charges for such services in most communities are about three dollars per picture and up. Although several such photographs add considerably to one's expense, money spent for illustrations is money well spent. Pictures not only add to the size of the check, but in many instances will help to sell articles. One may be able, however, to have the work done by commercial photographers whose prices will possibly be less, because they are equipped and accustomed to giving such service. Their names can be found in the classified section of the telephone book or in the city directory.

Picture syndicates, listed under directories in "The Free-Lance Writer's Library" in the Appendix, will furnish suitable illustrations on almost any subject, generally at a cost of three dollars for each print. Many Federal and state government departments will supply a writer with mimeographed lists of good photographs that they have available on the subjects in their departments. From the list, a writer may select the ones he thinks will be suitable; the costs are usually fifteen or twenty-five cents. A beginner obtained pictures from the United States Signal Corps in Washington to illustrate an Armistice Day feature; another used pictures from the United States Department of Agriculture for an article on better farm housing; and a third got excellent photographs from the office of his state conservation department for an article on reforestation.

Many commercial institutions, industries, advertising agencies, and publicity departments have pictures that they will supply for a small fee. In some cases they will give them to a writer because they are anxious to create a demand for their commodities, or they desire to make their clients better known. The advertising departments of concerns manufacturing silver, china, bedding, furniture, and other products often will send large photographs without charge. The writer, however, when making the request should suggest, of course, that he is willing to pay a reasonable amount for the pictures if he can use them. Sometimes the interviewee or the authoritative sources for the material in the article will provide pictures at a reasonable price or will give them to the writer.

Qualities Desired in Photographs. The writer must give thought to the pictures for his articles, whether he takes them himself, has a photographer take them, buys prints from a photographer, or gets them gratis. In the first place, each picture must tell a story and tell it at a glance. Its composition, or arrangement, is affected by the time of day. Light and shadow become a part of the photograph. There should be but one central or dominating point of interest in a picture. High lights, shadows, masses, and lines should be arranged according to principles of balance, symmetry, and harmony in art.

The photograph must be pleasing to the eye, artistic, and fascinating. Two bright spots or two dark spots should not be of the same importance. The center of interest, or the dominant part, should be just a bit away from the center of the picture. The horizon line in a landscape should never divide it into two equal parts. Meaningless backgrounds should be avoided, since pictures should utilize their space to advantage. In planning the picture, one must remember that the camera really is a device for making drawings with reflected light; therefore, one should utilize the high lights and the shadows to accentuate the meaning the picture conveys.

Careful thought should be given as to the most advantageous point of view in order to avoid too much or too little detail. The items to be photographed should be placed as close together as the telling of the story (or the process) and the principles of good art permit. The idea of size in a photograph may be presented by including a person, a hand, a finger, or some object the size of which is familiar to the reader. If one is showing a picture of a machine, he should show the operator working it, to give life and action to the photograph.

Testing the "Suitability" of a Photograph. If any one of the details are obscured by heavy shadows, those parts may appear black in the halftone illustration. The "suitability" of any part may be tested readily by covering up all of the print except the small area that appears black. If it is the subject's face that is somewhat obscured by the shadow, one should cover up all of the photograph except that part of the face. If that small area can still be recognized as a part of the subject's face, it is fairly safe to say that the picture will reproduce satisfactorily when the halftone is made.

Good Photographs Find Markets. There are only three reasons why editors reject photographs: (1) technically, they may be poor and inadequate; (2) they may not illustrate properly the subject the writer intended; and (3) they may not be slanted to the editor's particular publication. But a good photograph will find a market if it has (1) originality, (2) human interest, (3) broad appeal, (4) good composition, and (5) subject matter that helps to tell the "story" of the article.

Photographs Must Conform to Necessary Requirements. Reproduction of pictures by means of the halftone must conform to definite requirements. A ferrotype print, or "glossy print," as it is better known, is made by drying it on sheets of metal to produce a smooth shiny surface. It is more readily adapted to the engraving process than photographs made on rough papers; therefore glossy prints are required by editors. The picture on single-weight glossy paper should be unmounted; if it is not, the print has to be removed from its mounting.

If one is submitting an article to a publication that uses color, it is advisable to have two sets of photographs. One, the glossy print, for reproduction as a halftone; the other, an ordinary print to color with water colors or crayons. The staff artist will know then where the right colors should be placed on the "cut" in order to give the reader an accurate idea of the effect.

Size of Photograph Is Important. Since engravers can produce better halftones, or "cuts," by reducing the picture at least one-half, one should have photographic prints of the standard size. Photographers—professional or amateur—should have negatives for illustrations in the sizes of 5 x 7, 6½ x 8½, or 8 x 10 inches. Smaller ones are accepted by a few publications, but they should not be smaller than 4 x 5 or, at the very least, 3½ x 5½ inches. Should a free-lance use smaller photographs, he must have them enlarged to one of the standard sizes.

Photographs May Be Enlarged. Enlargements may be made from negatives if they are clear and sharp. They must be rich in "velvety" blacks and crisp in clear high lights, or the gloss print will not reproduce satisfactorily. As editors pay space rates for illustrations, it is profitable to have them enlarged as much as possible, and it saves considerable money. Engravers say, however, that even with all the modern equipment, it is more difficult to get a clear distinct halftone if the negative has been enlarged.

Rates of Payment. The usual allowance for photographs to illustrate articles is from $3 to $10 apiece. In many offices a completely illustrated article will bring more per word for the article than the same words sent without illustrations. If the editor has to find the illustrations by sending messengers scurrying around among photographic syndicate files to find six or more adequate and appropriate photographs for the writer's article, he is justified in paying the writer less per word. An idea, when completely worked out with words and photographs and other illustrations, is a real article of commerce that an editor is only too willing to pay for as generously as he can.

Developing Camera Technique. Like every good thing in life, picture taking and picture making requires study, observation, and painstaking care. If it did not, photographs would not bring attractive prices. A good camera is an essential part of a writer's equipment for feature writing. It will pay its way many times over if used with some knowledge and thought. By simplification, and by gradual improvement of cameras, and by the development of new types of films, successful photography has become so simple that every writer should take it up not only as a hobby but as part of his profession, because it reduces expenses and aids in making sales.

A journalist may acquire a good camera for any amount from twenty to eighty dollars. If one desires to purchase a camera, and knows but little about them, he should seek the advice of an expert before determining the kind of camera he wishes to buy. The important factors that a writer should consider in selecting one are (1) the kind of pictures that he wishes to take, (2) the best shape and size, and (3) convenience in carrying. Many writers use a press reflex type of camera equipped with the fastest type of lens and shutters. It is particularly useful in taking subjects in poor light or in taking rapidly moving objects.

As soon as one finds that he has developed a fair camera

technique, he will be anxious to learn to do his own finishing. He will find excellent guidance by reading the stimulating books and magazines on the subject listed in "The Free-Lance Writer's Library." He may be appalled at first at the seemingly intricate directions, but if he will follow an instruction book accurately, he will find it all quite simple. He should be content with small beginnings at first; when larger checks result from his combined labors at the typewriter and in the dark room, he may try more pretentious photographs. Nine-tenths of the fun of photography is in the developing and printing and planning the composition.

The amateur photographer will find photographic silhouettes, or shadow pictures, an aid in illustrating ideas. They can be made indoors very easily by the novice if he follows the instructions closely. A young woman wrote an article on posture and illustrated it with silhouette photographs. She sold it to *Hygeia*.

Amateur Should Use Professional Methods. Too many writer-photographers are content to make "satisfactory" pictures, with the result that they fail to add to their incomes as much as those who make exceptionally good pictures. The ambitious amateur photographer who wishes to do professional work gives study and thought to: (1) focusing the camera on the main point by measuring rather than guessing distances; (2) timing the exposure, under the given light conditions, as correctly as experience and the exposure-meter can make it; (3) avoidance of faster exposures than the motion of the subject requires, by using a tripod and making a slow automatic snapshot or even a time exposure in order to get sharpness and depth, the quality much desired in editorial offices; (4) having people in the pictures to give life and action; (5) making the pictures clear by giving more light to objects close to the lens and less light to those farther away; (6) making the pictures sharp in detail by cutting down the lens opening and giving it a longer exposure; (7) giving more exposure to objects dark in color than the same objects if they are white; (8) avoiding horizontal or vertical lines, because they will cut the picture in two; (9) viewpoint and balance; (10) learning how to reduce overexposed negatives, intensifying underexposed ones, and increasing or decreasing contrasts by the use of proper chemical solutions; (11) the use of different color filters, diffusion disks, photoflood lights, portrait attachments, films, and papers in control of natural and bizarre effects; and (12) taking interesting photographs and writing articles around them as well as writing interesting articles and taking pictures to illustrate them.

Using Drawings to Illustrate Articles. Pen and ink sketches, diagrams, floor plans, and working drawings often are necessary to explain and illustrate elements in a feature. Even though the writer may have excellent photographs, drawings may show the detail that the camera fails to emphasize.

If a writer has even a little skill in drawing, he may prepare rough sketches that will enable the staff artists to catch the idea to be illustrated and make the finished drawings. However, if a writer has any training or even some ability in making pen and ink sketches, he may prepare his own illustrations. The books listed in "The Free-Lance Writer's Library" will be suggestive. Publications pay for acceptable art work as well as for photographs. Even beginners have used simple skeleton lines representing the human figure, or rough sketches to explain an idea, and typewriters to represent figures by filling in the desired spaces with the letter x.

Line drawings, such as pen and ink sketches, are made into zinc etchings for reproduction and show no gradations in tone. Photographs, in order to show all the gradations of light and dark, are reproduced by the halftone. Drawings should be made on fairly light weight bristol board with black India or drawing ink. They should be at least twice or even three times the size intended to be when published.

Charts, Graphs, and Tables Add to Reader Interest. Many articles, particularly those slanted for the business papers or farm and home magazines, make use of other devices than photographs or drawings to clarify, condense, or explain points and to give a tone of authority. Editors use them because they build good will toward the publication. Subscribers appreciate having information in a concise form that they can clip and file. Some publications devote pages to recipes, household, and budget problems in chart and table form for convenient filing. Even the novice may, with the aid of the books listed in the Appendix, use these devices.

All lines, printing, and lettering should be done in India ink on bristol board. Statements or figures on record sheets or blanks intended for reproduction should be typed with a fresh record black ribbon.

Preparation of Illustrations for Mailing. A carefully planned caption, or "cut-line," adds much to the interest of the illustration and of the article. Periodicals vary in the style of their captions as much as they do in the style of the titles of the articles. If the caption is not appropriate, the editor will have to rewrite it. Before writing a "cut-line," one should analyze those in the periodical to which the article is slanted. Some publications use long statements as "cut lines"; others use short ones. Some are humorous; others are serious. Whatever style of captions the publication uses, it should serve as the pattern for the novice. One should also count the number of units, or letters, in the "cut-line" selected as the guide and use that number for a measuring stick for his own captions.

With a little practice and a great deal of thought, one will find it easy to write "cut-lines." The beginner should jot down the "story" of the picture or drawing in one sentence. After one finds the right idea to explain the illustration, he can give attention to word selection and caption length. He should keep in mind that every "cut-line" will be more effective if it has an actual or an implied verb.

"Cut-lines" should be typed on a piece of paper and pasted on the back lower edge of the illustration, in order that the "line" will extend down under the picture or drawing, as shown in Fig. 11. With a pair of scissors, its edges should be trimmed off so that they are even with those of the illustration. If the illustration has been obtained from a source that desires credit in lieu of payment, credit should be given by adding a credit line, such as "Reproduced by permission of the Alabama State Historical Society."

One should never write the identification on the back of the photograph. A sharp pen point or pencil point may ruin it for reproduction. The writer may type his name, address, and the title of the article which the photograph or drawing is to

FIG. 11. PHOTOGRAPH WITH CUT-LINE.

illustrate on a small piece of paper and paste it with thin, smooth paste on the back of the illustration—photograph, drawing, or chart. A wire paper clip should never be used to fasten the illustrations together. If the illustrations are small, enclose them in an envelope.

Some writers who sell many pictures place a reservation of rights on photographs submitted for publication. Using a rubber-stamp, they indicate on the back of each print the following: "WARNING. License to reproduce this photograph, on which a copyright is pending, will be granted upon acceptance of the terms quoted. If purchased, it is for your publication only, and must not be syndicated, rented, loaned, nor used for advertising purposes without written permission."

Since the writer mails the manuscript flat, all illustrations—photographs, drawings, charts, graphs, and tables—may be mailed in the same envelope. They must be protected with additional cardboard packing. One cardboard may be sufficient to keep the manuscript from becoming damaged, but there should be cardboard on both sides of the manuscript and illustrations, because the latter are damaged easily.

Accepted Photographs Are Not Returned. If the manuscript and the illustrations are purchased, they are not returned. For that reason, writers never promise to return illustrations that they obtain for an article. If persons furnishing them request that they be returned, the writer should have copies made from the originals. If one cannot get the negatives to have duplicates made, he may have the photographs rephotographed, but the process is rather expensive.

Exercises

1. Examine the publication to which you are slanting an article to see how many of the photographs are formal and how many are informal ones.
2. Are there any illustrations in the issues examined that were not well slanted—either to the article or to the periodical? If so, why not?
3. Classify the illustrations as to artistic and news types. How many of each did you find?
4. Are there any sources indicated for the illustrations used? If so, list them.
5. Did you find any illustrations that lacked the desirable qualities listed in this chapter? If so, what ones were missing?
6. Selecting some photograph or snapshot with heavy shadows that you have, apply the test for "suitability"? Can it be reproduced?

7. Talk with an expert and write a 300-word report on "A Good Camera For A Feature Writer."
8. How many drawings did you find in the publication to which you slanted your feature? List them as to kinds.
9. How many charts, graphs, or tables did you find in the periodical? List them as to kind and number.
10. Analyze the "cut-lines" as to length and style and place your tabulations in a table-like form.
11. Write one "cut-line" for each of the five or six illustrations that you have planned for your article.
12. Inquire the price from a local photographer for rephotographing a photograph. What would he charge for making an 8 x 10 picture of a garden?

Publication Analysis

Life, Mademoiselle, and *The New Yorker*

Do not spend more than 45 minutes on the preparation of this report.

I. Identification for each magazine: name, publishers, editors, where published, price.

II. Make-up: What to you, as a future magazine editor, are the interesting things about the make-up of the two magazines? Give reasons for your answers.

III. Advertising:
   1. From the point of view of what you know about advertising, do you think the copy in each publication will appeal to the reader?
   2. What did you like about the advertising in each publication and give reason?
   3. What did you *not* like about the advertising in each publication and give reasons?
   4. What tips were suggested to you by the advertising?

IV. General policy:
   1. To what types of readers do the three publications appeal?
   2. Why should you as a free-lance photographer know these magazines?
   3. What photographs might you have submitted?

4. Are there any illustrations of special interest in either publication?
5. Look at the illustrations in each magazine and list five suggestions for each that will enable you to select better pictures (15 suggestions in all).

V. Slogans: Write a slogan for each magazine.

VI. Four Tips for illustrations: source, authority, and three possible markets suggested by this study.

16

LEGAL RIGHTS OF MANUSCRIPTS

Writers Should Know Something of Their Rights. Although free-lance writers of feature articles do not need to be concerned greatly about the legal rights of their manuscripts, since publishers copyright their periodicals, such knowledge will benefit them financially. It also may save them worry about what they can or cannot do legally concerning their manuscripts.

A movement to revise copyright laws in the United States has been going forward for years, sponsored by both writers and publishers, who find much that is objectionable in the present law. Customs and practices are important in influencing interpretation of the law as it is now. There is a constant tendency to make the laws concerning literary property more liberal. Bills for revision of the law of copyright are introduced from time to time in sessions of Congress, because the present law is outdated in many respects.

Literary Rights Protect Author's Work. A feature writer who gathers facts from other sources does not own the facts. Legally they are considered public property. But he does own his mode of expression, or literary style, and this has literary rights. Legally the word "rights" means the right to use or sell elsewhere, and "American" rights means to use or sell in the United States. One's original ideas, even if they are copyrighted, are free. But the manner, arrangement, and combination of words—the style of one's writing—is the writer's own property. Although the laws concerning literary rights sound simple as one reads them, cases involving their infringement often are extremely involved.

Serial Rights Cover Wide Range. The majority of publications purchase "first magazine rights," or "first serial rights." The word "serial" in connection with rights in a manuscript means a magazine or newspaper that is published serially—weekly, daily, or monthly—and not a fiction serial. The term came into use to distinguish the right to publish articles in a periodical from the right to publish a book manuscript. Although an editor accepts an article, he does not have to print it unless there has been an agreement to publish. The only redress the author has for a long delay in publishing an unpaid manuscript is to demand its return. If the "first serial rights" are sold to a magazine along with the manuscript, the author retains all other rights.

"Second serial" or "syndicate" rights permit publication of a manuscript in some publication other than the one in which it first appeared. In addition to selling unpublished articles to magazines overseas, as suggested in Chapter 14, it is possible to gain additional income by selling second rights to manuscripts that have been published in American magazines. The author should submit the manuscript in typewritten form, however, because it is easier to handle in the editorial office and the composing room.

As a rule, a feature writer is not concerned with the other rights—dramatic, photoplay, book, foreign, and translation. He may be interested in "all rights," since a few magazines—but only a few—do buy all rights, even on fact articles. Their publishers generally are willing to pay somewhat in excess of what they would be willing to pay for merely the first serial rights.

Authors May Indicate Rights They Wish to Sell. It is advisable for an author to know what rights a magazine wants to buy. Today most magazines buy first American and Canadian serial rights. An author may retain all other rights by typing on the cover sheet, in the upper right-hand corner,

"First American and Canadian Rights only for sale." The majority of feature writers do not include that notation, since most feature articles do not possess more value than first serial rights.

Endorsement of Check Transfers Right. An author's writing and style is his own property until he sells or gives his property rights to another with or without restriction of rights. But if the writer sells his article and endorses the check for its payment, he always gives up his rights to the publication that bought them.

Many magazines do not have formal contracts of purchase. They do have printed notices on the check for payment of the article, however, and these state that endorsement of the check by the writer transfers specified rights to the publication. The notice may include the right for the new owner to make a minor revision. A writer should read the check carefully to see what rights he is transferring. A few publications enclose vouchers with the check, explaining the rights they wish to retain, as in the following:

ESQUIRE
The Magazine For Men
919 No. Michigan Ave.
Chicago

ARNOLD GINGRICH, *Editor*

April 18.

Mr. James F. Scheer,
216 North Carroll Street,
Madison, Wisconsin.

Dear Mr. Scheer:

Enclosed is check for $150.00 in payment for North American magazine rights on your manuscript, CHEATERS VS. EXAMS, including pocket-size digest rights for which you will receive full compensation, if and when sold.

Cordially,

HELENE RICHARDS
Secretary to Mr. Gingrich

HR:ef
Enc. check $150.00

Copyright Law Reveals Rights and Liabilities. A copyright insures to the writer or to a publication, which may buy and copyright the manuscript, full protection against reprinting the whole or in part for a period of twenty-eight years. It may be renewed within one year before the expiration of the original time for another period of twenty-eight years. The work can no longer be copyrighted after the expiration of the fifty-six years. Copyright protects only the literary style and not the content of the manuscript. It is merely a registration of property rights, and the copyright notice states that these rights have been registered and reserved by the copyright holder. If the manuscript is reprinted and sold without the author's permission, he may bring suit against the infringer and recover damages if he can prove in court that he has suffered.

Arrangements can be made with a publisher to copyright a manuscript, either in the name of the author or in the name of the publisher. In the latter case, the publisher will agree to transfer the copyright for a nominal sum to the author if he so requests. Although it is a simple process, yet it is impractical to ask that it be done, because most publishers would rather not buy a manuscript than to go to all the bother. The publisher's "blanket copyright," protecting each issue as a whole, affords ample protection to a feature writer.

If a writer wishes to secure protection under the copyright law, he must send a complete and exact copy to the Register of Copyrights, Library of Congress, Washington, D.C. It must be accompanied by an application for copyright on the correct official form and a postal money order for $2 for the fee. The former interpretation of the law required the payment of the fee, the giving of the notice for copyright, and the depositing of the copies before the copyright was in effect. But the decision in 1939 by the Supreme Court in the Drew Pearson case interpreted the copyright law to permit delay in depositing the copies in the copyright office, even though the law stated that the copies must be deposited at the time notice is given and the fee is paid.

Few writers apply for copyright in their own names. As

a rule, publications are honest, and it is not necessary to take it out; thus, few bother to make the application.

Most free-lance writers never are tempted to violate the law of copyright. The source of their material is available as public records. They may interview authorities, but if an interviewee asks a writer not to make public or not to print, he is liable to damages if the interviewee can show that the printing of the material has effected him financially.

Writer Has Legal Right to Use Facts. An author is permitted to make use of ideas expressed or facts presented in any published writing, whether or not it is copyrighted. If the material is not protected by copyright or if the copyright has expired, an author legally may take as much material, word for word, as he so desires, without acknowledging credit.

If the factual material is protected by copyright, he may take whatever content he desires, as long as he does not copy nor imitate the literary style or the manner in which the ideas are expressed. The encroachment of copyright lies in saying the same ideas in the same words as the author from whom one is taking the material.

Common Law Copyright Affords Protection. If a writer has acquired information entirely by his own efforts, as does the scientist who makes a discovery, he can take legal action by suing for damages under the law of unfair competition to prevent another writer from using his own material. Common law copyright protects him even though he does not have copyright secured by registry under the law of copyright.

Libelous Statements Must Be Scrutinized. An author is liable for damages if he makes any statements that injure one's character, reputation, or ability if he cannot prove that they are true, since the facts must be proven in a civil suit by the defendant. One cannot start a suit for libel unless the material said to be libelous is printed, or if the person said to be libeled cannot be identified, or if the defamatory words are not in themselves actually malicious, or if the circumstances do not make them malicious.

Even a beginner, if he has a high regard for accuracy and

ethics, is not endangered by libel suits. He will ascertain the truth before he writes anything that might be construed as libelous. Not only the truth but the lack of intention to defame must be proven by the defendant. In order to establish a lack of malice in using a fictitious name that might be the name of an individual, publications or authors explain that "All names used are fictitious and resemblance to or duplications of the names of living persons is coincidental." But even this statement printed in the book or periodical, or explained in the feature article, does not entirely protect the publisher. A writer may say the most unpleasant things about the work or the results of the work of "people who offer themselves for public approval." Legally authors, actors, singers, public speakers, and candidates for public office (but not always public officials) are included in the group seeking "public approval." A writer is not permitted to make uncomplimentary statements, however, about the personal life of "people seeking public approval."

Since libel laws are not the same in all states, a writer will do well to guard his writing against statements that might be said to be libelous anywhere concerning private individuals or groups of people.

Biographers, novelists, and short-story writers are more likely to write material consciously or unconsciously that may be considered libelous.

The right of "qualified privilege" gives a writer authority to print, without evil intention, true reports of public and official proceedings (but only public and official), and it prevents publications from being sued for printing such matter.

Using Quotations. Novices frequently ask how much material may be quoted from publications without obtaining permission. Legally the use of a single sentence may be considered a violation of the law of copyright. Short quotations, however, are made without permission. Although a short quotation has not been defined legally, many writers and publishers consider that a maximum of fifty words from one publication may be used without permission if full credit is given to the author and publisher.

A "reasonable proportion" of a government bulletin may be quoted without permission, but "reasonable proportion" has not been defined legally. Permission to quote should be requested if a writer is in doubt.

If a book printed in Great Britain does not contain a copyright notice, it does not mean that it is not copyrighted. British law does not require a printed notice in the book. Their copyright term differs from the American, in that British copyright is for the life of the author after publication and for 50 years following his death.

Plagiarism and Piracy. Plagiarism may be defined as the act of taking the language or the style elements of an author and using them as if they were one's own. It involves moral rights rather than legal. Thus, the author of the material said to be plagiarized has no redress in the courts. Piracy is an unauthorized reproduction of another's production, word for word, idea for idea, or the essence of the writer's work, and therefore is in violation of common law copyright.

Manuscripts May Become Public Property. If a writer makes mimeographed or other duplicate copies of his manuscript and distributes them to a number of persons, he makes it public without restriction and legally loses all right in the manuscript. If any one else so desired, he could submit it to a publication and accept payment for it without encroachment of rights. If a manuscript was delivered by its author as a speech before a public gathering, he likewise makes it public property.

Photographs May Be Copyrighted. The writer-photographer may have photographs that he believes will have a varied market and that some sales will be lost if the photographs are not copyrighted. Indiscriminate copyrighting of photographs is unnecessary and expensive in the long run, although they may be copyrighted for as little as fifty cents each. There can be little if any advantage in having a photograph copyrighted if the owner believes that he will never be able to sell it to more than one publication.

Some writers who sell pictures, as discussed in Chapter 15, place a reservation of rights on photographs submitted for publication by stamping on a "warning notice." Unless one really is going to have the copyright registered as soon as the photograph appears in print, he should not stamp on a copyright notice. The copyright law, Section XXIX, states that "Any person who inserts a false note of copyright with fraudulent intent . . . shall be guilty of a misdemeanor, punishable by a fine of from $100 to $1,000."

Writers Should Read Law on Author's Rights. The courts do not accept ignorance of the law as an excuse for violation of laws. Amateurs and professionals both must be well informed on the protection afforded authors and their manuscripts. They should be posted on the liabilities as well as the rights. Informative books on the subject are listed in the Free-Lance Writer's Library in the Appendix, and they may be obtained in any city or state library upon request.

Exercises

1. What have you read recently in the newspapers, writer's magazines, or other professional publications concerning changes in the law of copyright?
2. Do you recall reading recently in the newspapers or magazines for writers of any cases in the courts concerning the violation of literary rights?
3. List two publications in which you found notices of serial rights of any kind, and include the caption of the article and the kind of right listed.
4. What statement will you look for before you sign the checks that you will be receiving for your feature articles?
5. Go over your feature articles to see if you have violated the copyright law. List any point that you think violates it.
6. What is the law of "unfair competition"?
7. Check your manuscripts carefully for any libelous matter. If you find any material that you think could be said to be libelous, how could you prove the truth of your statements?

8. What is the libel law in the state in which you live?
9. Go over your manuscripts carefully to see if you have violated any rules concerning the handling of quotations. If so, what rules?
10. List the cases of plagiarism or piracy of which you have heard or read.
11. List the photographs that you have taken which you think you might want to have copyrighted, and tell why.
12. If the photographs which you have taken for publication have persons in them, did you get their permission to use them?
13. List five points concerning author's rights that you have read in one of the books listed in the Free-Lance Writer's Library. Give the title and the author.

Publication Analysis

American Boy, American Girl Magazine, and *Nature Magazine*

Do not spend more than 30 minutes on the preparation of this report.

I. Identification: name, publisher, editor, where published, price.

II. Make-up:
1. What do you like about the make-up of the magazine?
2. What do you dislike about it?
3. What changes would you make if you were editor?

III. Advertising:
1. If you were placing advertising, what appeals would your copy have to have?
2. In glancing through the advertising, do you think that the advertiser gets returns from his copy?
3. Give reasons for your conclusion.
4. List a tip suggested by the advertising in each magazine.
5. If you were editor, what changes would you make?

IV. Feature articles:
1. What types of articles do you find and to whom does each one appeal?
2. Analyze any article that you wish and in any way that you wish, but include the pyramid form of analysis.
3. What do you think are your chances of selling to this magazine?

V. Literary Rights:

1. What statement does each magazine carry concerning its copyright law?
2. Did you find any notice of serial rights of any kind in any of the magazines?

VI. Three Tips: source, authority for the article suggested, and three possible markets for each one that was suggested by the study of this magazine.

PART II

AMATEURS' ARTICLES ARE PUBLISHED

A few of the several thousand feature articles written by juniors and seniors in a feature writing course in a school of journalism are reprinted, by permission of the publishers and authors, in the following pages. They will give encouragement to the beginner, by showing him how the young authors got the ideas and how they developed them into features that editors were pleased to buy.

The beginners were paid anywhere from $25 to $150 for these manuscripts. Many of the features were the first ones that they had ever written. Most of the articles have been published recently, but a number of the same by-lines will be found in current publications. These writers have continued their free-lance writing since graduation from the university or since the completion of the course.

A wide variety of articles was selected, in order that the beginner might, by a careful analysis of the technique and the subject matter, improve his ability to see ideas, to gather material, and to write effectively. The relative merit of the articles is not indicated by the order in which they are listed. They are arranged in alphabetical order of the names of the periodicals publishing them.

(1)

This article was suggested to the author by murals in the student union depicting Paul Bunyan as a renowned, although mythical, lumberjack. Reminded of the legends of Paul as a farmer, she interviewed several historians and the curator of the museum to obtain material for the story. She made four line drawings to show Paul as a farmer, the bee-mosquitoes, the remarkable dog "Sport," and "Lucy," the cow, being milked in turn by the six milkmen. Because the writer studied the market and slanted the material to it, the article sold shortly after it was mailed.

FAME AS A FARMER

Belongs to Paul Bunyan *

This Mythical Lumberjack Beats Modern Record

By E. M. Shuart

Illustrations furnished by the Author

No farmer today can raise the animals or grow the corn that the famous Paul Bunyan did half a century ago, but any farmer can say that way back when Paul grew to be the mythical giant of the northwest, he was almost as much farmer as he was lumberjack.

For example take Babe the Blue Ox. Babe was as useful on Paul Bunyan's farms as he was in his camps. After the land had been cut over by the loggers, Paul used to send Babe out in the fields to stamp down the stumps that were left. Sometimes, too, Paul helped clear the land by taking a hammer and pounding down the stumps. That way Babe and Paul together could clear an acre a minute.

Of course it's common knowledge that the Ox was so big that the distance between his eyes measured forty-two axe handles and a plug of tobacco held lengthwise, and that even the print of his hoof weighed over a ton. Also, the shoes that Babe wore were so heavy that a man carrying them would sink a foot deep into solid rock at every step.

It was for one of the Bunyan camp farms in the west that Paul got a second ox to be company for Babe. This second ox was called Benny, and he came from a farm in Maine. The little ox was undernourished when Paul bought him, but after he had eaten a good square meal, he left his skinny two ton weight far behind and grew like a weed. In fact when Paul led Benny out west, the little ox

* Reprinted by permission of *American Farm Youth.*

grew so fast every time Paul looked around, he discovered that his new pet had grown a couple of feet taller.

On their way west Paul and Benny got to North Dakota about sundown, and just as Paul was beginning to wonder about setting up camp for the night, a young farmer offered to let Benny sleep in his barn. Paul thanked the young man and together they gave the little ox his supper of flapjacks and buffalo milk, bedded him down in fresh clean straw, and left him, they thought, comfortably fixed until morning.

However, the next day when Paul and the young farmer got up, there was no ox, and, furthermore, there was no barn to be seen. In fact where the barn had been, there was nothing at all, and yet the men couldn't see any signs of a struggle, and they knew that there hadn't been any cyclone. For a while they were very much puzzled, but finally Paul noticed a black speck far away on the horizon, and when he took out his field glasses and trained them on the speck, he saw that it was Benny with the barn on his back. The ox had grown so fast in the night that he had outgrown his barn and gone off with it on his shoulders. After that Paul always tied Benny to a fifty foot stake driven just outside the barn door. Then if he grew so fast that he broke down the building, he still wouldn't have a chance to run away.

Another animal that Paul always kept on his camp farm was Lucy, his favorite cow. She wasn't any relation to either Babe or Benny, but her size almost matched theirs. She gave enough milk to keep six men busy all day skimming off the cream. Paul thought that she was part Jersey and part wolf. She could eat practically anything and not be hurt by it. During the winter of the deep snow Paul equipped her with four snowshoes and a pair of dark goggles and turned her out to graze for her food. She survived, too, and gave as much milk as ever. Later when the snow melted a little so that she could get at the tops of the evergreen trees, her milk got so strong it had to be used for cough syrup. In fact it became famous as one of the best cough remedies in the country. Ordinarily Lucy's milk supplied the enormous tables at the lumber camps with both cream and butter, and sometimes the cooks got so much butter made up ahead that they gave some of it to the lumberjacks to use to grease their logging roads.

Anyone could guess that a man who managed both camps and farms and who was as fond of animals as Paul Bunyan was, would have a lot of dogs around and Paul Bunyan did. His hunting dog was Elmer and Paul trained him so that he could kill a moose by shaking it in his teeth. Elmer would just take the moose by the back of the neck and shake him until he was scared to death. The dog was too gentle ever to bite.

Another good dog was Sport, who was probably the most remarkable dog Paul ever had. At first he was quite ordinary, but one night Paul mistook him for a rat (rats grew as big as bears in those days), and when he threw his hatchet at him he cut him in two pieces. However, Paul discovered his mistake almost immediately and so he clapped the two pieces of the dog together. It was a good idea all right, but in his hurry Paul turned one half of the dog up-side-down, and when they got Sport out in the light they saw that his two hind feet stuck straight up in the air. For a while Paul was really worried about his mistake, but it turned out to be a good thing because the dog learned to run on two feet and whenever he got tired of using one pair of legs he simply reversed himself and used the other.

Another tireless dog was Snookum, who was a cross between a short legged Dachshund and a Russian Wolfhound. He was seven axe handles tall behind and only two in front and so he was always running down hill, and that, of course, was easy.

Fido was the watch dog at the farm. He was a shaggy beast, very gentle and kind with people he knew, but a terror to strangers. Paul used to make him fierce on purpose by feeding him on peddlers he caught hanging around the farm or the camp.

Perhaps the most extensive breeding experiment that Paul had anything to do with was the development of the bee-mosquito, and that experiment wasn't really intentional. It happened this way. One of Paul's camps got infested with mosquitoes—similar to our present day mosquitoes only many times larger. The present mosquitoes rarely grow to be longer than two feet and are only degenerate survivors of the early breed. Those first mosquitoes would take the shingles right off the bunkhouses and fly in at the men barking as they flew. For a while Paul was almost desperate. Then he got the idea of importing some bees. He figured he could keep the bees on his farm to make honey and at the same time they'd sting the mosquitoes to death and so rid him of an awful pest. Paul sent one of his camp men, Sourdough Sam, east to get the bees and Sourdough marched a three mile line of them across the country and back to camp. Their wings were stuck down so they couldn't fly away, walking shoes were provided for them, and Sourdough Sam carried their stingers so that they wouldn't be too tired to sting the mosquitoes when they got to camp.

Everything should have been all right, but the difficulty was that the imported bees and the fierce mosquitoes took such a liking to each other that they intermarried, and their children were worse than either the bees or the mosquitoes alone. In fact an entirely new species was produced. The bee-mosquitoes had stingers at both ends of their bodies, and they were as long as the mosquitoes and as fat as the bees. The situation was serious.

Finally a college boy working in camp for the summer thought that he had an idea for catching the mosquitoes, and so one Sunday afternoon he tried out his scheme. First he got a good strong hammer from Ole, the camp blacksmith, and then he hid himself under a kettle that he got from Creampuff Fatty, the cook. The kettle, by the way, was ten feet high.

The boy's plan was this. He thought that as soon as the bee-mosquitoes smelled a man under the kettle they would stick their stinger through the iron to get at him, and then he would bend over their stingers by pounding them with a hammer and have the bee-mosquitoes caught fast. At first it looked as though the idea might work, but as soon as three or four of the monsters got their stingers inside the boiler they were able to fly away with it, and the poor college boy was almost devoured by the other bee-mosquitoes before he could get under cover.

Bee-mosquitos like those at Paul Bunyan's farm and camp naturally attracted a lot of attention throughout the country, and one day a representative of the Barnum circus arrived to try to catch a few bee-mosquitoes for his menagerie. He was successful too, after a fashion, although the method he used wasn't practical for large numbers. As the bee-mosquitoes flew above him, the circus man shot cold turpentine exactly at their stomachs, and when they doubled up with shock the two stingers at either end of their bodies hooked together so that the bee-mosquitoes were tied in a circle. Then it was easy to put them in chains and send them back east for exhibition purposes.

To tell the truth though, it was actually the nature of the bee-mosquitoes that finally destroyed them. One of their weaknesses was that they could never get enough honey to satisfy them, and so one day when they smelled a sugar ship coming in on Lake Superior they all flew out and gorged themselves so thoroughly on the sweet that they were too heavy to fly back to land, and the result was that they all fell into the lake and were drowned. That is what made the Apostle Islands in Lake Superior and they are here to this day to prove that this story is true.

One of the best proofs of Paul Bunyan's farming ability was the incident of the Minnesota corn stalk. The King of Sweden, who knew that Paul was running farms in connection with his logging camps, wrote to ask about the fertility of the land in that section of the country. Paul was always a careful workman and in order to send an accurate report to the king he dug a four foot hole in the ground and planted a single grain of corn. Then he called for a couple of men to come and watch the corn grow, but by the time he had finished calling the corn was almost up to his knees and by the time the men got there the top of the stalk was out of sight. Also, when Sliver Jim, a camp man, tried to climb the stalk to find the top of it, he made no progress at all and even found it useless to try to come down the stalk after he had once started up because for every foot that he would slide down the growing stalk shoved him up three. While Sliver was up the cornstalk the men had to feed him by shooting doughnuts to him from Paul Bunyan's gun. Otherwise the poor man would have starved to death.

Another thing, they found that they couldn't chop the cornstalk down because no two cuts ever fell in the same place. The stalk grew faster than the men could chop.

It began to look as though Sliver was going to spend the rest of his life up in the cornstalk, but at last Paul thought of an idea to make the stalk commit suicide. To do this he circled the base with a bent railroad tie, and then when the cornstalk kept on growing, it simply cut itself in two. It took three days to fall, and Babe the Blue Ox spent almost a week stamping the stalk into the ground so that it wouldn't block the settlers who were going west, but at any rate it did convince the King of Sweden that the middlewest had fertile soil, and that is why so many of his subjects decided to emigrate and come to America.

Yes, Paul Bunyan was really a super farmer as well as a super lumberjack, and though he never could settle down to stay in any one place, he ran his camp farms wherever he logged.

(2)

To show the variety of types that one publication may use, the three following articles were selected from a home magazine. The first article's source was in interviews with two experts in wood of the United States Forest Products Laboratory. Because of its technical nature, the writer introduced the material with a "fiction" lead; and in writing the article, he translated the scientific material into terms that the average home-owner would understand. He secured from the laboratory's publicity department a gloss print, which was reproduced as a halftone to illustrate the points made in the care of the wood.

IS YOUR WOODWORK SAFE? *

Simple Precautions Will Make It Safe

BY PAUL H. WAGNER

Three days after Mr. Cavanaugh had left for northern Wisconsin to get the house ready for Mrs. Cavanaugh and the children after a winter's stay in Florida, Mrs. Cavanaugh received the following telegram:

"HOUSE A MESS STOP PLASTER CRACKED FLOOR BULGED VARNISH ON ALL WOODWORK AND FURNITURE RUINED BY WATER SPOTS STOP DELAY RETURN TEN DAYS.
DAD."

Mr. and Mrs. Cavanaugh didn't know it at the time, but their bungalow had been made "a mess" by the effect of moisture changes, an exasperating experience which sooner or later may come to all home owners who, through ignorance or carelessness, fail to take precautions against this destructive force.

There are hundreds of Mr. and Mrs. Cavanaughs in the United States and elsewhere who have learned or will learn through expensive experience the importance of guarding the woodwork of their homes against moisture changes.

Mr. L. V. Teesdale, senior engineer, and Mr. E. C. Peck, associate

* Reprinted by permission of *American Home.*

technologist, of the Forest Products Laboratory, Madison, Wisconsin, have spent years in diligent research into the mysteries and secrets of moisture changes in wood products and the ways and means of minimizing the effects of the change of moisture in woodwork and interior finish.

Let us take the case of Mr. Cavanaugh and with the help of Mr. Teesdale and Mr. Peck analyze more thoroughly exactly why Mr. Cavanaugh found his bungalow in a damaged condition.

When Mr. Cavanaugh left for Florida he made the very serious mistake of neglecting to arrange for the heating of his home during his absence. Without heat the air in his house assumed very nearly the temperature of the out-of-doors air, at the same time increasing its relative humidity or relative dampness. Consequently the woodwork in the house, being relatively dry, absorbed moisture from the damp air.

"When wood absorbs moisture," Mr. Teesdale explained, "it expands as did the woodwork in the Cavanaugh home. The force of this expansion caused the floors to buckle in the center, the plaster to crack when the joists and beams expanded, and the furniture joints to spread apart. The water which condensed in the home during the cold weather dripped on the floor and woodwork, ruining that. Later when the house was heated this moisture was removed and shrinkage occurred, causing cracks in the floors and the opening up of wood panels.

"Thousands of dollars are spent every year in temperate climates by home owners in repairing the damages done by moisture changes in the interior decoration of their homes. Once moisture changes have left bulges or cracks in your floors, or warped the panelings on the doors, there is only one way to correct the damage and that is the expensive way of replacement."

If you have ever been so unfortunate as to have forgotten to drain your car radiator in sub-zero weather, or if you have seen the buckling of huge slabs of pavement under the mid-July sun, you are well aware of the tremendous power exerted in the expansion of substances. In contraction the force is equally as great.

When wood, whether it be in your prized dining room suite or the newly laid hardwood floor, absorbs moisture it expands and when it loses moisture it contracts. That is the law of moisture change effects. In this expanding and contracting there is enough force to move brick walls and split huge boulders. (In some sections of the country rocks are quarried and split by the simple device of pouring water on a wooden wedge driven into a hole drilled in the rocks.) So it is obvious that when expansion occurs in the woodwork of your home it is going to cause considerable damage that cannot be overlooked.

Moisture conditions of woodwork are dependent on many things. Experiments conducted at the Forest Products Laboratory show that conditions vary according to the efficiency of the type of heating apparatus in the home, to the proper seasoning point of the wood on construction and to the amount of humidification which takes place in the home after occupancy.

"Woodwork in temperate climates suffers a great deal because of the drying effects of the artificial heating during the colder weather," Mr. Peck pointed out. "Thus it is important that a home be heated as evenly as possible so that the woodwork will not be subject to radical changes in moisture content."

"Artificial heating of homes is the basis of most moisture change troubles in woodwork. In the southern coastal regions," Mr. Peck explained, "there is little of this kind of damage to woodwork because homes there require little artificial heating, consequently the woodwork remains seasonally constant throughout the year and there is no swelling due to absorbed moisture."

To the home owner who takes pride in the sober opulence and beauty of a home well graced with protected and neatly kept interior decorations the Forest Products Laboratory offers a few rules of thumb which though not absolute protection against all moisture changes will offer reasonable security. They are as follows:

1. Be sure that the interior trim and plaster is dry before allowing the flooring to be laid or delivered.
2. Maintain some heat in the house from the time the flooring is laid until the painters finish. Temperatures comparable with those during occupancy should be maintained.
3. Never allow flooring or woodwork of any kind to be delivered during rainy weather.
4. Stains and wax finishes offer little protection in themselves against moisture absorption. All woodwork should first be covered with a coating of varnish or shellac if the best protection is desired.

"The home owner can do three things after occupation," Mr. Teesdale points out. "He can see to it that a good coat of varnish or shellac is always on his woodwork; he can avoid excessive and uneven heating which tends to dry out woodwork, and cause it to crack; lastly he can humidify the air of his home by evaporation of water by means of shallow pans or mechanical humidifiers. Never under any circumstances should the home owner or the landlord leave his home or building unheated during the winter. It is only inviting ruination."

The discussion of moisture content change in wood may seem a bit technical, but the matter is not so complex after all.

(3)

A department store-window display of bedding suggested to a young woman that an article on the subject should have wide reader-interest. In addition to talking to several store managers, she interviewed a professor of home economics, who explained how to determine the best values. She secured gloss prints from several manufacturers by writing to their advertising departments, and she had two pictures taken by a commercial photographer to illustrate the points that she made in the article. She gave thought to writing a clever caption, which added to the reader appeal in the article.

HOW DO *YOU* SHOP FOR A GOOD NIGHT'S SLEEP? *

By Virginia Van Brunt

This article is based on an interview with Mrs. Elizabeth Neal, assistant professor of related art in the home economics department of the University of Wisconsin. It deals with some of the problems met by the average layman who does not know how to determine the best values in sheets, blankets, or comforters.

Your sheets are ragged and thin; your blanket supply needs replenishing; your pillowcases have become objects from which you glance shamefacedly away; your springs squeak and mattresses are lumpy. You are met with the necessity of buying new bedding. And you dread it.

* Reprinted by permission of *American Home*.

Before I begin with the business of shrewd shopping for bedding, may we inject a moral that is so old it should be legend but actually seems almost to have been forgotten. Your bedroom is only as good as your spring and mattress. It can be smart in color scheme, smartly attired in crisp or luxurious bed coverings, but unless the beds themselves are truly comfortable, your bedroom has missed by a mile its sole reason for existence. Antiques are charming—but too many American homes cling fondly to the belief that antique springs and mattresses are also lovely. One finds comfortable chairs, where one spends at most three hours out of twenty-four, and in that same home eight-hour beds that groan and squeak with pain at the thought of supporting their tough, rigid old springs and mattresses for one more night. Truly, that groaning and squeaking is not a call for furniture oil—it is pain and agony over America's loyalty to antique springs and mattresses. Another year of it and I believe husbands will find some reason for spending at least two nights a week at a comfortable hotel! As Mrs. Blake said in these pages some time ago, "those hotels which advertise 'all the comforts of home' just haven't slept on home beds in some time." Begin with the spring and mattress. Eight hours out of twenty-four, one third of your life—figure it that way, figure it by any method—but begin with the spring and mattress

The first factors to consider when selecting any kind of bedding are, according to Mrs. Elizabeth Neal, appearance, durability, comfort, and laundering quality. The three materials used most frequently in sheets are linen, percale, and muslin. Linen, although often prohibitive because of its price, washes more easily than cotton, is particularly smooth and lustrous, and is more durable, if it is a good quality linen. Linen sheets are a particularly wise selection for summer since they are cooler than cotton. Of percale and muslin, the former, by virtue of being a better grade material and closer weave, is usually preferable in every way.

Laundering of sheets is not a major problem, since they may be boiled without injury to the fabric. In deciding upon sheets, it is wise to choose those which have been "torn from the bolt when manufactured rather than merely cut, for it insures a straighter, more even sheet," said Mrs. Neal.

Durability is perhaps the basic factor in determining final selection of bed linen, explained Mrs. Neal. Factors which contribute to the wearing span and service of sheets and pillowcases are thread count, or the closeness of the weave; the per cent of sizing, which includes excessive starches and waxes to increase the apparent weight and smooth finish of the article and help cover up blemishes; weight per square yard; tensile strength, that is the amount of pull it will stand before breaking; the kind of yarn used, and weaving fibers. Watch for these details.

"One usually finds the threads closely woven in the better grade material," she said. "Good yarn is required for weaving closely and, since there are also more threads to the inch, firmness is thus produced without heaviness." The satisfactory sheet should have from seventy-two to eighty threads to the inch in the warp and from sixty-four to seventy-six in the filling. The number of threads to the inch, both in width and length, will have to be determined by inquiry of the saleswoman or label on the sheet, but the closeness of the weave may be easily determined by merely holding a corner of the material to the light.

Occasionally the spaces in loosely woven sheets are filled with sizing, which washes out when the article is laundered and leaves the material limp and flimsy. Mrs. Neal suggests, as a simple test to determine the amount of sizing, that a piece of the sheet be rubbed briskly between the fingers to determine whether any powdery dust will sift out. If it does, the sheet has been too heavily sized and will not be durable.

The average weight per square yard is between 3¼ and 5¼ ounces, and, although as a rule the heavier sheets wear longer, if weight of laundry is a factor, the thrifty housewife may find that she will save money by selecting sheets that wear a shorter time but weigh less.

Another of the requirements for durability, tensile strength, can be determined accurately only by experts, although some manufacturers label their materials with the tensile strength on it. Two factors which contribute as much to the beauty of the sheet as to its durability are the kind of yarn used and the kind of weaving done. If the yarn stands up occasionally in bumpy knots, the sheet will not be as practical as one which is even and does not have alternating thick and thin places in it, or broken, split, and missing yarns. Many of the flaws of weaving or poor yarn also become apparent when the sheet is held up to the light.

Since there are few things more annoying than attempting to make a bed with sheets which are obstinately too short or too narrow, Mrs. Neal pointed out that most home economists agree that the most practical length for a sheet is 108 inches; in width fifty-four inches is desirable for a cot, sixty-three for a single, seventy-two inches for a three quarter, or eighty-one inches for a double bed. Pillowcases should be two inches wider and ten inches longer than the pillow to cover it.

In wool blankets, much the same rules and precautionary measures are concerned in wise buying as in sheets. Similar to the process of sizing used in sheets, sometimes small bits of wool from the napping machine are put into the poorer quality blankets to cover up the poor structure of the cloth. Later these small bits of wool are apt to come out and leave a bare, unfinished surface. To guard against such a possibility, it was suggested that the wool be rubbed and brushed to see whether tiny clumps of wool brush out, and to look carefully at the weave of the blanket to see whether it is firm and evenly woven.

The nap of the blanket is an almost indispensable feature however, if warmth is desired, for it creates more air space and hence holds the heat better, but the nap should be obtained from the long fibers themselves being brushed up, not merely pieces of wool transplanted into a poor article.

There are three grades of blankets which may be selected: wool, wool and cotton combined, or all cotton, and of the three, all-wool blankets of course take warmth precedence. The fact that a blanket is advertised as being part wool, however, Mrs. Neal emphasized, does not necessarily mean that it is any warmer than an all-cotton content, for from 20 to 25% wool is required to give cotton-wool blankets any additional warmth over cotton. A small per cent of cotton even in the all-wool is desirable, for it keeps the wool from shrinking. Often cotton and wool mixtures are stronger than low-grade all-wool and will launder better, since there is less shrinkage.

With the possibility of shrinkage in such an animal fiber as wool, meticulously careful laundering becomes essential. The best method of washing wool, Mrs. Neal outlines as this: "Have plenty of luke warm soapy water and 'suds' the woolen up and down through it. Never wash anything wool at a high temperature for the fibers become brittle and lose resilience." Neither should they be subjected to rubbing or wringing; instead the water should be squeezed out and the fabric shaken gently and shaped while drying. Before it is quite dry the nap should be brushed up carefully to keep it from becoming matted. Care should also be taken when blankets are packed, that they have plenty of space, for, if pressed tightly, they will become hard and the meshes which retain air and give them their warmth will close up."

In selecting comforters, Mrs. Neal suggested, resilience and buoyancy are important rather than heaviness. They may be tested by putting one hand on top and the other on the bottom and pressing. The amount that it can be compressed and speed with which it returns to its original shape is the criterion by which one may judge. And if it does not spring back into shape when new, then it most assuredly will not after it has been used.

(4)

For her first feature in the class, a young woman chose to write a utility article based upon her family's experience in moving. Not content with relating her own experiences, she interviewed several managers of transfer companies for information to aid the reader when he moved. Since she could not find attractive pictures, she asked an art student to make four sketches of movers at work. She typed out the cut lines on typewriter paper and pasted them on the bottoms of the drawings. When the article was published, she found to her surprise that the editor had used her article without any changes —a reward for careful planning and effective writing.

THESE MOVING SITUATIONS *

By Fannie M. Turnbull

Sketches by Jerry Erdahl

Moving need not mean a complete emotional upheaval. Even if your bed has been ripped up and your dishes are packed in barrels, don't let your nerves be torn or your sense of humor be placed in cold storage. Just give your apron strings another jerk and pitch in. It's fun. A new house, a new city to live in, a new apartment just around the corner—whatever the place, it's different and exciting.

But it won't be exciting if you live in a welter of excelsior and

* Reprinted by permission of *American Home*.

newspapers and unmatched dishes for three weeks before and ten weeks after the crucial day. If you have never moved before, don't be discouraged by its apparently insurmountable aspects. Everything will get packed and transported with amazing ease when the time actually comes.

First, call a reliable transport company, and be sure it really is reliable. A friend of mine once hired a company to move her furniture three doors up the street. The day was a nipping one in November and the movers arrived well-fortified to brave the blasts of winter. Indeed they felt so very jovial and athletic that they tipped her piano on end and rolled it on its side across the lawn between the two houses. The piano has a cracked sounding board to show for this careless treatment to this day.

But, if the company is reliable, you will have no such troubles. Here is practically the only time during the whole process that your husband will be useful to have at hand. The manager of the company will come out and make an estimate of what the transportation will cost you, but he may want to leave everything to a "gentleman's agreement." Your husband should not agree to this.

Insist on a written contract, particularly if you are moving from city to city and collection will be left to the foreman when the job is done. Remember that when you move you pay as the last piece of furniture goes in the door. If you don't give at least a substantial part payment it may all come out again. But don't pay the whole bill at once. Wait and check for any loss or breakage. If it is serious the company should make it good, but it is more likely to if you have not completed payment. Motor carriage is regulated by both intra-state and inter-state rules. A revokable license is usually required, cargo insurance protecting the owner of the property, and properly made out bills of lading. If things do go wrong and remain unsettled the public service commission should be notified for redress.

Moving is not a job for husbands, as any mover if he said what he thought, would tell you. Obligingly they will carry a mop and a broom into the front hall, then stand around smugly, having done their part; and at the other end of the route, they will be occupied with discovering their own belongings to the exclusion of everything else in the house. So if you possess a husband, get rid of him over moving day. Send him off to his business as usual if you possibly can, or let him buy some groceries, or walk the dog, or take the children to the movies. Dogs, cats, children, and husbands are equally distressing when your home is completely torn up.

Later on if you need a man's help in settling, it is better to get a boy in by the day, who can be ordered about, than to ask your husband. Above all, if your husband has business papers around the house, put them in a box by themselves, label them blackly, and carry them with you. It will save you future grief.

When you start to pack before the movers arrive, remember that you will have to live picnic fashion for a few days in your new home. If you are wise you will fix up a few dishes, just a cup and plate for each member of your family, a frying pan, and a sauce pan or two, and most important of all a can-opener and the salt. Keep track of your silverware. No one is going to walk off with it, but you will enjoy eating from it when you arrive. Silver spoons are much more attractive than tin kitchen ones, and a great deal nicer than quarter-sized measuring spoons as once fell to my lot.

If you take down your curtains yourself and pack them in boxes, chances are that you will be able to put them up again without having to send them to the laundry or cleaners. If the movers take them down they are quite likely to get creased and soiled. Pack your clothes in your trunk and chiffonier drawers. Also put all the knickknacks from the tops of your dressing tables and chiffoniers into the drawers. It is much easier to move tightly packed chests than light ones from which the drawers slide out.

In some place where they can be easily found again, put together a broom, a hammer and screw-driver, and some nails and screws for cleaning up and making repairs at the other end of the line. Put your bedding on your bedroom chairs and tie a sheet over the seat and around the back to hold it there. It keeps the chairs from being scratched and your blankets will be easily accessible when next you want them.

From then on, let the movers do the work. Don't fuss at them or direct them. They know their business and probably you don't. Above all, don't be helpful. Gathering up wastebaskets, end tables, lamps and pillows, and piling them all in the front hall to be taken out, only impedes progress. If the moving men are nice they won't swear *loudly* when they lug the buffet from the dining room and trip over a lamp cord in the hall, but they *will* swear.

Let them pack your dishes even if they want you to do it. If you pay a special packer by the hour he will do a good job. Moreover, all the risk will be taken by the moving company. Don't try to balance great-aunt Hortense's Spode tea set on your knee all across the country.

When you get into your new home, if you have much china and glassware, don't unpack your china barrels until you have had a day or two to settle larger matters, and don't be urged by importunate movers. They can pick up their barrels on the next trip to town. When you are more or less settled and not so tired that bending and climbing on step ladders is too arduous, buy shelf-paper and wash your shelves. There is no point in putting dishes away temporarily. On the other hand, don't bother to wash each piece of china and glassware as it goes on the shelf. Wipe off any dust on a towel and leave the washing until you have more time.

As you unpack each barrel, put the newspaper and excelsior in a box or previously emptied barrel and keep it. Check every teapot for its lid, and each cup for its saucer, before you throw the trash out or burn it—precaution pays.

It will be much easier for you if all cleaning and re-decorating is completed before you move into your new home. Remember also to leave a clean house behind you. If you hire someone for a few hours to come in and sweep away the dust, papers, and trash which moving entails, the next occupants will hold you in fragrant memory.

If possible, work out a schedule of where to put each article of furniture as it comes in, and station someone at the door to direct the movers as to where to set each piece. Movers are very obliging fellows and amazingly resourceful. They will do anything reasonable that you ask them and many things beside.

Once we had to move from city to city in January, when the countryside shivered at eighteen degrees below zero, and the streets were sheeted in ice. We arrived at eleven that night in a state of antarctic frigidity to find the movers had reached the house ahead of us. They had entered the house, broken the seal on the electric meter, and turned on the lights—against the law, of course, but "no one knew who did it." In the living room a fire fed with packing boxes and kindled with kerosene was burning on the hearth, and they were waiting before it for our arrival. We wrapped the children up in rugs from the car and settled them before the fire, and by two A.M. were completely moved in.

But that was an exceptional situation. It is better to move at reasonable hours. Remember to get a good night's sleep and plenty to eat. You will really need it. Don't let your exuberance get the better of your judgment and start putting down stair carpets at three in the morning as one woman I knew did. However, it is a good plan to hang pictures as soon as possible. They do not need to be in their ultimate location, but they will be out of the way of gouges and broken glass.

If you are a coffee addict, make yourself a cup now and then during the day and take some food with it. The dietitians tell us that we use up about a thousand more calories a day when we are very active than when we are quiet. That is rather a total to replenish, so don't be forgetful about eating. If you like tea, try the effect of a nice little brown pot steaming on top of a packing box.

Above all, don't wear yourself out with superficialities. Let the movers do the heavy work. If you smile sweetly upon them they will probably set up your beds for you, which you will deeply appreciate about ten o'clock that night. Don't try to unpack before your furniture is settled, and don't be discouraged by the mess. Taken easily there is nothing more fun than shifting homes.

(5)

Upon reading a brief item from a country correspondent in his home-town paper about the birthday of a miller, a young writer interviewed the miller the following Saturday. He first made a survey of possible markets. He selected the one that he thought his material would suit, and he wrote the article somewhat after the style of sketches in one of the large weekly magazines well known for its concise, crisp articles. He obtained a picture of the miller and one of the mill which added to the reader-interest.

86 YEARS OLD—STILL ACTIVE *

By Victor Schoen

There is a 59-year-old brick mill at New Holstein, Wis., where an 86-year-old miller still puts in about 8 hrs. of work a day. The mill is still the same that C. F. Dumke helped his father build back in 1877 and it still has many of the innovations which his father

* Reprinted by permission of *American Miller*.

brought along with him from Germany more than 80 yrs. ago.

Many of the little flour and feed mills that once dotted the Wisconsin countryside have disappeared and only an occasional heap of caved-in beams and debris along the road or on the outskirts of little villages marks the once widespread industry. But Dumke clung on, resisted the forward pressing of progress and still operates the same little mill like he did over half a century ago.

"A good many farmers still like to have their grist ground and have their own flour milled," says Dumke. He recalls the mills that used to, but no longer operate in Plymouth, Kiel, Chilton, Franklin, Centerville, and in many other neighboring towns. It used to be that there was a mill every couple miles.

"When the other mills closed down, I got many of their customers, and now some of my customers come from as far as 20 to 30 miles. The small mills have passed, but then some may return, because many farmers want their own grist ground and won't have it any other way," he opines.

Taking the lead in using new sources of power has always been Dumke's pride, and he points to the installation of a kerosene burner some 40 years ago, the first of its kind in the Middle West, he says. He has seen what he calls the "march of time" in milling, from the use of round, flat stones for grinding flour, much the same way as was used in the time of Christ and before, to the modern steel rollers which he uses today.

The power first used to turn the mill came from steam produced in a wheezy boiler, fed by cord-length wood. Not only was the wood burning boiler a lot of trouble in keeping the fires burning, but it was also pretty noisy and not too sure, he recollects. When coal became more generally used, he welcomed it with a sigh of relief, but soon found it was too expensive for his use and he abandoned the boiler altogether.

Next came the kerosene engine, whose upkeep was also too expensive and a gasoline motor was installed. When electric power became available, Dumke "switched" to a large electric motor whose steady hum is as familiar around New Holstein as the lightning rods on the community hall.

Not only is Miller Dumke familiar around the town with its 1300 inhabitants, but he is actually pretty much of a landmark. Generations have grown up sitting on the mill loading platform and watching the activity within. Several times a day he walks the three-block distance between the home of a daughter with whom he lives and the mill. Despite his age he still walks a sure, steady step.

Working hard and moderation in all things is Dumke's formula for health and long life. All his life he has known practically no illness. This he attributes to his rules of moderate living and the fact that he comes from hardy stock.

He was born in 1850 in the historic province of Brandenburg, Germany, from a long line of hardy Prussian farmers and millers. At the age of four he came to America with his parents. In 1876 father and son built their first mill at New Holstein, then only a settlement of 300, but in the richest farming section of Wisconsin, in the Fox River valley. The following year fire destroyed their mill, but in the following spring, in 1877, they rebuilt the mill which still stands today.

"I intend to continue every day at the mill whether I grind flour or feed each day or not. People say that I am the oldest miller in Wisconsin. I don't know. Anyway I come from hardy stock and have worked hard all my life. This is my job and I love it," says Dumke. "Every man should have some work to do every day of his life, no matter how old he is."

(6)

It occurred to a young woman who observed an old house being painted that the home-owner must have many problems in selecting the right paint. With that idea in mind, she talked to paint dealers and interviewed a chemist who is an authority on woods and paints. He was able to supply her with several photographs, and a paint manufacturer sent several gloss prints that aided in attracting the reader's attention. She asked to see the trade publications to which the dealer subscribed, and one of them she selected as a possible market.

HOW TO PREVENT THOSE PAINT COMPLAINTS *

By Marvel Y. Ings

There is no time quite as exciting as house painting time. Whether it comes in the spring, in hottest summer, or in the fall,

* Reprinted by permission of *American Paint and Oil Dealer*.

it brings with it a thrill of anticipation and a sense of exploration into the realms of color and balance and design. It is something to look forward to, and it is hard to wait to see the old house in all its new glory.

"No secret is divulged in pointing out that some house paint jobs, even with the best of house paints, fail to give satisfactory service," says Dr. F. L. Browne, senior chemist of the Forest Products Laboratory at Madison, Wisconsin. "If the failure takes place within a year or two the house owner often complains to the paint dealer or paint manufacturer. As a rule, the difficulty is not due to the quality of the paint but to some blunder in its use or unusual condition of service, but it is not always easy to convince the house owner that the paint was not at fault after the difficulty has arisen.

Mistakes Must Be Anticipated

"Some of the conditions that give rise to short-lived paint jobs are now known and paint salesmen, working in cooperation with their dealers and painters, can prevent many of the mistakes that would otherwise lead to complaints by seeing that customers are properly advised before the mistakes are made. Salesmen and paint dealers can do much to prevent future complaints by asking about the behavior of the previous paint used on the houses of their customers. If the last paint applied failed unreasonably soon it is not wise to promise that the new one will give good service until the house has been examined for the cause of the previous difficulty. If the former coating shows evidence of moisture failure and nothing has been done to alter the conditions the new paint will probably fail also. Under such circumstances a sale of paint without warning the customer about its probable failure amounts to an invitation for him to file a complaint a year or so later. A complaint represents loss even if no adjustment is made and it makes future sales more difficult.

"One of the most common causes of premature paint failure is moisture collecting in the sidewalls of buildings during the time of year when buildings are heated," Dr. Browne said. "The latter part of winter and early spring are the times of year when the damage is most often done, but the scaling of paint may not come to the houseowner's attention until the following summer when the walls have dried out again. Unfortunately there is much that is not yet known about moisture conditions in houses; for example, why one house develops the trouble while neighboring houses do not, and what steps can be taken to keep moisture out of the sidewalls of houses in which it collects.

"No one paint is superior in all respects. Experience proves that soft types of paint are less prone to rapid failure on houses whose sidewalls become wet than are harder paints. If a soft paint is applied over a hard paint, however, the coating retains the characteristics of the hard paint so far as resistance to abnormal moisture conditions is concerned.

"If hard types of paint have failed on a house because of moisture and no practicable means are discovered for making sure that the sidewalls will remain dry in the future, the safest procedure to recommend for repainting is to remove all the old coating and to repaint with a soft paint."

"There is no denying the fact that much has been said about the effect of different woods on the durability of paint," I suggested.

"It is not always appreciated that different kinds of old paint may exert even more effect on the durability of the new paint of different composition," the chemist replied. "That may be the case even though the old paint is still in very good condition as far as integrity of the coating is concerned. Some of the incompatible combinations of paints are known, the easiest one to recognize being a white or tinted paint applied over a full-cover paint such as brown, green or red. The incompatibility arises not merely from the difference in the nature of the pigments in white and in full color paints, but from the difference in total amount of pigments. As a rule full-color paints contain much less pigment by volume than white or tinted paints. The well-known case of yellow ochre priming under white paints is perhaps the most clearly recognized case of incompatibility.

Mistakes in Application

"Sometimes the harmful effects of an incompatible combination show up promptly the first time white paint is applied over a full-color paint; frequently, however, the white paint jobs merely prove slightly less durable for a time, but after two or three repaints, each less durable than the previous one, the surface develops such a bad case of deep cracking and curling that the whole coating must be removed before a satisfactory repaint job can be applied. For that reason painters should be advised to examine coatings on older houses that show bad cracking and report the uncertainties that may arise if strikingly different colors are found underneath."

"What about mistakes in thinning paint?" I asked.

"Paint salesmen and paint dealers can well afford to devote some time to getting acquainted with painters who use their paints and helping them to avoid bad practices in paint application," Dr. Browne replied. "Mistakes in thinning paint and in the amount of paint applied give rise to some of the common complaints about unsatisfactory service. Stingy application of paint and too much thinning of priming coats often cause difficulty in paint jobs on new wood surfaces, leading to inadequate hiding and spotted gloss, chalking and fading. Three-coat jobs, of course, are less subject to such troubles than two-coat jobs, but at the present time a large proportion of our painting of new wood is two-coat work.

"Too generous use of volatile thinners in priming coats is a common cause of unnecessarily early failure of paint. The mistaken notion that thinners are needed to increase the penetration and secure firmer anchorage of the paint fosters this blunder in paint. As a matter of fact linseed oil penetrates all woods more freely than is desirable and the object of good priming is to restrain, not to stimulate it. Special primers for wood now being offered by several manufacturers are designed with this object in view. In a good priming mixture with ordinary linseed oil paint there should be at least three times as much linseed oil as volatile thinner. It is entirely practicable to omit thinners in the priming coat mixture. Resinous woods such as southern yellow pine offer no exception to this rule; in fact, too much volatile thinner is particularly harmful in priming coats for such wood.

"For good painting a sufficient quantity of paint must be applied whether it is done in two or three coats. From experience it is known that the amount of paint should be enough to leave a coating about 1/200 inch thick even though a somewhat thinner coating of modern paints will hide the surface satisfactorily. As far as practicable the coating on wood should be kept in the neighborhood of this thickness. This can be done only if the old coating is given time enough to chalk and to erode materially before new paint is put on. Hard types of paint usually wear away less rapidly than soft types of paint, and, when repainted hard types of paint usually 'hold out' the new paint better than soft types, that is, the hard paints absorb less oil from the new paint.

Material Determines Program

"As a rule if repainting is done within three years only one coat of new paint should be put on. After four years soft types of paint may wear away enough to take two repaint coats, but hard paints may often be recoated to best advantage with one coat only, possibly with preliminary spot coating of patches where loose paint has been scraped off. The amount of paint applied rather than the number of coats is the important consideration. It is not good practice to apply two finishing coats in succession. Sometimes this occurs when a paint job is completed and the owner decides that he does not like the color. Paint salesmen and dealers should try to get customers to select color schemes carefully before starting the paint job so that the paint job can be properly designed to give good service.

"The failure of paint on protected parts of buildings, such as overhanging eaves, when the paint on the exposed parts is in good condition often comes from the fact that too thick a coating has been built up on the protected areas where the weather has a little chance to wear away the paint. Such areas should receive less paint than the exposed areas when repainted.

"It is likewise bad practice to spread a painting job out over six months or a year. Only the finish coat is designed to stand weather exposure; primers and body coats are not. Houses completed late in the winter, for example, are often primed perhaps in December, second coated in March and finished during the summer. It would be better in such cases to take great precautions in drying the plaster to avoid forcing moisture into the sidewalls and to complete the paint job in December by taking advantage of the warmer days of the month and confining paint application to the hours between 10 a.m. and 2 p.m."

And as we talked Dr. Browne explained the importance of priming, the reasons for flaking and the selecting of wood for painting characteristics.

"On woods that contain wide bands of summerwood, such as southern yellow pine and Douglas fir, paints as ordinarily applied fail by flaking from the summerwood sooner than they do on woods like cedar, cypress, redwood and white pine," he said. "Aluminum priming paint is especially suitable for the initial painting of woods like southern yellow pine and Douglas fir because it retards the flaking from summerwood.

"There is less reliable information about the use of aluminum paint in repainting. Where the old coating has come off sufficiently to leave the summerwood mostly bare, and the remnants of old coating are not too thick or too badly curled, aluminum paint should prove satisfactory in repainting, provided two coats of white or light colored paint are applied over it. With paints of dark color or gray paint, one coat may hide the aluminum color. There is no good reason for recommending aluminum paint for jobs on which paint failure has been caused by moisture. Unless the moisture condition is remedied any method of painting may prove disappointing. Failures under such conditions when aluminum paint has been used, tend to undermine confidence in its recommendation for its proper purposes.

Frequent Repainting Advised

"Modern mixed-pigment paints are made to give improved appearance during the useful life of the coating, to maintain their resistance to the passage of moisture longer, and to leave a surface that 'holds out' new paint better than softer paint when repainting comes due," Dr. Browne concluded. "These improvements are gained by careful control of physical properties of the coating that may be called 'hardness' for want of a better term. Quality paints of this kind, however, call for greater care on the part of the house owner to see that they are properly maintained because the hardness on which the improvements are based makes a coating that cracks and curls badly if repainting is neglected long after it comes due.

"The surface should be repainted before it begins to disintegrate seriously. Once disintegration has been allowed to go on through a period of paint neglect it may become difficult to repaint the surface smoothly and the new job may not last so long as it should. Those property owners who are accustomed to leave their paint in a shabby condition of neglect for several years before they repaint should be advised to use only a soft type of paint until they are willing to raise their standards of paint maintenance to a point justifying the use of mixed-pigment paints of a harder type."

(7)

An athletic director, enrolled for graduate study, based an article on material out of his own experience. He supplemented it with interviews with recreational directors, and thus broadened the appeal to readers. For illustrations, he used a picture of a box hockey game and made several line drawings to better explain the construction details.

SPECIAL ACTIVITIES *

for patrons endorsed by University of Wisconsin, Chicago Park District, and other prominent recreational bodies. This article is about Box Hockey, a novel, economical and attractive game.

By H. T. Friermood

Dayton, Ohio, Y.M.C.A.

Even Johnny Weismueller gets tired of swimming and takes to the shore occasionally for a sun bath or other activities.

Millions of other people from north to south and east to west in the United States, as well as throughout the civilized world, are continuing to swell the ranks of swimmers and sun bathers. Yet even the hardiest must rest; and just lying in the sand for a sun bath is essentially boring.

Alert beach and pool managements are on the look-out for additional attractions that will provide pleasure and create interest in their establishments.

The game of Box Hockey is an attraction that is novel, attracts attention, is economical, and may be used in a great variety of establishments.

Porter F. Butts, House Director of the Memorial Union, a million and a quarter dollar student social activity headquarters and club house at the University of Wisconsin, is constantly striving to better his excellent and unique services. He has instructed Charles Dollard, supervisor of the building and grounds, to keep continually on the watch for new ideas and wholesome attractions.

Mr. Dollard in commenting on their policy, recently said:

"For the past three years we have been working on the theory that the way to secure attendance and loyal patronage is to provide interesting activities and features of a positive nature. We want our students and friends to have such a good time that undesirable practices will not appear.

"Capable supervision is provided to instruct people rather than to censure them. With this plan of operation we need variety of

* Reprinted by permission of *Beach & Pool.*

equipment at not too great an expense. In addition to the beach and lake activities we have added deck tennis, lawn ball, dart baseball, and Box Hockey to our lawn terrace facilities. Refreshment facilities for bathers are also provided."

Robert R. Vernon, camp superintendent at George Williams College Camp on Lake Geneva, Wisconsin, has added several Box Hockey outfits to the equipment for camp guests. This camp is designed for conference groups as well as family summer vacationists and can easily accommodate 1000 people in its tents and cottages as well as serve them in the great dining halls.

"Games of this type that are self-entertaining is one of the greatest boons a camp management can have. They keep people interested and in a frame of mind that makes them more receptive to larger group activities. We are studying this problem with the view to making extensive additions. Our tennis court and golf course facilities are ample, but the beach type activities open up a whole new field," says Mr. Vernon.

Box Hockey is one of the many games and special activities that have been developed under the supervision of V. K. Brown, Chicago Park District, Chicago, Illinois. Originally it was devised as a leisure-time activity for use on the playgrounds, the back yard at home or in the basement. The outfit is simple to construct and provides action and fun for persons of all ages and of both sexes.

It is a small-scale combination of the old fashioned game of "shinny" and croquet. The action takes place in a box eight inches high that may vary in size from two and one half to three feet in width and from five to ten feet in length.

The object of the game is to maneuver a small block of wood, or puck, through the opponent's goal by means of a straight stick (a broom handle or a wooden wand) that is two and a half or three feet in length. The opponent is trying to guard his own goal and at the same time score on his adversary.

Parallel to the two ends of the box three more partitions are built into the box. Two of these are placed about four inches in from the two ends and are called the goal partitions, or goal panels, while the third partition goes exactly in the center of the box, and is called the center partition or panel.

The "goals" are small, arched openings cut into the goal panels. These openings are made large enough for the puck to slide through when pushed or struck by the sticks. The openings or goal holes, one in the center of each goal panel, are of course cut before the panel is fastened into the box. The center partition has two openings for the puck to pass through; one about four inches in from each side of the box.

Playing Rules

Two people play at a time and must stand on opposite sides of the box facing each other.

Each player has a stick about three feet long (a broom stick or wooden wand) and with a band painted around the stick twenty-four inches from the striking end. The players thus have a grip about twelve in length and must hold their sticks within this space. The stick may be held with one or both hands.

Start the game by placing the puck on top of the center panel. The players place their sticks on opposite sides of the center panel with the striking ends of the sticks resting on the floor of the box.

Then, like the old game "shinny," the sticks are brought up slowly and tapped together above the puck three times. The stick is returned to the floor of the box after the first and second tap, but after the third tap each player attempts to knock the block off the center panel down into the box and through the hole in the goal panel of his opponent.

Each player has a goal to defend; the game is ordinarily played right handed so each player defends the goal on his right and attempts to score through the goal on his left.

Games may be played on a time basis or for a certain number of points.

Players must stay on their own side of the box. It is not legal to step around to the end of the box to defend the goal.

Players must hold above the twenty-four inch painted band at all times. This is to prevent bruised fingers as well as to keep from taking unfair advantage.

As a safety measure players should never lift the striking end of their sticks more than six inches above the top of the box. Raising it higher may strike the opponent in the face when he is bent down to his task.

Usually players make arrangements to change sides and sticks during the course of the match.

Some of the same problems faced by public beach and pool managements are encountered by private and semi-private organizations.

Harvey I. Allen, a Y.M.C.A. physical director for the past thirty-five years, is in charge of the Dayton, Ohio, Y.M.C.A. physical education program. In a membership of 5,000 men and boys there are many who are interested in securing a healthy coat of tan during the summer months. A special roof solarium has been in use since 1929 when this ultra modern thirteen story building was opened for use.

The gymnasium roof is not finished in a manner that permits much activity. Besides a special wooden platform for the sun bathers to recline upon, a shower with cool water was the only other eqiupment provided. Balls and bats could not be used because they might go over the three foot safety wall. Deck tennis requires a certain amount of running that the roof could not stand. Other games were not practical.

"In spite of the fact that men and boys want a sun tan they find it monotonous to just lie in the sun and wait for results," Mr. Allen explained. "They like action either for themselves or for their observation. This season a Box Hockey outfit was provided and we have experienced a revival of interest and participation."

There is a certain amount of noise as the wooden sticks strike the sides of the wooden box. For this reason the outfit should be placed where this will not make it objectionable.

Box Hockey is only one of a type of games that have proved their popularity. Some beach and pool managements try out ideas on a small scale near the end of the season to see if they "take." In this way enlargements of proven attractions may be made for the opening of the next season. Box Hockey might be used as an experiment.

A known value of special attractions is the publicity that can be secured and played up. A special picture showing the mayor and the chief of police engaged in a "hot" game of Box Hockey would certainly attract attention and bring most any establishment favorably to the attention of its constituency through the local newspapers.

Box Hockey is a splendid game and, we repeat, attracts attention, and is economical.

(8)

A walk down Main Street, where she saw a window display of kitchen utensils, resulted in a young woman writing an article during the same week that she had to complete a paper on "Colonial Life" for a history course. An art student made a drawing showing the bright pots and pans hanging on a rack similar to those used in colonial days.

HIGHLIGHTS IN THE COLONIAL KITCHEN *

By Patricia Peverley

In the colonial or early period home an old-fashioned kitchen with its rack of brightly shining kettles is in vogue again. The glow of copper and the sheen of aluminum and steel not only add decorative charm to kitchen furnishings, but the arrangement is of practical service value as well.

A neat rack which keeps much-used pots and pans at hand has its place even in the compact completeness of an up-to-date kitchen. A wooden rack is easily made of two or more horizontal bars supported by two standards. Small brass hooks, from which the kettles hang, are spaced from 8 to 12 inches apart along the cross bars. The weight is supported by two short outspread legs attached to each standard. The size is variable and may be arranged according to the wall space and your individual needs. The most convenient height is from 4½ to 5½ feet. Equip the rack with casters so that it may be moved about easily.

Of course, only bright, spotless utensils may be so openly displayed. Some women will long to rearrange their kitchens in this manner, but will sigh, and vision tedious hours spent in polishing. Cleaning and scouring become an important factor in the daily routine, but by using the proper cleaning methods no extra time or work is necessary.

Care begins in cooking. Avoid spilling food on the outside, or letting it burn on the inside, of utensils. A good sudsy wash soon after utensils are used, with thoro rinsing and drying, will mean less scouring and stain-removing. Good scouring soaps and powders that don't scratch even the softer metals are on the market and are quick and effective for stained or burned utensils.

Copper kettles have particular charm on the old-fashioned rack. Remember that the cleaning process to keep that coppery luster is different from that used for other metals. Many good copper polishes are now available, or, if you prefer, you may mix your own

* Reprinted by permission of *Better Homes & Gardens.*

cleaning paste. One cup of vinegar combined with two tablespoons of salt and enough flour to make a smooth paste are all you'll need. The paste can then be transferred to a jar and kept ready for use. Place a small amount on a damp cloth and rub it into the copper. You'll be delighted with the speed with which the coppery glow is restored. After cleaning, the vessel should be rinsed well in cold water. Most modern copperware is manufactured with tin or chromium lining. If the lining is of tin it's best not to use steel pads for scouring, as the tin is easily marred.

Lined up on the rack with your copper kettles will be pans of aluminum, steel, and enamelware. Aluminum is a popular metal, as it never rusts, is a good conductor of heat, and is light-weight. There are attractive, bright, stain-resisting finishes. Steel pads may be used for scouring, for aluminum isn't as easily scratched as tin. Aluminum darkened by alkalis may be cleaned by boiling water and vinegar in the utensil.

Enamelware in white or bright colors will prove equally decorative. These pans shouldn't be thrust away into dark cupboards, or stacked carelessly in closed drawers where they're more likely to be chipped. The smooth glazed finish of enamelware is resistant to acids and seldom stains.

Stainless steel is an attractive and practical metal for cooking utensils. It's more expensive than other metals but gives years of service without becoming shabby or dented. If you purchase steel vessels you'll find their care is very simple. Stainless steel retains its sheen and never colors with extreme heat. Scouring can be done without scratching, and the pans emerge from the dishwater with a high polish.

Women thru the ages have prided themselves on the unblemished appearance of their cooking utensils. The small kitchen rack, with its galaxy of glistening pots and pans, can be a showcase for your taste and skill in kitchen management.

(9)

To show the variance in appeals and sources, the two following articles were selected from the same publication, although not from the same issue. The writer of the first article had sore feet and consulted a physician, who advised her to purchase a pair of orthopedic shoes. While having the shoes fitted she decided that here was a story. She interviewed the store owner and the doctor. The latter gave her pamphlets and books in order to supply a background in foot health. She studied several shoe-trade journals and selected the one that she thought would be the best market for the type of article she planned to write. She developed the article as a success story, in order to present the actual business methods in an attractive way. In revising the article, the appeal was broadened to include high-school and working girls as well as co-eds. A photographer took two pictures showing the owner and the interior of the store filled with customers.

SPORTS INFLUENCE COLLEGE STYLES *

This article is based on an interview with Harry B. Dyer, owner of Dyer's Orthopedic Shoe Store, Madison, Wis., and talks with women students at the University of Wisconsin.

BY C. E. IVERSON

Ten thousand students invade the city of Madison, Wis., each September to attend the University of Wisconsin. Of these, 3000 are young women, between the ages of 16 and 22, who need and buy shoes.

Each co-ed wants a pair or two for the campus; for formals, sandals are her favorite; and the Saturday night date has another type of requirement.

Where does the college freshman go to replenish her shoe wardrobe? What shoe store is likely to get the trade of these young women during their four-year stay in the college town?

"Dyer's Orthopedic Shoe Store makes a bid for it in Madison," answers Harvey B. Dyer, who has made a successful effort to build up co-ed appeal in his store. "My stock includes the kind of shoes that have proved favorites with University of Wisconsin women students, and to lead the co-eds from their classrooms and dormitories into my store, I've used all sorts of advertising and publicity methods."

* Reprinted by permission of *Boot and Shoe Recorder* and Miss Caroline E. Iverson.

Permanent resident customers are not neglected by Mr. Dyer in his attempt at developing the university trade. Rather, the value of his products has been enhanced in the eyes of the high school girl and the business woman because the co-ed has demonstrated approval of his shoes by buying them.

In a college town the co-ed sets the style: her younger sister in high school or her older sister in the business world both mimic her taste.

What does a college girl want in shoes? What special activities does she engage in which require particular types of shoes?

"The modern co-ed enters into more activities than her grandmother ever guessed existed," answers Mr. Dyer. "One can no longer picture an American girl without imagining her in some sport, and sports have had direct influence on her shoe buying. She plays hockey, golf, and tennis; rides horseback, skates or skis. For each of these sports she has found a type of shoe that is particularly well adapted to help her win or gain maximum enjoyment from the activities. The ski boot, the rubber-spiked hockey shoe, the riding boot, the golf shoe with fiber sole or steel spikes, or the improved tennis shoe are all for this purpose.

"Two common characteristics are found in each of these special shoes: there is enough room for the foot, and the shoe has low heels. These two qualities of the sport shoe have had more part in influencing the co-ed's choice of her school and date shoes than any other specific factors. Naturally, if she once finds shoes that are comfortable, she's likely to keep on wearing that type.

"First, public opinion clung to the high-heeled, ill-fitting shoe which made the young lady's foot look small; common sense dictated a change for everyday use; finally, common sense won. Today, the flat-heeled or low-heeled shoe is the general favorite for school wear on the University of Wisconsin campus."

Mr. Dyer has summed up the changing psychology in shoe selection that other shoe store proprietors have probably noticed on the college campuses with which they come in contact. The idea of comfort is paramount to students buying shoes.

"University life is busy and complicated enough without adding foot troubles to it," is the co-ed's attitude.

Comfort and health seem to go together in the students' minds, as far as shoes are concerned. How recent and extensive is this acceptance of health shoes?

"The new consciousness of personal hygiene that has been developed by schools, radio, and printed matter in recent years has had its effect on foot health as well as general body health," says Mr. Dyer. "Physical education teachers, school doctors, and interested shoemen have sponsored foot examinations of grade school and high school pupils. Pedographs have been taken; foot exercises to improve feet and posture have been prescribed. This childhood training is remembered by the college student."

"Here at the University of Wisconsin," Mr. Dyer continues, "corrective work plays an important part in the department of physical education for women. Under the direction of Dr. Helen Denniston, associate professor of physical education, who is known throughout the country for her corrective work, the subject has come to touch the life of every freshman girl who enrolls in the university.

"Dr. Denniston's special interest has been foot correction. Her main difficulty in this work was finding a suitable shoe to prescribe to the students who came to her. For several years she complained to me that there was no shoe on the market adapted for corrective work, which was very attractive and stylish."

Attractive shoes? Of course, the co-ed wants these. She believes in comfort and health, but what young lady can reconcile herself to complete disregard of style? Surely not the university co-ed.

Mr. Dyer and Dr. Denniston combined their efforts to design a shoe that a doctor could approve of and a shoeman could sell. Dr. Denniston supplied the orthopedic and shoe last ideas, and Mr. Dyer prescribed the colors and patterns acceptable from the style standpoint. It took several years of experimenting to develop the shoe, but there is no doubt that Wisconsin students like it. New stocks in the 30 different color combinations are sold out almost immediately after being received.

Granting that you have a shoe that college women are sure to like, you ask what methods of informing the student can you use?

"Contacts in the university have done much to promote my sales to co-eds," says Mr. Dyer. "My work with the physical education department gave my store a reputation not only for carrying the kind of shoes that doctors and physical education teachers recommend, but also for knowing how to fit these shoes correctly. Thus when this department or the hospital unit of student health has co-eds with foot troubles, they are sent to me for fitting.

"If the foot defect is found during the freshman medical examination, and the student is sent to me, I am likely to have her trade for the whole four years that she is in college. Even after she leaves school, very often a girl will continue to order her shoes here by mail, and she leads her mother and sisters to do the same.

"Physical education students graduated from the university go out as teachers in other colleges, and often send back to secure shoes from me for their pupils in need of foot correction. Just the other day we received letters from a teacher at Stephens College in Columbia, Mo., and one at the Mississippi State College for Women, who wanted to have the shoes they used in Madison for their students. In a case like this, an agent is appointed from among the students to handle the business end of selling the shoes, while the teacher supervises the fitting.

"By furnishing the shoes for demonstrations in the home economics department," continues Mr. Dyer, "our products are recommended in educational programs to home economics students."

Other means of stimulating sales to co-eds are collegiate window displays. Labeling the shoes according to the college dormitories proved effective, Mr. Dyer says. One popular shoe, having an inch heel and made of dark green bucko with brown alligator trim, was called "Barnard Hall"; another with rather a round toe, made of brown elk, trimmed with alligator and a "Scottie" shawl tongue, was called "Langdon Hall."

Sometimes the shoes are labeled: "I'm Connie," "I'm Jackie," or "I'm Skippy." During homecoming weekend, a display of shoes sprinkled with photos of former famous University of Wisconsin football players decorated the window.

"I believe in going to the student with my product, rather than waiting for her to come to me," says Mr. Dyer. "In the library of the physical education and women's building, I have a showcase with some of my shoes exhibited. Advertising in the *Daily Cardinal,* student newspaper, proves valuable, especially when the fashion editor cooperates with me. After-dinner talks and demonstrations at sorority houses and dormitories to display shoes that they are interested in stimulates business."

To Mr. Dyer, the 12 years that he has run Dyer's Orthopedic Shoe Store have been hard work, but it is work at a hobby. The atmosphere of this store suggests friendliness, sympathy for foot troubles, and a desire to satisfy. Enthusiasm about the value of orthopedic shoes never languishes, even when a customer sits for an hour and a half, "trying to make up her mind."

From the business standpoint, the store avoids competition of other shoe stores in Madison by its specializing. In the Fall and early Winter months of 1937, when business experienced a general slump, Mr. Dyer was going along, not at his usual pace, but with increased sales. People can't stay away from a druggist when their bodies are sick; neither can they do without the shoe druggist when their foot needs care.

Let's develop co-ed appeal, then, according to Harvey Dyer's formula:

Fit the co-ed with comfortable, healthful, attractive shoes, and she can't help coming back to you for more. Then your "college town" shoe store is sure to succeed.

(10)

The second feature in the same business magazine was based upon the writer's experience as a part-time shoe salesman. However, he thought the article would be more authoritative if he interviewed a number of store managers and through them told the story of "speeding sales." He obtained three gloss prints from three managers to show how each tried to improve his sales.

HOW TO SPEED SALES IN JANUARY *

Does the Slow Season after the Holidays Haunt You? Do you Idle Away Your Time During the Two and One-Half Month Period Before the Spring Season Opens? What Methods Do You Use to Stimulate Shoe Sales? Have You Made a Study of the Techniques Other Shoe Merchants Use to Cope With This Problem? How Madison, Wis., Shoe Managers Found Answers to These Questions.

By Alvo Albini

When shoe customers reluctantly enter the store, demand bargains, and keep the salesman on edge, then every shoe salesman

* Reprinted by permission of *Boot and Shoe Recorder* and Mr. Alvo Albini.

knows that January has come. When stores begin to cut down on their light bills, salesmen work half-days or alternate weeks, and counting inventory is the only way to keep busy, then every shoe store senses the beginning of a slump season which often lasts up to the middle of March.

Selling shoes in January is one of the mysteries of the shoe business. It is during this period that every effort is made to cut down the customer's resistance to a minimum. Every customer is a "must" customer.

Each January slump presents itself with different problems. To cope with this inevitable shoe phenomenon, shoe store managers have devised various methods for getting more sales.

From the expensive and sophisticated shoe departments to the lower price chain stores, techniques of a variegated kind are used to lessen the severity of the seasonal slump. Some stores concentrate on effective sales presentations. Some announce their wares through direct mail advertising, newspaper advertising, leaflets, and even through the radio.

Every effort is made to individualize the store. Window trims are more carefully set in. Interior displays are uniquely made up. Bargain counters are made attractive in order to catch the customer's eye.

Every shoe manager or owner has a few "trump cards" which he can rely upon during this inactive period of business. By prudently "playing his cards" the shrewd shoe man can lessen the severity of the slump. He can beat his last year's low figures and establish a new high for slow season volume turnover.

Because the shoe men of Madison, Wis., all agree that the January slump is inevitable there as elsewhere, each has his own distinctive way of increasing his business during this period.

Leonard Woolen, manager of the shoe department in Burdick & Murray, ladies' ready-to-wear specialty shop, uses what he calls the "courtesy card" technique to stimulate his slow Winter season.

"At the beginning of each year," explains Mr. Woolen, "we mail out 'courtesy cards' to every customer on the store's accounts and invite her to take advantage of a courtesy discount which we offer our customers only. By bringing the card with her, a special discount is given on every pair of shoes that she buys."

Approximately 4000 cards are mailed out each January. Over

50 per cent of the customers who receive the cards respond to the offer, says Mr. Woolen.

Another method which Mr. Woolen uses during January is to introduce some new Spring style to the customers who come in for galoshes, purses, or some other minor item.

"I always try to pick up a few new Spring patterns," says Mr. Woolen, "and make a special effort to keep them off our displays and out of our windows.

"When a customer comes in for a pair of galoshes, we inform her that we have a few new styles in shoes which we would like to show her. By inducing the customer to try on the shoe and make her feel as though she is really the only one to know about the new style, extra sales are often made."

The slow season in Madison, says Mr. Woolen, lasts from Jan. 1 to March 15.

Phil Applebaum, manager of the shoe department in the Harry L. Manchester department store, Madison, believes that time alters one's mind and ideas about January slumps.

"The drop in the January business can be avoided," says Mr. Applebaum, "by having new shoes come in during this month. However, the ability to introduce new styles is based largely upon the condition of your Fall stock. One must work ahead several months in liquidating the old Fall styles."

Over 50 per cent of the business of the Manchester shoe department comes from the Madison suburban areas. This consists of the middle class and better class of buyers. During the January season, Mr. Applebaum stocks up on plenty of "cruise shoe" styles.

An elaborate and colorful folder is prepared by the advertising department and is mailed to the vacationing customers. By keeping an alert eye on the society columns of the local papers, Mr. Applebaum draws his list of prospective "cruise shoe" customers and contacts them by telephone or by mail.

"Today," says Mr. Applebaum, "we don't have the people buying many pairs of shoes even if there is a sale in progress and if real values are offered."

In his department, Mr. Applebaum finds that his customers are not all sale-minded during the month of January.

"Because it is imperative for the women of today to have a complete line of accessories to match their shoes, they realize that although they may be saving several dollars on the sale shoe, they will have to spend twice the amount saved in order to get a complete new set of accessories to match. Consequently the customer is willing to pay more for the latest style in the color that matches the accessories."

The main problem in January, according to Mr. Applebaum is to promote and introduce new shoes for the coming season. People will become accustomed to look upon the store as the fashion center of the city and in this manner the slow season during the beginning of the year can be stimulated.

Mr. Applebaum's shoe department sells ladies' shoes from $5.50 to $14.75. The shoe brands that are featured are the I. Miller's and the Selby's Arch Preserver.

In an orthopedic shoe store, the sales strategy during January is somewhat different. Harvey Dyer, president of the Dyer Orthopedic shoe stores of Madison, Wis., Rockford, Ill., and Evanston, Ill., declares that the most successful way to boost January business is by clearance sales.

"Clearance sales," says Mr. Dyer, "definitely stimulate business. Competition makes it necessary today to have a sale during this month because it is being looked for by the public.

"If you want to lower the customer's resistance you must lower the price."

The lowering of prices depends largely on the merchandise that each store has on hand. Mr. Dyer cautioned that sensible reductions varying from 15 to 25 per cent of the original cost of the shoe must be made.

"A store that has its good-will firmly established does not go in for ridiculous price cuts," says Mr. Dyer. "It would be lowering the store's prestige to undertake such a risk."

Two sales a year are held by the Dyer Orthopedic shoe stores. One in January and one in August. The sales usually last three weeks.

Mr. Dyer calls the January period not a slump season, but a sale season. The weather, he declares, plays an important part in determining the sales during this time of the year. His sale season usually extends to Feb. 15.

M. W. Parkinson, manager of the shoe department in Miller's ready-to-wear store in Madison, is one of the users of the direct mail advertising.

From the personal mailing list collected by the store during the year, Mr. Parkinson sends out letters to all of the customers informing them of the bargains.

"Window trimming," says Mr. Parkinson, "is the main item I stress during the January period. I give my windows more care. Change the trim more often. Stress price and bargains."

Mr. Parkinson's shoe department features the Fashion Thimble shoe with prices from $1.99 to $4.95.

Situated on the lower campus of the University of Wisconsin, Mr. Edwin O. Olson's shoe department in the University Co-op department store, has 75 per cent of his trade dependent on college students.

Although Mr. Olson agrees that the slow period is from Jan. 1 to March 15, his shoe business does not have a great fall as do other merchants on "The Square." The second semester spurt adds considerably to the gap of business ordinarily present.

With new students entering the University during the latter part of January and the beginning of February, Mr. Olson's shoe business is stimulated by this student trade. This unique set-up lessens the drop in the business slump in his department.

"Because of the great drains on the college man's income," says Mr. Olson, "he is more value-minded. With more expenses to account for, he takes advantage of the sales during the slow season and loads up on bargains."

During the January season, Mr. Olson has his salesmen devote more time to their sales talk and in the showing of more styles. Prices are made attractive through the various sales campaigns.

The average price shoe that the college man today buys, declares Mr. Olson, is about $6.50. Mr. Olson's shoe department is for men only. Nunn-Bush, Edgerton, and Freeman shoes are sold. Prices vary from $4.00 to $10.50.

(11)

Analyzing the advertising as well as the editorial copy revealed to a beginner the magazine's lack of advertising of laundry equipment and of features pertaining to the subject. The appeal of the woman's section in this farm publication is to the housewife who does her own work. Thus, she reasoned that the editor might be interested in an article that the advertising solicitors could present as part of their sales argument to manufacturers of laundry equipment and supplies. She listed all the steps in the process of laundrying, not only to make her article have reader-appeal but to see what types of advertising could be "tied-up," as the copy writers say, with the article. A gloss print depicted modern laundry equipment operated by a charming housewife whose expression revealed she did not dread "washday." The tactful suggestion in the note to the editor hinted at the possibility of an advertising tie-up. The editor wrote the author that the article had enabled the advertising department to increase its lineage.

SHORTCUTS TO AN EASY WASHDAY *

By Marcelle Glassow

Fifty-two times a year all the soiled clothes of the family have to be washed. Someone must make them fresh, crisp, and spotless before they may be worn or used again, and in most families that someone is Mother.

Mother usually looks upon washing as the hardest task she has to do. It is a difficult and wearisome job if one gets all messed up in it. But with a little system and a happy state of mind, washday need not be one of drudgery.

First of all, keep your laundry, the kitchen, or wherever you do your laundering, bright and cheerful. Shining windows, gleaming paint, gay curtains, go a long way towards lightening the task of washday. The arrangement of equipment is something every woman must work out for her own convenience, but be sure to keep everything you need handy so as to save yourself time and steps.

Mending, stain-removal, and sorting are preliminaries of washday. It is desirable to mend rips and tears before washing to avoid the risk of enlarging the holes. Furthermore, mending before washing saves wrinkles after ironing. Washing "sets" some stains, thus making it more difficult to remove them.

The soil on clothes usually is dirt mixed with oily or greasy substances which hold it on the fabric. Were it not for these sticky substances, much of the dirt in clothes could be separated by mere shaking. Water alone will not take all this dirt and stickiness out

* Reprinted by permission of *Capper's Farmer*.

of clothes. Therefore it is necessary that attention be paid to using an effective soap, the agent which cuts away all dirt and grime.

There are many good brands of soap on the market either in bar form, chips or beads. They are made up of ingredients selected carefully and blended accurately with the object of strengthening their cleansing power in order to ease the laundry work. The quantity of soap to be used depends largely upon the character of the water in your locality. Hard water will require more soap than soft. It also is wise to remember that while too little soap handicaps the cleansing action, too much soap may produce an excess of suds which deters the cleansing.

By sorting clothes into piles of white cottons and linens, fast and unfast colored cottons and linens, and fine fabrics, one avoids troublesome delays. The white cottons and linens may be soaked in warm water and soap suds an hour or so, or even overnight, so as to loosen the dirt. The soaking method of washing clothes is based upon the principle that dissolved soap, which produces active suds, releases dirt thru its own action. Rubbing and boiling become unnecessary, for the dirt is urged out gently by the soaking. Put the dirtiest clothes at the bottom of the tub so they will have the longest benefit of the soaking.

Clothes that are known to be absolutely fast color may be soaked about 20 minutes. Be sure you test every new colored garment before mixing it with the rest of the clothes, for one unfast color may discolor an entire tubful of clothes. According to the United States Division of Textiles and Clothing, there are no effective methods of "setting" colors, and those ordinarily suggested are of doubtful value. It is easier to wash a doubtful colored garment separately than to spoil a tubful of clothes.

Silks require no soaking, and should be washed in much cooler water than ordinary cottons and linens. They need more delicate care, also, since any twisting may pull them out of shape.

If clothes have been soaked, thus getting rid of the oily and greasy matter, the water used in the machine may be hotter than with unsoaked clothes. A good rule is to have the water as hot as your hands can stand it.

Thorough rinsing removes all traces of the soap and loosened dirt from the clothes. If convenient, the first rinse water should be as warm as the wash water. The second rinse may be cold if it is more convenient. Remove as much water as possible from the clothes when transferring them from the first to the second rinse. Dirty rinse water left in the clothes leaves the clothes grimy in appearance.

Some women prefer using bluing in the final rinse. When bluing is used test the color of the solution by putting a small article into it, or by holding a little in the palm of the hand. Excess bluing may be removed only by boiling the articles.

Besides imparting a smooth and attractive finish to clothes, the use of starch helps to keep garments clean for a longer time by covering and holding down the tiny surface "fuzz" that catches dust and dirt. For white clothes the starch should be as hot as the hands can stand, since hot starch penetrates more evenly. A small lump of butter stirred into the hot starch gives the fabric more gloss when it is ironed, and the starch will not stick to the iron. Always starch garments wrong side out. For fine fabrics and laces use a dilute solution, and for colored garments have the starch lukewarm.

To save time in ironing pay particular attention to the drying. Be sure to wash the line each time before hanging the clothes. A new rope line may be softened by boiling a few minutes and rinsing in hot water. This also adds to its life. Shake as many of the folds and wrinkles out of the clothes as possible, and hang together pieces of similar type. Hang sheets by the two hems. This not only avoids wear and tear on the sheets, but it facilitates taking the dry sheets off the line. The sheets can be folded neatly, and with a swift ironing of the hems, they are ready for the linen closet. Fold all the pieces as you take them from the line and lay them into the basket. In this manner you may eliminate much ironing.

The ironing job will be lighter if your equipment suits you properly. Make sure your board is sturdy and rigid, and regulate its height so as to avoid having to bend or stoop. A smoothly padded board saves time. It is much easier to iron articles which have been dampened and rolled up tightly for a few hours than to iron clothes directly off the line. The garments should be smoothed out, pulled into shape and folded before they are rolled, as the ironing is easier if wrinkles are not rolled in. Sprinkle articles, one at a time, preferably with warm water, and roll similar articles together to make more convenient both the ironing and putting away the ironed articles. If electricity is not available there are highly efficient washers equipped with gasoline motors available at a reasonable price. Also, when contemplating the purchase of a washing machine, remember there is more to consider than price. Any man-made machine is bound to wear so make certain you can get service locally for only then can you enjoy a washer satisfaction at the least cost. In selecting a washing machine there are nine things well worth giving consideration: Where will the washer be used? What facilities for draining does it possess? To what extent will the washer be used? How many people are there in the family? What types of clothes will be washed? What water supply is available? What kind of water will be used? Are laundry tubs built-in? How much can you afford?

A stitch in time can save much more than nine in the care of clothes. Look over your soiled clothes for stains and spots before you begin to wash them, for an otherwise easily removed stain may become indelible if it meets with soap and water and heat. Stain removal at home is an easy matter if one takes the necessary precautions and follows a few simple rules. The first rule is promptness. A stain that is fresh is far easier to take out than one which has been set by drying and exposure to air.

The second rule is to be sure that you know what made the stain before you begin to treat it, for the procedure which would take out one stain may merely set another. The third rule is to know what the material is and to treat it with a cleaning agent which will not injure the fabric. Before you begin operations, test the cleaner on a piece of material like that which you intend to clean or on an inconspicuous part of the garment. A spot on the fabric is better than a hole or a discoloration caused by use of the wrong cleaner.

Try simple methods before you try complicated ones. If the fabric is safe in water, water may sometimes remove the stain. On fragile fabrics or for deep stains, solvents such as naptha and benzine will be effective, altho they are inflammable and must be handled carefully. Dry corn meal or talcum powder sprinkled on and then brushed off will remove light stains.

(12)

A writer may find that, in gathering material, he has many facts that do not pertain to the phase of the subject about which he plans to write. He often can write a second article from the additional material. Or, in collecting material for one article, he may find material for an entirely different market, as this journalism junior did. A halftone showed a family of four listening to the radio.

A SELECTIVE VIEW OF RADIO *

By R. A. Anderson

As parents most of us are careful to guide the experiences of our children—their companions and activities, their reading, and the motion pictures they see. But on the whole we are very likely to disregard the vital influence of radio, and more likely to ignore its possibilities. As individuals seeking in our own right a full and thoughtful existence, we seldom stop to examine this great flow of entertainment and information.

Perhaps we are still pleasantly amazed at the unlimited diversion which a twist of our radio dial brings into our homes, gratified at this "free" show, whatever its substance. If at times annoyed, we are mainly thankful for radio and fail to apply the full drop of precaution which in an ordered plan of Christian living we accord to other makers of character.

For while we may find much in radio broadcasting that is wholesome and enjoyable, there is also a great deal to be taken with the familiar grain of salt. Opinion, so plentiful on the air waves, comes often in half-truths, cloaked in some plausible garment of false authority. Propaganda, commercial and otherwise, is rampant. Radio advertising commonly reduces the principles of health and right living to a succession of cold and headache tablets and morning-after beverages. We are taught the claims of patent medicines instead of the principles of sound health and the proper treatment of ills. This, ironically enough, takes place in a world which is wont to recall with much amusement the tricks of the old-time medicine shows!

"Much radio advertising," declared Harold B. McCarty, director of Wisconsin's state station WHA, "tends to make the individual feel inferior and lose the realization of his own unique social worth. He hears constant haranguing from all sides about the relation of his appearance and condition to social position and success in life.

* Reprinted by permission of *Christian Home*.

"This incessant reference on the air to the real or imagined ailments, which are usually minor, to complexion and teeth, to weight, baldness, and the loss of youthfulness, to looks and daily habits, is a vicious negative appeal which can only contribute to the feeling that one doesn't belong. A person has got to feel, on the other hand, that he does belong."

This very evening you may turn your dial to a radio station of enormous power that lies just across the Mexican border, from which a physician discredited by the American medical profession broadcasts several hours nightly, and advertises to millions of Americans the miraculous benefits of an operation panacea in which he specializes.

Radio is no respecter of boundaries. But even within our own country there is no agency active in protecting the listening public from quacks and nostrums. In a few cases, the Federal Trade Commission has been impelled to act. The Federal Communications Commission has exercised little or no control over program content. Still one commonly hears a listener say, "It must be true—I heard it on the radio." Such a listener is a victim of the absolutely unfounded notion that what is on the radio has passed some test of authenticity.

"Let's have a little more critical, skeptical listening," Mr. McCarty pleads, "and not be misled by radio itself, nor by any kindly, anonymous radio voice. Let's ask 'Who?' 'Why?' 'On what authority?' For on the other side is the picture of an abundance of good things if we simply have the interest and the information necessary to seek them out."

Now that's a wise caution. But the selective radio listening we should all seek to develop, as Mr. McCarty hints, is not founded upon skepticism alone. There is indeed an abundance of good things, which it should be our purpose to learn to recognize as such. Radio broadcasts are so varied as to defy adequate classification. They perish with each passing moment. But perhaps we can formulate some enduring yardstick with which to measure and evaluate these fleeting offerings.

Radio's "stage" is an imaginative one; thus radio is well adapted to fantasy. But let's insist that a clear line divide it from the portrayal of reality. Many children's programs illustrate this point admirably. When the *Singing Lady* (NBC Blue network) tells her nursery tales in song and story, no claim is made to simulate life. This simple and charming broadcast, given with a rare understanding of what young children like, is a pleasant diversion for them and a fine stimulus to their imagination. Much the same may be said of the Columbia Network's program *Let's Pretend,* in which fairy tales are dramatized by children. *The Silver Flute* (NBC Red network) is a weekly series of folk-tale dramatizations, suitable for both children and adults, which stays well within its province and has many delightful narratives.

There are few finer examples of how first-class radio drama may be drawn from down-to-earth reality, without assistance from incredible external events or trumped up situations, than *One Man's Family,* a weekly NBC Red network broadcast. Here is the genuine play of wholesome human emotions, true and goodhumored, never descending from its high dramatic standard.

When the spheres of real and unreal are confused, on the other hand, the result may be ridiculous. "Aw, he always gets into trouble and always gets out," was the way one young listener summed up a certain Wild West series.

We ought to ask of a dramatic series, furthermore, that we come to the end of a broadcast with something we did not have at the beginning—a new bit of knowledge, a different slant on some subject, or simply the residual pleasure from a wholesome emotional experience. For example, one program of the *Columbia Workshop,* an experimental drama series, took its listeners on an imaginary sightseeing tour of the slums of a large city. It was so well written and so tinged with reality that some of it did not make a pretty picture. Yet, it was forceful and purposeful, and must have led many listeners to a fresh insight.

Radio drama may increase our knowledge of the past, and our appreciation of tradition in such historical and biographical series as *There Was a Woman* (NBC Blue network), *American Portraits* (NBC Red network), and *Brave New World* (Columbia), which brings Central America into the scene.

For children, the emotional emphasis of a program is important. Emphasis upon violence, mystery, and pursuit is the most intriguing, and in the extreme of violent drama, to a sensitive child can likewise be the most harmful. In certain surveys more than half the child listeners observed were reported to lie awake thinking of the stories they have heard. One should think twice before depriving a child of a well-liked program; at the same time one should realize how very vital make-believe seems to children, and try to expose them to the better types. Though such programs as the Mutual network's *Witch's Tale,* and *Lights Out* may be diverting bits for grown-ups, horror tales of the sort have little place in the young child's radio diet.

Fortunately some radio time is allotted to political and economic forums, like *America's Town Meeting of the Air* (NBC Blue Network) and the *University of Chicago Round Table;* and to individual persuasive talks by anyone from the President himself to his bitterest opponent. To these we must carry the criteria of reason and tolerance and sincerity. When listening to an opinionated address we should continually ask ourselves: Is he sincere or merely bombastic? Is he telling the whole truth? Does he resort to catchphrases and melodious but empty generalities? Is the trend of his argument logical, or simply cleverly organized? Is he tolerant?

One may keep intelligently abreast of events through regular listening to such sound commentators as Lowell Thomas, Boake Carter, Dorothy Thompson, Hendrik Van Loon, and Howard Marshall, a British journalist who broadcasts *They're Saying in England* (NBC Blue network). *Press-Radio* is fine for fast, concise, unbiased reporting, though not very complete. Local "newscasts," it is well to remember, are likely to reflect the editorial opinion of the newspaper sponsoring them.

While we should beware of anonymous or virtually anonymous broadcasts on health or any other subject, particularly when there is some product constantly referred to and offered for sale, we ought to welcome with equal force such reliable programs as the New York Academy of Medicine's *Talks for the Layman* (Columbia) and the dramatized *Your Health,* of the NBC Red network. The *American School of the Air,* a daily Columbia school-hours broadcast, and such series as *Science on the March* (NBC Blue network) and *New Horizons* (Columbia), produced by the American Museum of Natural History, should be sought in the program listings as sources of interesting, objective information.

Music must depend upon taste alone. Opera in season, the *New York Philharmonic* (Columbia) and other civic symphonies, choral singing, like Columbia's *Choral Quest,* the *Marine Band* and others —all these are available to music lovers, and we are *all* music lovers.

Selective radio listening, finally, requires regular access to advance program listings. Daily newspapers can usually give neither sponsor, adequate description, nor criticism of programs, though Sunday editions often list them a full week in advance. Better sources are the National Broadcasting Company's *Monthly Educational Bulletin,* mailed to anyone requesting it (Address: RCA Building, New York City). *Radio Guide,* a weekly periodical having separate regional editions, classifies, describes, and criticizes network and local radio offerings. It may be purchased in your vicinity for ten cents.

These sources will help us to discard any habit of aimless, indiscriminate listening we may now have. Alert to radio's failings, conscious too of its power to enrich the lives of all the family, we may begin to plan our listening and not let a single good thing escape us.

(13)

After gathering the material for the preceding article, the writer found an idea for a second one on a different phase of the subject. He had a photographer take pictures of two "school rooms of the air" and obtained a photograph of the Director. This is just one of many examples where one feature leads to another.

VOICES FROM THE "OUTSIDE WORLD" *

Radio Brings Them Into City and Rural Schoolrooms in Wisconsin, Among Other Places, and So Supplements the Instruction Which the Teacher Provides

By Robert A. Anderson

Wisconsin, for more than six years now, has offered teaching daily by radio to its remote and urban classrooms alike, in a voluntary plan of supplementary education designed to vitalize the work of elementary school pupils and stimulate them to a further interest in their subjects.

To those pupils, comprising still less than half the schoolrooms of the State, radio is now an accustomed event but never a commonplace. They take it eagerly and responsively.

Focal point of the Wisconsin School of the Air is state-owned

* Reprinted by permission of the *Christian Science Monitor Weekly Magazine Section.*

station WHA, situated on the campus of the University of Wisconsin in Madison.

* * *

Station Director Harold B. McCarty, former president of the National Association of Educational Broadcasters, is founder and director of the Wisconsin School of the Air.

"Radio has been building up heroes and impressions in the thoughts of children who listen in their homes," he declared. "Its program characters have come to be real figures in their lives, with a definite influence on their language and habits.

"Why shouldn't there be a like influence under guidance, with heroes of a different type? Here is a radiant teaching talent which exerts itself in a small classroom; I was interested in distributing such talent over a wide area."

Nature and music are the subjects currently enjoying greatest popularity with the youthful listeners, of the 10 regular programs covering half a dozen general fields. Wakelin McNeel, conservationist and Wisconsin 4-H Club leader, takes well over 10,000 pupils "Afield with Ranger Mac" in weekly discussions of trees and forests, of birds and weeds and flowers. Children join in a virtually statewide chorus in their "Journeys to Music Land," under the leadership of Prof. E. B. Gordon, of the University of Wisconsin School of Music.

Radio, while proceeding advisedly as a classroom aid, is little aware of subject-limitations. "Let's Draw!" teaches a purely visual skill in art and craft-work through a plan of stimulating the imagination of the child by means of legend and music. "State Capitol Visits" lifts civics and government out of the textbook as an experienced announcer interviews and thus humanizes leading legislative and executive figures.

"Trailer Travels" provides a vital presentation of national geography. "Rhythm and Games," conducted by Mrs. Fannie Steve, Health Education Director of the Madison public schools, is a recreational program but ever with a purpose: the development of bodily grace and poise.

"Though radio has a permanent place in the schoolroom," said Mrs. Lois Nemec, State Elementary School Supervisor, "that place —whether one preponderantly of direct teaching or simply of stimulation—has not yet been determined. That is going to depend principally on how the individual teacher uses it."

Many out-of-the-way rural schools have seen little change over decades. The same brisk, pleasant teacher is seated at her desk in front of rows of pupils whose ages and grades we gather only from their neatly graduated order, the smallest ones in the first row, and successive seats and rows holding the older and larger ones, to the age, perhaps, of 12.

One observes a flag and naive crayon sketches and posters, "Be Kind to Animals," "Well Begun is Half Done." There is a squat iron stove, and elsewhere a low, home-painted table on which repose the miscellaneous souvenirs of children's rambles: cocoons and curling leaves, forked twigs, dry butterflies, and pebbles. Somewhere in the room one sees a radio, often the lone symbol of change.

During classroom reception, listening pupils are allowed, preferably, to be at ease, ready to respond to the spirit of the broadcast, and to their radio teacher's leadership.

"The poor classroom teacher may dull the air of expectancy and eagerness which should surround a program," Mr. McCarty says. "The more efficient teacher realizes that nothing should be done to mar a quality of pleasure and vitality like that attending the coming of a well-liked guest. An easy listening attitude should be developed out of the beauty and appeal of the music at the outset, without disciplinary measures."

* * *

The pupils thus relaxed, the moment such music opens a program the visitor seated behind the class may see all the rows of feet begin, unconsciously, to tap the time. No classroom teacher's command to "Sit up tall and straight!" could be followed, it would seem, with quite the same smartness as is that of this impelling radio voice; and yet such an order on the air connotes to the child no sense of imperiousness.

Similarly, listening pupils are asked from time to time to show their hands. "How many of you have ever seen a live bat closely?" the query might be, or "How many of you would like to go down in a salt mine?"

When the broadcaster has returned with, "Well! Not a great many, it seems," or, "I knew you all would!" more than once some smaller member of a group has been moved to ask, incredulously:

"Gee, can he see us?"

The child's ability to retain radio teachings has often been remarked upon. One teacher of a consolidated country school declared: "Several times I have tried to teach to my seventh-grade class certain material in agriculture that has later come over the air. I couldn't make the facts stick the way Ranger Mac did; they seemed to take on new meaning coming from a fresh source."

John Callahan, State Superintendent of Public Instruction, remarked on this point: that we all learn from experiences, and that radio is simply an experience in which children are strongly interested.

Broadcasters are chosen largely on the basis of character and personality; often they are not those who write the script. Novelty, moreover, is admittedly a force. Programs are 15 minutes long, except for those of participation, like music, which may be longer. No student listens to more than three or four broadcasts a week as a rule.

* * *

"At first I was concerned about the possibility that the novelty might wear off," said Mr. McCarty. "From the beginning we have felt that radio could enrich the work of the classroom and assist the teacher, not by supplanting her in anything, but by providing extra stimulus and inspiration. Nothing in our experience since then has indicated that the use of radio can diminish her importance."

The teacher must "set the stage" before each broadcast and cultivate an eager, receptive attitude in her class, as by queries which she purposely leaves unanswered, on the subject at hand. Similarly, since a broadcast is admittedly a fleeting matter, she must joint its threads immediately after, while the material is still fresh, and in the discussion recall points not remembered by the children. The value of any program is thus enhanced by her part.

"Most of my children will never leave the farm," one appreciative rural teacher told me, "and I am so pleased to see them pursuing subjects now, under the influence of the radio, which will widen the scope of their interests for years to come."

(14)

The appeal of the unusual and the extraordinary interested a senior. She looked about for subject matter that would lend itself to that type of treatment. She found it in her own home town. A snapshot enlarged sufficiently to reproduce as a half-tone was taken by the amateur. The editor added a drawing in color to show the subject of the sketch as a justice holding court.

THEY SAID HE COULDN'T LIVE *

But Geneva man, after 43 operations, has served as mayor twice, holds court, and is always busy

BY HILDA BALDWIN

So you think you have a right to brag about "my operation"? Then meet L. E. Evans of Geneva, O., who has had 43 major ones in the past ten years and still has had time to become one of the busiest and most prominent men in his town and county.

In 1920, when Mr. Evans was 33, married happily, with two fine children and a good job, he was just beginning to realize how satisfactory life can be.

Then on St. Valentine's Day, while he was charging the soda water tank in the waiting room store of the C. P. & A. Railroad, the tank exploded. One leg just below the knee was blown off, the other seriously mangled. Three doctors held out no hope for his life.

But he did live, and for a year, although he was bed-ridden, he managed his store, sold magazine subscriptions, and with the help of his capable wife earned a satisfactory income.

For several years before the accident, Mr. Evans had been studying law, and when he took stock of the legal knowledge he had acquired along with his other business experiences, he decided he had the qualifications for mayor of Geneva, a town of 4,000.

At this time he was recuperating in a wheel chair, so his campaign, which elected him over three other candidates, was called the "wheel-chair campaign" by the newspapers. After his election, papers for miles around carried the story of his various handicaps and achievements.

During his first term as mayor (1923–1925) he was mainly concerned with the problem of the unemployed. He made a news-

* Reprinted by permission of the *Cleveland Plain Dealer Sunday Magazine*.

paper appeal to the citizens and soon they fell into the habit of calling up Mayor Evans when they had an odd job or two to be done. For many of the idle men the odd jobs formed their sole source of income, and Mayor Evans was often blessed for his part in helping to make the work available.

After the close of his term Mr. Evans started a wholesale candy business, and then operated a restaurant for a year and a half. Both, like all the ventures in which he had had a hand, were successful.

Despite his seeming successes in business, however, he has never collected much of a bank roll. "All my operations," he says with a twinkle in his eye, "cost real money. And the surgeons don't give quantity discounts in spite of my repeated visits."

His operations have been mainly re-amputations and skin grafting, and their cost has run into thousands of dollars.

After the restaurant experience, Mr. and Mrs. Evans started a neighborhood grocery store. He was now able to walk on artificial legs, but just as the store became a paying proposition, the doctors ordered him not to be on his feet so much. So he was forced to sell the store.

After this he was appointed superintendent of Geneva Township Park, the village owned park five miles from town, along Lake Erie. This position he has held ever since.

In 1931 he was again elected mayor by a big majority and his accomplishments during this term are the few achievements he is willing to discuss at length. Through his efforts an appropriation was obtained for a new $75,000 postoffice, to replace a small store-like affair, scarcely worthy of a town the size of Geneva. The old town hall was replaced by a new and larger one, and in the same year (1931) a new $25,000 town bridge, on Federal Route 20 was built, in addition to the widening of the highway at both ends of the town. He was also able to get $4,100 more from the state for operating expenses for the county.

He was the first mayor to institute an advisory board of one Democrat and one Republican, and this board has successfully functioned ever since.

In 1931 also when unemployment figures rose to unprecedented heights in the town, he devised an original employment system. Whenever some person who had read the mayor's pleas in the papers telephoned for a man to shovel snow, cut wood, or do some odd job, the mayor would put a slip of white paper, containing name, address and telephone number, in the window facing the street, behind his desk. Thus he could take the phone call as he held court in his justice of the peace office (he was mayor and a justice at the same time) swing around in his swivel chair, put the paper in the window, and still not interrupt the session.

Some idle man who had been watching for this white signal flag of hope throughout the day could then rush into the office, be silently handed the slip and hastily depart without disturbing the proceedings.

In the course of his term he found various citizens willing to donate the wooded lots they owned to the cause of the unemployed. He put 25 men to work cutting and selling the wood and by this means they netted themselves some $800.

Perhaps his intense sympathy for these jobless men can be attributed to the fact that he himself has known well what it was to be penniless.

A similar sympathy for children who "never got a break" was expressed a few years ago when, with the help of merchants' donations, Mr. and Mrs. Evans undertook to entertain over 100 youngsters at Township Park for a day's outing. The parents of none of these children had been able to afford them a holiday at the lake.

It doesn't take much of a psychologist to realize that his interest in unfortunate children is related to his own childhood.

"I was born in Battle Creek, Mich., on Feb. 1, 1887," he says, in summarizing his early years. "When I was 3, my father, a foreman in a steel mill near Cleveland, died. When I was 8 I had to get up at 4 a.m. to sell papers to earn money for my breakfast. After the eighth grade I continued my studies at night school, working daytimes for a judge. I had always wanted to be an attorney, so the judge loaned me law books and helped me over the rough spots.

"I had worked ten years for the C. P. & A. Railroad when the explosion occurred, and only a year and a half later when I was running the store from my wheel chair, another explosion took place in the basement. Fortunately the only damage done was to property that time."

One cannot help feeling this man's boundless vitality, enthusiasm and courage as he talks, his hands expressive and strong, his blue eyes lighting up with sincerity, and frequently twinkling with humor. He is always just coming into his office, just hurriedly driving away, or busily holding court, taking phone calls, and writing messages on his memorandum. Even to pin this soul of activity down long enough to obtain an interview is quite a feat.

When he was outlining his daily schedule, he told of an average day's work as casually as you or I would say, "Yesterday I washed the car."

"I always get up at 6 o'clock," he said. "Come here and attend to my cases before noon. I spend afternoons at Township Park, and after dinner I usually spend three or four hours studying law. I go to bed at 11:30 or 12 o'clock. At intervals throughout the day I drink my usual nine cups of coffee."

His wife, his 22-year-old daughter and his 25-year-old son are quite accustomed not to see much of him. Although he enjoys going to movies, he seldom gets much opportunity with such a self-imposed schedule. His family realizes that he finds as much excitement and pleasure in work as most men find in their hobbies and leisure pastimes.

Despite his interest in the man who is down, he states in brisk terms that he has no sympathy for the person who lets a bad break or two keep him licked. In fact, his theory of what a little ambition and work can do for a man has caused him to carry the principle to the point where he comes into conflict with his doctors.

Always they are telling him not to attempt so much, but he laughs and keeps right on—proving that some men exist who can take defeat, mold it in their strong hands, and return it to the dealer. Life, in a new shape, with a new covering—the shining coat of success.

(15)

A young man noticed a fleet of grocery trucks bearing the sign of the owner's store. He interviewed the grocer and obtained facts that he was confident would interest other merchants. Looking over the trade publications on the grocer's desk, he found that the retailer was a member of the association that published one of the journals. He wrote the article to appeal particularly to association members and, since the magazine used many illustrations, sent five gloss pictures to be reproduced as halftones.

YOUR DELIVERY TRUCK . . . MAKE IT BUILD SALES *

BY JACK HAND

A few years ago someone invented an advertising device which hung on a string in a grocery store doorway, and moved abruptly up into the view of the customer when the door was opened. It was a simple little gadget, but it was good advertising, because it moved, and the motion caught the eye of the customer. The same principle—motion—is used by the nation's greatest advertisers today. These moving signs are called "spectaculars" and they are the most effective outdoor medium known to the advertising profession.

The individual grocerman himself has a valuable "spectacular" and a very economical one. It is his delivery truck, an advertising medium with motion and with a circulation even larger than the newspaper or the outdoor sign.

At least four or five hours a day your delivery truck is out on the streets, moving from one end of the community to another, stopping, starting, mingling with traffic, not only on the busy streets but on the streets of residential districts where signs are not ordinarily allowed.

But like any other advertisement, your truck may be effective and pull customers, or it can do your business more harm than good. One NROG member in the middle west who calls his store the "Diamond Grocery" bought a new truck five or six years ago. The first couple of years, while his truck was new, customers were attracted to his store by just that advertising. But as the truck got older, he noticed that these new customers weren't as numerous as before. Last year he bought a new, good looking truck and, with an almost startling suddenness, the records showed that new customers were again numbering among the Diamond Grocery's patrons.

Many grocers have customers on their delivery lists who may never actually visit the store more than once or twice a year—some who may never have been inside the grocery store where they buy their foodstuffs. Their only contact with the store is through a friend who recommends the grocer to the customer—and incidentally, the customer to the grocer—and through the truck which comes each day with the groceries. The impression they have of

* Reprinted by permission of *The Co-Operative Merchandiser.*

your truck is bound to be the impression they have of your store. A modern truck, a modern store. A clean and attractive truck, a clean and attractive store. But, a rattling, dirty, ill-kept truck leaves a feeling that the store is likewise unclean and poorly managed.

That is why the wise grocer has a new looking and modern truck. It is his contact with the customer—a sort of trademark that the customer comes to recognize.

Naturally, a policy of a new truck every year might be a hard one to live up to, in some cases. The depreciation on commercial vehicles for the first year is about 50 per cent. For two years it is approximately 60 per cent. At the end of four years your truck still has a trade-in value of nearly 40 per cent of its original cost.

During those last two years the upkeep has been considerably higher; new piston rings; perhaps a cylinder reboring; possibly a new transmission, for deliveries stop and go a lot; certainly new tires. All in all, you would have been better off to trade it in at the end of the first or second year, for a new truck with newer, more effective advertising power, and with less upkeep!

Most grocers figure the cost of delivery at no more than 2 per cent of their credit business—about 1 per cent of their entire turnover. So the delivery truck, serving its double duty as a customer service and an advertising medium, is mighty cheap advertising expense. You might as well make the most of it.

But, if you can't afford a new truck every year with your present business, you can at least afford a new paint job. Trucks become marred and rusty more quickly than passenger cars. They spend too much time in operation to avoid wear and tear on the finish, and too much time in traffic to avoid all minor accidents. Their all-weather, all-season use is bound to result in dull finish, rust, and tarnish.

A professional auto trimmer will paint your truck for $35 to $40 and, although you could do it yourself, the professional job will be worth the difference in cost. The auto trimmer knows the tricks of his trade. He knows how to cover rust spots so the paint will stick, and how to remove small dents. He is equipped with sprays and brushes to give you a paint job that looks factory made. Nothing gives the notion of cheapness to a truck more quickly than a homemade-looking finish. Almost better to leave it dingy and rusty!

Color, in the advertising your delivery trucks offer you, is just as important as color in other outdoor advertisements. More grocers buy black trucks every year than any other color. The streets are filled with black sedan deliveries and, although a sedan delivery draws more attention than a passenger car, remember, in buying or painting your truck that some distinctive color will attract more attention than black. The NROG colors of cream and green, either for the entire body or for decoration and emblem, could be used and be just that much more of an advertisement.

Above all, never re-letter a truck without a complete new paint job, unless, as is very infrequent, the old finish can be made to look decent with a good polishing. If a shiny, modern, new lettering is framed by a marred, dull finish, people will be more likely to notice and remember the paint job, and wonder if your store also needs paint.

The sign painter to whom you take your truck for lettering will have a variety of types of letters to show you. Never stand close to a sign to judge its legibility or attractiveness, but step back from the samples and pick a type of letter that is easily read at a quick glance—one that is as modern as you want your store to be.

Just as important as the paint job or the lettering or the newness of your truck from the standpoint of advertising is its conduct on the streets. You, yourself, are annoyed by a noisy driver with bad street manners, sounding his horn unnecessarily, or a reckless one speeding down narrow streets, darting in and out of traffic, stopping at stop-and-go lights with a screeching of tires, or a thoughtless one blocking driveways and parking haphazardly.

Your deliveryman should remember that the pedestrian, the motorist, the taxi or bus passenger, all are prospective customers—or perhaps already patronize your stores. He should be careful to be courteous at all times. The pedestrian that he narrowly misses as he hurries away with the green light may be the best account you have, and he may stop buying from you if one of your trucks causes him sufficient annoyance. The driver of the car whose fender your truck nicks may be the husband of a woman who is serving your groceries on the table he is going home to. And when he tells her that the nick on the fender was caused by "that damnable Smith Grocery truck" she may call another grocer tomorrow.

A fellow member of yours in NROG has operated two twin trucks for over five years, has traded them in every other year, and has had them repainted the odd year. He has realized an annual increase in business from the time he started using modern delivery trucks. In those five years his business has gone up 55 per cent. In the last year his increase has been 18 per cent. Since January of the year just passed this grocer has gained 36 new, and steady, every-day customers. Some of these customers he has never seen—they have never been to his store. But every day he sends his store out to them, in the form of a neat, well lettered truck. The old customers stick and the new ones keep coming, because this grocer shows the customers a sample of his fine, modern store when he sends a fine, modern truck to their homes with quality merchandise.

(16)

A student's hobby supplied the idea; her familiarity with literature and her knowledge of the value of psychological appeals enabled her to write an interesting lead. Her ability to interview, to write enthusiastically, and to slant accurately resulted in the following article. Halftones of Orchesis members rehearsing a dance and a portrait study of the interviewee were almost as interesting as the article.

DANCING TOWARD CAP AND GOWN *

How Margaret H'Doubler Made Dance a Part of Education

BY FANNIE MUIR TURNBULL

* * * "I see America dancing," Walt Whitman sang years ago. Could he step into the colleges of America today he would find his prophecy coming true.

Rising in the Middle West, in Wisconsin, and sweeping out across America to California, to Texas, to Massachusetts, the philosophy and technique of dance education developed by Professor

* Reprinted by permission of *Dance*.

Margaret N. H'Doubler at the University of Wisconsin holds its pioneer place against the European and Eastern ideas which have pushed after it as firmly as Whitman could have asked.

Education is much like the building of an art form. Ideally it develops all the possibilities latent in man, both of his soul and of his body, so that he may unfold freely and fully. In the teaching of dance, perhaps more than in the teaching of any other art form, these possibilities come closest to realization since it involves both mental and physical growth.

But for many years the only university in America to recognize this fundamental urge to movement was the University of Wisconsin, where Margaret H'Doubler pioneered.

In the twenty years since the first classes were scheduled, the dance philosophy as well as the external teaching forms developed at Wisconsin have spread like oil into both educational and professional dance fields.

Today, graduates are teaching in nineteen different states, Orchesis groups have been organized in most of the larger colleges and universities, and a summer school session at Wisconsin under Margaret H'Doubler has come to mean one of the greatest incentives to her work that any dance instructor can have.

The start of Miss H'Doubler's new educational theories in dance was quite accidental. "Basketball was my passion," she confesses, laughing. The sheer coordinated motor joy of the game appealed to her to teach, and dance was farthest from the thoughts of the young graduate in biology.

But Blanche Trilling, director of the women's physical education department then as now, was out of patience with old, artificial dance forms. She suggested that Miss H'Doubler spend her graduate study at Columbia looking for something to take its place.

Unenthusiastic at first, Miss H'Doubler went East in 1916. Except in a few instances she could find nothing but ballet training offered. Through contact with Gertrude Colby, the late Bird Larson and Alys Bentley, who taught music through the aid of movement, she caught some glimpses, but nowhere was there a sound philosophy for cutting away from the old formal, five-positioned technique.

What efforts were being made, as in the case of Isadora Duncan's followers, were cultish or blindly imitative of personalities. There was no medium of expression for the individual.

Deciding that at least she was learning what not to do, Miss H'Doubler did research in anthropology and art history to learn the development of the art impulses of groups and individuals through the ages, and to add to her previous knowledge of anatomy, kinesiology, philosophy and biology.

In 1917 she returned to the University of Wisconsin to teach what her pupils thought a very queer kind of dancing. But these "guinea-pig" students soon became enthusiastic and carried their interest into other classes on the campus. Faculty members in other departments became interested and informal discussion-recitals grew up, where the students danced and the instructors talked over each problem from the point of view of their own branch of education.

As an educational field the dance is not concerned with the theatre, but with the individual student, creating a balance between his inner and outer expression. The stress upon the manufacture of "concert dancers" which has cursed dance studios for years has never been felt at Wisconsin. Margaret H'Doubler says:

"The dance of a student may not be good from the standpoint of artistic perfection, but it is her own. Psychologically speaking, her creation may answer as great a need for expression as that of a concert dancer.

"In our schools we may not be able to reach the highest artistic perfection, but by holding to high amateur standards there can be developed keen artistic integrity, and the appreciation essential to the art of those who are the greater artists. We can develop intelligent appreciators who are artists by avocation."

On these principles—that dance education to be vital and not superficially imitative must spring from the experience of each individual: emotional, intellectual and physical—is based the whole organization of dance instruction at Wisconsin.

"Man fashions as he knows," explains Miss H'Doubler; "he is true to his particular stage of development."

There are three of these stages: the first primitive, child stage, emotional and formless, but genuine and potentially good; second, the discovering and experimenting stage in which form often obscures the spontaneity; and the third stage, psychologically mature, technically perfect so that technique may be forgotten, capable of the widest communication.

The major course for women is an eclectic one, since artistic integrity as well as mastery of movement must be developed and it covers a wide academic field. But beyond the curriculum lie deeper teaching aspects, those aiding the student to construct her own pattern of personality, individually determined by the ideal of the sort of self into which one wants to grow.

This personality-growth is just as important as the achievement of an art form, according to Miss H'Doubler, and is reached in the same way. The sources of personality are three, the emotions through which we feel, the intellect by which we clarify, the physical body through which we express ourselves. Personality becomes the expressive total of these three energies.

The body becomes the perfect expressive agent for personality through motor integrity, the complete comprehension and command of the fundamentals of movement. To every experience there is a motor phase, be it catching a street-car or balancing a tea cup. That is what gives dance its hold on man.

Visiting dancers broaden the teaching scope in addition to the staff work given under Miss H'Doubler and under Elna Mygdal and Beatrice Hellebrandt, both graduates of the department. Miss Hellebrandt's position is unusual, her special function being the correlation of dance and music. Such dancers as Harald Kreutzberg, who has taught classes two years in succession during his Madison visits, Shan-Kar, Ted Shawn and Bertha Ochsner, a graduate of Wisconsin in 1919, have been brought to Madison by the dance department and the Wisconsin Union.

Nor is instruction limited either to the dance majors or to women. The spacious dance studio has room for men and women whose campus interests are as diversified as law, journalism and home economics. Under Elna Mygdal they learn better coordination through use of their own bodies, and gain a satisfying appreciation of the dances of others that comes when the little Cinderella of the senses, the kinesthetic one, is also given a chance to grow.

Daily classes are much too short for the rapid advancement many students desire, so Junior Orchesis meets once a week to take care of the request for an intermediate technique class where step and rhythmic patterns, analysis of music, improvisation and elementary choreography can be worked out.

Orchesis itself is the next step, an informal group without pin or pledging, the idea of which has spread from Wisconsin into colleges throughout the country. Knit only by the common interest of its members in dance, it has a high technical standard for entrance requirements, including the presentation of two original dance compositions.

Having proved her technical right to belong, each Orchesis member is given opportunity to create other dances for herself and to receive competent criticism on them. All types of subject matter, evolving from the diverse backgrounds of the students, find expression, from satire to tragedy according to the mastery of her medium possessed by the student.

Improvisation is continually encouraged. Miss H'Doubler explains it as an index to the individual's development, and a pleasurable experience, a sort of free-wheeling of the coordinated mind and body.

Through this method of teaching there is no fear of forgetting on a program. Always there will be something to take the place of the forgotten motion,—something, moreover, equally good, arising at the moment out of kinesthetic memory.

The so-called natural dance has no place in this scheme, however, says Miss H'Doubler. It has not been disciplined toward perfected movement. It may arise from the laws of the individual's own body as developed during her life time, but it is not according to the physiological laws of our structure which should form the groundwork for all expressive motion.

From the students' own dances, and problems specially presented by the instructors, grows the public presentation, Dance Drama, given each Spring at Wisconsin.

Though in a sense a culmination of the year's work, it is not a goal in itself. The students do not exist through the winter simply for the opportunity of being seen publicly in the Spring. Rather, Dance Drama is a sort of personal check-up, an opportunity to see both one's faults and excellencies and to progress from them.

It offers another line of development in the educative process whose highest aim Margaret H'Doubler defines as the achievement "through action and experience, through knowledge and participation, of the freest, fullest and most fearless unfoldment of the individual."

(17)

With an aptitude for working with figures and uncovering elusive facts from every possible source, a student, for his first article, wrote about fads that sweep the country. He secured snapshots of the fadists indulging in the craze of the moment. The article was used on the first page of the magazine section along with several colored drawings, made by the staff artist, depicting the "bees in the bonnets."

BEES IN UNCLE SAM'S BONNET! *

Recalling How Mah Jongg Swept U. S.,
And Rise and Fall of Pee Wee Golf,
Jigsaw Puzzles and Knock, Knocks,
Who Knows What the Next National
Craze to Strike Us Will Be?

By C. Carlton Brechler

Back in 1924 you were spending your evenings with your friends matching up the winds, seasons, characters, and dragons of Mah Jongg.

You abandoned the movies in 1930 to amuse yourself in a nearby vacant lot with a golf club, braving water and sandtraps, slicing around boulders, ricocheting off of backboards, and putting through pipes and tree trunks.

In 1933 you sat up until the early hours of the morning trying to put a 500-piece jigsaw puzzle together in less time than it took the neighbor from whom you borrowed it.

"Faith, hope, and charity" was your motto in 1935, and for a while each mail brought you another chain letter or two.

And the next year you were all acting even more strangely. You started out by singing a queer song which you may remember as beginning: "You push the first valve down." From there you proceeded to do strange things with your hands and fingers, and then, looking at your neighbor, asked with a very pleased expression on your face, "What's this?"

More recently you went in for Monopoly, a real estate game in which you bought, mortgaged, sold, and rented lots and houses, and counted out paper money until you were blue in the face—yet you enjoyed it.

* Reprinted by permission of the Detroit *News* Feature Section.

THEN 'KNOCK! KNOCK!'

When next observed you were singing another song, this one entitled "Knock Knock, Who's there?"; and everywhere you went you would repeat those two magic words, "Knock-Knock," and try one of your newest puns.

Yes, you have been doing some mighty strange things. Mah Jongg was an ancient Chinese gambling game. Jigsaw puzzles were for children and mental cases. Chain letters were mathematically impossible. And most of the others were absolutely senseless.

Yet there is one satisfaction; you weren't the only one. I was doing them, too, and so were millions of others the country over.

* * *

At the time that you were playing Mah Jongg, thousands of others in the country were not, merely because manufacturers could not work fast enough to supply them with games.

During the period that you were sitting up nights fitting together little pieces of cardboard, 100,000,000 other jigsaw puzzles were also spread out on the card tables of the land.

When you were most interested in minature golf, they were setting up about 800 courses a day in the United States.

And when you bought your copy of "The Music Goes 'Round and Around," they were selling at the rate of a copy a minute.

These are all members of a strange category of phenomena which prevail in America, and are known as "national crazes." There is not a great deal of explanation of why we have such crazes. After the ball once starts rolling, we know that it is a case of "monkey sees, monkey does." But no one knows what the next craze will be; no manufacturer is prepared for the next one; and when it is going at high speed, no one is capable of judging whether it is at its height and will tumble soon, or whether it will continue to scale new heights.

RICHES AND RUIN

Thus it is that national crazes develop into mushroom industries which surprise many by making them wealthy overnight, at the same time that they ruin many others. They suddenly put a great strain upon the manufacturers in a certain field by making unheard of demands, and after the manufacturers are finally organized and producing at peak efficiency, the demand suddenly dwindles to nothing.

Previous to the American adoption of Mah Jongg, the Chinese had for centuries been making sets by hand for the limited number of Chinese who could afford them. Then unexpectedly, and much to their astonishment, orders began to pour in from America at such a rate that they could not fill, in a decade, the orders they received within a few days.

"No can do," said the Chinese as they laid down their tools.

IN PRODUCTION

But American industrialists got behind them, and soon with a little organization, and much persuasion, Mah Jongg sets were pouring out at a reasonable rate of speed.

There was sufficient bamboo to supply their needs, but the ivory ran out. At first the shin bones of Chinese calves were used in place of ivory, but the supply was far from sufficient to supply an American craze. Orders and reorders in 10,000 lots continued, and the beef packers of Chicago, Omaha, and Kansas City came to the rescue and shipped tons of shin bones to China.

From coast to coast, and throughout Europe for that matter, everyone was playing Mah Jongg, and paying absurd prices for sets. Since the demand was so great, and since many were very elaborate, $12 sets were common, and $40 ones were not at all uncommon. But suddenly, as swiftly as it came, Mah Jongg was gone and forgotten.

The president of one of America's leading game manufacturing companies says Mah Jongg is today coming back. Maybe in a year or so we will dust off our old Mah Jongg sets and have another try at the game.

The rise of miniature golf is a romance of American business. In the fall of 1929 this country had been plunged into one of the severest depressions in all history; but while great enterprises were failing, and others were glad to keep out of the red, the miniature golf industry was born and flourished—many of the courses earning 300 per cent a month.

During the winter, peewee golf was a toy. By mid-summer it was a big business and a social problem. It stood out as the one shining success story in a year of gloom—1930.

$250,000,000 INVESTED

Miniature golf was probably the most intensive national craze this country has as yet gone through. Before it died out, close to $250,000,000 was invested in courses and spent by players—in spite of the depression. Official Government statistics published in about the middle of the summer of 1930 reported the establishment of 25,000 courses, representing an investment of $125,000,000.

Every vacant lot became a golf course. Within a radius of four blocks in New York City, there were 22 courses at one time, and at the peak of the craze more than 5,000 miniature courses were laid out in a single week.

Three plants in the country were manufacturing miniature golf equipment. One of these employed 200 men and occupied five acres of floor space. These manufacturers sold and installed complete courses at about $4,500 apiece.

A certain tennis court owner in New York was extremely reluctant to replace his courts with a golf course. He was finally convinced, however, and shortly afterwards he wrote the manufacturer reporting that he had cleared $1,500 the first week, and that even then he had to turn away almost 100 customers a night.

* * *

In 1933 the country had a "run" on jig saw puzzles. This craze got started when some enterprising fellow began punching puzzles out of cardboard instead of cutting them out of ply wood with fine saws as had been the custom. The idea rapidly took on the form of national lunacy as advertisers began sending in orders for as many as 1,000,000 puzzles at a time to give away or use as premiums, and as manufacturers began putting weekly puzzles on sale at all news stands.

Within a couple of months civilized America was demanding 10,000,000 new puzzles each week, and some 300 firms had rushed in to meet the demand. Three of these firms punched out almost 70,000,000 puzzles during the craze, and another claimed to have produced 1,000,000 a week at its highest point.

10,000,000 A WEEK

It is probably safe to say that between September, 1932, and March, 1933, the producers manufactured nearly 100,000,000 jig saw puzzles in the United States.

The jig saw puzzle mania collapsed the same as all the others had, leaving thousands of unsold puzzles in warehouses. On the whole, however, more persons were satisfied at the close of this craze than at the close of many others. Industry had been aided, advertisers had found a suitable medium, movie stars had cashed in for one cent a puzzle where their likenesses were used, and millions of hands had been put to work.

THE CHAIN LETTERS

You were probably introduced to your first chain letter in 1935 when you received one in the mail.

You may remember that it contained the names of five persons, and instructed you to make five copies of the letter and mail them to the friends to whom you wished prosperity.

"In omitting the top name, send that person 10 cents as a charity donation. In time as your name leaves the top, you should receive 15,625 letters with donations amounting to $1,562.50," the letter would read. In closing it admonished you to "Have faith, the faith your friends have, and this chain will not be broken."

MASS HYSTERIA

It was with the advent of the dollar letter that this scheme took on the form of mass hysteria. In many Middle Western cities chain letter "factories" were set up, employing a staff of clerks and notary publics, and inaugurating a type of dollar letter which eliminated the necessity of selling the letters to your friends. If you purchased one of these letters and had your signature duly notarized, the "agency" undertook to sell your two letters to the next two customers in line, and their four letters to the next four in line, ad infinitum.

One of these "agencies" claimed to have mailed more than $15,-000. Outside the building would be a line extending for blocks. You could explain to any of these persons standing in line that 15,000,000 persons would have to follow him before he could receive any return. But he would continue to wait, undaunted by mathematics, willing to take a chance at getting the $1,024 which theory had promised him.

* * *

"The Music Goes 'Round and Around" was merely a foolish song originally featured by a couple of musicians in a night club orchestra. Yet it took the country by storm. They sold 45,000 copies of the song the first three weeks, and later were selling a copy a minute.

A tie, hat, dress, sofa, movie, and cigaret holder were named after the song. It could be heard over the radio once every five minutes, and one station, WHN, played it 28 times on one all-night broadcast in response to 428 requests.

But the song not only died out soon, but fell completely out of the favor of the public which by this time could no longer stand to listen to the piece.

BOOM IN MONOPOLY

Monopoly hardly attained true national craze proportions. There was a sudden demand for the game which made it impossible at times to obtain sets in several of the large cities.

Handies, the "What's this?" game you play with your hands, probably was the most foolish, had the quickest rise and spread, and the earliest downfall of any of the recent crazes. Much of its popularity and the speed with which it traveled is due to mentions by national columnists, the offering of prizes for original handies, and a book by Milt Gross entitled "What's this?"

KNOCK-KNOCK

Knock-Knocks revived the good old indoor sport of punning. National columnists did a lot to spread this craze, as did the many newspapers that offered prizes for winning puns.

The idea was originated and popularized by a dance tune and capitalized upon by advertisers, Hollywood and the radio. A typical knock-knock pun would run like this:

"Knock Knock!"

"Who's there?"

"Tarzan!"

"Tarzan who?"

"Tarzan stripes forever."

People soon became tired of this foolish craze, however, as evidenced by this one:

"Amsterdam who?"

"Amsterdam tired of these knock-knocks I could scream!"

WHAT'S NEXT?

This national whim reached the point where one columnist described it as "a devastating mania and mental disease." The Columbia Broadcasting Company banned the song from all sustaining programs, newspapers stopped offering their cash prizes, and very quietly the knock-knock craze drifted off to nowhere.

And that is a brief survey of the high points of our national crazes during the past dozen years—each one evidencing a slight touch of national insanity. I have not gone back to mention ping pong, nor have I even touched upon backgammon, crossword puzzles, imp, "Where's Elmer," "Little Audrey," "I'm in business," and a dozen others.

What will be the next craze? Only time will tell. Jig saw puzzles or Mah Jongg may have a return engagement, some new game may suddenly rise, or perhaps some old game such as dominoes may at last come into its own. There is plenty of opportunity in this field for a clever and shrewd business man to make his fortune within a few months.

(18)

An antique shop that a young woman passed daily on her way to class suggested to her a "tip" on collecting early American glass. Reading all available material gave the writer the necessary background to interview antique collectors and the curator of the museum. She received permission to photograph six historic pressed glass cup plates in the museum, which made a most attractive halftone in the magazine section on "Glass and China."

LET'S COLLECT EARLY AMERICAN GLASS *

Some Tips to the Beginner

BY MABEL WALKER

That blue hobnail sauce dish which Cousin Sue gave your mother when you were visiting the old family home last summer is a thrilling clue to a first class collecting hobby. Or perhaps the gift

* Reprinted by permission of *Hobbies—The Magazine for Collectors.*

was an old pressed glass tumbler with the barley pattern, or a lacy glass cup plate that has interested you in finding a complete set or certain occasional pieces which you need for that space in the corner cupboard, or window shelf to complete a decorative unit. Some collect old things because they are old, but whatever the motive, you will collect more intelligently and derive greater enjoyment from it if you know something more than surface facts.

Glass making is the first recorded industry to be established in what is now the United States. The London Company brought "eight skillful workmen from foreign parts", to teach the colonists how to make glass, tar and pitch, and soap ashes in a glass house established in Jamestown in 1608.

Glass is so commonplace in the twentieth century every day life that many rarely stop to think of the romance inseparably linked with its history. The small glass objects found in the tombs of the Pharaohs are a link in the history of the plate glass window of the twentieth century, just as are the opal glass plate, the blue hobnail bowl, the pressed glass covered dish in Westward Ho pattern, which you want to match or add to your collection. There is still a challenge to one's imagination in the modern factories which specialize in such varieties of glass as unshatterable; rough and ribbed, bullet proof, safety glass that can be rolled up like a rubber mat, and spun glass that can be used in making dresses. The modern industry of glass making was enjoying a vigorous youth in the days of Stiegel and Sandwich, whose names have come to be synonymous with early American glass.

In the making of glass, America is the "heir of all the ages," for the first glass factories brought with them information, as well as skilled workers from Europe. As early as 1739, and earlier, the slogan "Made in America" could be applied to glass, since at that time the industry began in earnest at the Wistar factory in New Jersey.

A beginning collector may think that early glass to be of the type desired must be a product of Wistar, Stiegel, or Sandwich since these three were the earliest and best known manufacturers of glass. But over one hundred other glass factories were in operation before 1850. This ware went into peddlers' carts for distribution to remote farms and villages, to ornament the corner cupboard or the "sitting-room" whatnot. Perhaps your Cousin Sue's mother bought a set of dishes from Johnny Peddler in exchange for a basket of fruit, or a dozen hens, and this same piece is now the leaven in the hobby that will cause your collection to grow into a thing of beauty and permanent joy.

"But how shall I know that I am collecting the early glass and not some modern imitation?" is a query asked by the beginning collector. In the first place early American glass for household use was manufactured in two phases; one for table, included pitchers, sugar bowls, salt cellars, sweet meat dishes, cup plates, drinking glasses and similar things, while the other represented utensils for kitchen and pantry such as glass for canning and preserving fruit, and pans for cooling milk and raising cream for butter and cheese.

Tests for identifying old glass have been in the popular notion such factors as the pontil mark, the resonance or ring of glass, signs of wear, family history, and touch, but glass can not always be dated by any of these because marks may be duplicated, signs of wear may be effected, and no glass works held a monopoly on resonance.

A few general hints of help in identifying old glass are that it is seldom true to form. It is brilliant and full of life, and has a mellowness just as old wood acquires a patina. Flaws in form do not mean chips or cracks. Old clear glass is never entirely colorless. There is no positive way of telling when and where all pieces were made because there were migratory workers who carried designs from one factory to the other, and also carried their own pontil rods.

Pressed glass is always smooth on the inside, since the design for the pattern is cut into the mold and is thus on the outside of the piece. This glass was produced in such quantities that the term "early Woolworth" has been applied to it, but there is no need to apologize for the quantity which was produced from 1837 to 1864. The perfection of the process of making pressed glass rather than blown glass was due to the ingenuity of an American who began experimenting as early as 1820. It is true that the art of pressing glass into molds was known to the ancient Egyptians, and that machine pressed glass was known in England, but the credit for perfecting the process goes to a Yankee. By 1840 factories for making pressed glass ware sprang up like mushrooms in the various states, and thus was distributed the great quantities of pressed glass table ware which collectors today seek when matching old pieces.

The recognition of glass patterns is an assurance that the beginning collectors like to feel. This recognition can come only through seeing the pieces, or studying very good photographic plates through conversations with informed persons, and reading from reliable sources of information at every opportunity. Though we may not be able to tell positively when and where patterns were made there are certain available patterns which can be identified. In the pressed glass the Bellflower is one of the first patterns in glass tableware. Many other patterns are accurately described with accompanying photographic plates in "Early American Pressed Glass" by Ruth Webb Lee, which makes a valuable reference for the collector, since there are more available patterns in pressed glass than in blown glass due to the invention of the machine method of pressing glass.

The Dewdrop group of patterns, Hobnail, Opaque White glass, and frosted glass are popular patterns for collecting. The Dewdrop patterns which appeared in the 60's and were produced until the 80's are unsurpassed in duration and popularity. This group is characterized by the entire dish being covered with small pointed hobnails.

Dewdrop and Star, Plain Dewdrop, and Popcorn are variations of the pattern. Large numbers of plates in various sizes, goblets, sauce dishes, honey dishes, and bread plates are found in these patterns in both colored glass, and clear glass, blue yellow and amber being the most used colors.

The Hobnail is similar to the Dewdrop pattern, the Pointed Hobnail being the earliest in this group, and is credited to a factory near New York City during the late 60's. The hobnails have blunted rounded ends in the patterns except the pointed, and pieces are found in brilliant clear amber as well as blue. In matching Hobnail sets one should compare either the top edge or the base. Some of the pieces were made with ball feet, and were heavy in weight, brilliant and sparkling.

Flattened Hobnail is a later pattern made in the usual pieces. The Opal Hobnail is generally of a yellowish tinge, or blue, and is chiefly made in one of the four types—frilled edge, round standing on three ball feet, square standing on square feet, or octagonal. The Hobnail pattern was widely copied by different factories in a number of variations. The frosted type in plain color, as well as in combination of colors was made later than the opal variety

Opaque White glass is an available type in a variety of bowls, plates, cups, and other pieces. Plates are found with plain and lacy edges, or open edged designs which are also applied to other pieces. The American Opaque glass generally gives forth a ruddy glow when held against the light; it is generally thinner than the English made glass and is extremely fragile, and takes on a bluish tinge around the edge. Old time trade names of this glass were *white enamel, opaque white, opal, opalescent,* and *alabaster.* The term white glass is confusing for in some of the old factories the term meant milk white glass, while in others white meant clear glass or crystal. This type glass was probably made before the War of 1812, and by 1870 was quite popular. Milk White glass is known to have been made at the Sandwich factories, and since it was a popular type it was also made by other pressed glass factories.

Collectors of early glass ware find a variety of pieces in which to be interested, but two which have furnished much interest have been cup plates and salt cellars. The little cup plates are chiefly of two kinds—those bearing historical and commemorative designs, and those having conventional decorative patterns. In size the cup plates are two and three-quarters to three and three-quarters inches in diameter. The true cup plate has a flat bottomed surface, while other small occasional plates were larger and not flat on the bottom. The original purpose of the cup plate was to keep tea from dripping from the cup on to the table top or cloth, because it was the custom to drink one's tea from the saucer. Tea cups did not have handles, and it was impossible to hold the hot cup in the hand and drink from it, so the little cup plate solved the problem of the dripping cup. An old workman's record shows that a man and a boy could make 1600 of these little plates in a day, which fact is a joy to collectors of these fascinating pieces. The first plates out of the molds were sharp and clear in outline, while the last were softer as the outlines in the molds became softer and blurred. This has caused a discussion as to the value of the first or the last made, but there is not an agreed opinion.

Cup plates, hobnail sauce dishes, opal glass bowls, or any of the other pieces of old glass used for table ware may provide the exact fascination needed to build up a set or to accumulate occasional pieces that will repay their cost in the romance of their past.

(19)

Even arguments with one's friends may be stimulating to a writer. A young woman had become a bit irritated in a discussion on correct posture. She decided to interview the professor of the corrective class in physical education to find out how she could improve her own. It occurred to her that if she was interested, wouldn't hundreds of others be? The professor suggested a list of books to give the young writer background, and asked her to come back for the interview after she was better informed. She developed it along the lines of a utility article, but with the point of view of how-not-to-do. The article sounded "preachy," because she had written it in the second person. In revising the manuscript, she injected a slightly humorous angle to detract from the dictatorial tone. She had six silhouette drawings made of correct and incorrect postures to illustrate the points she set forth in the article.

IT'S THE WAY YOU WALK *

Correcting Faulty Posture Takes a Certain Amount of Time, But Luckily There's Nothing Hard About It

BY JANE PRIESTLY

Little things can determine another's opinion of you: the way you do your hair, the tone of your voice, your dress and—the way you walk.

The next time you find yourself waiting in a hotel lobby or a railroad station, look at the people around you. Notice the ones that you like, that seem alive. They walk firmly, with their heads up and their shoulders straight; and when they sit down they don't sprawl all over the chair.

Then look at the others. Here comes poor Miss Question-mark. Her eyes are fixed on the floor just ahead of her, and her neck and shoulders are pulled forward, leaving her feet dragging behind. Across the room sits Miss Debutante, her weight centered on the middle of her spine, her chin on her collar bone. When she walks

* Reprinted by permission of *Hygeia*.

she drifts along like a weeping willow. Clickety-click, Mrs. Fuss-and-bustle trots past you, the direct antithesis of Miss Debutante. Her shoulders are thrown back too far, and her spine curves in at the waist, giving her hips the appearance of a tea tray.

Now look at yourself. Do you walk and stand like some one you'd like to know? Are you living up to the smart new dress you plan to buy? Here are three simple tests by which to find out:

First, to learn whether you lean toward the Fuss-and-bustle type, try the back-to-the-wall test. Stand against a wall with your heels three or four inches away from it, and with the back of your head, your shoulders and your hips touching it. If your back is properly shaped there will be just room enough for some one to put a hand between the small of your back and the wall. If your back is too flat, as is Miss Debutante's, it will go against the wall almost all the way.

The second test will tell you where and whether you're out of line. Stand as straight as you can in a doorway, with your back against the corner of the jamb, and pull the door toward you until it touches you. If it touches your chin or nose first, your head and neck are too far forward. If it bumps against your stomach, your pelvis is tilted at the wrong angle, and you're probably hollow chested. Now pull yourself up until you occupy as little space as possible. This is correct posture, and the door will probably touch your chest first.

For the third test you will need a three-panel mirror. If there isn't one where you live, try the one at your favorite dress shop the next time you go. Stand in front of the mirror, and assume the best posture you know. Now look at yourself. Are your feet parallel? Do your ankles turn in? See whether your hips are in line with each other and whether your shoulders are the same height. Your arms should hang loosely, slightly bent, so that your hands are a little to the front.

Now fix the mirror so that without moving your head you can see yourself in profile. If you are standing as you should the tip of your ear, the point of your shoulder, your elbow and your ankle bone should be exactly in line. Look at your back. Does it seem to curve too much? Or do your shoulders curve forward so that you're slightly camel-backed like Miss Question-mark? Your neck should be straight and your chin down and in, not stretched out as if you were hearing the call of the wild.

If you have been honest with yourself in these tests, nine chances out of ten you have found at least one point that will bear improvement. Correcting faulty posture takes a certain amount of time, but luckily there's nothing hard about it.

The first thing you will want to know is how to assume correct posture. You should stand by the following six rules:

Keep your neck straight, so that it feels as if you were almost stretching the back of it.

Feel your chest come up and out between your shoulders.

Keep your shoulders down and back, but easy.

Keep your abdomen in.

Keep your knees straight, but don't lock them back.

Keep your feet pointed straight ahead with your weight over the middle of your foot, not on your heels.

When you walk, hold yourself just as when you stand, and use your whole foot for each step. Control your hips so that you won't wobble, and walk on one line rather than on two, to keep from swaggering. Let your arms swing freely. Try to transfer your weight smoothly from one foot to the other by pushing off forward from your big toe on each step.

When you sit, keep your head and chest up, your chin and stomach in. The hips, knees and ankles should be almost at right angles to one another.

Learning to practice good posture is half the battle. The other half is won by doing simple exercises for a few minutes every day. What did you find wrong with yourself in the tests?

If you were round-shouldered, here are two answers to the question: First, stand up as straight as you can, clasp your hands behind your back, and roll your shoulders back as far as you can. Then relax, and do it over again. Sitting down, clasp your hands on the back of your head, with your elbows back as far as they will go. Stretch upward, then extend your arms above your head, keeping them back. Relax, and repeat.

If your left shoulder is higher than the other, try this: Stand with your right hand on the base of your neck, your elbow back. Put your left hand on your hip, and bend your body to the left, pushing your right elbow up and back. Return to position, and try it again, but don't twist or let your hips swing to the right, because you won't use the right muscles if you do. If it's your right shoulder that's higher, just reverse the process.

Your back curves in too far? Then try standing as you did for the back-to-the-wall test. Now pull your back against the wall by contracting the muscles in your abdomen and pelvis. Try walking away from the wall while holding this postion.

Another one for your back is this: Lie on your back on the floor with your hands at your sides. Flatten your back as you did against the wall. Bend one knee up over your chest, straighten your leg upward, and lower it as slowly as you can, keeping your back flat and your knees straight. Then do it with the other leg. This is a good exercise for keeping the stomach flat, too, because it strengthens the abdominal muscles. Another exercise with similar effect is done lying in the same position. Raise and lower both legs at once without bending your knees. Do so as slowly as you can.

If your back is too flat, do this exercise instead: Lie prone on a table with the edge under your hips so that your legs hang down. Put your hands under your chin, keeping your neck straight and your elbows out to the sides. Now, by using only your back muscles, raise your legs and head simultaneously as high as you can, then relax. You won't get very far with this at first, but in time you'll be able to feel like a chair rocker.

Picking up marbles with your toes and walking on a straight line with your toes curled under as if holding marbles are two of the best exercises for keeping your arches high and your ankles straight.

Now suppose that you've been exercising faithfully, and you find your carriage positively regal. Keep it that way. You feel better, and you tire less easily, since your muscles are no longer being strained out of shape. You look better. You are graceful, and your clothes fit you twice as well. The way you walk, sit and stand is a little thing—unless you are Miss Question-mark or Miss Debutante or Mrs. Fuss-and-bustle.

(20)

Planning the questions carefully, cutting and running off 100 questionnaires (which she distributed to her classmates), and correlating the answers provided material for a student's first article. A clever line drawing of youngsters on their way to school with their books under their arms and a lad's dog following behind fitted the idea of the article admirably.

THEY GREW UP . . . *AND LIFE INSURANCE IS TAKING THEM ON* THROUGH COLLEGE *

A student's report of life insurance at work in a large middle-western university

BY BETTY BRYAN

I suppose that most fathers are thoroughly convinced of the value of a college education. They know that to young people it gives added breadth, vision, and assurance, through which their lives will be made richer.

In addition to these points they believe that it has an appreciable money value, that it decidedly increases the earning power of an individual and will bring greater material comfort.

Everett Lord, dean of College of Business Administration, Boston University, has made an impartial study of the subject, and his analysis fixes the average lifetime earnings of a college graduate above those of a high school graduate by $56,000. He has proven that the average man with only an elementary education must fight hard for a bare living, while the high school graduate never reaches the $3,000 a year level. On the other hand, he points out that the average college man's earnings go up and up until at the age of sixty-five, his yearly income is $6,000 and still rising.

Another educational analysis is that made of 31,991 persons listed in "Who's Who in America." Of this number 27,996 attended college, 2,230 had a high school education or equivalent, and 1,795 had only common school educations.

As the daughter of a life insurance man, I have heard all my life of the value of insurance. I know that I am in school on the funds secured by policy loans on my father's policies. Combining these two facts, it is only natural that one of my first reactions on entering a large middle western university was an active curiosity as to what effect the institution of life insurance might be showing in the lives of my fellow students.

* Reprinted by permission of *The Insurance Salesman.*

Casual conversations revealed so much interesting data, that the following brief questionnaire was submitted to one hundred of our students:

THEY GREW UP. *and life insurance is taking them on*

Through College

A student's report of life insurance at work in a large middle-western university

By BETTY BRYAN

I suppose that most fathers are thoroughly convinced of the value of a college education. They know that to young people it gives added breadth, vision, and assurance, through which their lives will be made richer.

In addition to these points they believe that it has an appreciable money value, that it decidedly increases the earning power of an individual and will bring greater material comfort.

Everett Lord, dean of College of Business Administration, Boston University, has made an impartial study of the subject, and his analysis fixes the average lifetime earnings of a college graduate above those of a high school graduate by $56,000. He has proven that the average man with only an elementary education must fight hard for a bare living, while the high school graduate never reaches the $3,000 a year level. On the other hand, he points out that the average college man's earnings go up and up until at the age of sixty-five, his yearly income is $6,000 and still rising.

Another educational analysis is that made of 31,991 persons listed in "Who's Who in America." Of this number 27,996 attended college, 2,230 had a high school education or equivalent, and 1,795 had only common school educations.

As the daughter of a life insurance man, I have heard all my life of the value of insurance. I know that I am in school on the funds secured by policy loans on my father's policies. Combining these two facts, it is only natural that one of my first reactions on entering a large middle western university was an active curiosity as to what effect the institution of life insurance might be showing in the lives of my fellow students.

Miss Bryan distributed questionnaires to 100 students of the university she attends in order to discover what percentage of them were attending school directly from the proceeds of life insurance.

Casual conversations revealed so much interesting data, that the following brief questionnaire was submitted to one hundred of our students.

Are you receiving your education through:

1. Proceeds of deceased father's or mother's policies.

2. Proceeds of matured endowment policy.

3. Money borrowed on policies of living parents.

4. Loans made from individuals on security of life insurance policy on the life of the student (student will pay after completion of education out of his salary and in case of death, the proceeds of the policy will pay, either by assignment or by beneficiary nomination).

Result of Survey

Three percent of the students interviewed were attending school by reason of proceeds of life insurance which had been carried by the deceased father or mother, where the insurance was taken with the specific purpose of providing funds for the education.

Seven percent were in school by reason of funds provided out of the proceeds of a matured endowment policy, either on the life of a parent or the student himself.

Eight percent of the students interviewed were attending school on funds procured by loans on living father's or mother's policies.

Three percent of the students who answered the questionnaire were in school by reason of loans that they had been able to secure from friends or relatives on security of their promise to repay funds advanced for their education out of earnings after said education was completed, backed up by a life insurance policy payable to the loaner, thus guaranteeing the payment of the loan in case of the death of the student before repayment.

The total of the preceding percentages reaches 21 percent, which indicates that 21 percent of the 100 students interviewed are attending school directly from the proceeds of life insurance. As the students interviewed were average young men and women, the responses to this questionnaire are reasonably representative for the entire student body.

The modern father may choose one of four means of planning ahead for his child's education. First, he can go ahead without planning and depend on his child to work his way through school, paying expenses out of his earnings. This has been done, but educators throughout the world have definitely advised against it; mainly because the earning of a university degree is, in itself, a serious undertaking, and the actual value of the person's education may be seriously affected by the time spent in earning his expenses.

(Continued on page 58)

FIG. 12. THE SIMPLE LINE DRAWING AIDED IN SELLING

Are you receiving your education through:

1. Proceeds of deceased father's or mother's policies.

2. Proceeds of matured endowment policy.
3. Money borrowed on policies of living parents.
4. Loans made from individuals on security of life insurance policy on the life of the student (student will pay after completion of education out of his salary and in case of death, the proceeds of the policy will pay, either by assignment or by beneficiary nomination).

Result of Survey

Three percent of the students interviewed were attending school by reason of proceeds of life insurance which had been carried by the deceased father or mother, where the insurance was taken with the specific purpose of providing funds for the education.

Seven percent were in school by reason of funds provided out of the proceeds of a matured endowment policy, either on the life of a parent or the student himself.

Eight percent of the students interviewed were attending school on funds procured by loans on living father's or mother's policies.

Three percent of the students who answered the questionnaire were in school by reason of loans that they had been able to secure from friends or relatives on security of their promise to repay funds advanced for their education out of earnings after said education was completed, backed up by a life insurance policy payable to the loaner, thus guaranteeing the payment of the loan in case of the death of the student before repayment.

The total of the preceding percentages reaches 21 percent, which indicates that 21 percent of the 100 students interviewed are attending school directly from the proceeds of life insurance. As the students interviewed were average young men and women, the responses to this questionnaire are reasonably representative for the entire student body.

The modern father may choose one of four means of planning ahead for his child's education. First, he can go ahead without planning and depend on his child to work his way through school, paying expenses out of his earnings. This has been done, but educators throughout the world have definitely advised against it; mainly because the earning of a university degree is, in itself, a serious undertaking, and the actual value of the person's education may be seriously affected by the time spent in earning his expenses.

Second, the father can, if he chooses, make no advance provision whatsoever, and depend entirely on current earnings to supply the necessary funds. This plan also may be carried out, but the average man's current earnings cannot supply college expenses without a great deal of inconvenience and very often lowering the standard of living in his home. Then again, sickness or death can prevent the carrying out of this idea.

Third, the father can gather the necessary money in a savings fund especially set aside for this purpose; but in all such funds, every emergency or need will prove a temptation that human nature will probably yield to and in the end there will not be any such fund.

Problem of Education

Fourth, a man can guarantee his child's education through life insurance. In addition to the means included in the questionnaire, regular educational policies are obtainable in many companies. These policies take care of the educational problem in a father's life either in whole or in part, making any proportion of the face value of the policy payable in convenient installments throughout the four year period. In case of the premature death of the father, these policies pay in installments of both principal and interest during his child's education.

More than ever it seems that the most valuable heritage that a parent can leave his child is a higher education. After the experiences of the depression and the terrific loss of capital, the majority of people agree that higher education is the one heritage that can be left for a son or daughter which cannot be dissipated, squandered, misappropriated, or lost.

When one thinks of the added joys and pleasures in life that are the result of a college education; of the increased earning capacity and the resulting independence, one wonders more and more why a larger number of parents do not avail themselves to the service of the life insurance companies, which seem to be the only source from which this service can surely be received.

(21)

A number of graduate students were relating methods of "cribbing" that they had observed at the colleges they attended before entering professional school. A student in feature writing was impressed by the interest of the undergraduates present. If they are so interested, why wouldn't others be, reasoned the embryo journalist. He looked about to see what publications were most read by his classmates. He interviewed a number of professors who previously had taught in smaller colleges, and thereby added to his store of material. Then he was confronted by the problem of illustrations. He could use drawings, but they would not be as convincing. A number of his classmates agreed to pose, and a fellow student taking photography snapped the pictures and developed and enlarged them. The editor purchased four of the six pictures and ran the article just as colleges across the land were giving final examinations. Proctors found the information given a real aid—which, of course, prevented the students' benefiting from the ideas if they had read the article.

STUDY OF COLLEGE CRIBBAGE *

Any dope can memorize Latin conjugations for an exam, whereas it takes a really brilliant student to figure out a new and foolproof way to cheat. Photography, psychology, and sheer stockings are utilized by the new-way cribbers. Cleaning your glasses is one way to jog a failing memory or a blank mind. Only one professor found the perfect system for foiling them all.

By James F. Scheer

Between sips of beer and bites of the hamburger sandwich, the boys "bull-session" about the student who tinkered for a few days inventing the "dummy watch" system of cheating rather than learn to conjugate his Spanish verbs.

With a semester's average slightly above failing, he knew he would have to "crib" if he wanted to pass; so he removed the intestines of his pocket watch, installed a small spool and connected it with the stem. On the spool he wound a tiny scroll bearing all

* Reprinted by permission of *Ken* and Mr. James Scheer.

the "tough" verb conjugations from *aprender* down through the alphabet.

Seated in the back of the room, he consulted his watch often, turning the stem and copying the necessary information. On the basis of his excellent exam paper his semester grade was raised to a "B."

Now the "dummy watch" method has gone professional. A student at a large eastern university manufactures wrist watch models for $35 apiece. Clients are glad to pay the price, for they understand what a difficult and tedious task it is to record a semester's outline of physics, or any other subject, on a tiny scroll. Because he practices the fine-brush technique, he can squeeze far more information in a limited space than can a penman or printer.

Most colleges and universities have at least one proctor who is suspicious that every exam-writer beneath the sweep of his eye is trying to cheat. When a certain instructor became particularly objectionable in this respect, a brilliant student in the class decided to cure him once and for all.

An important six weeks test came on the first day of April. Pencil in hand, the student kept looking at a watch held in the other. Eager to catch someone "cribbing," the instructor bounded down the aisle and pulled the watch from the fellow's hand. His face reddened like a ripe tomato when he saw the words written on the crystal: "April Fool."

Even that didn't end it. Within a few minutes the student was again glancing slyly at the timepiece. Thinking the prankster had played the trick as a part of "cribbing" strategy, the proctor hurried back to investigate.

Written on the crystal was: "Fooled again."

No matter how sound a "cribbing" system may be in theory, it sometimes slips up in practice, as a lazy student of physical geography found. Certain that knowledge of rainfall statistics in the various climate zones from tropical to polar would be necessary, he prepared accordingly. On the night before the final exam, he shaved clean a rectangle of skin on the calf of his leg and spent two hours inking in the complete data.

Next day in the exam room, the "cribber" chose a seat against the back wall. Two of his classmates, in the know, acted as shields by sitting at his left and right. No one would be able to see him pull up his trouser leg and copy.

When the mimeographed exam sheets were passed out, his confidence disappeared. Both shielders turned toward him, grinning. The rainfall questions had been omitted from the examination.

Since ink is too hard to wash off, bare leg system has been revised. A small sheet of paper, slipped around the calf and held in place by two rubber bands, contains the contraband information.

The girls, too, use their legs to get around difficult examinations. A co-ed who had difficulty memorizing poetry wrote excerpts from Chaucer's *Canterbury Tales* on a sheet of paper and slid it across her thigh under one of her sheer stockings. She had parts of *Paradise Lost* under the other. Seated in an obscure corner, she pulled her dress above the "crib" notes and wrote perfect answers to the memory questions.

"True and false" or "yes and no" tests offer opportunities for mass cheating.

Sometimes a whole row of students can make perfect scores on their "true and false" questions by prearranged signals with a brilliant classmate who is willing to co-operate. It is a simple system. The brains-of-the-scheme raises his right foot for "true" and his left for "false." There are a few variations. A pencil tilted to the right means "yes" and tilted to the left, "no." Nods of the head, too, can indicate the same thing.

A co-ed who dislikes having to remember anything but week-end dates writes famous years in history on the crystal of her man-sized wristwatch with grapefruit juice.

To eliminate the hand-cramping work of writing tiny words and figures on small sheets of paper to be held in his palm during the exam, a chemistry student worked out his campaign in a more modern manner.

He wrote the most difficult formulae on a blackboard and photographed them all on one exposure. He then had the picture reduced in size to fit the palm of his hand.

Glasses not only help a student's vision, but the case in which they come can aid his memory. After studying the question sheet, he removes the small cloth from the case and cleans his glasses while referring to the crib-sheet within.

Not long ago a psychology student evened the score with an instructor who had accused him of cheating consistently throughout the semester.

Shortly after the blue-books for the final test had been passed out, the suspected student eased a scrap of paper from the pocket of his suit coat and glanced stealthily at it.

The instructor saw him and started forward. "Give me that paper!" he demanded. The student handed him the slip: "Is it true you were secretly married on December 4th?"

A "cribber" at a large mid-western university perfected what he calls the "lavatory system." Before entering the exam room, he thumb-tacked an outline of his American History course on the inside of a lavatory booth in the building. He posted a friend at the door to guard against its possible occupancy.

Then he went to write his test. Scribbling down the answers to all the questions he knew, he suddenly waved a hand in the air, holding his stomach with the other.

The proctor accompanied his student to the lavatory. Remaining in the booth long enough to find the answers he wanted, the student went back with enough knowledge to finish his paper satisfactorily.

One way for a poor student to pass a test is not to take it at all. Rather than fail the course, a substitute is hired. Rates are usually $5 and up. Of course, the trick can work only in large examination rooms in which five or six quiz section groups have gathered to take their exams. The proctors collect the papers at the door. The professional exam-taker is careful to hand the completed paper to someone other than his employer's instructor.

But the dangers do not end with turning in the paper. A student who took his best friend's mechanics exam will testify to that. During the heat of answering questions, he phrased his ideas too well, made too few mistakes, and failed, in spots, to imitate his friend's penmanship. The corrector of the tests read the paper and was suspicious. It couldn't have been the work of the person whose name was attached to it. He compared the handwriting and exposed the trick.

Rather than pace the aisles to keep his students from "cribbing" on the exam, a cagey professor at a west coast university solved the old problem in a new way.

After passing out the test questions, he walked out of the room. Asked why he was loafing in the halls, he answered:

"I'm giving a final examination."

"Aren't you afraid the students will exchange answers?"

"No. I turned in their grades yesterday," he laughed.

(22)

Experience with a group of community players suggested an article to a writer. By use of a quotation to serve as the point of presumable interest, a "fiction lead" to widen the reader interest, and the interview form to hold the interest, the writer developed an interesting article in which are combined the elements of several types. The editor selected two of the four pictures showing the players on the stage.

BIGGER AND BETTER DRAMATICS *

How to Launch a Little Theater Movement in your City

BY LEONE M. BUECHELE

All the world's a stage, and all the men and women merely players . . ."

Light-hearted conversation charged the atmosphere in the city's largest motion picture house. The audience bore a certain distinction more associated with the opera than the movie. Generous illumination revealed eagerness and excitement on every face. A white-haired woman was heard to whisper in hushed, genteel tones, "It's just like the theatre!"

There was a sudden lull as the lights were dimmed and the stage curtains opened for the presentation of the bi-annual major dramatic production of the Community Players, little theatre group of Sheboygan, Wisconsin, a representative mid-western city of 40,000. The play to be given was Anna Cora Mowatt's "Fashion", that delightful comedy of New York life in 1850.

"I do wish we had brought the children, after all," said Mrs. Bothwell, the woman with the white hair, to her attractive daughter-in-law, adding "I feel that this play will be eminently worth-while."

"Yes, the Community Players have worked long and hard to make it a success. I heard that they practiced until after midnight nearly every evening for six weeks," replied the younger Mrs. Bothwell quietly. She and her husband, accompanied by the latter's mother, had traveled thirty miles on a winter evening to see

* Reprinted by permission of *Leisure*.

"Fashion." Young Mr. Bothwell had said that the Community Players tried to accomplish for Sheboygan—on a comparative scale—what the Theatre Guild has done for New York.

Bigger and Better.... Dramatics

How to Launch a Little Theater Movement in Your City

by Leone M. Buechele

"All the world's a stage,
And all the men and women merely players . . ."

LIGHT-HEARTED conversation charged the atmosphere in the city's largest motion picture house. The audience bore a certain distinction more associated with the opera than the movie. Generous illumination revealed eagerness and excitement on every face. A white-haired woman was heard to whisper in hushed, genteel tones, "It's just like the theatre!"

There was a sudden lull as the lights were dimmed and the stage curtains opened for the presentation of the bi-annual major dramatic production of the Community Players, little theatre group of Sheboygan, Wisconsin, a representative mid-western city of 40,000. The play to be given was Anna Cora Mowatt's "Fashion", that delightful comedy of New York life in 1850.

"I do wish we had brought the children, after all," said Mrs. Bothwell, the woman with the white hair, to her attractive daughter-in-law, adding "I feel that this play will be eminently worth-while."

"Yes, the Community Players have worked long and hard to make it a success. I heard that they practiced until after midnight nearly every evening for six weeks," replied the younger Mrs. Bothwell quietly. She and her husband, accompanied by the latter's mother, had travelled thirty miles on a winter evening to see "Fashion." Young Mr. Bothwell had said that the Community Players tried to accomplish for Sheyboygan—on a comparative scale—what the Theatre Guild has done for New York.

Further conversation was interrupted by the introduction of Frederick W. Hilgendorf, the dramatic director and the man behind the throne of the Sheboygan Community Players. Mr. Hilgendorf is a man of middle-age with boyishly-combed gray hair, sensitive, even features, and not-too-serious blue eyes. His bearing bespeaks the artist and on this occasion his voice held an unmistakable animation. There was not a sound in the whole theatre as he welcomed the capacity audience in behalf of the Community Players.

"Fashion," unfolding against a vivid background of the social '50's, was a worthy contribution to the little theatre movement and won the sincere praise of local and visiting critics and students of drama.

A social hour followed the play and it was then that Mr. Hilgendorf was asked by some of the visitors just how to go about starting a "Little Theatre" movement, an organization which would propose to elevate the standards of the drama, but still keep it within the understanding of the interested public.

The dramatic director's eyes lighted with pleasure as he was about to tell of the creation of an organization very close to his heart. It was nearly midnight and lightly-falling snow could be glimpsed through the long windows of the Community Players' club-

FIG. 13. SHE SAW HER ARTICLE IN PRINT

Further conversation was interrupted by the introduction of Frederick W. Hilgendorf, the dramatic director and the man behind the throne of the Sheboygan Community Players. Mr. Hilgendorf is a man of middle-age with boyishly-combed gray hair, sensitive, even features, and not-too-serious blue eyes. His bearing bespeaks the artist and on this occasion his voice held an unmistakable animation. There was not a sound in the whole theatre as he welcomed the capacity audience in behalf of the Community Players.

"Fashion," unfolding against a vivid background of the social '50's, was a worthy contribution to the little theatre movement and won the sincere praise of local and visiting critics and students of drama.

A social hour followed the play and it was then that Mr. Hilgendorf was asked by some of the visitors just how to go about starting a "Little Theatre" movement, an organization which would propose to elevate the standards of the drama, but still keep it within the understanding of the interested public.

The dramatic director's eyes lighted with pleasure as he was about to tell of the creation of an organization very close to his heart. It was nearly midnight and lightly-falling snow could be glimpsed through the long windows of the Community Players' club-room. Logs crackled merrily in the old-fashioned hearth as Mr. Hilgendorf began his story.

"I believe that in talking to a group of theatre-minded individuals who are eager to launch a difficult project and who are anxious for a successful outcome, it will be necessary to hold to the practical side of the facts which will help to build up your organization and increase its membership. You may not agree with me in all things, but that will make it so much more vital and inspiring before you make your final decision in the matter.

"To be more explicit, let me tell you the anecdote of the German, the Frenchman, the Englishman and the American who spent several months elephant hunting in Africa. They all did the same things at the same time, carried the same sort of gun, lived in the same tent, ate the same food, and wore the same kind of clothes during the time they were in Africa together. When they returned to their respective homes, each turned his attention to the writing of a book. The German wrote three volumes on 'The Origin of the Elephant'; the Frenchman wrote a book, had it bound in lovely red velvet with pages edged in gilt and called it 'The Loves of an

Elephant'; the Englishman wrote a book on 'The Preservation of the Elephant'; and the American's book was entitled 'Bigger and Better Elephants.'

"So your point of view may differ from my point of view due to the fact that we must adjust ourselves to our home environments.

"There is however one common factor necessary for success no matter what your viewpoint may be and that is sincerity of purpose. With that as a basis the project cannot help promoting itself in all the phases it undertakes. It will have its 'ups' and 'downs', often threatening to vanish altogether, and it is at such crucial moments that the test of sincerity proves itself."

The snow was coming down thicker and faster; the fire blazed high; it was past the usual hour for departure. Everyone in the room, however, seemed oblivious to all else except the words of the speaker.

Mr. Hilgendorf was saying that the functions of the little theatre were two-fold; First, to provide a means of social and cultural development; and secondly, to bring about maximum development of artistic skill on the part of its members in the various theatre arts—not just to give the idle members something to do.

He went on to add that the little theatre should try to become professional, but never professional in the Broadway manner. It should aim to be "non-professional," in the sense that the word takes away the amateur sting and grinds off the rough edges. The second fundamental desire of the little theatre should be to remain democratic.

The dramatic director now paused for a moment to see if there were any questions and Mr. Bothwell queried about the organization, methods and business of a little theatre. He asked how a director works, where the patronage comes from and whether it works on a subsidy or entirely on box-office receipts.

"In some theatres the director is in sole charge. The only restriction is that he must make the activities and subscriptions pay all the expenses including rent, royalties, costumes, etc. And leave a balance instead of a deficit at the end of the year. There may be a deficit on one or two productions, but if there is a balance at the end of the season, all is well. So the director selects his plays with care. He casts the plays, designs scenery and costumes, plans the music, directs the songs and dances, and works out every detail of each production.

"There are theatres in which the dramatic director supervises the various phases of the work through distinct committees, giving the heads of departments full power after all work has been laid out for them. No matter what the system may be, the best results are obtained only when the dramatic director is recognized as monarch of production co-operating with the promotion director who holds down and balances the budget.

Mr. Hilgendorf declared that finances has always been a major problem of most little theatres. On the debit side are rent, salaries, maintenance (telephone, light, etc.), stationery and postage, permanent equipment, costumes and make-up, scenery and properties, scripts, royalties, library fund, incidentals. All these must be balanced by subscriptions, donations, festivals, tournaments, plays, and advertisements.

At this point, someone in the audience suggested that Mr. Hilgendorf tell something about the Sheboygan Community Players, who are beginning their third year as an organized unit. As if leading up to this topic during his entire discourse, the dramatic director enthusiastically began:

"The Sheboygan Community Players' organization is operated by the Recreation Department under the auspices of the Board of Education. It has no patron memberships and no donations of money have ever been received. Membership to the organization is one dollar.

"The force which moves the players to success lies in the enthusiasm of the Director of Recreation, Superintendent of Schools, Dramatic Director and Dramatic Executive Committee comprised of prominent citizens, plus the loyal members of the organization.

"Sheboygan is a drama-minded town and about five years ago the time was ripe to conduct a city-wide drama tournament. An executive drama committee was appointed by the Director of Recreation. On this board were placed the Superintendent of Schools, two members of the School Board, the president of the American Association of University Women, the president of Fireside Players, an active dramatic group, the chairman of the Women's Drama Committee, a man from a Catholic group who had been director in his parish for thirty years, the leader of church plays in the Methodist church, a banker to act as treasurer, a minister to give 'prestige' to the group, and the city editor of the local newspaper.

"Under this committee the one-act play tournament operated successfully. It was the first step toward the little theatre.

"It was then that the executive committee began to realize the importance of improving the one-act plays with respect to staging and acting, so Professor Cloak of Lawrence College at Appleton, Wisconsin, was engaged to give a course of lectures on 'The Directing of Amateur Plays.' The attendance at these lectures proved conclusively that Sheboygan was ready to launch a Little Theatre—city wide in nature."

"How was the organization to take place?"

Answering his rhetorical question, Mr. Hilgendorf stated that in raw materials there were $200 which the tournaments had brought in and a goodly share of moral support. The problem now was to raise enough money to pay a full-time professional director, and a momentous one it was.

The Superintendent of Schools, who was deeply interested in the project, came to the rescue. After taking up the matter with the Director of Recreation, an agreement was made between the Board of Education and the Recreation Department that a professional director would be engaged by the school board to teach some English classes in the high school and direct plays for the Community Players. The major portion of his salary was to be paid by the Board of Education and the balance from the funds of the Players. The Board of Education was also to give the use of rooms in the schools for rehearsals, try-outs, building of scenery and storing of costumes. The school auditoriums were open for conducting lectures, monthly theatre nights, workshop nights and also for staging major productions unless a local theatre could be rented.

"It was at this time that I was asked to be the first director of the adventurous project," Mr. Hilgendorf told the group. "A program was laid out for the entire year, the benefits of which were received by those who joined at a nominal fee of one dollar. Pamphlets were sent to 1000 citizens who had once belonged to a Civic Music Organization and to all drama groups which were then in organization.

"However, when our first monthly theatre night arrived, we played to an audience of thirty-seven only. We were disappointed, but not discouraged. To get people interested, we gave a free performance and filled the auditorium, resulting in a membership of more than 100.

"At the end of the year we had 283 members, last year we had 650, and this year we expect to reach the 1000 mark. Last year 250 members expressed a desire to participate actively in the productions; the rest were content to be entertained for their dollar membership fee."

Seated between her son and daughter-in-law, the elder Mrs. Bothwell appeared intensely interested in everything being said. As the speaker glanced in her direction, she queried:

"What is the nature of the repertoire offered your members and just how are your expenses met?"

"We have two major productions each year, four monthly theatre nights, eight workshop nights, weekly radio plays over our local radio station, and weekly lectures on acting.

"The final check on all matters pertaining to finances falls to the Director of Recreation or promotion director. He and his secretary receive membership fees. The promotion director sees to the rental of theatres, expenses relating to the building of scenery, paying of union stage hands, paying of royalties, advertising and publicity.

"In the past we have charged our non-members twenty-five cents admission for the Monthly Theatre Nights and fifty cents for the major productions. Our average attendance at the big plays was 1100. This year we are charging non-members seventy-five cents for each major production, but a member uses his dollar membership fee for admittance with an additional reservation fee of twenty-five cents made essential by our budget limitations as we no longer draw revenue from the play tournaments.

"Things have not always been easy for those responsible for the success of the Community Players. Many are the times we had the feeling that we were playing with a huge bubble about to burst any moment and destroy all we had built. However, seemingly momentous problems are forgotten in the thrill of achievement and if all ends well, how soon troubles pass into oblivion! You no doubt will find similar hardships and some difficult bridges to cross, but keep on like the American in the Elephant hunt and produce bigger and better plays, get bigger and better audiences, and above all see to it that your box office receipts become bigger and better."

(23)

Stories of the superstitions connected with seventeen-year-locusts were related to a student writer. She became so interested in the legends that she decided to use the idea for her first feature article. She read encyclopedias, excerpts from books pertaining to the subject, and several United States Government bulletins. She interviewed a professor of entomology, the chief apiary inspector for the state, and the director of the state museum. Before writing the article, she analyzed three magazines and two newspaper magazine sections to ascertain the opportunities of selling. She selected one of the five for the possible market, and obtained ten gloss prints of insects. The editor bought five of them, which added to the attractiveness of the article when it was published.

MORE THAN MERE INSECTS *

Cicadas, ants, wasps and beetles glorified as soothsayers

By Joyce M. Jaeger

War, want and woe can be seen in the wings of an insect, not by a Biblical prophet, nor by a graybeard seer of questionable reliability, but by any layman who examines closely the lightly-veined wings of a 17-year cicada, and recalls the stories related to him by his grandfather.

There, in deeper color near the margin of the coral-veined front wings, he can undoubtedly see a "W," and, if he possesses an unblinded faith in the teachings of age, he will read into it the warning that for hundreds of years has excited credulous and superstitious individuals.

The 17-year locust, more properly but less popularly known as the periodical cicada, actually is not among the close acquaintances of the average citizen. He could hardly be so, for only once in 17 years, or five times in a human lifetime, does an individual of the same brood regularly appear, to set tongues a-wagging with portents of misfortune. Then, without a note of warning, he and millions of his brethren burst forth from the earth where they have been metamorphosing for more than 16 years, swarm about the trees and shrubs, and fill the woodlands with their shrill, insistent song that is startling when first encountered.

C. D. Adams, Wisconsin State Department of Entomology, hav-

* Reprinted by permission of *Nature Magazine*.

ing witnessed a Kansas epidemic of periodical cicadas in the '80s, recalls vividly the odd noise they make.

"We passed along a heavily-wooded road," he relates, "and heard millions of them singing and buzzing in the trees. I didn't know then what they were, and I asked my father.

" 'That's the 17-year locust,' he told me. 'It's been a long time since I've heard them.' "

More than anything else, the individual insect seems to sing, "Pharaoh, Pharaoh." The group song resembles the humming of a resonant telephone pole when its wires are vibrating in a strong breeze. The sudden and unexpected appearance of the cicada is largely responsible for the growth of the superstitions related to it.

"It was only natural," says Dr. Charles L. Fluke, professor of entomology, University of Wisconsin, "that when the cicada appeared suddenly in great numbers where there had been none before, superstitious and ignorant persons, seeing the 'W' on the wings, should say, 'War!' But lately, as popular education is spreading, that belief is dying out."

And with the dying out of the belief has come a lessening in numbers of the insect itself. In some places where it was once common enough to be a serious pest to fruit growers, it has, for the past brood or two, barely appeared—a happy omen to believers, who know now that, in spite of continued armament races, world peace is inevitably in view. But for hundreds of years, war or no war, the insects have in late May of every 17th year emerged to enjoy their few weeks of life above ground; and for hundreds of years, wars have been heedlessly fought with an unwholesome indifference to the habits of the 17-year cicada.

The majority of insects, however, are not credited with having such a significant influence on human destinies. Most of them, according to "those who know," are merely symbols of good or bad luck and affect our lives only superficially.

Has a fly persisted lately in flying about your face? A stranger wishes to meet you. Have you had a spider come down in front of your face or spin a web over your head, or have you seen a honey bee flying before you? You will receive a letter. Did a butterfly fly into your house? You will have a lady visitor who will be wearing a dress of the same color as its wings.

You must under no circumstances tear off the wings of a butterfly —that is very unlucky. The same butterfly left whole may bring you good luck by settling on your head, money by settling on the palm of your hand, a new suit or dress by settling on your shoulder, or a new sweetheart if he alights on your clothing.

A spider, too, to most people an insect, is a potent carrier of good luck if properly treated. Although, at various times, all black and all bright-colored spiders have been thought poisonous, it has long been known that you should "carry a dead spider (color unspecified) in your shoe for luck." To walk through a web or to have a spider crawl on you is the height of good fortune, and a bride receives a blessing in having a spider on her wedding gown. Killing the spider is extremely inexpedient for it reverses the consequences.

The "cricket on the hearth" has been immortalized as a carrier of happiness and good fortune to the household in which it dwells. As a matter of fact, crickets are more likely to favor as an abode the dampness and protective seclusion of the bottom cellar stair to the hearth, especially as they like the potatoes that may be found in the cellar. But Dr. Fluke, after enjoying the benevolent presence of a solitary cricket under his basement stairs for years, moved into another home where there was no cricket, only to find that "I've been luckier than ever this year."

It may be well to forsake a house, leaving the cricket, but if a cricket forsakes your house, leaving you, it's a sure sign death will occur among your family. Sickness or dire calamity is also foretold by a moth singeing its wings in a candle flame.

The death-watch, a beetle that bores in the timbers of buildings, portends death with equal certainty, according to the legend. In boring, the little insect makes a ticking sound by striking its jaws or head against the walls of its burrow—a soft but persistent tick that can be heard only in the dead still of night, at which time the only persons awake and eligible to hear are watchers at sick-beds. These circumstances facilitate belief in the gruesome legend.

If coincidence strengthens that superstition, it is a short step to believe that a white moth hovering about at night is the spirit of the dead relative or friend. If the death has occurred in a family that keeps bees, haste must be made to inform the bees of it, or they will all leave.

Not only the lives of human beings, but also the welfare of their cattle and crops has been attributed arbitrarily to insects and their kin. To kill a "daddy-long-legs" is to court disaster. Your harvest will be poor, and you'll lose all your cows, or your cows will go dry. But if you hold the creature by two legs, he will point with the others where the cows are, and if you throw over your shoulder one that has crawled on you, good luck is yours. A poor crop is foretold, too, by a white cabbage butterfly flying in the garden early in the season.

German housewives once called a moth a "butterhex." Because of night flying habits, moths were identified with witches, and bewitched (hexed) butter by crawling into churns, milk pans, and butter jars. A more modern belief is that small moths called "millers", other than the clothes moth, cause injury to clothing and fabrics.

Regarded with horror were walking sticks, relatives of the grasshopper. They were thought to be sticks come to life. Children have more frequently feared damselflies, or "darning needles," which reputedly are evil spirits sent by Satan to work mischief, and which sew up children's ears. To earwigs, insects that sometimes become serious pests around the house, is also attributed the habit of creeping into the ears of sleeping persons and sewing them up.

A favorite with children is the lady-bug, or lady-bird, a common beetle. They know it is bad luck to kill a lady-bug, and good luck to have one in the house in winter, or to have one crawl on their hands. Tossing it into the air, they chant:

"Lady-bug, Lady-bug,
Fly away home.
Your house is on fire,
Your children will roam."

It is just as definitely known that fireflies seen after dark are "fairies hurrying to a dance," and that if a dragonfly sits on your fishpole or line while you are fishing, you might as well go to school for the fish will not bite.

A sure sign of the coming of cold weather is a butterfly seen in the late fall, and 90 days after the first katydid there will be a frost. Warm weather, on the other hand, is promised by noisy locusts; and rain, by the biting of flies.

An easy short-cut to prosperity is to dream about ants, or to carry a spider in your pocketbook. You will lose your "pot of gold" however, if you disturb yellow butterflies settled in a puddle.

The nests of wasps can be useful both to old people and young.

If a girl wants her sweetheart to love her more, she need only wear a piece of a wasp's nest in her clothing. Some old people find that the paper from such a nest makes the best possible wiper for spectacles. A housewife is careful not to knock down or remove the nest of a "mud-dauber," for such an act presages the breaking of all her dishes.

Even the well-informed housewife, realizing the difficulty of getting rid of flies, also knows that "kill a fly and ten flies will come to its funeral." She may believe that bedbugs are carried in to the house by bats, or that to get cockroaches to leave a building she need only impale one on a pin. It is certain that her equally well-informed husband will believe that his dog must have a flea or two to be really active in his master's interest. If he keeps bees, he knows that he must not count his hives or all the bees will die.

Those undoubtedly lead a precarious existence who must consider the reaction of the insect world to their every movement. The same persons, being believers, find the medicinal uses of insects highly beneficial and economical.

Dusty cobwebs, the superstitious say, have been used to stop the flow of blood from a cut, and pills made of cobwebs, to stop hemorrhages. Headaches have been cured by swallowing a bit of spider web. The clay from the nest of a wasp is reputedly excellent as a cure for boils. There is nothing like a bee sting to cure rheumatism, in the opinion of many who have never been stung or had rheumatism. To remove warts, the bite of a katydid or cricket is effective. Cockroaches, crickets, and earwigs, variously bruised, burned, or boiled, and properly compounded and applied, so tradition recalls, will cure earache, dropsy, ulcers, and weak sight, thereby doing as well as or better than concoctions offered by barkers in medicine shows of a decade or two ago.

Perhaps the most strangely prepared and all-encompassing cure is "specific medicine Apis." This preparation is extracted from the bodies of honey bees by killing them in alcohol while they are intensely excited. The bodies are digested in this medium at a warm temperature for a month, until the final strength represents two ounces of bees to one pint of medicine. That hives, diphtheria, scarlet fever, dropsy, erysipelas, and all kinds of œdema accompanied by swelling and burning could be cured by "specific medicine Apis," was the belief of our forefathers.

And so, in medicine as well as in mythology and legend, insects have their place—and a large place it is, for there are more species of insects than there are of all other living forms, including plants. The legitimacy of this place might be questioned by skeptics, but skeptic or believer, it is probably best to play safe and not tempt fate—or the insects.

(24)

A newspaper account of a successful druggist suggested a historical sketch of the store and its owner. The managing editor gave the four gloss prints they had used for the newspaper to the journalism student, and the editor of the trade publication used two of them.

WISCONSIN'S UNIQUE PIONEER *

By William Ender

Uniquely picturesque and a monument to the harmony of drug stores of the early pioneer days, the C. C. Sniteman Company of Neillsville, Wisconsin, is outstanding both for its achievement and for its unaltered beauty. In 58 years of operation, one of the most striking changes was the installation of modernistic electric lighting fixtures. The owner and founder of the company, Charles C. Sniteman, is an active druggist for 66 years, and has been in Neillsville since the time before a railroad penetrated the area.

Primarily fascinating and successful feature of the store is its prescription department, believed to be the largest in the state for a city under 2,500 population. By the first weeks of last October, the department was filling its 455,600th prescription. More than 300 bottles of basic drugs line the shelves at the left interior of the store, and an equal number of rare drugs are stored in specially provided drawers below, in addition to the regular stock on the shelves in the compounding room. The fixtures in this room are built of solid oak, and the shelf of the table is covered with a double plate glass which is so heavy that five men were required to lift it into place. Originally a single plate, the glass was sent to the factory for another plate several years ago after a bottle had fallen from a shelf and broken it.

Constant need has been found for two registered pharmacists

* Reprinted by permission of *North Western Druggist.*

during the day. Two of them, H. L. Sontag and George Parry, have been with the company for the longest time. Mr. Sontag, a graduate of the Philadelphia College of Pharmacy, has been with Mr. Sniteman's since 1882 as a druggist, and previous to that time, as a boy, worked at odd jobs in the store. Mr. Parry joined the staff in 1922. Out of the complete file of prescriptions filed in small boxes on a shelf in the rear room of the store, the company experiences an occasional call for a refill of a prescription first compounded 20 years ago.

Double and triple filling of orders was commonly requested years ago because of the thorough stock of rare drugs Mr. Sniteman's consistently maintained. At one time, a traveling man, after trying futilely to have his prescription filled in St. Paul, Minnesota, and in Eau Claire, Wisconsin, finally succeeded at Neillsville. To be convinced that he was told the truth, the attendant had to show him the drugs, and let him watch the compounding process.

Open Continuously

The present brick building in which the store is located was built around a small frame structure in 1891 progressively, so that the company never lost a day's business. The display windows are close to one story high, and at the top have been painted in a rolled parchment effect. The top of the building, painted in silver, is highly ornamental and is surmounted by a flagpole. Two silver mortar and pestles, two signs flat against the front, an electric bulb sign, and a neon sign face the street from the second story. The latter was erected this year, and is one of a very few neon signs that light the main business district. Up to the time of the World War the company was labeled the "Deutsche Apotheke," but because of war-time sentiment it was found expedient to take it down in preference to the "Federal Drug Store." Until recently the store was known as the "mammoth silver front store."

Solid mahogany fixtures are used throughout the entire interior of the main store. These cases and shelvings were built by the Phoenix Manufacturing Company of Eau Claire fifty-five years ago at a cost of about $2,500. Aisle showcases rise approximately four feet, and are glassed at the sides and top, while the wall cases, which rise to within two feet of the high ceiling, have two large glassed doors. At a point at the right of the store where a stairway to the second floor causes a right angle to the first floor, the cases were built to wind around, neatly eliminating the angularity. The wall case was fitted with specially constructed drawers, and the floor showcase is fitted with curved glass. Because of the great difficulty encountered in formation, the Phoenix company refused to make another case of this nature. A back wall was artistically decorated with two large mirrors, and two entrances to the prescription department were adorned with curved spoke archways.

Until 1920 a small portion of the left front half of the store was occupied by a jeweler, Henry Clough, who also had one display window. The stock was withdrawn after the death of the operator, but his fixtures, including a high mahogany rail near which his workbench was located, still remains.

Early Lighting

During early years of operation the store was lighted by carbon arc lamps, which were discarded when electricity came into use. Sniteman's was one of the first stores to be electrically lighted in the state, for this area had one of the first power plants in the state. Five years ago the original incandescent light fixtures were discarded for a single bulb modernistic type ceiling light.

Although the store has a full length basement, no central heating system has ever been installed. Two coal stoves, one in the center of the store, another in a rear room, are utilized in cool weather. The basement space is used wholly for storage of wallpaper, paints, and oils which the store carries as an auxiliary line. Originally the wallpaper was displayed on 40 to 50 feet of top shelving, but this was discontinued in favor of the rear room. So carefully are the wallpaper rolls figured that the store never has more than a half dozen odd pieces at one time. During the popularity of the phonograph the store carried a complete line, and for a time had a stock of radios, which were later dropped because of extra labor required in sales and service.

Many outmoded drug accessories possessed in duplicate were sent to the State Historical Library at Madison. Among them were a drug mill, a druggist's retort, and a mortar adorned with glass prisms. During National Drug Week the store devoted one of its windows to a display of the many rare pieces it possesses.

To the right of the prescription department through a small curtained archway is a little private office of Mr. Sniteman. On one side are shelves lined with books, among which is a library of drug materials, an encyclopedia, and private papers. At the rear stands a safe which had to be hoisted through a side window because it was too wide for store doors.

Competition has been successfully staved off during the history of the store, with the exception of a sole competitor, the Kearns Drug Store, which carries an auxiliary line of ice cream and soft drinks. During recent years a chain drug store entered the town, but during six months of operation filled slightly more than 50 prescriptions.

The operator of the store, Charles C. Sniteman, was born in New York on Sept. 17, 1851, and graduated from the Philadelphia College of Pharmacy in 1871. After spending about eight years at Peoria, Ill., he came to Neillsville on Jan. 15, 1879, to recoup his failing health. Mr. Sniteman first worked in the store of Henry Myers, but purchased his interest within a year and took in Isaiah Myers for partner. Shortly afterwards Mr. Sniteman purchased his interest and organized a corporation in 1891, known as the C. C. Sniteman Company, which is still operating.

Active in civic and military affairs during his 58 years in Neillsville, Mr. Sniteman has served as secretary and director of the Neillsville Furniture Company, treasurer of the old lighting company, and treasurer of the Neillsville Opera House. During the war he served as hospital steward in the medical department of the third regiment, W. N. G. Hard hit by the depression, Mr. Sniteman is confident of "coming back again," and comes down to the store faithfully every day, determined to be of service to the last.

(25)

Studying a personal-experience article in a magazine for her weekly Publication Analysis, a major in English, who was taking the feature course, decided to write about her own experiences in learning the value of money. The subject matter did not lend itself to illustration, but the writer used four tables, or budgets, to give variety to the make-up.

I KNOW THE VALUE OF MONEY *

The story of a girl who has managed both her business and personal affairs since the age of twelve.

BY JEAN R. MCDUFFIE

My parents wanted me to grow up independent; capable of managing my possessions and my life. So when I was still a child, they began their training which has accomplished just the object they had in view.

On my twelfth birthday Mother and Daddy sat me down for a talk which I shall always remember. "It isn't just age that makes a person wise and capable," they told me. "Nor is it having lots of money and a fine social position. Knowing your own mind, your own affairs, and the value of money is one of the greatest things to which a person can aspire, and this is what we want to teach you."

So with $15 a month for my very own I began my life as a person within myself. With that money, $10 of which I got from Daddy the first of the month, and $5 from Mother on the fifteenth, I had to take care of all my expenses, clothes included. It was rather difficult at first, buying all my own things, but any important article I brought home and had Mother put on the final approval.

Fifteen dollars seemed enormous to me, but I soon discovered that I couldn't persist in eating sweets and ice creams to any great extent if I wanted to be dressed as well as the other girls and have my clothes in repair. Money just didn't go anywhere near that far. I was lucky to have a considerably well stocked wardrobe when I started out, for I didn't have to worry about needing such a thing as a coat, which would have been a little too expensive for me to know how to budget.

My parents took care of the expense of my school books, so I was relieved of that large burden. A typical monthly account for me from the ages of 12 to 14 was as follows:

Clothes	$10.
Cleaning & repair	$2.
Spending	$3.
	$15.

* Printed by permission of *Parents' Magazine.*

Through those years, my father was making a comparatively small salary, and I couldn't have had more even if it was merited. So when I was 14 years old and Daddy was given a raise, my allowance underwent a similar change.

As prices of wearing apparel went up considerably at that time, my family felt I needed a little more money to make ends meet, so I was given $5 more, making my monthly allotment $20. Despite clothes being more expensive, I contrived to buy fewer, thereby spending only slightly more for this item than I had in the previous two years.

I also learned to sew, and made four or five summer dresses each year, which carried me through the brunt of the season at a greatly reduced cost. By doing this, I was also able to have more during the winter, for I prodigiously saved whatever I could. From the time I was 14 until I reached 17, my expenses were:

Clothes	$13.
Cleaning & repair	$ 2.
Spending	$ 5.
	$20.

Daddy usually gave me a heavy coat at the beginning of the winter, and that was supposed to last clear through, but when I found I needed another for spring or fall, as a rule I bought one on the installment plan, paying $5 a month for it until the bill was repaid. Only once did I have a charge account, and that was responsible for the only time I slipped up on my obligations.

There was a small all-purpose shop near where we lived, and there I did most of my shopping. For Christmas, I had many friends, aside from my family, to whom I wished to give presents.

Wanting to try my luck at a charge account some months before December, I opened one at the shop and proceeded to charge everything I bought. The end of the first month my pocketbook permitted the payment, but on conclusion of the second month it was slightly in the reverse.

I wasn't a bit worried, for I figured I could stint through December and settle at the close of that month. There I didn't reckon with the Yuletide spirit; for when my bill came the second of January, I was $50 in debt. That was the only time I was forced to seek family aid. Daddy gave me $35 for a Christmas present, and I added $15 to finish charge account once and for all.

When I was 17, I was given a car at Christmas time, an inexpensive, but late model sedan. All the family's friends looked askance at this seemingly absurd present—an automobile for a 17 year old girl although I had just learned to drive.

Daddy said that he would prefer to give me a car when I had just become acquainted with its wonder, and would be more enthusiastic about driving than when I was older and might be somewhat bored with it. I feel he was right, for surely I enjoyed it more at that time than I ever will again.

This added expense brought me another raise in my allowance, at the same time that Daddy received one in salary. On $30 a month I was to continue to pay all my expenses and about one third of the cost of the car's operation and upkeep.

I always washed it myself, so that much was taken care of, but too frequently I drove to the service station Daddy patronized and had the gasoline put on his bill.

This car was entirely my own. With it I was privileged to take trips at will. Whenever I felt like driving some place for a weekend with a friend, I just told my parents where I was going and left. They never questioned nor forbade my departures, because I was wise enough not to plan wild goose chases or silly jaunts.

About this time I began to want more substantial articles. I saw a beautiful radio one day for $65, and nothing would do but I should have it. Have it I did, on the installment plan, and I thought I would never finish paying for it. To bolster my depleted pocketbook, I undertook to teach ballroom dancing lessons in the recreation room of our home throughout the winters when I was 17 and 18.

This brought me from three to five dollars a week and gave me enough to save money occasionally. My expense account ran about like this:

Clothes	$20.
Cleaning & repair	$ 2.
Spending	$ 5.
Car expenses	$ 5.
	$32.

With most of the money earned from my dance instruction I bought victrola records which I used both in the classes and for my own pleasure. The rest of it was distributed proportionately to each of the above items. However, as I took many trips, a great deal of it was spent on those.

Making my own decisions was wonderful training. My parents never gave me any advice on any of them. When I asked their opinions they simply discussed the case from both sides, leaving the ultimate issue to my own discretion. Only once have they vetoed any of my plans. I had chosen to go to a private high school for girls in my home town, and not being a particularly brilliant student, found that I was spending almost all my time on studies.

I asked to change schools, and there my enterprise was blocked, for my parents realized that I was really learning something, aside from making the best grades I have ever made in my life.

When I was graduated from high school, I was given the opportunity to go to any school in the United States. After some debating, I decided on a midwestern state university. Although my parents would have preferred my attending a smaller college nearer home, they voiced no protest, and selling my car for $250 I embarked upon my higher learning.

As we were at that time living a considerable distance from the school I had chosen, $40 went for my transportation. With $100 I bought a fur coat, and with the $110 remaining, equipped myself with necessary campus clothes.

As a recognition of my being grown up, my allowance was increased to $50 a month, just for the extent of college days. The expense of books put me in adverse financial straits the first month of school, but after that I fared admirably.

On this $50 I must live independently. Despite the fact that it seems enormous to some people, I have found that the girl dependent on her family, with $5 a week to spend, actually has more money for trivialities than I. This has been an average budget for me:

Clothes	$15.
Cleaning & repair	$ 3.
Appearances (cosmetics & hair)	$ 4.
Transportation	$ 4.
Notebooks, paper	$ 4.
Spending	$ 5.
Sorority bills	$15.
	$50.

This last item may seem absurd to some people, yet with all the pleasure I get from my sorority life, I would rather have less money to spend and fewer clothes. I seldom spend the total $15 a month for clothes, for my needs are limited to occasional skirts, sweaters, and shirts.

From this management of my own money, I feel that I know its value more than the average girl with whom I come in contact. Not a one of my close associates have any where near my knowledge of just what money will buy, and how far it will go. I have learned how and where to shop to get the most for the smallest sum. I know good quality from poor, and I am sure that when I marry, no matter how little money my husband may have, I will be able to get along on it and handle it efficiently.

My parents wanted me to grow up independent; capable of managing my possessions and my life. They have accomplished their purpose.

(26)

An errand took one of the seniors into the building where the art department is housed. He saw two pianos that aroused his curiosity. Upon inquiry, he found material that he was confident would interest readers, because it concerned the new and the unusual. He had a photographer take two pictures, which the editor used. When the writer received the check, he agreed that "there was gold in every class room."

COLOR PIANO PLAYS MELODY ON RODS OF GLASS *

BY CLARENCE LUND

Vivid splashes of sunset-red and shafts of cool green play along a hanging curtain of glass rods bathed in a deep purple background. The color piano is translating music into tones of the spectrum. On an orthodox piano a musician plays. At the keyboard of a companion piano Prof. William H. Varnum, chairman of the art department of the University of Wisconsin, fingers keys that actuate floodlights and spotlights interpreting in color the moods of the audible music. Each key is the electric switch for a color light mounted in the wings of a small stage and focused on the row of

* Reprinted by permission of *Popular Mechanics*.

fifty glass rods. Each octave on the piano represents one color of the spectrum. Three switches above the keyboard control major "chords" of color, floodlights above the stage that envelop the set in the fundamental hue of the musical composition. Foot pedals operate rheostats controlling the volume of each color octave. Professor Varnum, the inventor, has grouped various colors according to their physiological or psychological effect on human beings. He lists the emotional aspects of color thus: Red, very exciting, irritating, bloody, passionate; orange, hot, warm, glowing, lively, suffocating; yellow, gay, extreme opposite of sickly; green, peaceful, neutral, tranquil; blue, cool, sedate, sober; violet, stern, hard, unyielding, gloomy; purple, stately, pompous, impressive. The color pianist listens to the theme of the musician and adapts that mood to his color stage. The instrument is opening new avenues for the study of music and color coordination and the development of stage lighting.

(27)

The experiences of an amateur dramatic group in making its stage-lighting equipment afforded material for a senior's first feature. She knew that if she kept the appeal of the article to interest only college students, she would have difficulty in finding a market. She broadened the material to interest high-school boys, whom she knew to be avid readers of the popularized scientific and mechanical magazines. The illustrations included diagrams from blueprints, four line drawings showing construction details, and two photographs of the suitcase-switchboard and one of a stage setting showing the switchboard operator throwing the lights on the amateur "star."

It Doesn't Cost Much to Make Your Own

STAGE LIGHTING EQUIPMENT *

Ease of construction, flexibility, ruggedness, portability, low cost, and safety are among the features of the amateur stage lighting equipment illustrated in the accompanying article. The switchboard has been used very successfully by Wesley Players, an amateur dramatics society conducted by students at the universities of Wisconsin and Purdue

BY M. M. WOODSON

Do you feel that your club's amateur dramatic productions are losing some of their appeal because you haven't been able to obtain the proper lighting equipment?

Yes, you may answer, but we haven't the money to buy expensive equipment, so what can we do about it?

Here's what you can do, you amateur electricians: construct your own switchboard and stage-lighting set. The board proper shouldn't cost more than ten dollars.

The first thing to do is to get enough galvanized iron to make a box and panel, or if you prefer to have the outfit portable, it may be placed in a small suitcase 21 by 12 by 5½ in. If you use the suitcase, reënforce it with a strap-iron frame that will slip inside. A metal box has the advantage over the suitcase that it makes the set fireproof and shockproof when provided with a proper ground wire.

All the equipment, with the exception of the board light, will be bolted directly to a panel cut from five-ply wood. Fasten this light to the back of the case so that only the top portion of the bulb extends through the hole in the panel. The wiring is all on the underside of the panel, so if repairs are necessary at any time, the panel with the frame can be pulled out of the case. Get some sheet asbestos and put it on the bottom of the panel as well as inside the case between the frame and the wiring, where its use is most important.

* Reprinted by permission from *Popular Science.*

There will be three main control sections on the switchboard. The first is the footlight section. This should consist of four individual units, all having the same common return wire. Each unit may be either dimmed or cut completely, or the whole section may be dimmed and cut by one switch and dimmer.

The second section is for special lights such as spots, floods, and overheads. The flexibility of this unit is the same as that of the footlights.

The third section is for the purpose of producing effects such as lightning, bells, telephones, and horns. A push-button switch in the 110-volt circuit provides for the lightning, while a 6-volt transformer with adequate push-button switching affords proper voltage for bells.

The capacity of the board, while not over 25 amperes, is adequate for general use. A No. 10 wire is suggested, but the capacity can be made larger by using a larger wire.

The footlight cable, which must be designed especially for use with the board, is made of five individual wires twisted together, one being the common return.

At 20-in. intervals, short leads to the sockets should be tapped on to each of the four circuits in rotation. Make them any length you wish.

Plugs in this footlight cable are ordinary two-prong male plugs with both prongs—and this is important—fastened to the one wire to which the plug is attached. It is a good idea to paint the plugs different colors so as to differentiate the several circuits from the common return.

The special-light leads consist of common lamp cord of sufficient capacity.

For dimmers, one small, comparatively high-resistance wire dimmer may be used where the current is not too great; where the power handled is higher, a variable impedance coil can be used with less heat dissipation. This can be made by winding a helix of No. 12 magnet wire, and binding together with tape a core of short iron wires in such a way that the latter may be slipped in or out of the helix. You can put this in a space of about 15 by 5 by 5 in.

An alternate method of making a dimmer is to use a 1-gal. crock filled with salt water. Cut a sheet-metal triangle just large enough to go into the crock. Attach a cord to the triangle, and by means of a pulley or wooden shaft, provide for moving the sheet-metal triangle in and out of the salt solution as shown. For the other connection, merely bend a strip of sheet metal over the top of the edge of the crock so that the metal extends down into the salt water. This is a cheap type of dimmer, easily constructed. By experimenting with the proportion of salt in the water, you can determine the amount necessary to carry the load.

If you wish to build your switchboard in a galvanized-iron box and use a galvanized-iron panel, the basic plan is the same, but there are a few minor changes. The controls in each circuit are mounted so that the supporting bracket for each row of outlet switches and dimmer plugs forms a continuous strip of metal, which acts as a stiffener.

When the circuits are assembled, one side of each outlet and switch should be wired with one continuous wire, and the opposite side of the outlets and switch provided with leads as illustrated. The leads are bolted to the panel so that they are in a position to be connected to a No. 10 main-line wire leading to the main switches.

Because of the possibility of shorts and shocks on open knife switches, it is advisable to use standard parts of a sufficient capacity in all circuits, and the switches should preferably be of a silent type. The transformer, bells, and buzzer can be mounted on the back of the box, and long enough leads can be provided to allow the panel to be swung on hinges at right angles to the box.

The cost of the two types of switchboards is approximately the same, and the weight is about 20 lb. each.

Baby spots can be easily made. Get a No. 10 can and fasten it to a piece of "two-by-four" about 18 in. long. In the bottom of the can fasten a two-piece sign socket, or hold the socket by means of wires. At the end of the board, in front of the open can, nail a piece of tin doubled over twice so as to hold a slide made of transparent cellulose wrapping material in a pasteboard frame. By using such frames, you can have any color of light you need. If you desire a more powerful reflection, paint the inside of the can with aluminum paint. Use a 60-watt bulb.

If you want to project and converge the light, a can may be slit lengthwise, the top and bottom removed, and the tube inserted in the open end of the baby spot, telescope style.

For portable footlights, if required, get two No. 10 cans, cut them in half lengthwise, and nail them to a piece of "two-by-four," 6 ft. long. This will make four reflectors about 18 in. apart. The top of each half can should be slit down and doubled over to form an arched top, as shown.

APPENDIX

THE FREE-LANCE WRITER'S LIBRARY

References and Guides for the Journalist

ALMANACS AND YEAR BOOKS

Ayer, N. W. & Son, *Directory of Newspapers and Periodicals.* Philadelphia: N. W. Ayer & Son, published annually.

Editor and Publisher, International Year Book Number. New York: Editor and Publisher Company, published annually.

Irvine, E. Eastman, Editor, *The World Almanac and Book of Facts.* New York: World-Telegram, published annually.

Soils & Men Yearbook of Agriculture 1938. Washington, D. C.: United States Department of Agriculture, 1938.

Standard Rate and Data Service. Chicago: B. & B. Service Corporation, published monthly.

The New York Times Index. New York: The New York Times, published annually.

The Official Index to the Times. London: Times Publishing Company, published monthly.

BOOKS ON TECHNIQUE AND STYLE IN WRITING FEATURES

Bakeless, John, *Magazine Making.* New York: Viking Press, 1931.

Bartlett, John, *Familiar Quotations.* Boston: Little, Brown, and Company, 1937.

Batten, H. A., Goodrich, Marcus, and Toogood, Granville, *The Written Word.* New York: Greenberg, 1932.

Beckman, F. W., O'Brien, Harry R., and Converse, Blair, *Technical Journalism.* Ames, Iowa: Collegiate Press, Inc., 1937.

Bell, Ralcy H., *The Mystery of Words.* New York: Hinds, Hayden, and Eldridge, Inc., 1924.

Benbow, John, *Manuscript and Proof.* New York: Oxford University Press, 1937.

Bierce, Ambrose, *Write it Right.* New York: Union Library Association, 1937.

Bingham, Walter V. D., and Moore, Bruce V., *How to Interview.* New York: Harper & Brothers, 1934.

Bleyer, Willard Grosvenor, *How to Write Special Feature Articles.* Boston: Houghton Mifflin, 1920.

Bond, F. Fraser, *Breaking into Print.* New York: McGraw-Hill Book Company, Inc., 1933.

Brennecke, Ernest, and Clark, Donald L., *Magazine Article Writing.* New York: Macmillan, 1930.

Brownell, W. C., *The Genius of Style.* New York: Charles Scribner's Sons, 1924.

Campbell, Walter S., *Professional Writing.* New York: Macmillan, 1938.

Charnley, Mitchell V., and Converse, Blair, *Magazine Writing and Editing.* New York: The Cordon Company, 1938.

Chase, Stuart, *The Tyranny of Words.* New York: Harcourt, Brace and Company, 1938.

Clapp, John M., and Nugent, Homer H., *How to Write.* New York: The Ronald Press Company, 1930.

Crawford, Robert P., *The Magazine Article.* New York: McGraw-Hill Book Company, Inc., 1931.

Cushing, Charles P., *If You Don't Write Fiction.* New York: Robert M. McBride & Company, 1921.

Dobrée, Bonamy, *Modern Prose Style.* Oxford: Clarendon Press, 1934.

Fenby, Thomas, *Handy Dictionary of English Synonyms.* Philadelphia: David McKay Company.

Frederick, J. George, *The Psychology of Writing Success.* New York: The Business Bourse, 1933.

Harrington, Harry F., and Watson, Elmo Scott, *Modern Feature Writing.* New York: Harper & Brothers, 1935.

Hollingsworth, H. L., *The Psychology of the Audience.* New York: American Book Company, 1935.

Hyde, Grant M., *Handbook for Newspaper Workers.* New York: D. Appleton-Century Company, 3rd edition, 1939.

Irwin, Godfrey, *American Tramp and Underworld Slang.* New York: Sears Publishing Company, 1930.

Laird, Donald A., *How to Use Psychology in Business.* New York: McGraw-Hill Book Company, Inc., 1936.

Mencken, H. L., *The American Language.* New York: Alfred A. Knopf, 1935.

Nixon, H. K., *Psychology for the Writer.* New York: Harper & Brothers, 1928.

Park, Clyde W., *English Applied in Technical Writing.* New York: F. S. Crofts & Company, 1927.

Partridge, Eric, *Slang, Today and Yesterday.* New York: Macmillan, 1934.

Patterson, Helen M., *Advertising "Tie-Up" with Editorial Matter in Twenty-One Magazines.* Unpublished manuscript.

Pitkin, Walter B., *The Art of Rapid Reading.* New York: McGraw-Hill Book Company, Inc., 1929.

Quiller-Couch, Sir Arthur, *On the Art of Writing.* New York: G. P. Putnam's Sons, 1916.

Reed, Perley I., *Writing Journalistic Features.* New York: McGraw-Hill Book Company, Inc., 1931.

Rickard, T. A., *Technical Writing.* New York: John Wiley & Sons, 1931.

Sherman, L. A., *How to Describe and Narrate Visually.* New York: George H. Doran Company, 1925.

Smith, Henry J., *"It's the Way It's Written."* Chicago: Daily News, 1921.

Smith, S. Stephenson, *The Command of Words.* New York: Thomas Y. Crowell Company, 1935.

Spencer, Herbert, *Philosophy of Style.* New York: D. Appleton-Century Company, 1933.

Stevenson, Burton, *The Home Book of Quotations.* New York: Dodd, Mead & Company, 1937.

Taintor, Sarah A., *The Secretary's Handbook; a Manual of Correct Usage.* New York: Macmillan, 1929.

Tillett, Nettie S., *How Writers Write.* New York: Thomas Y. Crowell Company, 1936.

Walser, Frank, *The Art of Conference.* New York: Harper & Brothers, 1933.

Webb, Ewing T., and Morgan, John J. B., *Strategy in Handling People.* Chicago: Boulton, Pierce & Company, 1931.

Weekley, Ernest, *Adjectives—And Other Words.* New York: E. P. Dutton and Company, 1930.

Weseen, Maurice H., *Words Confused and Misused*. New York: Thomas Y. Crowell Company, 1932.

White, Wendell, *The Psychology of Dealing with People*. New York: Macmillan, 1937.

Wilhelm, Donald, *Writing for Profit*. New York: McGraw-Hill Book Company, 1930.

Wooley, Edward M., *Free Lancing for Forty Magazines*. Passaic Park, N. J.: Edward Mott Wooley Associates, 1927.

Woolf, Douglas G., *The Business Paper Editor at Work*. New York: McGraw-Hill, 1936.

Wright, Milton, *Getting Along with People*. New York: McGraw-Hill Book Company, 1935.

VOCABULARY AIDS

Fowler, H. W., *A Dictionary of Modern English Usage*. Oxford: Clarendon Press, 1926.

Mawson, C. O. Slyvester, Editor, *Roget's International Thesaurus of English Words and Phrases*. New York: Thomas Y. Crowell Company, 1933.

Murray, James A. H., Editor, *A New English Dictionary on Historical Principles*. Oxford: Clarendon Press, 1933.

Neilson, William A., Editor, *Webster's New International Dictionary of the English Language*. Springfield, Mass. Merriam Company, second edition, 1937.

New Standard Dictionary of the English Language. New York: Funk & Wagnalls Company, 1929.

Onions, C. T., Editor, *The Shorter Oxford English Dictionary*. Oxford: Clarendon Press, 1933.

BOOKS ON PHOTOGRAPHY AND ILLUSTRATIONS

Arkin, Herbert, and Colton, Raymond R., *Graphs—How to Make and Use Them*. New York: Harper & Brothers, 1936.

Bement, Alon, *Figure Construction*. New York: Gregg Publishing Company, 1921.

Brahdy, Joseph, *Perspective Drawing*. New York: D. Van Nostrand Company, Inc., 1929.

Brinton, Willard C., *Graphic Methods for Presenting Facts*. New York: McGraw-Hill Book Company, Inc., 1914.

Dalzell, J. R., and McKinney, James, *Architectural Drawing and Detailing*. Chicago: American Technical Society, 1936.

Deschin, Jacob, *Making Pictures with the Miniature Camera.* New York: McGraw-Hill Book Company, Inc., 1937.

Deschin, Jacob, *New Ways in Photography.* New York: McGraw-Hill Book Company, Inc., 1936.

Elementary Photographic Chemistry. Rochester, N. Y.: Eastman Kodak Company, 1924.

Ezickson, A. J., *Get that Picture.* New York: National Library Press, 1938.

Foster, W. R. Maxwell, *Drawings for Advertisements, Book Illustrations, Etc.* London: A. & C. Black, Ltd., 1928.

Guptill, Arthur L., *Freehand Drawing Self-Taught.* New York: Harper & Brothers, 1933.

Guptill, Arthur L., *Sketching and Rendering in Pencil.* New York: The Pencil Points, Inc., 1922.

Haskell, Allan C., and Breaznell, Joseph G., *Graphic Charts in Business—How to Make and Use Them.* New York: Codex Book Company, Inc., 1922.

How to Make Good Pictures. Rochester, N. Y. Eastman Kodak Company, 1936.

Karsten, Karl G., *Charts and Graphs.* New York: Prentice-Hall, Inc., 1933.

Kincaid, James C., *Press Photography.* Boston: American Photographic Publishing Company, 1936.

Mudgett, Bruce D., *Statistical Tables and Graphs.* Boston: Houghton Mifflin Company, 1930.

Neblette, C. B., Brehm, Frederick W., and Priest, Everett L., *Elementary Photography.* New York: Macmillan, 1936.

Nesbit, William, *How to Hunt with the Camera.* New York: E. P. Dutton & Company, 1926.

Norton, Dora M., *Freehand Perspective and Sketching.* Brooklyn: Published by the Author, 1925.

Price, Jack, *News Photography.* New York: Industries Publishing Company, 1932.

Rosenberg, Manuel, *Practical Art.* Cincinnati: The Signs of the Times Publishing Company, 1924.

Stubbs, G. G. Blaxland, General Editor, *The Modern Encyclopedia of Photography.* Boston: American Photographic Publishing Company.

Trew, Cecil G., *Figure & Animal Drawing.* London: Adam & Charles Black, Ltd., 1938.

Woellner, Robert C., and Wittick, Eugene C., *General Mechanical Drawing for Beginners.* Boston: Ginn and Company, 1932.

The Author and the Law

Bouvier, John, Revised by Rawle, Francis, *Bouvier's Law Dictionary and Concise Encyclopedia.* St. Paul, Minn.: West Publishing Company, 1914.

Siebert, Frederick S., *The Rights and Privileges of the Press.* New York: D. Appleton-Century Company, 1934.

Wittenberg, Philip, *The Protection and Marketing of Literary Property.* New York: Julian Messner, Inc., 1937.

Encyclopedias

Hastings, James, Editor, *Encyclopaedia of Religion and Ethics.* New York: Scribner, 1927.

Hooper, Franklin H., Editor, *The Encyclopaedia Britannica,* Fourteenth Edition. London: The Encyclopaedia Britannica Company, Ltd., 1936.

McDannald, A. H., Editor revised edition, *The Encyclopedia Americana.* New York: American Corporation, 1936.

Seligman, Edwin R. A., Editor, *Encyclopaedia of the Social Sciences.* New York: Macmillan, 1930.

The Catholic Encyclopedia. New York: Robert Appleton Company, 1907.

The Lincoln Library of Essential Information. Buffalo, N. Y. The Frontier Press, 1931.

Guides to Selling Articles

Kane, A. N., Editor, *The Manuscript Market Guide.* Book Hill, Highland Falls, N. Y. The Editor Magazine, published quarterly.

Mathieu, Aron M., Editor, *The Writer's Market.* Cincinnati: Writer's Digest, published annually.

The Writers' and Artists' Year Book. London: A. & C. Black, Ltd., published annually.

References and Source Books

Almack, John, *Research and Thesis Writing.* Boston: Houghton Mifflin Company, 1930.

Bates, Mary E., Editor, *Annual Magazine Subject-Index.* Boston: The F. W. Faxon Company, 1938. (1907 to the present)

Bible.

Bok, Edward W., *A Man from Maine.* New York: Charles Scribner's Sons, 1923.

Desmond, Robert W., *Newspaper Reference Methods.* Minneapolis: University of Minnesota Press, 1933.

Dougan, Alice M., Bertha, Joel, and Moore-Smith, Jeannette, Editors, *Readers' Guide to Periodical Literature.* New York: The H. W. Wilson Company, 1938, published annually.

Drewry, John E., *Some Magazines and Magazine Makers.* Boston: The Stratford Company, 1924.

Fletcher, William I., and Poole, Mary, Editors, *Poole's Index to Periodical Literature.* New York: Peter Smith, 1938. (1802 to 1906)

Howes, Durward, Editor, *American Women.* Los Angeles: American Publications, Inc., 1939.

Howes, Durward, Editor, *America's Young Men.* Los Angeles: American Publications, Inc., 1938.

Kane, Joseph N., *Famous First Facts.* New York: H. W. Wilson Company, 1934.

Marquis, Albert N., Editor, *Who's Who in America.* Chicago: A. N. Marquis Company, 1938.

Monthly Catalogue United States Public Documents. Washington, D. C.: Superintendent of Documents, published monthly.

Mott, Frank L., *A History of American Magazines 1741–1850.* New York: D. Appleton, 1930.

Mott, Frank L., *A History of American Magazines 1850–1865.* Cambridge, Mass. Harvard University Press, 1938.

Mott, Frank L., *A History of American Magazines 1865–1885.* Cambridge, Mass. Harvard University Press, 1938.

Muench, Alice F., and Joseph, Bea, Editors, *International Index to Periodicals.* New York: H. W. Wilson Company, 1938, also published monthly.

Rand McNally Commercial Atlas. Sixty-Sixth Edition. New York: Rand McNally & Company, 1935.

Thorpe, Willard L., Editor, *Dun's Review.* New York: Dun & Bradstreet, Inc., published monthly.

Who's Who. New York: Macmillan, published annually.

Writers' Publications

Abbott, Richard K., Editor, *Writer's Digest.* Cincinnati, 22 East 12th St., published monthly.

Bowler, A. N., Editor, *The Writer.* Boston, 8 Arlington St., published monthly.

Brown, James W., Editor, *Editor and Publisher.* New York, 1700 Times Building, published monthly.

Esenwein, J. Berg, Editor, *The Writer's Monthly.* Springfield, Mass., 29 Worthington St., published monthly.

Hawkins, Willard E., Editor, *Author and Journalist.* Denver, 1837 Champa St., published monthly.

Kane, A. N., Editor, *Editor Magazine.* Highland Falls, N. Y. published monthly.

Hawkins, Lucy R., Editor, *The Matrix.* Chicago, 35 East Wacker Drive, published bimonthly.

Peters, Ralph L., Editor, *The Quill.* Chicago, 35 East Wacker Drive, published monthly.

Periodicals

Local Newspaper
Nearest Metropolitan Newspaper
News-Week
New York Times
Time

OPPORTUNITIES TO SELL FEATURE ARTICLES

To show the beginner in free-lance writing the scope and the opportunities to sell his feature articles, the following tables are presented. They were compiled by making a study of the number of periodicals listed in the directories of Standard Rate and Data Service * and the number of feature sections listed in N. W. Ayer and Son's *Directory of Newspapers and Periodicals* † for the year 1938.

OPPORTUNITIES TO SELL TO MAGAZINES

Type of Publication	Number of Them	Number of Times Issued Per Year	Total Annual Issues
Antiques	1	12	12
Business-Executives	14	1– 4 8–12 1– 6 1–26 3–52	288
Art	1	6	6
Athletics	2	12	24
Aviation	3	12	36
Baseball	2	1–12 1–52	64
Birds	1	6	6
Civil Service	1	52	52
Clubs	14	12	168

* Standard Rate and Data Service, *Directories.* Chicago: B. & B. Service Corporation, published monthly. 1938.

† N. W. Ayer & Son, *Directory of Newspapers and Periodicals.* Philadelphia, 1938.

OPPORTUNITIES TO SELL TO MAGAZINES (*Continued*)

Type of Publication	Number of Them	Number of Times Issued Per Year	Total Annual Issues
Collegiate	2	1–12	18
Dogs	5	1– 6 4–12 1–52	100
Dramatic and Theatrical	5	4–12 1–52	100
Educational	12	12	144
Fashions	13	2– 4 1– 5 2– 6 7–12 1–24	133
Florists	1	24	24
Fraternal	11	9–12 1–24 1–52	184
General	270	3– 1 2– 4 32– 6 185–12 5–24 2–26 41–52	4,727
Home and Landscape	18	1– 4 17–12	208
Golf	4	1– 5 1– 6 2–12	35
Horse and Hunting	9	1– 6 6–12 2–52	182
Juvenile	34	24–12 10–52	808
Mail Order	6	4–12 2–52	152
Military and Naval Service Men	11	1– 6 6–12 2–24 2–52	230
Miscellaneous	9	1– 4 6–12 2–52	180
Motion Picture	17	16–12 1–52	244
Motoring	17	1– 4 1– 9 15–12	193

OPPORTUNITIES TO SELL TO MAGAZINES (*Continued*)

Type of Publication	Number of Them	Number of Times Issued Per Year	Total Annual Issues
Music	4	1–6	
		3–12	42
Radio and Wireless	14	1–4	
		1–6	
		6–12	
		6–52	394
Railroad Employees	32	1–6	
		31–12	378
Society	12	7–12	
		1–24	316
		4–52	
Sports	34	1–1	
		1–6	
		27–12	
		5–52	591
Tennis	1	12	12
Travel	8	1–6	
		7–12	90
Women's	40	1–4	
		1–6	
		37–12	
		1–52	506
Yachting and Motorboating	5	12	60
Total	632		10,807

OPPORTUNITIES TO SELL TO BUSINESS PAPERS

The following table represents the 157 classifications of trade journals. They are compiled in reference to the number of papers rather than by type of classification, as in the tables preceding and following.

Number of Magazines and Papers	Number of Times Issued Per Year	Total Annual Issues
94	1	94
9	2	18
34	4	136
1	5	5
27	6	162
10	9	90
6	8	48
58	10	580
3	11	33
1,044	12	12,528
8	13	104
1	18	18
2	22	44
41	24	984
31	26	806
195	52	10,140
3	104	312
18	313*	5,634
1,585		31,736

* Daily except Sunday, etc.

OPPORTUNITIES TO SELL TO RELIGIOUS PAPERS

Type of Publication	Number of Them	Number of Times Issued Per Year	Total Annual Issues
Baptist	21	1–10	
		2–24	
		18–52	994
Catholic	75	1– 1	
		1– 4	
		1– 8	
		2–10	
		3–11	
		18–12	
		49–52	2,830
Christian	11	5–12	
		1–26	
		5–52	546

OPPORTUNITIES TO SELL TO RELIGIOUS PAPERS (*Continued*)

Type of Publication	Number of Them	Number of Times Issued Per Year	Total Annual Issues
Congregational	1	12	12
Episcopal	8	2– 4	
		3–12	
		1–24	
		2–52	172
Evangelical	3	1–12	
		2–52	116
Inter-and Undenominational	20	1– 4	
		1– 6	
		1–11	
		7–12	
		1–35	
		9–52	608
Jewish	14	5–12	
		9–52	528
Lutheran	7	1–11	
		1–12	
		5–52	283
Methodist	36	9– 4	
		5–12	
		1–24	
		21–52	1,092
Presbyterian	9	2–12	
		1–26	
		6–52	362
Reformed Church	3	52	156
Unitarian	1	52	52
United Brethren	5	2– 4	
		1–12	
		2–52	124
United Presbyterian	8	4– 4	
		2–12	
		2–52	144
Zionist	1	52	52
Missions and Miscellaneous	9	1– 4	
		5–12	
		3–52	220
Combinations (not in survey)	5	5– 4	20
Totals	237		8,311

OPPORTUNITIES TO SELL TO FARM PAPERS

Type of Publication	Number of Them	Number of Times Issued Per Year	Total Annual Issues
General	72	1– 8 2– 10 29– 12 10– 24 23– 26 7– 52	1,578
Dairy	13	6– 12 4– 24 1– 26 2– 52	298
Fruit	7	12	84
Vegetables and Small Fruit	2	12	24
Live Stock	12	4– 12 1– 24 1– 52 2–316 4–365	3,210
Breed Publications	16	1– 9 9– 12 3– 24 2– 52 1– 64	357
Poultry	21	1– 6 1– 10 17– 12 1– 26 1– 52	298
Pigeons — Pet Stock	4	12	48
Bee	2	12	24
Farm Newspapers	3,766	2– 52 2–104 3,762– 52	195,936
Special Farming	6	1– 6 5– 12	66
Power Farming	3	1– 9 2– 12	33
Cooperative	1	12	12
Farmers' Associations	31	1– 6 19– 12 4– 24 7– 52	694
Totals	3,974		202,662

TOTAL OPPORTUNITIES TO SELL FEATURES

Based on the Five Surveys Tabulated

Type of Publication	Number of Them	Total Annual Issues
General Magazines	632	10,807
Business Papers	1,585	31,736
Religious Papers	237	8,311
Farm Papers	3,974	202,662
Newspapers Using Features	8,141	1,058,590
Total	14,569	1,312,113

INDEX

INDEX